This book is the second in a series of four published by Polity Press in association with The Open University. The complete list is:

Knowing Women: Feminism and Knowledge
edited by Helen Crowley and Susan Himmelweit

Defining Women: Social Institutions and Gender Divisions
edited by Linda McDowell and Rosemary Pringle

Inventing Women: Science, Technology and Gender
edited by Gill Kirkup and Laurie Smith Keller

Imagining Women: Cultural Representations and Gender
edited by Frances Bonner, Lizbeth Goodman, Richard Allen, Linda Janes and Catherine King

The books are one component of the Open University course *U207 Issues in Women's Studies*. Details of the course are available from the Central Enquiry Service, The Open University, PO Box 200, Milton Keynes MK7 2YZ. Telephone: 0908 653078.

The Open University U207 *Issues in Women's Studies* Course Production Team

Amanda Willett, Barbara Hodgson, Cathering King (Chair), Diana Gittins, Dinah Birch, Felicity Edholm, Fiona Harris, Frances Bonner, Gill Kirkup, Harry Dodd, Helen Crowley, Joan Mason, Judy Lown, Kathryn Woodward, Laurie Smith Keller, Linda Janes, Linda McDowell, Lizbeth Goodman, Maggie Riley, Maureen Adams, Meg Sheffield, Melanie Bayley, Randhir Auluck, Richard Allen, Rosemary Pringle, Siân Lewis, Susan Crosbie, Susan Himmelweit, Susan Khin Zaw, Tony Coulson, Veronica Beechey, Wendy Webster

External Assessor: Elizabeth Wilson, Professor of Policy Studies, Polytechnic of North London

Cover illustration by Christine Tacq

DEFINING WOMEN

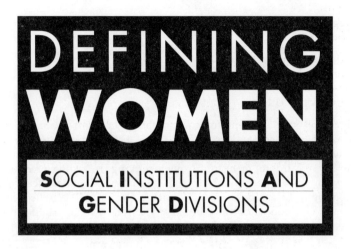

SOCIAL INSTITUTIONS AND
GENDER DIVISIONS

Edited by Linda McDowell and Rosemary Pringle

POLITY PRESS   in association with    The Open University

First published in the United Kingdom by Polity Press in association with
Blackwell Publishers and The Open University

Editorial office:
Polity Press
65 Bridge Street
Cambridge CB2 1UR, UK

Marketing and production:
Blackwell Publishers
108 Cowley Road
Oxford OX4 1JF, UK

20 0 0 0 0 4   7 74

Edited and designed by The Open University

ISBN 0 7456 0979 1
ISBN 0 7456 0980 5 (pbk)

A CIP catalogue record for this book is available from the British Library
and the Library of Congress.

Typeset in 10 on 12 pt Palatino
by Photo·graphics, Honiton, Devon
Printed in Great Britain by T.J. Press, Ltd., Padstow, Cornwall

This book is printed on acid-free paper.

CONTENTS

PREFACE

Defining Women is the second in a series of four books that together make up the Open University's undergraduate course *Issues in Women's Studies* (U207). The focus of this book is on the ways in which social institutions, their practices and discourses define women and their position in a number of contemporary industrial societies, although in the main the examples are drawn from the UK. We have selected a range of articles that deal with these issues, primarily from recent British, Australian and US feminist writing. Based around three pairs of dichotomous concepts – the public and private, dependence and independence and equality and difference – we look at relations of power and the nature of gender divisions in families and households, in the labour market and in the state, particularly in the welfare state. In each case we ask how feminists have theorized, analysed, used and challenged these key dichotomies, focusing on the interconnections between the chronological development of feminist thought and changes in the material world. We also indicate the ways in which, over the last two decades and more, feminism has challenged conventional notions in the various social science disciplines that have also addressed the questions we raise here.

The book is divided into four parts. The first introductory section establishes the framework of the argument and shows how women are defined and constrained by the sets of social relations and institutional practices that construct gender divisions in contemporary societies. In the second part the focus deepens to show that not only are women and the characteristics of femininity defined in opposition to men and masculinity, but that there are significant differences between women themselves on the basis of, for example, their class position, their race or ethnic identity, age, sexuality and the part of the country in which they live. This recognition has been one of the most challenging issues facing the women's movement and women's studies as it has developed as a discipline. And in recent years, grappling with questions about difference, diversity and multiple cross-cutting interests has been a common feature both of the feminist and post-modern theories that have had an impact on the development of the social sciences.

In Part III we interrogate the notion of work. Feminists have challenged conventional definitions that equate wage labour with work and so exclude the caring and nurturing work that women undertake 'for love' in the home and in their community. We focus here on the development of a gender division of labour in industrial societies that constructs this caring work as private 'women's work' based in the home and sees the public world of the workplace as a masculine arena to which women are admitted only as subordinate or secondary workers, confined within a relatively narrow range of 'female' occupations.

In Part IV we turn to an examination of women's political struggles. We focus on the ways in which women have alternately emphasized, argued, organized and campaigned for equality with men and for differential treatment based on their particular circumstances and needs as women. We look at a number of specific examples of women's political mobilization both within and against the institutions of the state. The role of the state in defining and controlling women has been a central element of feminist analysis. In particular, the institutions of the welfare state have played a key role in the construction of a particular definition of femininity and of women's position in post-war Britain. We examine this and show how feminists have had a contradictory relationship to the welfare state, the institutions and practices of which have both deepened women's subordination and provided at least the prospect of greater independence. We also look at how women have used the legal process in particular to improve their labour market position, and how they have organized on a more informal basis in struggles that emphasize women's particular interests as women deriving from a set of 'female' values and attitudes, for example against war. Finally, we return to the question of diversity and ask in what sense and in what ways might women continue to organize on the basis of their gender. Is it possible still to find a unity or commonality of interest among women, despite an acceptance of the diversity between us?

This book is the product of an enjoyable collaborative venture. We, the editors, have written introductions to each of the parts of the book and the chapters within them and we have each benefited from the critical but supportive approach of the other. Selecting the articles from the wealth of good material that is available was a mammoth task but one which reflects the enormous progress that has been made within women's studies throughout the 1980s. One of us is a geographer and the other a sociologist but we tried hard not to let our own disciplinary predispositions influence us. One of us lives and works in the UK, the other in Australia. The problems that such a transnational collaboration posed were eased by an all too short visit to the Open University by Rosemary Pringle at a crucial point in the production of this book. The postal system and the fax machine were disappointing substitutes thereafter for the excitement and challenge of closer contact. We each learned a lot from the other and enjoyed ourselves in the process. We hope that you too, the reader, will find the results of our work equally stimulating and enjoyable and might be persuaded to go on and read all those articles we would have liked to have included but could find no space for.

We would also like to acknowledge the support of our colleagues from the U207 course team and Chris, Sophie, Hugh and Sarah who lived with us as we struggled with what often seemed like impossible deadlines – thanks.

Linda McDowell   Rosemary Pringle
The Open University   Macquarie University
Milton Keynes   Sydney

PART I
DEFINING WOMEN

INTRODUCTION:
WOMEN AS 'OTHER'

The focus of this book is the social definition of women. The ways in which social institutions, practices and discourses[1] define women in contemporary societies are examined. Institutions such as the family, the economy and the state, as well as institutionalized patterns of sexuality and norms of appropriately 'feminine' behaviour are addressed in the readings that follow.

Women are constantly defined in relation to men. Whether they are similar to men, different from or complementary to them, men, masculinity and male behaviour are always the reference points. Most obviously, women are defined in familial terms as carers and nurturers. Their identity and status derive from their relation to the explicitly gendered categories of mothers, daughters and wives. Women are thus defined not only in relation to men, but as dependent on men and subordinate to them. Men, on the other hand, are not defined in relation to women, or in purely familial terms, but in relation to a larger 'public' world in which they operate as workers, colleagues or citizens. As Black and Coward put it: 'Women are precisely defined, never general representatives of humanity or all people, but as specifically feminine, and frequently sexual, categories . . . Being a man is an entitlement not to masculine attributes but to non-gendered subjectivity' (Black and Coward, 1981, p. 83). Men's specific gender is thus ignored: they represent the universal and the human to which women are 'Other'. This perception of woman as 'the Other' has been taken for granted in most social and political thought as well as in everyday life. It was first examined in detail by Simone de Beauvoir whose book *The Second Sex*, published in France in 1949, became one of the founding texts for 'women's studies' as a distinct area of enquiry.

The statuses of men and women have been constructed around a whole series of dichotomous categories: the 'one' and the 'other', the public and private domains, work and home, rationality and emotionality, culture and nature, mind and body, autonomy and dependence, to name just a few. The first of each of these pairs tends to be associated with men and positively valued, while the second is associated with women and negatively valued. The interpretation of social reality in this way, as a series of opposites, leaves little room for gradation or overlapping categories. Women

3

represent what men are not; thus reason and emotion are treated as incompatible, home is presented as the domain of women, the public world of politics the domain of men, and so on. What is the significance of this dichotomizing process for an understanding of power relations between the sexes? Are women and men to be understood as fundamentally different from each other, even as polar opposites? Or are the differences between them relatively minor compared with what they have in common?

In this book, we concentrate on three dichotomous relationships which are of particular importance in the social definition of women. The first is the relation between public and private spheres, which are conventionally associated with men and women, respectively. Secondly, there are relations of dependence and independence. Women have been defined as dependent on men, both financially and in the sense of being under their care and protection, rather than as independent individuals. But, at the same time, women are likely to have children, husbands and, increasingly, aged parents dependent on them, and to undertake a great deal of the emotional, psychological and nurturing work within households. In other words, relationships of dependence are multiple and complex. Thirdly, there is the question of sameness, or equality, and difference. Do their differences from men disadvantage women or are these differences to be celebrated as a source of strength? Should women focus their political demands on equality with men or demand differential treatment? As well as the question about differences between women and men, there is also a question of differences between women, differences which at times seem so vast that they threaten to undercut the very notion of 'woman'. We shall be tracing these three themes in relation to the categories of work, the welfare state and political action.

Work, welfare policies and political action all appear to fall into the domain of 'public' life. But feminists have challenged women's marginality in all three areas, and in the process have challenged the very categories themselves. They have broadened the definition of 'work' to include much that was previously perceived as private and hence undertaken for 'love' and not for wages, and have expanded the notion of politics way beyond its formal boundaries. The idea of politics and state intervention as being separate from domestic and everyday life has also been questioned. Notions of 'worker' and 'citizen', apparently gender-neutral terms, have been shown to be masculine in so far as they embody masculine attributes and behaviour outside the so-called private world. Feminists have also questioned the idea that power is concentrated in the political sphere, arguing that power is constitutive of all social relations. Many feminists are wary of overstating the impact of the state or formal powers in the public sphere on private life, stressing instead the continuities of men's power across all domains (Allen, 1990). The exercise of power within personal relationships – especially abuses of power as seen in domestic violence and child abuse, for example – has also been redefined by feminists as a *political* question.

Feminist thinking on all these questions obviously has not remained static over the past twenty years. We shall therefore be tracing connections between a number of levels: changes in feminist practice are linked to the development of a body of feminist theory and to shifts in the actual conditions of women. For example, the Thatcherite restructuring of the economy and the welfare state during the 1980s affected the position of women in Britain. While our vantage point is primarily British, we shall be concerned throughout with the question of what women do and do not have in common in a range of societies. Where appropriate, we draw on the experience of other countries and on a range of sources and examples to explore the commonalities and differences between women, mainly in the contemporary world but also in the past.

WOMEN'S STUDIES

Women's studies originated outside academia with activists (including students) who wanted to draw on women's collective experience to understand and to change the prevailing power structures. The earliest tertiary courses arose as a result of demands from students and junior staff rather than from formal institutional initiatives. At the same time, in adult and community education women active in feminist and community politics pushed for the introduction of new material and teaching methods. At all edu- cational levels, women criticized their exclusion from course content, as well as the hierarchical structures and authoritarian teaching methods which tended to exclude women. They wanted not only to change course content but to make knowledge accessible to women. This included both bringing more women into higher educational institutions and taking women's studies into the schools and the wider community. The subject matter quickly became more complex and, especially in the USA, the area started to become professionalized and to move in universities towards discipline status. Yet the links between women's studies and feminist politics remain strong. The women's movement of the 1960s onwards differed from the earlier movement in its emphasis on 'sexual politics' and its critique of domestic life and personal relationships. It was concerned with psychological oppression, the structures of femininity, and women's responsibility for housework, child care and emotional well-being, rather than with the focus on political representation of earlier times. As feminists began to theorize these areas themselves, they became critically engaged with virtually all

5

the social sciences and humanities. Women's studies has thus been constituted in the context of a series of political, professional and theoretical battles.

That it is usually called 'women's studies' rather than 'gender studies' indicates how strongly linked this area is with feminist theory and practice. Women's studies has its origins in the emphasis on women's experience and women's standpoint which were felt to have been excluded from what passed for 'knowledge'. To rename it 'gender studies' could be seen to depoliticize it, to draw it back within the confines of existing disciplines, to abandon the radical challenge to the existing ways in which knowledge is organized, and to deny the specificity of women's oppression. While 'gender' became a key category for feminists, it did not embody notions of power and domination in the obvious way that 'class' did. And yet, as gender became more carefully theorized, the potential arose for the focus to shift from women. Was it not important for feminists to study the powerful? Feminists have continued to differ on how exclusively they focus on women; certainly many have felt strongly that the relation between women and men is an important part of the study, while for others the very categories 'woman' and 'man' have been problematized, and the differences *between* women examined. Many feminists have also stressed the importance of studying masculinity and exposing the supposed gender neutrality of many discourses, social practices and institutions. And feminist work has actually opened up the area of gender studies to men as well as to women.

Women's studies has drawn on many disciplines in the process of itself becoming a discipline, a branch of knowledge, or an area of concentrated study. Whether we call it a 'discipline' does not matter greatly, for much depends on what we mean by that term. 'Disciplines' are not fixed and static; rather, their content and frameworks undergo constant change, as do their relationships to each other. New disciplines frequently grow out of older ones, as more specialized branches or as offering a fundamental challenge to existing paradigms. Psychology grew out of philosophy, politics out of history, biochemistry out of chemistry, and so on. There are also a number of 'applied' disciplines which may draw their theoretical frameworks from a variety of sources and apply them in a distinct way. In focusing on social institutions in this book, we have drawn on a wide range of disciplines, including sociology, history, anthropology, geography, economics, law, social policy, philosophy and politics.

Women's studies is not unusual in building on existing disciplines. Where it is unusual, perhaps, is in the range of disciplines it uses (just about everything is potentially relevant), and in the ways in which it deliberately sets out to challenge and

6

reconstruct the existing organization of knowledge. Feminists have frequently found that the most interesting questions emerge on the margins of existing disciplines; key questions for feminism often have been excluded or trivialized precisely because of this marginalization. Sexuality, which has been central for feminists, is perhaps the best example of this. Ignored by political theory, by industrial relations and organization theorists, relegated to the sociology of family and of deviance within sociology, virtually denied a history by the historians, reduced to questions of sexual functioning by the psychologists, it has been a major achievement of women's studies to make questions of sexuality and power central to all these disciplines. In this it has, of course, been helped by developments in critical social theory and by the renewal of interest in psychoanalysis (see the companion volume, *Knowing Women: feminism and knowledge*, Crowley and Himmelweit, 1992).

Note

1   The term 'discourse' is used to refer to the specific structure of statements, terms, notions and beliefs that categorize women. These are found in institutional and organizational behaviour as well as in language and texts.

1
DEFINING PUBLIC AND PRIVATE ISSUES

POWER AND DEPENDENCE

The three articles in Chapter 1 introduce the three themes identified in the Introduction; namely, dependence/independence, equality/ difference and public/private, and provide some evidence and theory on the question of power. In the first article, Irish feminist Aveen Maguire raises in straightforward terms the question of power. How do we recognize it? Starting with the experience of an individual woman subjected to domestic violence, Maguire applies the three-dimensional framework of left liberal Stephen Lukes to consider the various levels of the operation of male power. She builds up a multi-faceted account which moves from the individual to the institutional, from simple brute force to the subtleties of false consciousness and manipulation. Power, she makes clear, operates most effectively when we are unaware of its presence and believe that we are doing what we choose. Male reactions to men's abuse of power are often to deny or to 'rationalize' its origins. For example, in cases of rape that come to trial great play is often made of men's 'natural' sexual urges and the way in which women 'arouse' these by their behaviour.

Men's sexual and physical violence is supported by the institutional power of the courts and of judges to define 'appropriate' behaviour. For example, a man is 'entitled' to respond violently if his wife attempts to depart from very narrowly prescribed norms of marriage and motherhood. Men's power within the family is also exercised over children as well as over women. Difficult questions about the rights and responsibilities of individual household members are raised by the issues of domestic violence and child abuse – and by the extent to which formal agencies, such as the police and social workers, should have the right to intervene in so-called private or family matters.

However, power is not to be identified solely with violence or coercion. If power were always identified as coercive and unpleasant, people would surely be able to resist it much more strongly. And violence may actually be a 'weak', in the sense of last resort, form of power. If men need to use violence to get their way, it may well be because they have lost access to other, perhaps more effective, control measures. While many feminists have necessarily drawn attention to the incidence of rape, domestic violence, incest, child abuse, and sexual harassment, there is also a strand of feminist thought that has focused on desire and pleasure and how this is connected to relations of unequal power. Power may be operating most effectively when we are unaware of it or experience it as pleasurable.

UNDERSTANDING GENDER RELATIONS

In developing their understanding of gender and power, feminists have taken three broad approaches. The first regards knowledge as empirically or experientially based, deriving from careful observation of attitudes, behaviour, events and hypothesis testing. This approach tends to focus on the individual and her conscious activities as the source of knowledge. 'Consciousness-raising' in the early days of the women's movement was an important part of expanding women's knowledge of their shared experience. For many, the next step was to move beyond what was empirically verifiable to theorize the underlying structures of women's oppression. Although power may be experienced in individual terms, it also has a systemic quality about it. The actions of individual men have institutional, ideological and discursive backing.

In the 1970s and 1980s, feminists developed the term 'patriarchy' to refer to the systemic nature of men's power. Patriarchy has been defined as 'a set of social relations between men, which have a material base, and which though hierarchical, establish or create interdependence and solidarity among men that enable them to dominate women' (Hartmann, 1981, pp. 14–15). Marxist feminists in particular were attracted to various versions of structuralism that became popular in the 1960s in linguistics, anthropology, psychoanalysis and Marxism. Structuralism emphasizes the determining characteristics of the system rather than the actions of individuals, and stresses that surface events and phenomena are to be explained by sets of structures and relations that lie deep beneath the surface. Structuralism stresses that it is the system as a whole and not its individual elements that needs analysis. Marxist and socialist feminists were particularly concerned with identifying the structures of patriarchy and specifying their relation to the structures of capitalism.

A number of different analyses of patriarchy were developed, some emphasizing the economic basis of male power (control over women's labour), while others stressed the ideological level or the sexual control of women. Sylvia Walby, in *Theorizing Patriarchy* (1990), has attempted to develop an analysis of patriarchy as a system analogous to capitalism: by including all these levels or structures as she refers to them. She identifies six structures that constitute patriarchy as a system: the patriarchal mode of production, patriarchal relations in paid work, patriarchal relations in the state, male violence, patriarchal relations in sexuality, and patriarchal relations in cultural institutions. However, her analysis is primarily descriptive and is limited by its basis in contemporary British society. Twenty years earlier, Juliet Mitchell in *Women's Estate* (1971) had drawn on structuralist versions of Marxism and on psychoanalysis to develop a similar analysis, although she argued there that patriarchy is located primarily at the ideological level and capitalism at the economic level, in contrast to Walby. However, Mitchell also analysed the position of women in terms of structures – in her case four: production, reproduction, sexuality and child care.

The relationship between patriarchy, or what Cynthia Cockburn has called sex/gender systems (in her introduction to *Gender at Work*, Game and Pringle, 1984), and modes of production (that is, slavery, feudalism, capitalism and 'state socialism') is still far from understood. Feminist theorists differ, for example, in their views as to whether patriarchy is indeed a system analogous to a mode of production or is part of that mode of production. Thus some feminists hold to a single systems view of capitalist patriarchy, or patriarchal capitalism, whereas other feminists take a dual systems position, differing in the extent to which they regard the structures of male power and dominance as related to or dependent on the mode of production.

While structuralism provided more complex accounts of how the system worked, it seemed to many to be too deterministic, leaving no space for individual action to challenge the systemic structures of domination. It also led to the building of more and more abstract models which seemed to have little demonstrable relation to 'reality'. In recent years, feminist social scientists have shifted the theoretical object away from 'patriarchy' and towards 'gender' as the category that may be more useful for ensuring that we look at all social relations and not only at those concerned with family relations or with waged work (see, for example, Acker, 1989). And 'gender' itself is now theorized in more sophisticated ways than the 'sex role stereotyping' approaches of the 1970s (see Crowley and Himmelweit, 1992). There has been a shift from the definition of gender as a set of attributes connected to individuals to a wider understanding of gender as a set of meanings and discourses. This shift is linked to the expanding interest in post-structuralist ideas in the social sciences and humanities since the 1970s.

'Post-structuralism' was eagerly taken up by some feminists who saw it as having much in common with feminist concerns with power, plurality and diversity and the breaking down of oppositional categories, such as those used to define 'women', as central issues. Post-structuralism does not advocate a return to empiricism but it does point to the instability of structures, stressing their open-ended and partial nature and variability over time and space. Post-structuralists, such as the French writers Michel Foucault and Jacques Derrida, have been critical of claims to understand the system as a whole, and of the structuralists' claims to universal truths. For them, discourses are always necessarily about power and strategy, and meaning is contextual and multiple, in the last resort probably impossible to pin down.

Post-structuralists insist that reality cannot be known independently of language and discourse. It is through language that we make sense of reality, and language does not simply describe reality, it actively orders it. Those who take this position are likely to give much more attention to texts and discursive strategies than are those who assume a 'real world' of empirical events. Feminists, who had long been interested in the power of language to shape the world, began to challenge the most fundamental assumptions, categories and methods of their disciplines and to scrutinize the key texts that had dominated teaching and research within each discipline. There has been the beginning of a shift from claiming to study real structures in the world, to an examination of how 'the world' is constructed in discourse. The analysis of 'patriarchy' as a solid set of structures existing in the real world is being complemented by accounts of the 'phallocentricity' of texts: that is to say, the way in which texts were constructed from the point of view of men, with women present only as 'Other' or object. Textual strategies have become extremely important. This means going beyond the surface sexism of texts to understand the ways in which women have been systematically excluded or marginalized. Feminists have argued that the exclusions are deliberate, that 'male-stream' theory (O'Brien, 1981) is dependent on an opposition to women and the feminine and is unable to include them. In Article 1.2 Beverly Thiele analyses the strategies whereby women have been rendered invisible in social and political theory. If social and political theory actively constitutes its subject, rather than just describing what it is, it is clear that the deconstruction of texts takes on a central political importance, writing itself becomes a political action. As Thiele shows, the classical theorists of social and political thought rely on conceptual categories that exclude women from their analyses.

Many feminists had already registered the power of language and myth to construct reality. Their political practice had shown that myths cannot be shifted merely by showing that they are wrong or inaccurate. Take the example of rape, which we have already raised. It is surrounded by numerous myths: that women secretly want to be raped, that a struggling woman cannot be raped, that rapists cannot help themselves. All of these can be contested with masses of social science evidence. But the myths remain. We have therefore to understand the larger symbolic function of myth and what might be involved in dismantling such myths. Ideas about representation, language and textual strategies in constructing and challenging these myths were attractive to feminists already grappling with such issues. There has been a shift from 'establishing the facts' to making visible the connections between discourse and power.

Feminist textual strategies could also be scrutinized. Classifications, it should be noted, inevitably understate the differences within particular categories – within radical feminism or within socialist feminism, for example, which are often defined in opposition to each other – as well as ignoring the overlaps between them. We need to be aware that these tendencies do not exist independently of the way we think about them. Rosemarie Tong (1989), for example, has delineated seven varieties of feminist thinking: liberal, marxist, socialist, radical, psychoanalytic, existentialist and post-modern. In doing so, she imposes an order on them that is not clearly pre-given. While this provides a useful tool for thinking about theory and political actions, we need to be aware that other categories (cultural feminism, lesbian feminism, separatism, for example) could equally have been used, creating a different constellation. This raises a further question about whether 'conservative feminism' is possible or is a contradiction in terms. Certain of the appeals to 'feminine values' and to the virtues of family life from the 'moral majority' in the USA, or from conservative critics in the UK, have a great deal in common with other feminist re-evaluations of family life. Similarly, conservative women's appeals to notions of individual liberty have parallels in liberal feminism. Bea Campbell in her book *The Iron Ladies* (1987) raises the question of whether women, active in the Conservative Party of the late 1980s in the UK, and demanding equal rights with men, should be classified as feminists.

EQUALITY OR DIFFERENCE: BOTH OR NEITHER?

Feminist debates about equality with and difference from men have taken a different turn in the context of post-structuralism. The history of feminist thought can be characterized by shifts in emphasis between equality and difference, but for most feminists it has become apparent that it is more complex than an either/or situation. Increasingly, feminists have realized the importance of avoiding the either/or, both forms of which may be regarded as male-identified. Whether women are defined as the same as men, or different from them, men remain the reference point, the ungendered 'norm' against which women are compared.

Many feminists in the early 1970s saw difference as largely a matter of socialization and believed that changes in the socialization of men and women might lead towards greater equality. However, by the end of the decade there was developing a concern that 'equality' seemed to imply women conforming to masculine standards and giving up what was distinctive to their gender. In particular, there was a re-evaluation of mothering and an acknowledgement that 'equality' should not be achieved by renouncing the pleasures of motherhood. Adrienne Rich's *Of Woman Born* (1977) eloquently put the case that, for women, motherhood is a source of strength and pleasure as well as of oppression and dependence. Should women renounce motherhood – a characteristically 1970s feminist position – or rather contest the relations within which it was experienced?

As the seventies drew to a close, the emphasis among some feminists shifted from equality to difference (Eisenstein, 1984). Radical feminists – or cultural feminists as they began to be known – celebrated women's culture and frequently denied that there was anything of value connected to men or masculinity (Daly, 1978a). Feminist sociologists and philosophers emphasized women's unique standpoints. On the other hand, many liberal and socialist feminists continued to stress the value of arguing for equality, particularly in the political sphere and in the labour market, while recognizing that some of the points about difference should be taken on board. These issues are explored in more detail in Part IV.

Feminists have come to use the term 'difference' in a variety of contradictory ways. Michèle Barrett (1987) identifies at least three main ways it is used: the experiential, the psychoanalytic and the semiotic. The first is largely descriptive and refers to the different experience of inhabiting a female body rather than a male one. But it can also lead to a concern with differences in women's experience, depending on class, race, sexuality and so on. Difference in this sense is addressed in Part II. Meanwhile, it has been through feminist critique and engagement with psychoanalysis, especially in France, that the most powerful emphasis on difference has come. Luce Irigaray (1985) has criticized psychoanalysis for operating as if there were only one sex, namely men. She refers to this as 'phallocentrism' and identifies three distinctive forms of it in psychoanalytic thought: the two sexes are conceived as identical, as opposites or as complements. That is to say, women are defined always in relation to men, either as the same (the pre-oedipal phase), as different from men (the oedipus complex) or complementary to them (mature femininity). Irigaray stresses the importance of claiming an autonomous self-defined identity as women, an identity which is no longer derived from a negative comparison with men, but stands on its own, putting female sexuality, female desire, into

14

discourse. The emphasis is thus more accurately on autonomy than difference.

PUBLIC AND PRIVATE

The public and the private constitutes another of the key dichotomies that not only structures this book but which has been central to the development of western political thought, to the definition of 'woman', to feminist theorizing (and retheorizing) and to feminist political actions. The notion that the public and private are separate spheres, each appropriate to the different sexes, has a long and contested history but has been of particular importance since the development of industrial capitalism and urbanization in advanced economies which resulted in the increasing separation of men's and women's lives. The separation was never complete and was most marked for the middle class, but the assumption that 'a woman's place was in the home' had a marked impact on all women because of its embodiment in social and political theory and practice. Appeals to women's supposed irrationality, lack of reason, their special responsibilities, their intuitive and caring natures and so on, were the basis of their exclusion from waged work, or at least from professional work and from the sphere of formal politics throughout the nineteenth century. This theme is returned to in several places, not only in this book but in the companion volume *Inventing Women: Science, technology and gender* (Kirkup and Keller, 1992).

The particular distinction between the public and the private that developed with industrial capitalism in western societies resulted in women's exclusion from the 'rights' of citizenship and therefore constructed them as less than full individuals. The prevailing ideology was that men would govern the society and women the homes within it. The result was a model of social life that separated the 'private' domestic sphere from the 'public' sphere, reflected in and influenced by nineteenth-century social theory and the developing disciplines of the social sciences. Contemporary nineteenth-century notions of the obligations and duties of fatherhood and motherhood further reinforced the domestic/public separation and women's dependence on men because of their status as non-citizens. These assumptions continue to be reflected in contemporary legislation and social welfare policies, as will be shown in Part IV.

The importance of the domestic or private and public separation led to women's restriction to the domestic sphere being advanced as a universal exploration for women's subordination. It has been a particularly pertinent divide in anthropology where the assumption that women are 'closer to nature' is linked to their restriction to 'domestic' activities and to their reproductive roles. Michelle Rosaldo was one of the earliest exponents within feminist anthropology of the argument that the public/private division is universal. She suggested that, although this opposition will be more or less salient in different social and ideological systems, it does provide a universal framework for conceptualizing the activities of the sexes (Rosaldo, 1974, p. 23). She defined private or domestic activities as those institutions and activities which are organized around mother/child groups, whereas public activities are based on hierarchical structures that construct women and children as inferiors. There have been criticisms of Rosaldo's universalist assumptions and she, herself, later modified her theory (Rosaldo, 1980), but the domestic/public division remains not only a salient feature of many types of analysis within the social sciences, as Beverly Thiele in Article 1.2 shows, but also a way of marking clear domains for women's political action, albeit often to challenge this very division. While feminists have demonstrated the interconnections between the public and the private – for example, in the ways in which familial and gender relations are also part of the organization of waged work (as will be shown in Part III) – it is also important to be able to theorize the reasons for and the ways in which the public/private division has been constructed and changed. As Leonore Davidoff (1990), a feminist historian, has argued, demonstrating the ways in which a taken-for-granted division between the public and private is a central notion within the social sciences has been a major part of feminist retheorizing. In the initial stages of their critique, however, feminists themselves took these divisions as natural givens, inserting the private domain of women into historical analyses. This insertion was no simple task for, as she argues, historical source material reflects the division, because of the ways in which information has been collected and recorded.

The second stage in the critique was to deconstruct the division and show how, rather than being a 'natural' and universal division, categories such as the public and private are themselves socially constructed. In politics, sociology and economics, key concepts such as the state, civic society, citizenship and the market reflect the public domain and masculinist (i.e. those social attributes associated with men and masculinity) values such as rationality, abstraction and individualism. By questioning the public/private division, feminist theory has been able to raise new questions about the gendered nature of key social institutions. However, questioning and deconstructing the division does not mean that it should be abandoned. Linda Nicholson, in Article 1.3, summarizes the case for feminists continuing to theorize the division, albeit in a way that draws attention to its variety rather than its universality. Only when we have understood the origins and variety of the public/private distinction, Nicholson suggests, will we be able to assess intelligently the future of such divisions.

We need to ask such questions as: Are some kinds of public/private distinctions synonymous with male domination, and how do these distinctions change historically? Would some such distinction persist in a 'non-patriarchal' world? The feminist slogan, 'the personal is political', seems to imply that feminist politics is concerned with breaking down any qualitative distinction between public and private, placing personal or 'private' matters on the 'public' political agenda. However, Jean Bethke Elshtain (1981) has attacked some radical feminists for blurring all distinctions between public and private identities. She argues that it is a condition of democracy that some separation should be kept between the two as a safeguard against fascism. But, as Nicholson makes clear, the point is not to break down the division but to challenge its ideological hold by looking at its historical origins and changing dynamics.

Article 1.1
POWER:
NOW YOU SEE IT, NOW YOU DON'T.
A Woman's Guide to how Power Works

Aveen Maguire

We all recognize power when we see it – or do we? We know the exhilarating feeling of exercising power ourselves. We also recognize the feeling of being on the receiving end of power. But do we see clearly how power operates in our society? Irish women have learned much over the last twenty years about power. We have organized around issues like family violence, housing conditions, education, contraception, social welfare, maternity services . . . and, even where our declared aims have not been achieved, we have gained strength through the exercise. But in spite of our efforts, the way we in Ireland still experience power as women is through the lack of it.

[· · ·]

Consider Anne, who has fled her husband's violence to take refuge with her children in a hostel for battered women. Some weeks later, she returns home, armed with a barring order and her supplementary welfare allowance. She knows what powerlessness is. The ineffectiveness of the barring order would be a laugh if it were not so tragic. As her outraged husband creates a ruckus outside the house, day and night, she juggles the desire not to upset the children any more with the shame of having to ask the neighbours to call the guards and with the dread of another beating if she lets him in. The amount of her supplementary welfare allowance is another sick joke – in no way does it allow her to cope on her own. As Anne's anxiety mounts and her exhaustion increases, the response of the medical profession is to adjust her, not her problems. She is put on valium, librium or some other tranquillizer to lessen her anxiety, literally to quiet her down. Her power to create a fuss, to do something drastic about her drastic situation, is undermined. It can rightly be said, in the appropriate technical jargon, that the institutions of her society are not responsive to her needs.

The reality of our everyday lives is conveyed to us through social and political institutions. They are the skeleton, the framework, on which the flesh of our reality hangs. Religion, language, health care, the courts, trade unions, welfare schemes, business corporations, local government, political parties are the everyday context in which we live and function.

As women working to replace present social institutions with a more responsive social and political life, one which facilitates our *ex*pression not *re*pression, we know that we are struggling against the exercise of someone else's power. Sometimes our awareness of this is vague, sometimes very much more precise and specific. . . . Our reality, 'the way things are', is the result of someone's successful exercise of power. Someone's will has been successfully translated into action to create this reality. Reality is not 'just the way things are', 'the way the world wags', 'the way life is'. Reality is the result of a use of power.

It is an obvious, but liberating, insight to realize that institutions are made by people. Most of us tend to think first of an institution as a place with a purpose, like a hospital or a prison. But think of our education system, geared to schooling and training us to fit into society; our economy, commerce and advertising, geared to the profit motive first and the fulfilment of human desires second; the law, tending more and more to control rather than to protect the freedom of the people; our language, reflecting the dominant images and values of society and conditioning us to go on accepting them. All these are institutions, constructed with just as much intent of purpose as a prison or a hospital. And in so far as they are made by people, they can be remade by people.

It would be naïve to jump from this insight to the belief that all that is required is to have the will to reshape our reality and to take unto ourselves the power to do so. No one can doubt that the women's movement possesses the will to change our society. But the successful exercise of our power has been limited. The reverses we have experienced and the slow speed of our progress need to be analysed. We need to take a critical look at why so many of the issues which have been raised have not been pushed through to a resolution which satisfies us. We need to know how power is being exercised against us.

According to Weber's classic definition, power is 'the probability that one actor within a social relationship will be in a position to carry out his own will, even against resistance' (note use of 'his'). Thinking of power in this way allows us to think of it as something diverse, changing, a collective term for many facets of the same thing. You have power when you're able to force people to do what you want even when they don't want to. You also have power when people do what you want without your even thinking whether they want to or not. This is quite distinct from the situation where you discuss and gain a consensus on an issue.

In analysing how power is being used against women in our society, a well-established sociological model may help. This model suggests that we can best identify power at work by examining three possible guises or 'faces' that power wears (Lukes, 1975).

The first face of power is visible in direct action, where force or might are used, or in public decisions, taken on publicly discussed issues. The second face of power can be seen in attempts to stifle an issue as it emerges, or in attempts to redefine or reshape an issue into something less threatening. The third face of power is the hardest to discern. Power in this third dimension is used to manipulate people's perceptions so that they are unaware of having a grievance. The history of women's oppression is littered with examples of all three.

Examples of the first face of power are the most obvious. Power may be exercised in direct action, as in violence against women. A woman may submit to physical force which she is unable to resist or she may submit because of more subtle moral pressures. For example, a married woman may give in to rape or a beating by her husband rather than face the sanctions that will follow if she publicly discloses the state her marriage is in.

Power at this first level may also be exercised in open decisions taken on publicly discussed issues. Putting Anne on valium is an exercise of power of this kind. The issues involved – violence, broken marriages, and the right to an income above the poverty line – have been discussed publicly at length. Our society has decided to keep the situation under control rather than change it. To change the situation would threaten the status quo, so those with power in the status quo use it to maintain things as they are.

Anne's problems are not unique or rare. It is possible to devise better solutions to them than our society offers: to have a more equitable distribution of wealth and income; to give equal status and resources to alternatives to the nuclear family structure for the many whom it does not suit; to eradicate institutionalized violence and foster a sense of self-esteem in society so that women and men need not so often be brutalized by the receiving and giving of violence.

Of course, these 'solutions' are glib, grandiose, radical, unrealistic, easier said than done. But the reason they are not attempted is not because they are difficult; it is because they are a threat to the way things presently are.

... Because these issues pose a threat, those with power to take a decision on them decide not to respond to the issues but instead control them so that the threat is contained. ... Anne's tension and anxiety – the symptoms of her problems – are dealt with; she is helped to 'cope' with the way things are, not to change the way things are. Her personal power to create enough fuss to have her demands attended to is undermined by the help she is offered. This is power being used directly to exercise social control.

It is important to realize that we do not have to invent a whole conspiracy of knowing actors who, once threatening issues are raised, consciously exert their power to stifle those issues. Once a power structure is set up, its momentum is maintained on the basis of a set of values and beliefs, an ideology, the same ideology by which the decisions to set up the structure were made in the first place.

This ideology is most easily recognized in the range of taken-for-granted notions which shape our day-to-day lives. To illustrate from Anne's situation again: the doctor prescribing valium for Anne *may* be doing so because s/he wants to maintain the existing social order; but not necessarily so. It is more likely that s/he believes that someone else is doing 'something' about the broader social issues involved. What is required, as this doctor sees it, is to act in her/his professional capacity to prevent Anne from having an even more serious breakdown. This doctor is, most likely, unconsciously operating *within* the dominant ideology; s/he is merely acting in the grip of the structure of the society.

Most uses of power are complex. They contain elements of two or all three faces of power. For instance, Anne's case was a definite illustration of social issues which had been raised in public and were met by a 'No' from those with the power to make it stick. This is the first face of power. But there is an element of the second face of power there as well. To respond to those issues by saying 'violence is part of human nature', 'there will always be marriages that don't work', 'those who work harder than others should get more than others' is an evasive attempt on the part of those with the power to disguise their real intention of refusing to resolve the issues. The desire to disguise the true intent of one's actions is characteristic of the second face of power.

Power wearing this second face is a dissembling creature; it tries to hide its true motives. Those who exercise it may often appear ready to embrace an issue, to resolve a grievance when, in fact, they have seen that issue as a threat to their own security and are working to suppress it as it emerges into the public arena. If they cannot suppress the issue, they will use their power to mould, to divert, to distort it into something less threatening. At this second level, power is most successful when it can prevent a threatening issue from getting 'onto the agenda' at all.

Just such an attempt was made by the proposers of the anti-abortion amendment to the Irish constitution in 1982. Aware that EEC membership might make legal abortion an issue in Ireland, they attempted to pre-empt the whole debate. The fact that the attempt backfired into a more sophisticated discussion of abortion than would have seemed possible a year or two earlier does not alter the fact that it was an attempt to stifle the issue.

If an issue manages to get onto the agenda for decision making, power of the second dimension still has other tricks in its repertoire. Those with power to take decisions on the issue will frequently give the impression of wanting to resolve it. What they are really doing, however, is consolidating their own position as best they can in the face of this threat to the status quo. The Health (Family Planning) Act of 1979 is a good illustration.

The Act was a response to various demands for action on the availability of family planning services in Ireland. Ever since the days of the 'contraceptive train' protests in the early 1970s, when women from the Republic attempted to bring in contraceptives from Northern Ireland, women were in the forefront of the campaign to make family planning services available for all who wished to avail [themselves] of them. Women demanded that in a supposedly pluralist, non-confessional state their right to decide whether and how to plan their pregnancies should not be pre-empted by an official ban on the sale of contraceptives. . . . A large section of the medical profession, particularly general practitioners, were worried that a significant portion of their practice was being lost to the increasingly popular family planning clinics. The Roman Catholic church, itself internally split on the issue of contraception, wished to have contraception restricted to 'natural methods' for married couples only. The other churches in Ireland insisted that the state should facilitate the right of their members to plan their families by whatever method they favoured.

In passing the Health (Family Planning) Act 1979, the government took a decision aimed, not at resolving the issue of availability of contraceptives, but at taking the heat out of a politically difficult problem. By limiting the supply of contraceptives to those with bona fide family planning reasons, the Act implied strongly that only married couples could avail [themselves] of them and so pleased the Roman Catholic church. By insisting that all contraceptives, including condoms, could be obtained only on a doctor's prescription and from a qualified pharmacist, the Act could be seen to be responding to GPs' anxieties about family planning clinics and, at the same time, to be giving a boost to those independent pharmacists who wished to avail [themselves] of this new addition to their trade. By making all forms of contraceptives technically available, albeit by a cumbersome and expensive route, the government could claim to be responding to demands for contraceptive services.

That the government's intention was to deflate the whole issue rather than do anything positive about extending family planning services, became clear in the following weeks and months as a blind eye was turned on the family planning clinics, who were technically in breach of the law as they continued to sell contraceptives. That the infamous 'Irish solution to an Irish problem' is a hypocritical absurdity is irrelevant. The decision to pass that Act deflated the issue in a way which best served the existing power structure.

The second face of power can also undermine an issue by distorting, reshaping, redefining it as it emerges so that it is perceived by the public as something quite different from what its supporters originally intended. For example, the whole attempt by women to liberate ourselves from repressive sexist stereotypes has often been redefined and distorted into a demand for sexual freedom, for liberation of our sexual selves alone. Where we have been demanding freedom to define our own roles in society, we are treated as if we want to cast off the shackles of reasonable responsibility so as to indulge ourselves and feed our every desire. Where we are seeking in all the aspects of our lives alternatives which would be more humane, for women and for men, we are sneered at as if we were irresponsible, fickle, promiscuous, even amoral. The richness and importance of what we are saying is heard selectively and is re-broadcast in a way which trivializes it out of recognition. The message is undermined, distorted, but the manner of its distortion is significant, too. Our society would like to turn us, even in our struggle for liberation, back in to the sex symbols and sex objects which characterize the dominant attitude to women in our society.

Part of the effectiveness of this strategy is that those who have pushed to translate their grievance into a publicly discussed issue, find themselves forced to dissipate their energies in reclaiming and salvaging the distorted issue. Inevitably they lose momentum, and often heart, in this struggle to bring the issue back on course.

Another manifestation of the second face of power occurs in deliberate misinformation on an issue. If an issue is unwelcome to those in power, they can deliberately misinform the public about it. This has the attraction of at best misleading some and at worst confusing others. For example, when it is pointed out that women are more generally found in poorly paid jobs, that they have less access to training and poorer promotion prospects than men, time and again the response will come back that equal pay for equal work is now a legally safeguarded principle which is being implemented throughout the paid workforce. This is clearly not a response to the complaint being made. It is a blatant attempt to misinform and confuse. Although it can easily be refuted, it takes time and energy to do so.

The third face of power is the most insidious. The first face is identified by asking who took what action or decision on an issue being debated. The second face is uncovered by asking who prevented this issue from emerging into the public arena or who distorted, remoulded, diverted it. The third face is much harder to locate.

23

The third face of power operates by controlling our perceptions of ourselves, our awareness of reality, by exercising manipulative control over our minds. Perhaps this is beginning to sound a bit paranoid? But if power is exercised in such a way that we sometimes fail to perceive that we are enduring a grievance, then the circle of power is complete.

For example, many women live in the chronic misery of low self-esteem. The complexity of reasons for this is obviously huge but consider the influence of just one factor, advertising. The dominant female images in advertising are of women either as alluring objects of sexual gratification or as the successful housewife and mother who tends her beautiful and happy family and house and still has time and energy to be as soft and gentle to her husband and children as the skin on her cleverly protected hands. Women who fall short of these ideals are encouraged to feel dissatisfied with themselves. Ludicrous as these images are upon reflection, they are bombarded at us with such intensity that it requires a lot of energy to resist them. It is difficult not to feel dissatisfied with ourselves, difficult to refuse to judge ourselves by these standards. Here a patriarchal understanding of women, of sexuality, of the family and of a consumer-oriented economy conspire to create a sense of inadequacy in women. Encouraging women to spend their energy in combatting this false sense of inadequacy, in attempting to live up to these false ideals, is a very effective method of controlling them. . . .

Knowledge is power. Certainly, all knowledge gives access to power of some kind, if it is skilfully used. Knowledge of the mechanisms by which power is exercised is no exception. Knowing something about the ways in which power is used against us gives us a choice.

It is perfectly possible, for instance, to use the knowledge of how the system works to play the system better. Many women have taken this option. They have chosen the combination of available roles which suits them best. They have become successful careerists, brilliantly attractive sexual partners or the reliable and esteemed lynch-pin of a successful, happy household – some have managed the superwoman combination of all three. But to succeed in this way, in terms defined by a male-oriented society, requires accepting a set of values and attitudes which men, not women, have defined. We *can* accept this set of values and attitudes defined by men. But to do so consciously is a cynical and perfectly reasonable choice for which we pay a price.

Knowing that power can be exercised against us at every level, from the crudest to the most subtle, may be, quite simply, too daunting. Either it is time to despair, or we accept a certain loss of hope and settle down to accommodating ourselves to the best deal we can get.

A third option, and one which is far more positive for women, is to deviate from the accepted notions, the established values, the norms. Instead of using our energies in a struggle where the ground rules are stacked against us, we can apply them to the active creation of alternatives. But even in this option, where we choose to turn our backs on society, society will not ignore us. Those who take a course of action which deviates from the accepted codes and practices will be pursued; and deviance is seen by those in power as a very threatening thing.

Those whose power base is being endangered by deviant behaviour will respond in one of two ways. They will either colonize the 'deviant' behaviour, take it over, adopt it, absorb it into acceptable practice in society. Or they will label it as something undesirable. Our creative new activity – our attempt, as women, to get away from the way things have been done – will be labelled deviant, weird, perverse, sick, queer, marginal. This is an attempt to undermine its appeal, to isolate those involved. But deviance, like beauty, is in the eye of the beholder. What is deviant behaviour to a secure group will be perfectly rational behaviour to those for whom the very security of that group means repression. Take the example of women's campaign to reclaim the night: why should women be terrorized off the streets? Why agree to control the problem of men's violence and harassment by compliantly staying at home? It is rational to organize to have the problem eradicated, to get out and confront the 'bully in the playground'. That is not deviance, that is common sense. This is the strength Mary Daly exhorts us to experience by repossessing our language which has long been used against us. For example, what is a nag but a person characterized by her persistence and conviction? Deviance has been a very dirty word. We need to reclaim it and cultivate it as the virtue it is.

Women and men want delight, fulfilment, self-respect, satisfaction. Power presently operates to prevent us from living full, self-directed lives. It is rational, not deviant, to fight for an alternative society. Learning how power operates against us is not just a negative, passive exercise. It liberates us from the constraints of an old framework and empowers us to create one better suited to our needs.

[· · ·]

25

Article 1.2
VANISHING ACTS IN SOCIAL AND POLITICAL THOUGHT: TRICKS OF THE TRADE
Beverly Thiele

It is common knowledge among feminists that social and political theory was, and for the most part still is, written by men, for men and about men. The classic theorists of political philosophy are all firmly within what O'Brien (1981, p. 5) calls the 'male-stream': their subject matter reflects male concerns, deals with male activity and male ambitions and is *directed away from* issues involving, or of concern to, women. As a consequence, women themselves do not appear as actors in the realm of social and political thought. Where she is present, woman is either a partial figure engaged in activities which can easily be described by direct analogy to men (as with the Marxist worker – a sexless creature), or she is an ideological construction of the male theorist's imagination – we see 'Woman' in all her glory rather than *real* women. . . . What women are, do and can become are not the central concerns of male-stream theory nor are they considered appropriate concerns for such theory.

[· · ·]

Artemis March (1982) began an investigation into women's disappearance from male-stream scholarship by identifying the forms their invisibility takes in androcentric sociology. I want to extend this analysis to political theory and go a little further by disclosing the tricks which help theorists to eliminate women from 'the discourse' (Smith, 1979). . . . The three forms of invisibility March identified were exclusion, pseudo-inclusion and alienation.

Exclusion

Invisibility of this form involves women being completely ignored or neglected because the subject of such theories are explicitly male or male-dominated institutions and activities. Women are excluded by default; they become invisible by being disregarded. . . . March (1982, p. 100) suggests that Weber, for example, structurally excludes women from his theory by setting priorities in subject matter and data which focus attention on social processes and activities in which women are only marginally involved, if at all.

There is . . . another far less subtle form of exclusion practised in political theory, . . . when women are, for no given reason, simply dropped from the discourse. Their disappearance is magical. In this second form women may in fact get mentioned but, to the extent that theoretical propositions about women bear any relation to the main thesis, they might just as well not be there at all. In such cases the theory's shortcomings are frequently all too apparent. Hobbes is an example. He assumes an initial State of Nature in which men and women are explicitly equal and in which women have natural authority over children, but he ends up with a Commonwealth entirely inhabited by men. Women's absence is so marked that Brennan and Pateman (1979, p. 187) have described the Hobbesian family in civil society as a 'one parent family' where that parent is a father. Why women never make it into membership of the Commonwealth is never explained, and their relation to civil society has continued to plague liberal and social contract theorists ever since (Brennan and Pateman, 1979; Pateman, 1980a).

It should be stressed . . . that the exclusion of women is an active process rather than a result of passive neglect. It is not a simple case of lapsed memory: these theorists don't just forget to talk about women; rather, women are structurally excluded from the realm of discourse or, for the sake of theoretical preoccupations and coherency, they are deliberately dropped.

[· · ·]

Pseudo-inclusion

Pseudo-inclusion differs from exclusion in that the theory appears to take women into account but then marginalizes them. Women become defined as a 'special case', as anomalies, exceptions to the rule which can be noted and then forgotten about. What is normative is male. . . .

March's choice of Durkheim's *Suicide* is an excellent one, particularly given his treatment of the statistics on female suicides. This data contradicts Durkheim's thesis about why people commit suicide, but rather than change the theory or admit that it is not universally applicable, he embarks on a long explanation of the peculiarities of woman's nature. We are, to quote March (1982, p. 103), 'too primitive to absorb the niceties of male civilisation, too dense to be deeply affected by the unweavings and reweavings of the social fabric, too self-contained to be socially vulnerable'. For these reasons we become unsuitable subjects for Durkheim's study and, as Beth Pengelly's (1981) careful analysis of *Suicide* reveals, he actually deletes the statistical data on women halfway through the text.

[· · ·]

Alienation

The third form of invisibility ... refers to those theories which Clark and Lange (1979, p. ix) call 'extensionally male'. That is, they include women as subjects but they do not speak of the parameters of women's lives without distortion. Women's experience is interpreted through male categories because the methodology and values of the theorists remain androcentric. Despite any commitment these scholars have to the subject of women, their perspective interferes with their interpretation of women's experience, in particular by underwriting the selection of that part of women's lives which is deemed significant. How else can Mill see education as women's gateway to liberal equality and freedom, and fail to see that their continued responsibility for childrearing constrains both their access to education and, once they've got it, what they can do with it (e.g. Pateman, 1980b, p. 31).

Some of the best examples of women's alienation in theory come from the Marxist tradition; for example, Engel's description of women's oppression as *class* oppression. Similarly, Marxist-feminist attempts to use Marxism to understand women's oppression have often resulted in this type of invisibility for their subjects: our domestic labour, once seen as non-productive, is now thought to 'produce use-values' for capitalism rather than service the need of men in a patriarchy; procreation is not race regeneration but 'reproducing the labour-force'; and our position within the family and relations with other family members are significant only as part of the 'social relations of production' not reproduction. . . . Women's activity is still treated from an androcentric perspective and there is no effort to shift the grounding of the analysis away from male ego and experience, and onto female ego and experience. Women *qua* women remain both invisible and eccentric.

[· · ·]

TRICKS OF THE TRADE

Although March does not discuss the mutual exclusivity of each of these types, it is fairly clear that they cannot be seen this way. . . . It seems then that the best value can be gleaned from March's work if it is treated less as a classificatory scheme for social and political theorists and more as a typology of possible approaches. This is even truer of the second series of categories, the techniques of invisibility. These are invariably used in combination with each other to bring about women's exclusion, and in some cases are consistently paired. Not only is this second list not composed of mutually exclusive items, it is also far from exhaustive. The techniques are simply the ones I and my feminist friends have come across in our forays into social and political theory so far.

Decontextualization

By decontextualization, I am referring to the practice in theorizing of abstracting from real people, real activities and events in order to make generalizations about 'Man', 'Society' and so on. The important problem with this process is that it allows a theorist's commonsense assumptions about the world and reality to intervene between the real and ideal, the particular/concrete and the universal or general. . . .

C. Gould (1976, p. 9) has suggested that one of the most important deletions which takes place between the concrete and the abstract is gender: that being male or female is considered irrelevant to being human. This may be so, but what has traditionally occurred is that the abstraction from gender difference to what is truly human – to what is supposedly shared in common by both sexes – has been distorted by the intrusion of male-stream consciousness. What is *male* becomes the basis of the Abstract, the Essential and the Universal, while what is female becomes accidental, different, other.

[· · ·]

Universalisms

Decontextualization and universalisms are closely linked because, just as the claim of objectivity obscures the value-laden nature of theorizing, the claim to universality disguises the different treatment of men and women in social and political thought. . . .

Language is a great facilitator of universalisms. Terms such as 'man' and 'mankind' are used as if they were *generic* when in effect they are *genderic*. 'He' is assumed to be the all-inclusive pronoun, even though a close examination of the text makes it all too apparent that the author literally means 'he'. As Moller-Okin (1980, p. 5) pointed out, 'the dangerous ambiguity of such linguistic usage . . . [is that] it enables philosophers to enunciate principles as if they were universally applicable, and then to proceed to exclude all women from their scope'. Sexist language disguises the omission and denies the exception being made of women.

Naturalism

Perhaps the most common and persistent of the techniques used to separate women from men and exclude the former from the central grounds of theory is the recourse to the excuse proffered by 'Nature'. . . . In the first place, what is 'natural' ceases to require a social or political explanation; it is simply given, a constant which can be taken for granted. Marx, for example, uses this ploy to eliminate reproduction from dialectical materialism. Although a necessary condition for the 'reproduction' (sic) of capital, the propagation of the species, he says, need not concern the capitalist as it can be safely left up to the labourer's natural instincts (Marx, 1954). When reproduction is conceptualized as 'natural' it becomes incapable of generating social change and is written out of historical materialism. . . .

The irony in this deletion of reproduction was nicely exposed by Mary O'Brien in *The Politics of Reproduction* (1981). She points to the selectivity of such a rationale:

> Clearly, reproduction has been regarded as quite different from other natural functions which, on the surface, seem to be equally imbued with necessity: eating, sexuality and dying, for example, share with birth the status of biological necessities. Yet it has never been suggested that these topics can be understood only in terms of natural science. They have all become the subject matter of rather impressive bodies of philosophical thought; in fact we have great modern theoretical systems firmly based upon just these biological necessities . . . [Dialectical Materialism, Psychoanalysis and Existentialism] . . . The inevitability and necessity of these biological events has quite clearly not exempted them from historical force and theoretical significance.
>
> (O'Brien, 1981, p. 20)

And yet it has, in the eyes of the male-stream, for reproduction and women.

This raises the second important feature of naturalisms in social and political thought; the considerable ambiguity in the implications and significance of what is designated 'natural'. Natural men and natural women often imply quite different things to a political theorist, and this inconsistency is very clearly related to his political intent. When Rousseau, for example,

> refers to the natural man and to the natural woman, he has two distinct reference points in mind. Natural man is man of the original state of nature; he is totally independent of his fellows, devoid of selfishness, and equal to anyone else. Natural woman, however, is defined in accordance with her role in the golden age of the patriarchal family; and she is, therefore, dependent, subordinate, and naturally imbued with those qualities of shame and modesty that will serve both to make her sexually appealing to her husband, and to cause her to preserve her chastity as her most precious possession.
>
> (Moller-Okin, 1979, pp. 401–2)

Male nature is independent, active and truly human while female nature, conveniently for the status quo, fits her only for a narrow domestic role. The convenience is on man's part: his nature is such that he may transcend his animality by escaping into the human political realm of civil society, but only because women, trapped by their biology into remaining in the private sphere, oversee all the animal-like functions of mastication, defecation and copulation. He may still have to do the number one and two but she will clean the loo.

Dualisms

... Dualisms are very common motifs in western social and political thought – mind/body, nature/culture, emotion/reason, subject/object, public/private, individual/social, concrete/abstract, and so on. All of them should be approached with extreme caution because more often than not they line up with that fundamental dichotomy, male/female. Women are all body and no mind, closer to nature than culture, in the private realm not the public, emotional rather than rational, etc. etc.

There are two important points to recognize about dualisms. In the first place the dichotomous terms are commonly regarded as separate and opposed. Nancy Jay (1981, p. 44) noted that instead of being viewed as mere contraries (A/B), which can recognize continuity between the terms without shattering the distinction being drawn, most dualisms are regarded as logical contradictions (A/Not A). One can be *either* subject *or* object, either rational or emotional, never both. . . . The fuzzy middle ground between male and female, nature and culture, public and private is lost to view.

The second important feature of logical contradictions is that they contain an implicit value judgment. One pole (A) has positive value, the other (Not A) is negative.

[· · ·]

For the feminist critic of social and political thought, dualisms provide useful ways of disclosing the male-stream nature of discourse. Their appearance in a text frequently embodies women's oppression and exclusion. When J.S. Mill outlines in *On Liberty* (1972, p. 75) the relationships between public and private realms, he reveals, for all his undoubted feminism, his male perspective. The private realm as an arena of freedom and autonomy, as compensation for the compromises of the public sphere, has meaning only for men. Women exist principally in the private sphere, an arrangement which is, for Mill, both normative and ideal. For them the private sphere expresses control not freedom, submission not autonomy; it is the realm in which they consent to be ruled by the exercise of *male* autonomy and freewill. . . .

Appropriation and reversal

One final tool of patriarchal scholarship is what Mary Daly (1978b, p. 8) has termed 'reversals'. These are images and symbols of women-centred processes which, as part of the male method of mystification, are 'stolen, reversed, contorted and distorted by the misogynist mix-masters' (Daly, 1978b, p. 75). Reversals ensure that women's activities and contributions to society and life are denigrated and trivialized, and they do so by appropriating the imagery and symbolism of those women-centred processes for male activities. Marx's use of the term reproduction – the reproduction of daily life, the reproduction of the labour force – is an example of reversal. It is more than mere analogy because by appropriating the symbolism for male process the original activity (birth) is deprived of its meaning and significance; for Marx, men make history and themselves, women *merely* make babies.

FEMINIST CRITICISM AND FEMINIST SCHOLARSHIP

[· · ·]

From what we have seen about the practices of male-stream theorists and the nature of their theories about women, two things are clear. First, the exclusion of women from the realm of discourse is not simply a sin of omission – a simple matter of neglect or forgetfulness which can be rectified by putting women back in – because we've seen that even when women do constitute part of the subject matter of political theory they are still rendered invisible by the orientation, techniques and methodology used by the theorists (that is, pseudo-inclusion and alienation). Presence, *being there*, is no guarantee of visibility, of accurate or appropriate treatment by the discipline.

Second, it is clear that invisibility cannot simply be a case of bias or unexplored assumptions or simple misogyny (although undoubtedly many of these theorists were misogynists). If this were the case then a commitment to overcoming bias or a feminist consciousness should be enough to write integrated political theory, and yet, it isn't. Mill, in spite of his feminism, was unable to write into liberal theory women who were, like men, free and equal individuals; and Marxist-feminists still produce theory in which women are alienated from themselves.

[· · ·]

The opposition of women, family and nature on the one hand, to men, civil society and politics on the other – is fundamental to the definition of what is political, of what is an appropriate subject for political theory. To include women requires a fundamental change of direction for the discipline. . . . Social and political theory is part of the praxis of men. It is both indicative of, and an agent in the oppression of women by men.

[· · ·]

We would appear then to have grounds for scepticism about the extent to which social and political philosophy may be redeemed. The exclusion of women is a foundation stone of the discipline and must therefore have profound implications for its 'logic of knowledge'.

So what are our alternatives? It seems fairly obvious that if women's lives cannot be adequately theorized about by androcentric thought, then we could in the first instance try to write theory from a gynocentric perspective, one which instead of being grounded in the experiences of men has at its centre a female ego. On the surface this would seem to beg the question of an integrated, truly universal political theory and lend credence to criticism that our reading of the tradition of western political thought is negative, accusatory and narrow (Tenenbaum, 1982, p. 137). Such a view, I think, is both inaccurate and misrepresents feminist ambitions. As Mary O'Brien's theorizing in *The Politics of Reproduction* (1981) illustrates so well, gynocentric theory is more than a mere counterbalance. . . . It is a turn of a spiral, not the flip of a coin.

More importantly for feminist scholarship, gynocentric theory not only challenges and transforms the *content* of political philosophy; it also challenges and transforms its *methodology*. In taking off from our critique of male-stream thought we are sensitized to the political uses of the male-stream's magic tricks and do not have to perform on the same terms. . . . With Mary O'Brien (1981, pp. 1–11) we write theory out of our experience and back into our experience. We are not only looking at a different subject: we are also doing a different type of scholarship.

Table 1.2.1 Forms of invisibility

(Active) Exclusion	Pseudo-inclusion	Alienation
Disregards women	Makes women a special case	Reinterprets women's experience
Problematic assumptions Data consists of external, visible acts Male ego is the assumed centre from which theory is spun out	*Problematic assumptions* That male data is normative and therefore interpretations and models based on men are adequate Women don't really count, therefore can delegitimate as 'anomalous' the female data or gender differences Single set of social relations exists	*Problematic assumptions* Same as pseudo-inclusion
Women as objects of analysis Data on women not collected Data on women not analysed	Women as objects of analysis Judge/interpret women's actions in male-centred activities/organiz-ations by male norms	Women as objects of analysis Incorporation of women into male categories (e.g. 'bourgeois') Women as converted to data/roles in conceptual schema which are male-centred (e.g. reproducer of labour force)
Women as subjects/actors Women not conceived as political actors – acting in self-interest Priorities given to male activities/actors	Women as subjects/actors Women seen only in marginal relation to male activities/spheres	Women as subjects/actors Male naming of female experience, women forced to think through their experience via male categories (e.g. femininity as penis envy)
e.g. Weber, Hobbes	e.g. Durkheim, Rousseau	e.g. Marx, Marxist-feminists, J.S. Mill

(Source: Extracted from March, 1982, p. 107)

Table 1.2.2 Tricks which bring about invisibility

Decontextualization	Universalism	Naturalism	Dualism	Appropriation/reversal
Abstracts from reality Ideology, consciousness determine what is important, essential, universal (male) and what is deleted as insignificant and irrelevant (female) e.g. Weber Differential treatment of men and women – what men are/do/can be vs what women are for	Obscures bias in decontextualization e.g. Language which claims to be generic obscures partiality	What is 'natural' ceases to require an explanation (e.g. Marx) Ambivalence regarding 'nature' and 'natural' reflects the purpose of naturalism in theory, i.e. to exclude women	Differentiate male from female and invest male pole with positive value and female with negative value viz. A-not A dichotomy They embody women's oppression and exclusion and exemplify mainstream character of social and political thought, e.g. Mill	Images/symbols/descriptions which are stolen from woman-centred processes and reversed for male scholarship e.g. Marx: men make history, women make babies. Weber: men act, women react

(Source: From the HAG feminist discussion group)

Article 1.3
FEMINIST THEORY:
THE PRIVATE AND THE PUBLIC

Linda J. Nicholson

The primary purpose of this [article] is methodological: to clarify certain confusions in feminist theory connected with the use of the categories 'private' and 'public'. These categories have played an important role within feminist theory, and I believe rightly so. Many feminist theorists have correctly intuited that these categories point to societal divisions that have been central to the structuring of gender in modern western society, at least. Some theorists have even argued that a more general separation, expressed in the opposition between 'domestic' and 'public', has been universally important in organizing gender.

Even so, I sense among feminist theorists a suspicion of such categories conjoined with a suspicion toward employing dualistic frameworks altogether. The following remarks by Rosalind Petchesky illustrate this tendency:

> This, in turn, led to a further analytical insight: that 'production' and 'reproduction,' work and the family, far from being separate territories like the moon and the sun or the kitchen and the shop, are really intimately related modes that reverberate upon one another and frequently occur in the same social, physical and even psychic spaces. This point bears emphasizing, since many of us are still stuck in the model of 'separate spheres' (dividing off 'woman's place,' 'reproduction,' 'private life,' the home, etc. from the world of men, production, 'public life,' the office, etc.). We are now learning that this model of separate spheres distorts reality, that it is every bit as much an ideological construct as are the notions of 'male' and 'female' themselves. Not only do reproduction and kinship, or the family have their own historically determined products, material techniques, modes of organization, and power relationships, but reproduction and kinship are themselves integrally related to the social relations of production and the state; they reshape those relations all the time.

(Petchesky, 1979, pp. 376–77)

Iris Young's article on dual systems theory elaborates this position (Young, 1980, esp. pp. 179–81). She notes that Marxist feminists, in their attempt to make Marxism more explanatory of gender, have often merely added onto the Marxist categories an additional set, creating models composed of two systems. Thus, many have tended to think in terms of 'production' *and* 'reproduction', 'capitalism' *and* 'patriarchy'. The specific oppression of women is then accounted for by appealing to the interaction of these basically separated spheres of social relationships. Young persuasively points out the many problems with this type of approach. She notes that the 'production/reproduction' model, or those similar to it, tends to universalize the division of labour peculiar to capitalist society. Only in capitalism has 'production' become separated from 'reproduction', or have some of those activities associated with the making of food and objects been separated from such domestic activities as childbearing and childrearing. To make this separation the basis for one's theoretical model is thus to project onto much of history a separation unique to modern society. Moreover, Young argues that dual systems theory suffers from other major problems: it obscures the integration that exists between the separated spheres; it fails to account adequately for the nature of women's oppression outside the home; and at the most fundamental level, it leaves unchallenged the assumption that women's oppression is a separable and thus peripheral element in social life.

Michelle Zimbalist Rosaldo has also criticized early work by herself and others that stressed a 'domestic/public' opposition as helpful in explaining the social organization of gender (Rosaldo, 1980). Rosaldo has argued that this opposition . . . tended to explain gender in psychological, functional terms . . . [and to] obscure cross-cultural diversity in the structuring and evaluation of gender.

All these arguments are extremely helpful and need to be taken seriously. I do, however, see a possible confusion in the conclusions that might be drawn. From such arguments we might be led to abandon oppositions, such as 'private' and 'public' that, properly interpreted, do provide an important clue for understanding gender. What is wrong with some of the dualisms Petchesky and Young pointed to, in particular the opposition of 'production' and 'reproduction', follows not from their duality, but from the fact that the categories chosen obscure history. As Young correctly notes, the use of the opposition 'production/reproduction' inaccurately projects backward onto all human history a division of labour specific to capitalism.

[· · ·]

If we interpret such oppositions historically, that is, as separations rooted in history and not in some biological or otherwise stipulated cross-cultural division of labour, we might then retain tools to help us understand important components of our own past history of

37

gender. Moreover, by so historicizing these separations we may be able to see what is wrong with much existing social theory, which tends falsely to universalize aspects of these separations.

Marxism, for example, tends to universalize the modern separation between family and economy. Thus Marx, and many Marxists following him, have tended on occasion to assert that changes in the family can be understood as effects of changes in the economy. The difficulty with such a position is that it assumes one can cross-culturally separate claims about the 'family' from claims about the 'economy'. Yet not until the establishment of a market economy in the modern period, did activities emerge on any significant scale, concerned with the production and distribution of food and objects that are organized separately from activities considered the province of the family. Indeed, part of what we mean by the term 'market economy' is that such activities become freed from governance by such institutions as family, church and state, and become organized only by the laws of the market. Of course, this separation, even in our own times, has never been complete. For example, even within contemporary society, where fast-food chains absorb ever more of the final stages of food production, this activity is still largely carried out within the home. . . .

By ontologizing the separation of family and economy, we . . . lose sight of the kinds of connections that have existed between the separated spheres, connections that have occurred in the very process of their separation. Thus, as many feminists have pointed out, even while many women have left the home for wage-earning activities in the course of the twentieth century, the social relations of their paid jobs often replicate the social relations of the homes they have left. This transference of gender roles from the home to the work world has been described by some feminists as the rise of 'public patriarchy' and may indicate certain weaknesses in the traditional Marxist cure for ending women's oppression: 'Get thee to the workplace!'

If Marxism has been guilty of obscuring our understanding of gender by universalizing the separation of the family and the economy, liberalism has been equally guilty of providing a comparable obstacle, that of universalizing the separation between the family and the state. Again it appears that the task for feminist theory is to disprove the universalization of this separation while also elaborating the grounds for its development.

What is meant by the claim that liberalism universalizes the separation of family and state? A basic explanation is that theorists associated with the liberal tradition assume that there are two different kinds of human needs best satisfied by two different kinds of institutions. On the one hand are the needs of intimacy, affection, sexuality, and the various kinds of aid and support that other human beings can provide. The family is the institution best designed for satisfying such needs. Within liberalism's history, the exact specification of these needs has varied, corresponding to real changes in the institution of the family. For example, the need for intimacy and affection on the part of all family members begins to become stressed only during the eighteenth century. . . . What is consistent is the claim that there exist some needs, naturally present in whomever they are allocated to, that can best be met through the family.

In conjunction with the claim that the family exists to satisfy certain natural human needs is a further claim that the family alone is insufficient to regulate social life adequately. Early liberal 'state of nature' theorists, such as Locke, while admitting families within the state of nature, did not believe them capable of preventing or solving the problems endemic to that condition. Locke and others have argued that some type of political institution, such as the state, is also necessary. The most fundamental purpose of the state is to prevent or resolve conflict arising among individuals who are not members of the same family. According to this theory, if the human population were small enough and constituted by only one family or by a few families widely scattered (a situation Locke attributes to the beginning days of human history), states would not be necessary. Given, however, a human population composed of more than one family, and given the problems Locke and others attribute to a stateless society, the need for a state arises.

It is important to stress that for liberal theory, while the state 'organizes' relations between members of different families in a manner somewhat analogous to the way families 'organize' their individual members, states are *not* families writ large. Not only is there a difference in size between the two institutions, they also differ widely in purpose and in terms of the nature of the relationships that constitute both. Of course, within liberal theory, there has been much diversity in the description of the extent and nature of the differences between families and states. . . . In Locke's writings, one finds arguments supporting both the similarities and differences of familial and political relations. For example, Locke argues against Sir Robert Filmer, for the contractarian nature of political relationships, in part through a claim about the contractarian nature of the marriage relationship. He also points to certain differences between the two, such as the rights over life and death, which states, but not families, have over their members. In general, however, all liberal theorists assume certain dissimilarities in the governance of families and political institutions based upon a belief in certain qualitative differences in the nature of the two institutions. While these differences are not always made explicit, a not untypical list would include reference to such features as their respective sizes and purposes, the composition of their members, the respective relation of their members to property, etc.

The point I believe feminist theory needs to make against this position is not that families and states are similar. While the slogan . . . 'the personal is political' may aid us in seeing certain similarities between personal and political relationships and between families and states, we cannot ignore the real differences between both personal and political and family and state. In opposition to liberal theory, however, feminist theory needs to show the historical nature of these differences. Liberal theory has been correct in describing the social divisions that have existed, and sometimes its arguments on the normative implications of these divisions are sound. What has remained untested, however, is the thesis of the inevitability of such divisions.

[· · ·]

The . . . point can be demonstrated by examining certain work by feminist scholars and others in the history of the family. One example is an analysis of the relationship between the family and the state by Marilyn Arthur. While Arthur's focus is primarily on the evolution of the Greek city-state, she perceives certain parallels between that evolution and the development of the early modern state in western Europe. In both cases, a basically aristocratic or feudal society organized around kinship gave way to a society dominated by a more egalitarian state. She describes the changes occurring in a pre-classical Greece as follows:

> Aristocratic or feudal society is usually dominated by a landholding nobility defined by birth whose social relationships preserve many of the features of tribal society. . . . In the midst of this society a class of commercial entrepreneurs arises. They derive from all social and economic groups: wealthy landowners interested in trade, younger or illegitimate sons of the nobility involved in maritime ventures, craftsmen and other specialists and wealthy, independent peasants. In archaic Greece the rise of this class was associated with the discovery of iron, whose ready availability made possible small-scale cultivation of land and thus transformed the method of production. The artisans worked the new materials, the merchants traded in it, and agriculture was intensified through its use. This new middle class was thus still strongly tied to the land (the economic base of society was agriculture throughout all of antiquity), but it was a larger and more diverse group than the landowning aristocracy. At this point in history the small household emerged as the productive unit of society, and any head of a household (who was

40

simultaneously a landowner) automatically became a citizen or member of the state. Conversely, the state itself, the *polis*, was defined as the sum of all individual households.

(Arthur, 1977, p. 67)

One can carry a parallel between pre-classical Greece and early modern Europe only so far; too many obvious factors differentiate the two periods. On a very general level, however, there is one important similarity: in both periods a connection appears between the development of a democratic state and the emergence of a relatively nuclearized household/familial unit. This connection makes sense conceptually if we consider the extension of political power in the early modern period and in the pre-classical period. Political power, in both cases, rather than resting in a tribal chief or head of kin, becomes more widely shared among the diverse constituents of a new middle class, whose justification for political representation lay in a position as head-of-household. Thus the growth of a more widespread political representation and the development of a more nuclearized household/familial unit appear as correlate phenomena. This thesis on the interconnection of a more democratic state and a more nuclearized family unit finds support in the work of others. Hannah Arendt (1958, p. 24), for example, . . . pointed out that the foundation of the *polis* was preceded by the destruction of all organized units resting on kinship, such as the *phratria* and the *phyle*. In reference to the early modern period, Lawrence Stone (1979, pp. 99, 100) has argued that kinship, lordship and clientage, the forms of social organization that structured medieval aristocratic life, were antithetical to the functioning of the modern state.

[· · ·]

Stone claims that one of the tools used by the emerging state in its battle for power with existing feudal lords was to transfer the idea of 'good lordship' from these lords to the individual male head-of-household. The subordination of the household members to their head was in turn described as analogous to and supportive of the subordination of subjects to the sovereign. Thus, Stone notes that the principle of patriarchy was transformed by the state from a threat to its existence into a formidable buttress for it (Stone, 1979, p. 111).

Both Arthur and Stone derive implications from their analyses for changes in gender roles. Arthur, . . . after noting the status of woman as object of exchange in the period prior to the one with which she is concerned, argues that the transformations that resulted in the rise of the household's importance as a political unit in ancient Greece in turn added a new dimension to this status. As the integrity of each individual household came to possess political significance, so also did the biological activities of women, who could potentially violate that integrity. Adultery, for example, when practised by women, became seen as a crime against society and not merely as a personal transgression (Arthur, 1977, p. 69). The corollary to the legal sanctions against adultery by women was the idealization given to the citizen wife who produced legitimate heirs. This idealization has caused some to argue that the overall status of women in classical Athens was not all that bad (Pomeroy, 1975, pp. 58–60). Arthur's position is that the idealization given to the citizen wife does not mitigate the fundamental misogynistic attitude of classical Athens. The proper Athenian housewife may have been praised when she acted as she ought, but beyond the praise stood the fear that she might not.

[· · ·]

In so far as the polis depended upon the autonomy and inviolability of the individual household and thus the legitimacy of each man's heirs, it is understandable that women's sexuality would be highly feared. Women, whose sexuality had the power to disrupt the political order, were idealized for acting rightly while being hated and feared for their power to do wrong. In such a context it follows that women's activities generally would be closely watched. . . .

Stone similarly argues that the nuclearization of the family unit in the early modern period had certain distinct implications for gender roles. Women's declining ties to an extended kinship system meant a loss of their countervailing power to their husbands' authority. An increased power of the male head-of-household was also brought about during this period as a consequence of other related phenomena. The Lutheran Reformation increased the spiritual authority of the father and husband while reducing the countervailing authority of the priest and the Church.

While Arthur's and Stone's analyses seem to suggest that the rise of a democratic state is on the whole bad for women, I do not want to be taken as committed to that claim. The status of women is always an extremely complicated phenomenon, and while the kinds of broad generalizations I have been delineating may be helpful for providing a first step in understanding gender relations, they provide only a first step. To go on we must pay more attention to the specificities of the particular period in question. In the case of early modern Europe such specificities must include reference to the fact that if, as in classical Greece, the production unit was a household, it was a very different kind of household. The idealization of marriage as a type of partnership, for example, which began to emerge in the early modern period, importantly differentiates the status of women in early modern Europe from the classical era, as

42

does also the emergence of the concept of the individual with natural rights. . . . The point is that unless we view the family and the state in historical relation to one another, the status of women must remain for us, as it does in much of liberal theory, an unsolvable mystery. In other words, within liberal theory the social relations of the family are assumed as universal and a function of such facts, to quote Locke, that men are 'stronger' and 'abler'. In the seventeenth century, while liberalism was breaking new ground in extending political representation to male heads-of-households, it had little to say on why women were not also to be included in the political sphere. Even by the twentieth century, when women's rights to political participation were becoming recognized, liberalism has provided little insight into its previous position. The failure of understanding in all cases can be attributed to an inability to see the family in conjunction with the state as a social institution, with two sharing inter-related histories.

. . . The conclusion I wish to draw . . . is primarily methodological: that an important task for feminist theory is to show the historical origins and evolution of those divisions others have assumed to be inevitable. Phrasing the project in this way enables us to clarify certain confusions. Rosalind Petchesky . . . stated that the separation between the public and the private, between the family and work, is ideological. This claim is similar to what was intended by the . . . slogan 'the personal is political'. In both cases it was recognized that such divisions as between the private and the public or the personal and the political do obscure our understanding of the dynamics of gender. The ironic point . . . is that, to prove such claims, we need to show how the private did become separated from the public or the personal from the political. In other words, to break the ideological hold that such divisions maintain over our lives, we need to show their historical origins and their changing dynamics. . . . While feminist analyses have brought us to recognize much of women's oppression within existing personal and familial relationships, and have enabled us to recognize the entanglement of at least a part of this oppression with the very separation of these relationships from political and economic relationships, the continued analysis of such divisions need not entail their complete rejection. Unless we can begin to see these divisions in historical terms and not as universal givens outside analysis and change, we will be unable to influence intelligently the future of such divisions.

PART II
DIVERSITY AND DIFFERENCE

INTRODUCTION:
RECOGNIZING DIFFERENCE

One of the most important, and challenging, issues that has faced the women's movement and women's studies as it has developed as a discipline, has been the need to recognize, describe and explain the extent to which there are differences *between* women. As a political practice and academic subject, feminism in the UK and in the USA has been open to the criticism that it has prioritized the concerns and issues of white western and middle-class women, ignoring the ways in which women are differentiated and divided by their class position, their ethnic origin and colour and by their residence in different countries of the world, with widely varying living standards, differences in religion and culture, and in political control – all affecting the social definition of women, women's place in society and their political priorities. As western women, the majority living in urban or urbanized areas, it is often hard for us to remember that the majority of women in the world live in rural areas, often at or little above subsistence levels, and, in many countries in the Third World, subject to famine, natural disasters and political instability.

In this section of the book we focus on some of these differences between women. Within the British context, a debate about varying political priorities arose within the women's movement from the mid-1970s onwards. Initially, there seemed to be relative unanimity about the range of issues that were important for women, from equal pay to a woman's right to control her own fertility. However, gradually a greater awareness developed of the effects of these particular demands on different categories of women and of their different needs. This critique was initiated, in particular, by black feminists. They argued that the demands of the British women's movement were based on the needs and desires of white middle-class women. These are the women, for example, who have gained most from the expansion of job opportunities, especially in the professions. These are the women, too, who have dominated the ranks of academic feminism, controlling the major women's studies journals and, until recently, the new feminist presses and publishing houses that grew up from the early 1970s. Black feminists pointed out that the right to abortion and contraception was often less relevant to them as they struggled for their rights to have children and against sterilization policies. In their everyday lives in a racist society, the issues that are most immediate for women of colour[1] are frequently different from the concerns of white women. But white women, too, from different ethnic backgrounds, also have varying experiences. For women who are Jews or Cypriots, for example, or from other groups, less visible because of their skin colour but still 'different', the UK's is also a racist society.

The British women's movement and academic feminism in this century have also been criticized for their ethnocentrism – that is, their sole focus on the UK, or at best on other highly industrialized societies. Too often the experiences of British women, the social conditions of contemporary Britain and the nature of family and kinship relations in this country have been assumed to be universal. The key conceptual categories developed in British or western feminist theory – for example, the significance accorded to the public/private divide or the attention paid to the particular relationship between capitalism and patriarchy in advanced industrial societies – may not have the same purchase in explaining gender relations and the specific form of women's subordination in other societies and at other times.

The material circumstances of women in societies that are distinguished from that of the UK by religion, ideology and levels of development, vary significantly from those experienced by their sisters in the UK. For women in Muslim societies, for example, the restrictions imposed by their religion affect their lives greatly, structuring personal relations between women and men, limiting access to forms of education and waged work and, in countries such as Saudi Arabia, preventing women from driving cars. In less developed countries, enormous regional variations in living standards exist, from traditional agricultural economies in the rural areas to rapid industrialization in urban areas, which affect women's daily lives and their opportunities. Elsewhere, women are facing political upheavals. In Eastern Europe, for example, the shift from communism to capitalism during the 1990s will restructure women's access to a wide range of goods and services, not always to their benefit. The women of the former German Democratic Republic, for example, may lose their liberal abortion legislation and their access to higher education, although the eventual availability of a wider range of everyday items and consumer durables may raise their living standards. In yet other parts of the world, in South Africa for example, where *apartheid* still divides women on lines of race and colour, political change will radically restructure the future society.

This recognition of difference and diversity – that women are a heterogeneous group divided by class, race and ethnicity, by nationality and religion, by age and sexual preference – was a slow and often painful process for many women involved, in whatever ways, in the second wave of feminism and in the rise of the women's movement in the UK from the 1960s onwards. The initial burst of energy, organizing and theorizing, the marches and the consciousness-raising groups were based on the assertion of the common basis of women's experiences, on women's sisterhood in oppression:

> Sisterhood expressed the idea that in general women have interests opposed to those of men, that men generally dominate women, and generally benefit from this domination. During the 1970s, however, feminists produced new knowledge of women's lives. Instead of establishing women's shared oppression as women, they began to emphasise the differences between women. Once attention was given to the diversity of women's experience, to the power of some women over other women, and to the political and economic interests shared by some men and some women, problems were created for feminism. Differences of interest between women challenged feminist theory's assumption of women's shared oppression. They also undermined the basis of feminist political practice. If women do not have interests in common, then it is not clear how feminist politics can change all women's lives for the better.
>
> (Ramazanoglu, 1989, p. 3)

But gradually, a new set of knowledge has been accumulated, and is, of course, still being added to. Feminists are constructing a greater understanding of the differences and diversities between women's lives in different places and at different times. Gradually, we are forging new bodies of theoretical knowledge and a new politics that builds on difference and finds strength in alliances. At the theoretical level, women's studies now no longer focuses solely, or mainly, on the difference between women and men but also on differences between women – in Chapter 1 we argued that the deconstruction and reconstruction of key dichotomies is the current focus of feminist theorizing. As Joan Scott argues in the conclusion to her paper 'Equality and difference' included in Part IV: '. . . the generalised opposition male/female serves to obscure the differences *among* [our emphasis] women in behaviour, character, desire, subjectivity, sexuality, gender identification and historical experience' (p. 262). And, as she continues, '. . . we must open up to scrutiny the terms women and men as they are used to define one another in particular contexts . . .' (p. 262). Thus we may no longer assume that the terms 'women' and 'men' have a universal meaning, nor that the associated attributes of masculinity and femininity are timeless and placeless. Rather, they are defined and used in particular ways in particular circumstances and the historical context of gender relations must be specified. Apparently timeless notions such as mother love have their own history, and are not as universal as we might like to think!

But not only the terms 'man' and 'woman' must be opened up to scrutiny. We also need to be aware that the other key dualisms and concepts that are crucial to women's studies and feminist theory (and that run throughout this book) – equality (or sameness) and difference, the public and the private, notions of power and dependence – have particular meanings at different times and in different places. Being a woman, a worker, a mother, for example, has a certain meaning in a specific context and is not universally invariant. As Nicholson has argued in her article in Part I: 'Unless we can begin to see these divisions in historical terms and not as universal givens outside analysis and change, we will be unable to influence intelligently the future of such divisions' (p. 43). The aim of influencing the future, of course, is what distinguishes women's studies from many other areas of academic study. It has a political as well as an academic purpose.

Note

1   The politics of language and terminology is important. In the UK, common usage has moved from 'coloured' (now regarded as offensive), through black, which people of Asian origin argue excludes them, albeit recognizing that a black/white distinction summarizes the racist attitudes prevalent in contemporary Britain, to terms such as Afro-Caribbean and Asian to refer to people's origins, now frequently joined by the term British to remind us that many non-white people are British. Similarly in the USA, terms such as African–American were in common usage at the time we wrote this in 1991. 'Women of colour' is also used in the USA, although seldom in the UK, as a generic term to refer to non-white women, subsuming and yet allowing the recognition of their multiple identities and origins. Donna Haraway has suggested that this phrase 'women of colour' is a post-modern concept, creating 'an identity constructed out of a recognition of otherness and difference' (Haraway, 1990, p. 12). The white population is sometimes referred to as 'Anglos' in US texts. Look out for the different terms used in the articles associated with this section.

2
PERSONAL EXPERIENCE, FAMILIES AND HOUSEHOLDS

The two chapters in Part II examine some of the major lines of division between women, with examples drawn, in the main, from contemporary societies. In selecting the articles, we have tended to focus on some of the broad structural differences between women: on the connections between class, gender and ethnic origins at different times and in different places. But women also differ by age, in their sexual preferences, in their marital status and in their physical health and abilities. Some of these issues are addressed in other parts of this book or in the companion volumes *Knowing Women* (Crowley and Himmelweit, 1992), *Inventing Women* (Kirkup and Keller, 1992) and *Imagining Women* (Bonner *et al.*, 1992).

Space precludes consideration here of all the dimensions of difference that differentiate women. We had to be selective. The voices of older women and of lesbian women are absent (although present elsewhere in this book), and neither can those women, of different ethnic origins for example, whose voices are included, speak for all 'minority' women. Thus in no sense are the articles that follow 'representative' in a formal social science sense. The first article in Chapter 2 is a personal statement from Nancy Mairs, a feminist writer and teacher living in Arizona in the USA. In her essay, 'On being a cripple', she writes of how she feels about the increasing restrictions on her mobility that the progress of her disease imposes. In the extract included here she makes pertinent comments on the oppressive nature of the idealized images of women that are current in the USA: images which almost all of us fail to live up to. Her essay touches on a whole range of experiences, many of which, as women living in contemporary Britain, we may share with her, but others with which we differ because of our own race, class, age, sexuality and life-time experiences. Mairs lives in a conventional 'family' in the USA, an advanced industrial society. But family and household forms vary – not only within societies but also between them. Feminist analyses in anthropology have been important in drawing our attention to the differences that exist in living arrangements between places and societies.

Geography, which deals with differences between places, perhaps of all the social sciences, has been the last to be influenced by a feminist critique of its subject matter, concepts and theories.

However, throughout the 1980s, feminists working within the discipline began to demonstrate how the built environment and the economic and social structure of cities, localities and regions, both reflects and affects gender relations. Thus Linda McDowell (1983) argued that urban land use and housing policy play an important part in the construction of women's subordinate and 'private' position in contemporary Britain. Writing with Doreen Massey, she also showed how the division of labour, in the workplace and in the home, varies over space and time within England, resulting in different conceptions of femininity and masculinity and different sets of gender relations in distinct localities. Thus in the north east and the north west of England, in East Anglia and in Greater London, gender relations took a different form at particular times in the last century (McDowell and Massey, 1984).

In anthropology, places, often unknown and exotic, are also the focus for analysis. Anthropologists have added enormously to our understanding of cross-cultural variations in gender divisions. Their subject matter – family and kinship systems, wealth, inheritance, work and trading patterns, ritual and symbolism in other societies – is, after all, centrally concerned with the nature of femininity and masculinity, with power and gender divisions. In this discipline the problem has been not so much one of the exclusion of women altogether, as it was in some of the social sciences, but rather one of representation and interpretation. Anthropologists interpret other societies through the lens of their own society and their individual positions within it. Usually, although not always, white, from advanced industrial societies, and male, they have brought their own prejudices to bear on the interpretation of other societies, often privileging information from key male informants or ignoring male/female differences altogether. Sometimes, of course, male anthropologists are excluded by their sex from gaining access to women and from observing and understanding women's rituals, but the specificity of their focus is seldom made plain and results are presented as if they apply to everybody in the area being studied.

In common with other social science disciplines, the first task of feminist anthropologists was to collect information on women and women's activities. However, as Henrietta Moore has argued in a review of the impact of feminism on her discipline, this 'could only be a first step – albeit a very necessary one – because the real problem about incorporating women into anthropology lies not at the level of empirical research but at the theoretical and analytical level. Feminist anthropology is, therefore, faced with the much larger task of reworking and redefining anthropology theory' (Moore, 1988, p. 2). Feminist anthropologists, like feminists in history, geography, economics or sociology, quickly found that the 'add women and stir' approach was insufficient to dismantle the male biases in their discipline and that additional steps were necessary. In the short extract below, Moore outlines the phases through which feminist anthropology has passed:

> Looking at the relationship between feminism and anthropology, we can see that feminist anthropology began by criticizing male bias within the discipline, and the neglect and/or distortion of women and women's activities. This is the phase in the 'relationship' which we can refer to as the 'anthropology of women'. The next phase was based on a critical reworking of the universal category 'woman', which was accompanied by an equally critical look at the question of whether women were especially well equipped to study other women. This led, quite naturally, to anxieties about ghettoization and marginalization within the discipline of social anthropology. However, as a result of this phase, feminist anthropology began to establish new approaches, new areas of theoretical enquiry, and to redefine its project not as the 'study of women' but as the 'study of gender'. As we enter the third phase of this relationship, we see feminist anthropology begin to try to come to terms with the real differences between women, as opposed to contenting itself with demonstrations of the variety of women's experiences, situations and activities worldwide. This phase will involve the building of theoretical constructs which deal with difference, and will be crucially concerned with looking at how racial difference is constructed through gender, how racism divides gender identity and experience, and how class is shaped by gender and race. In the process of this, feminist anthropology will be involved not just in reformulating anthropological theory but in reformulating feminist theory. Anthropology is in a position to provide a critique of feminism based on the deconstruction of the category 'woman'. It is also able to provide cross-cultural data which demonstrate the Western bias in much mainstream feminist theorizing. The third, and current, phase of the relationship between feminism and anthropology is thus characterized by a move away from 'sameness' towards 'difference', and by an attempt to establish the theoretical and empirical grounds for a feminist anthropology based on difference.
>
> *(Moore, 1988, p. 11)*

Moore defines feminist anthropology as concerned with 'what it is to be a woman, how cultural understandings of the category "woman" vary through space and time and how these understandings relate to the position of women in different societies' (ibid.,

p. 12). This is a definition which feminists working in a range of social sciences might find acceptable as a description of their own approach. Moore then defines feminist anthropology more specifically: 'The analysis of women's subordination is dependent upon some consideration of gendered relations. Anthropological analyses approach the study of gender from two different, but not mutually exclusive, perspectives. Gender may be seen either as a symbolic construction or as a social relationship' (ibid., p. 13). In both areas, that of gender symbols and sexual stereotypes and in the analysis of the social relationships between men, women and children, anthropologists have demonstrated the extent of variation in attributes of gender and accepted behaviours in a wide range of different societies. Sexual ideologies and stereotypes vary greatly, but certain symbolic associations between gender and many other aspects of cultural life do occur across a wide range of societies.

Moore suggests that feminist anthropology is dominated by a single debate, although the participants in it take different theoretical positions: is sexual asymmetry universal or not? In other words, are women always subordinate to men? We must, however, be wary of assuming that the common distinctions that we, as western feminists working in contemporary societies, believe to be significant – for example, between the public and private spheres, or the association of women with nature and men with culture – apply in other societies. Sometimes the relationships are quite different. A good example is the notion of motherhood. In contemporary Britain we define motherhood as necessarily based on maternal love, daily child care and co-residence. Yet, this is a historically specific idea. Work in African–American communities in New York City has found that mothers may not live in the same space as their children but rather in a looser kin-network, often composed of their female families (Stack, 1974). In Article 2.2 Diana Gittins picks up this question and examines the range of variation in 'families', kinship and motherhood at different times in different societies.

In the next article (2.3), Ann Phoenix provides a challenge to the assumptions that (what seem like obvious) differences between women – in this case on the basis of ethnicity – are explanations for their behaviour. By focusing on a comparison of young women of Afro-Caribbean origins and young white women, all of whom are pregnant, she demonstrates that 'cultural' explanations for the behaviour of the black women are based on inadequate, and often dated, stereotypical views of the Caribbean. As she shows, the motives and behaviour of both groups of young women were similar and were a response to their realistic assessment of alternative prospects for young, unskilled women in the UK. We return to the question of divisions between women based on race and ethnicity in the next chapter.

Anthropologists, but also sociologists and often geographers, tend to focus on particular societies and small places within them for their fieldwork, analysing the symbolic and social structure of gender relations on a local scale. International comparative data about the position of women are far harder to come by. However, despite problems of data comparability, of different definitions, or just plain absence of the relevant figures, it is apparent that the subordinate position of women is *universal*. Although the particular nature of this subordination varies between countries, women everywhere are second-class citizens. Two US geographers, Joni Seager and Ann Olson (1986), have collected what data are available and have produced a fascinating atlas of women's position in the world, based on a range of indicators from educational participation, through age of marriage and numbers of pregnancies to participation in waged work and political institutions. Some of the maps from this atlas are reprinted in the companion volume *Inventing Women* (Kirkup and Keller, 1992). Here, we illustrate the international commonality that arises from women's subordination, but also from their determination to struggle for a better world, through the poem 'Bocas: a daughter's geography', in which African–American feminist poet and novelist, Ntozake Shange, stresses the commonalities that exist between women in their fight against 'the same old men'. She touches on a wide range of struggles by women to create a new and better world for their children and themselves, from Nicaragua to South Africa and from Chile to the UK.

Article 2.1
ON BEING A CRIPPLE

Nancy Mairs

To escape is nothing. Not to escape is nothing.
Louise Bogan

The other day I was thinking of writing an essay on being a cripple. I was thinking hard in one of the stalls of the women's room in my office building, as I was shoving my shirt into my jeans and tugging up my zipper. Preoccupied, I flushed, picked up my book bag, took my cane down from the hook, and unlatched the door. So many movements unbalanced me, and as I pulled the door open I fell over backward, landing fully clothed on the toilet seat with my legs splayed in front of me: the old beetle-on-its-back routine. Saturday afternoon, the building deserted, I was free to laugh aloud as I wriggled back to my feet, my voice bouncing off the yellowish tiles from all directions. Had anyone been there with me, I'd have been still and faint and hot with chagrin. I decided that it was high time to write the essay.

First, the matter of semantics. I am a cripple. I choose this word to name me. I choose from among several possibilities, the most common of which are 'handicapped' and 'disabled'. I made the choice a number of years ago, without thinking, unaware of my motives for doing so. Even now, I'm not sure what those motives are, but I recognize that they are complex and not entirely flattering. People – crippled or not – wince at the word 'cripple' as they do not at 'handicapped' or 'disabled'. Perhaps I want them to wince. I want them to see me as a tough customer, one to whom the fates/gods/viruses have not been kind, but who can face the brutal truth of her existence squarely. As a cripple, I swagger.

But, to be fair to myself, a certain amount of honesty underlies my choice. 'Cripple' seems to me a clean word, straightforward and precise. It has an honourable history, having made its first appearance in the Lindisfarne Gospel in the tenth century. As a lover of words, I like the accuracy with which it describes my condition: I have lost the full use of my limbs. 'Disabled', by contrast, suggests any incapacity, physical or mental. And I certainly don't like 'handicapped', which implies that I have deliberately been put at a disadvantage, by whom I can't imagine (my God is not a Handicapper General), in order to equalize chances in the great race of life. These words seem to me to be moving away from my condition, to be widening the gap between word and reality. Most remote is the recently coined euphemism 'differently abled', which partakes of the same semantic hopefulness that transformed countries from 'undeveloped' to 'underdeveloped', then to 'less developed' and finally to 'developing' nations. People have continued to starve in those countries during the shift. Some realities do not obey the dictates of language.

Mine is one of them. Whatever you call me, I remain crippled. But I don't care what you call me, so long as it isn't 'differently abled', which strikes me as pure verbal garbage designed, by its ability to describe anyone, to describe no one. I subscribe to George Orwell's thesis that 'the slovenliness of our language makes it easier for us to have foolish thoughts'. And I refuse to participate in the degeneration of the language to the extent that I deny that I have lost anything in the course of this calamitous disease; I refuse to pretend that the only differences between you and me are the various ordinary ones that distinguish any one person from another. But call me 'disabled' or 'handicapped' if you like. I have long since grown accustomed to them; and if they are vague, at least they hint at the truth. Moreover, I use them myself. Society is no readier to accept crippledness than to accept death, war, sex, sweat, or wrinkles. I would never refer to another person as a cripple. It is the word I use to name only myself.

I haven't always been crippled, a fact for which I am soundly grateful. To be whole of limb is, I know from experience, infinitely more pleasant and useful than to be crippled; and if that knowledge leaves me open to bitterness at my loss, the physical soundness I once enjoyed (though I did not enjoy it half enough) is well worth the occasional stab of regret. Though never any good at sports, I was a normally active child and young adult. I climbed trees, played hopscotch, jumped rope, skated, swam, rode my bicycle, sailed. I despised team sports, spending some of the wretchedest afternoons of my life sweaty and humiliated, behind a field-hockey stick and under a basketball hoop. I tramped alone for miles along the bridle paths that webbed the woods behind the house I grew up in. I swayed through countless dim hours in the arms of one man or another under the scattered shot of light from mirrored balls, and gyrated through countless more as Tab Hunter and Johnny Mathis gave way to the Rolling Stones, Creedence Clearwater Revival, Cream. I walked down the aisle. I pushed baby carriages, changed tyres in the rain, marched for peace.

When I was twenty-eight I started to trip and drop things. What at first seemed my natural clumsiness soon became too pronounced to shrug off. I consulted a neurologist, who told me that I had a brain tumour. A battery of tests, increasingly disagreeable, revealed no tumour. About a year and a half later I developed a blurred spot in one eye. I had, at last, the episodes 'disseminated in space and time' requisite for a diagnosis: multiple sclerosis. I have never been sorry for the doctor's initial misdiagnosis, however. For almost a week, until the negative results of the tests were in, I thought that I was going to die right away. Every day for the past nearly ten years, then, has been a kind of gift. I accept all gifts.

Multiple sclerosis is a chronic degenerative disease of the central nervous system, in which the myelin that sheathes the nerves is somehow eaten away and scar tissue forms in its place, interrupting the nerves' signals. During its course, which is unpredictable and uncontrollable, one may lose vision, hearing, speech, the ability to walk, control of bladder and/or bowels, strength in any or all extremities, sensitivity to touch, vibration, and/or pain, potency, co-ordination of movements – the list of possibilities is lengthy and, yes, horrifying. One may also lose one's sense of humour. That's the easiest to lose and the hardest to survive without.

In the past ten years, I have sustained some of these losses. Characteristic of MS are sudden attacks, called exacerbations, followed by remissions, and these I have not had. Instead, my disease has been slowly progressive. My left leg is now so weak that I walk with the aid of a brace and a cane; and for distances I use an Amigo, a variation on the electric wheelchair that looks rather like an electrified kiddie car. I no longer have much use of my left hand. Now my right side is weakening as well. I still have the blurred spot in my right eye. Overall, though, I've been lucky so far. My world has, of necessity, been circumscribed by my losses, but the terrain left me has been ample enough for me to continue many of the activities that absorb me: writing, teaching, raising children and cats and plants and snakes, reading, speaking publicly about MS and depression, even playing bridge with people patient and honorable enough to let me scatter cards every which way without sneaking a peek.

Lest I begin to sound like Pollyanna, however, let me say that I don't like having MS. I hate it. My life holds realities – harsh ones, some of them – that no right-minded human being ought to accept without grumbling. One of them is fatigue. I know of no one with MS who does not complain of bone-weariness; in a disease that presents an astonishing variety of symptoms, fatigue seems to be a common factor. I wake up in the morning feeling the way most people do at the end of a bad day, and I take it from there. As a result, I spend a lot of time *in extremis* and, impatient with limitation, I tend to ignore my fatigue until my body breaks down in some way and forces rest. Then I miss picnics, dinner parties, poetry readings, the brief visits of old friends from out of town. The offspring of a puritanical tradition of exceptional venerability,

I cannot view these lapses without shame. My life often seems a series of small failures to do as I ought.

I lead, on the whole, an ordinary life, probably rather like the one I would have led had I not had MS. I am lucky that my predilections were already solitary, sedentary and bookish – unlike the world famous French cellist I have read about, or the young woman I talked with one long afternoon who wanted only to be a jockey. I had just begun graduate school when I found out something was wrong with me, and I have remained, interminably, a graduate student. Perhaps I would not have if I'd thought I had the stamina to return to a full-time job as a technical editor, but I've enjoyed my studies.

In addition to studying, I teach writing courses. I also teach medical students how to give neurological examinations. I pick up freelance editing jobs here and there. I have raised a foster son and sent him into the world, where he has made me two grandbabies, and I am still escorting my daughter and son through adolescence. I go to Mass every Saturday. I am a superb, if messy, cook. I am also an enthusiastic laundress, capable of sorting a hamper full of clothes into five subtly differentiated piles, but a terrible house-keeper. I can do italic writing and, in an emergency, bathe an oil-soaked cat. I play a fiendish game of Scrabble. When I have the time and the money, I like to sit on my front steps with my husband, drinking Amaretto and smoking a cigar, as we imagine our counterparts in Leningrad and make sure that the sun gets down once more behind the sharp childish scrawl of the Tucson Mountains.

This lively plenty has its bleak complement, of course, in all the things I can no longer do. I will never run again, except in dreams, and one day I may have to write that I will never walk again. I like to go camping, but I can't follow George and the children along the trails that wander out of a campsite through the desert or into the mountains. In fact, even on the level I've learned never to check the weather or try to hold a coherent conversation: I need all my attention for my wayward feet. Of late, I have begun to catch myself wondering how people can propel themselves without canes. With only one usable hand, I have to select my clothing with care not so much for style as for ease of ingress and egress, and even so, dressing can be laborious. I can no longer do fine stitchery, pick up babies, play the piano, braid my hair. I am immobilized by acute attacks of depression, which may or may not be physiologically related to MS but are certainly its logical concomitant.

These two elements, the plenty and the privation, are never pure, nor are the delight and wretchedness that accompany them. Almost every pickle that I get into as a result of my weakness and clumsiness – and I get into plenty – is funny as well as maddening and sometimes painful. I recall one May afternoon when a friend and I were going out for a drink after finishing up at school. As we were climbing into opposite sides of my car, chatting, I tripped and fell, flat and hard, onto the asphalt parking lot, my abrupt departure interrupting him in mid-sentence. 'Where'd you go?' he called as he came around the back of the car to find me hauling myself up by the door frame. 'Are you all right?' Yes, I told him, I was fine, just a bit rattly, and we drove off to find a shady patio and some beer. When I got home an hour or so later, my daughter greeted me with 'What have you done to yourself?' I looked down. One elbow of my white turtleneck with the green froggies, one knee of my white trousers, one white kneesock were blood-soaked. We peeled off the clothes and inspected the damage, which was nasty enough but not alarming. That part wasn't funny: the abrasions took a long time to heal, and one got a little infected. Even so, when I think of my friend talking earnestly, suddenly, to the hot thin air while I dropped from his view as though through a trap door, I find the image as silly as something from a Marx Brothers movie.

I may find it easier than other cripples to amuse myself because I live propped by the acceptance and the assistance and, sometimes, the amusement of those around me. Grocery clerks tear my cheques out of my chequebook for me, and sales clerks find chairs to put into dressing rooms when I want to try on clothes. The people I work with make sure I teach at times when I am least likely to be fatigued, in places I can get to, with the materials I need. My students, with one anonymous exception (in an end-of-the-semester evaluation), have been unperturbed by my disability. Some even like it. One was immensely cheered by the information that I paint my own fingernails; she decided, she told me, that if I could go to such trouble over fine details, she could keep on writing essays. I suppose I became some sort of bright-fingered muse. She wrote good essays, too.

The most important struts in the framework of my existence, of course, are my husband and children. Dismayingly few marriages survive the MS test, and why should they? Most twenty-two- and nineteen-year-olds, like George and me, can vow in clear conscience, after a childhood of chicken pox and summer colds, to keep one another in sickness and in health so long as they both shall live. Not many are equipped for catastrophe: the dismay, the depression, the extra work, the boredom that a degenerative disease can insinuate into a relationship. And our society, with its emphasis on fun and its association of fun with physical performance, offers little encouragement for a whole spouse to stay with a crippled partner. Children experience similar stresses when faced with a crippled parent, and they are more helpless, since parents and children can't usually get divorced. They hate, of course, to be different from their peers, and the child whose mother is tacking down the aisle of a school auditorium packed with proud parents like a Cape Cod dinghy in a stiff breeze jolly well stands out in a crowd. Deprived of legal divorce, the child can at least deny the mother's disability, even her existence, forgetting to tell her about recitals and PTA meetings, refusing to accompany her to stores or church or the movies, never inviting friends to the house. Many do.

But I've been limping along for ten years now, and so far George and the children are still at my left elbow, holding tight. Anne and Matthew vacuum floors and dust furniture and haul trash and rake up dog droppings and button my cuffs and bake lasagna and Toll House cookies with just enough grumbling so I know that they don't have brain fever. And far from hiding me, they're forever dragging me by racks of fancy clothes and through teeming school corridors, or welcoming gaggles of friends while I'm wandering through the house in Anne's filmy pink babydoll pyjamas. George generally calls before he brings someone home, but he does just as many dumb thankless chores as the children. And they all yell at me, laugh at some of my jokes, write me funny letters when we're apart – in short, treat me as an ordinary human being for whom they have some use: I think they like me. Unless they're faking. . . .

Faking. There's the rub. Tugging at the fringes of my conscious-ness always is the terror that people are kind to me only because I'm a cripple. My mother almost shattered me once, with that instinct mothers have – blind, I think, in this case, but unerring nonetheless – for striking blows along the fault-lines of their children's hearts, by telling me, in an attack on my selfishness, 'We all have to make allowances for you, of course, because of the way you are.' From the distance of a couple of years, I have to admit that I haven't any idea just what she meant, and I'm not sure that she knew either. She was awfully angry. But at the time, as the words thudded home, I felt my worst fear, suddenly realized. I could bear being called selfish: I am. But I couldn't bear the corroboration that those around me were doing in fact what I'd always suspected them of doing, professing fondness while silently putting up with me because of the way I am. A cripple. I've been a little cracked ever since.

Along with this fear that people are secretly accepting shoddy goods comes a relentless pressure to please – to prove myself worth the burdens I impose, I guess, or to build a substantial account of goodwill against which I may write drafts in times of need. Part of the pressure arises from social expectations. In our society, anyone who deviates from the norm had better find some way to compensate. Like fat people, who are expected to be jolly, cripples must bear their lot meekly and cheerfully. A grumpy cripple isn't playing by the rules. And much of the pressure is self-generated. Early on I vowed that, if I had to have MS, by God I was going to do it well.

61

This is a class act, ladies and gentlemen. No tears, no recriminations, no faint-heartedness.

One way and another, then, I wind up feeling like Tiny Tim, peering over the edge of the table at the Christmas goose, waving my crutch, piping down God's blessing on us all. Only sometimes I don't want to play Tiny Tim. I'd rather be Caliban, a most scurvy monster. Fortunately, at home no one much cares whether I'm a good cripple or a bad cripple as long as I make vichyssoise with fair regularity. One evening several years ago, Anne was reading at the dining-room table while I cooked dinner. As I opened a can of tomatoes, the can slipped in my left hand and juice spattered me and the counter with bloody spots. Fatigued and infuriated, I bellowed, 'I'm so sick of being crippled!' Anne glanced at me over the top of her book. 'There now,' she said, 'do you feel better?' 'Yes,' I said, 'yes, I do.' She went back to her reading. I felt better. That's about all the attention my scurviness ever gets.

Because I hate being crippled, I sometimes hate myself for being a cripple. Over the years I have come to expect – even accept – attacks of violent self-loathing. Luckily, in general our society no longer connects deformity and disease directly with evil (though a charismatic once told me that I have MS because a devil is in me) and so I'm allowed to move largely at will, even among small children. But I'm not sure that this revision of attitude has been particularly helpful. Physical imperfection, even freed of moral disapprobation, still defies and violates the ideal, especially for women, whose confinement in their bodies as objects of desire is far from over. Each age, of course, has its ideal, and I doubt that ours is any better or worse than any other. Today's ideal woman, who lives on the glossy pages of dozens of magazines, seems to be between the ages of eighteen and twenty-five; her hair has body, her teeth flash white, her breath smells minty, her underarms are dry; she has a career but is still a fabulous cook, especially of meals that take less than twenty minutes to prepare; she does not ordinarily appear to have a husband or children; she is trim and deeply tanned; she jogs, swims, plays tennis, rides a bicycle, sails, but does not bowl; she travels widely, even to out-of-the-way places like Finland and Samoa, always in the company of the ideal man, who possesses a nearly identical set of characteristics. There are a few exceptions. Though usually white and often blonde, she may be black, Hispanic, Asian or Native American, so long as she is unusually sleek. She may be old, provided she is selling a laxative or is Lauren Bacall. If she is selling a detergent, she may be married and have a flock of strikingly messy children. But she is never a cripple.

Like many women I know, I have always had an uneasy relationship with my body. I was not a popular child, largely, I think now, because I was peculiar: intelligent, intense, moody, shy, given to unexpected actions and inexplicable notions and emotions. But as I entered adolescence, I believed myself unpopular because I was homely: my breasts too flat, my mouth too wide, my hips too narrow, my clothing never quite right in fit or style. I was not, in fact, particularly ugly, old photographs inform me, though I was well off the ideal; but I carried this sense of self-alienation with me into adulthood, where it regenerated in response to the depredations of MS. Even with my brace I walk with a limp so pronounced that, seeing myself on the videotape of a television programme on the disabled, I couldn't believe that anything but an inch-worm could make progress humping along like that. My shoulders droop and my pelvis thrusts forward as I try to balance myself upright, throwing my frame into a bony S. As a result of contractures, one shoulder is higher than the other and I carry one arm bent in front of me, the fingers curled into a claw. My left arm and leg have wasted into pipe-stems, and I try always to keep them covered. When I think about how my body must look to others, especially to men, to whom I have been trained to display myself, I feel ludicrous, even loathsome.

At my age, however, I don't spend much time thinking about my appearance. The burning egocentricity of adolescence, which assures one that all the world is looking all the time, has passed, thank God, and I'm generally too caught up in what I'm doing to step back, as I used to, and watch myself as though upon a stage. I'm also too old to believe in the accuracy of self-image. I know that I'm not a hideous crone, that in fact, when I'm rested, well dressed, and well made up, I look fine. The self-loathing I feel is neither physically nor intellectually substantial. What I hate is not me but a disease.

I am not a disease.

And a disease is not – at least not singlehandedly – going to determine who I am, though at first it seemed to be going to. Adjusting to a chronic incurable illness, I have moved through a process similar to that outlined by Elizabeth Kübler-Ross in *On Death and Dying*. The major difference – and it is far more significant than most people recognize – is that I can't be sure of the outcome, as the terminally ill cancer patient can. Research studies indicate that, with proper medical care, I may achieve a 'normal' life span. And in our society, with its vision of death as the ultimate evil, worse even than decrepitude, the response to such news is, 'Oh well, as least you're not going to *die*'. Are there worse things than dying? I think that there may be.

I think of two women I know, both with MS, both enough older than I to have served me as models. One took to her bed several years ago and has been there ever since. Although she can sit in a high-backed wheelchair, because she is incontinent she refuses to go out at all, even though incontinence pants, which are readily available at any pharmacy, could protect her from embarrassment. Instead, she stays at home and insists that her husband, a small quiet man, a retired civil servant, stay there with her except for a quick weekly foray to the supermarket. The other woman, whose illness was diagnosed when she was eighteen, a nursing student engaged to a young doctor, finished her training, married her doctor, accompanied him to Germany when he was in the service, bore three sons and a daughter, now grown and gone. When she can, she travels with her husband; she plays bridge, embroiders, swims regularly; she works, like me, as a symptomatic-patient instructor of medical students in neurology. Guess which woman I hope to be.

At the beginning, I thought about having MS almost incessantly. And because of the unpredictable course of the disease, my thoughts were always terrified. Each night I'd get into bed wondering whether I'd get out again the next morning, whether I'd be able to see, to speak, to hold a pen between my fingers. Knowing that the day might come when I'd be physically incapable of killing myself, I thought perhaps I ought to do so right away, while I still had the strength. Gradually I came to understand that the Nancy who might one day lie inert under a bedsheet, arms and legs paralysed, unable to feed or bathe herself, unable to reach out for a gun, a bottle of pills, was not the Nancy I was at present, and that I could not presume to make decisions for that future Nancy, who might well not want in the least to die. Now the only provision I've made for the future Nancy is that when the time comes – and it is likely to come in the form of pneumonia, friend to the weak and the old – I am not to be treated with machines and medications. If she is unable to communicate by then, I hope she will be satisfied with these terms.

Thinking all the time about having MS grew tiresome and intrusive, especially in the large and tragic mode in which I was accustomed to considering my plight. Months and even years went by without catastrophe (at least without one related to MS), and really I was awfully busy, what with George and children and snakes and students and poems, and I hadn't the time, let alone the inclination, to devote myself to being a disease. Too, the richer my life became, the funnier it seemed, as though there were some connection between largesse and laughter, and so my tragic stance began to waver until, even with the aid of a brace and a cane, I couldn't hold it for very long at a time.

After several years I was satisfied with my adjustment. I had suffered my grief and fury and terror, I thought, but now I was at ease with my lot. Then one summer day I set out with George and the children across the desert for a vacation in California. Part way to Yuma I became aware that my right leg felt funny. 'I think I've had an exacerbation,' I told George. 'What shall we do?' he asked. 'I think we'd better get the hell to California,' I said, 'because I don't know whether I'll ever make it again.' So we went on to San Diego and then to Orange, up the Pacific Coast Highway to Santa Cruz, across to Yosemite, down to Sequoia and Joshua Tree, and so back over the desert to home. It was a fine two-week trip, filled with friends and fair weather, and I wouldn't have missed it for the world, though I did in fact make it back to California two years later. Nor would there have been any point in missing it, since in MS, once the symptoms have appeared, the neurological damage has been done, and there's no way to predict or prevent that damage.

The incident spoiled my self-satisfaction, however. It renewed my grief and fury and terror, and I learned that one never finishes adjusting to MS. I don't know now why I thought one would. One does not, after all, finish adjusting to life, and MS is simply a fact of my life – not my favourite fact, of course – but as ordinary as my nose and my tropical fish and my yellow Mazda station wagon. It may at any time get worse, but no amount of worry or anticipation can prepare me for a new loss. My life is a lesson in losses. I learn one at a time.

And I had best be patient in the learning, since I'll have to do it like it or not. As any rock fan knows, you can't always get what you want. Particularly when you have MS. You can't, for example, get cured. In recent years researchers and the organizations that fund research have started to pay MS some attention even though it isn't fatal; perhaps they have begun to see that life is something other than a quantitative phenomenon, that one may be very much alive for a very long time in a life that isn't worth living. The researchers have made some progress toward understanding the mechanism of the disease: it may well be an autoimmune reaction triggered by a slow-acting virus. But they are nowhere near its prevention, control, or cure. And most of us want to be cured. Some, unable to accept incurability, grasp at one treatment after another, no matter how bizarre: megavitamin therapy, gluten-free diet, injections of cobra venom, hypothermal suits, lymphocytopharesis, hyperbaric chambers. Many treatments are probably harmless enough, but none are curative.

The absence of a cure often makes MS patients bitter toward their doctors. Doctors are, after all, the priests of modern society, the new shamans, whose business is to heal, and many an MS patient roves from one to another, searching for the 'good' doctor who will make him well. Doctors too think of themselves as healers, and for this reason many have trouble dealing with MS patients, whose disease in its intransigence defeats their aims and mocks their skills. Too few doctors, it is true, treat their patients as whole human beings, but the reverse is also true. I have always tried to be gentle with my doctors, who often have more at stake in terms of ego than I do. I may be frustrated, maddened, depressed by the incurability of my disease, but I am not diminished by it, and they are. When I push myself up from my seat in the waiting room and stumble toward them, I incarnate the limitation of their powers. The least I can do is refuse to press on their tenderest spots.

This gentleness is part of the reason that I'm not sorry to be a cripple. I didn't have it before. Perhaps I'd have developed it anyway – how could I know such a thing? – and I wish I had more of it, but I'm glad of what I have. It has opened and enriched my life enormously, this sense that my frailty and need must be mirrored in others, that in searching for and shaping a stable core in a life wrenched by change and loss, change and loss, I must recognize the same process, under individual conditions, in the lives around me. I do not deprecate such knowledge, however I've come by it.

All the same, if a cure were found, would I take it? In a minute. I may be a cripple, but I'm only occasionally a loony and never a saint. Anyway, in my brand of theology God doesn't give bonus points for a limp. I'd take a cure, I just don't need one. A friend who also has MS startled me once by asking, 'Do you ever say to yourself, "Why me, Lord?"' 'No, Michael, I don't,' I told him, 'because whenever I try, the only response I can think of is "Why not?"' If I could make a cosmic deal, who would I put in my place? What in my life would I give up in exchange for sound limbs and a thrilling rush of energy? No one. Nothing. I might as well do the job myself. Now that I'm getting the hang of it.

Article 2.2
WHAT IS THE FAMILY? IS IT UNIVERSAL?

Diana Gittins

[DEFINING THE FAMILY]

Until recently, most sociologi[sts] . . . have argued that the family is a universal institution which performs certain specific functions essential to society's survival. Murdock, for instance, defined the family as a 'social group characterised by common residence, economic co-operation, and reproduction. It includes adults of both sexes, at least two of whom maintain a socially approved sexual relationship, and one or more children, own or adopted, of the sexually cohabiting adults' (G. Murdock, in Morgan, 1975, p. 20). The four basic functions of the family . . . are seen as: common residence; economic co-operation; reproduction; sexuality. Let us examine each of these in more detail.

Household is the term normally used to refer to co-residence. Murdock's assumption is that it is also a defining characteristic of 'the family' and vice versa. It is generally assumed that a married couple, or parent and child(ren) will form a household, and that family implies and presupposes 'household'. Yet this is by no means always so. Margaret Mead (1971) showed how Samoan children chose the household where they wanted to reside, and often changed their residence again later. . . .

There are numerous examples in contemporary society of families who do not form households, or only form households for periods of time. Families where the husband is in the armed services, is a travelling salesman or travels frequently abroad may only have the husband/father resident for short periods of time. Families where partners have jobs some distance away from one another may maintain a second household where one of them lives during the week. Children who are sent to boarding school may spend little more than a third of the year residing with their parent(s). . . . Obviously people can consider themselves 'family' without actually co-residing, and can also co-reside without considering themselves to be 'family'.

On the other hand, households might be characterized by a shared set of activities such as sleeping, food preparation, eating, sexual relations, and caring for those who cannot care for themselves. Some have argued that household can be defined to some extent in terms of a range of domestic activities. 'Sharing the same pot' has traditionally been the boundary drawn by census enumerators for demarcating one household from another. Yet these activities need not necessarily, and often do not, occur within one household. Some members of a household may eat there all the time, while others only part of the time. . . .

There is no hard and fast rule, much less a definition in universal terms, that can be applied to household in terms of domestic activities. Whether in modern industrial society or in Africa or Asia 'there is no basis for assuming that such activities as sleeping, eating, child-rearing and sexual relations must form a complex and must always occur under one roof' (Smith, 1978, p. 339). Household is thus in some ways just as nebulous a term as family, although it lacks the ideological implications that 'family' carries.

Murdock further posits 'economic co-operation' as a defining characteristic of all families. This is a very broad term and can encompass a wide range of activities from cooking to spinning to resources in terms of people and skills. Economic co-operation is something which can, and does, occur throughout all levels of society and is not specific to the family. Economic co-operation frequently occurs *between* households as well as between individuals within households. Undoubtedly households do entail an economic relationship in various ways; in particular, they entail the distribution, production and allocation of resources. Resources include food, drink, material goods, but also service, care, skills, time and space. The notion of 'co-operation', moreover, implies an equal distribution of resources, yet this is seldom so. Allocating food, space, time and tasks necessitates some kind of a division of labour; different tasks need doing every day and may vary by week and by season. . . .

All resources are finite and some may be extremely scarce; some form of allocation therefore has to occur, and this presupposes power relationships. Food, work and space are rarely distributed equally between co-residing individuals, just as they differ between households and social sectors. Most frequently, the allocation of resources and division of labour is based on differences according to sex and age. Rather than using Murdock's definition of 'economic co-operation', it is thus more useful to understand families in terms of the ways in which gender and age define, and are defined by, the division of labour within, and beyond, households. These divisions also presuppose power relationships and inequality – in effect, patriarchy – rather than co-operation and equality.

Power relationships define and inform concepts of sexuality, Murdock's third defining category. His definition of sexuality is *hetero*sexuality, although this is only one of various forms of sexuality. Presumably this is because the final – and perhaps most important – 'function' of families as seen by such theorists is reproduction, which necessitates heterosexual relations, at least at times. Sexuality is not something specific to families; rather, the assumption is that heterosexuality *should* be a defining characteristic of families. It also, according to Murdock, presupposes a 'socially approved relationship' between two adults.

Social recognition of mating and of parenthood is obviously intimately bound up with social definitions and customs of marriage. It is often assumed that, in spite of a variety of marriage customs and laws, marriage as a binding relationship between a man and a woman is universal. Yet it has been estimated that only 10 per cent of all marriages in the world are actually monogamous; polyandry and polygyny are common in many societies, just as serial monogamy is becoming increasingly common in our own. Marriage is not always a heterosexual relationship; among the Nuer, older women marry younger women. The Nuer also practise a custom known as 'ghost marriages', whereby when an unmarried or childless man dies, a relation of his then marries a woman 'to his name' and the resulting children of this union are regarded as the dead man's children and bear his name (see Edholm, 1982, p. 172).

Marriage customs are not only variable between cultures and over time, but also vary between social classes. Moreover, Jessie Bernard (1973) has shown that the meanings which men and women attribute to the same marriage differ quite markedly. Undoubtedly marriage involves some form of status passage and public avowal of recognizing other(s) as of particular importance in one way or another, yet it does not occur universally between two people, nor between two people of the opposite sex, nor is it always viewed as linked to reproduction. Marriage, in the way in which we think of it, is therefore not universal.

[· · ·]

Murdock's definition does not take adequate account of the diversity of ways in which co-residence, economic relations, sexuality and reproduction can be organized. Various theorists have made amendments and refinements to Murdock's definition of the family, but all tend to make similar errors. In particular, they translate contemporary western (and usually middle-class) ideas and ideals of what a family should be into what they assume it is everywhere.

[KINSHIP]

Far more precise attempts at definition and analysis have been made by anthropologists who prefer the term kinship to that of family. A feminist anthropologist . . . defined kinship as:

> the ties which exist between individuals who are seen as related both through birth (descent) and through mating (marriage). It is thus primarily concerned with the ways in

which mating is socially organised and regulated, the ways in which parentage is assigned, attributed and recognised, descent is traced, relatives are classified, rights are transferred across generations and groups are formed.

(Edholm, 1982, p. 166)

This definition of kinship is a vast improvement on functionalist definitions of family because, first, it stresses the fact that kinship is a social construction, and, second, it emphasizes the variability of kinship depending on how it is defined.

[· · ·]

In many poor families in western Europe and America well into this century it was not uncommon for children to be raised by a grandparent, other kin, or friend, and such children often thought of those who raised them as their parents, even though acknowledging that they also had biological parents who were different. . . .

Others have shown the ways in which kinship is a social construction, and how those who are not biologically related to one another come to define themselves as kin:

Liebow, Stack, Ladner and others describe fictive kinship, by which friends are turned into family. Since family is supposed to be more reliable than friendship, 'going for brothers', 'for sisters', 'for cousins', increases the commitment of a relationship, and makes people ideally more responsible for one another. Fictive kinship is a serious relationship.

(Rapp, 1980, p. 292)

It is possible to argue that this is how all kinship began and becomes constructed. Kinship, whether we choose to label it as 'biological', 'social' or 'fictive', is a way of identifying others as in some way special from the rest, people to whom the individual or collectivity feel responsible in certain ways. It is a method of demarcating obligations and responsibility between individuals and groups.

It is thus essential to get away from the idea that kinship is a synonym for 'blood' relations – *even though it may often be expressed in those terms* – and to think of it as a social construction which is highly variable and flexible.

[· · ·]

[MOTHERHOOD]

Because fatherhood is always potentially unknown, and always potentially contestable, it is therefore also always a social category.

70

Motherhood, on the other hand, is always known. Yet apart from carrying and giving birth to a child, the biological base of motherhood stops there. The rest is socially constructed, although it may be – and often is – attributed to biology or 'maternal instinct'. Whether or not women breastfeed their children has been historically and culturally variable. Baby bottles are no modern invention, but were used in ancient Egypt and in other cultures since. Historians have noted the number of babies given to 'wet nurses' in earlier times in Europe as a sign of lack of love and care for infants on the part of mothers. But we can never really know the emotions felt by people hundreds of years ago or their motivations for their practices. The most we can do is to note that their customs were different. To use our own ideology of motherhood and love and apply it universally to all cultures is a highly ethnocentric and narrow way of trying to understand other societies.

Notions of motherhood and 'good mothering' are highly variable:

> in Tahiti young women often have one or two children before they are considered, or consider themselves to be, ready for an approved and stable relationship. It is considered perfectly acceptable for the children of this young woman to be given to her parents or other close kin for adoption . . . The girl can decide what her relationship to the children will be, but there is no sense in which she is forced into 'motherhood' because of having had a baby.
>
> (Edholm, 1982, p. 170)

Who cares for children and rears them is also variable, although in most cases it is women who do so rather than men. Often those women who rear children may well claim some kinship tie to the biological mother – for example, grandmother or aunt, but this tie may simply be created as a result of rearing another woman's child. Motherhood, therefore, if taken to mean both bearing and rearing children, is not universal and is not a biological 'fact'.

Nor can it be argued that there is such a thing as maternal 'instinct', although it is commonly believed to exist. Women are capable of conceiving children today from the age of 13 or 14, and can continue to bear children approximately every two years until they are 45 or 50. This could mean producing around eighteen or nineteen children (although fecundity declines as women age), and this, of course, seldom occurs. Few women in western society marry before they are 18 or 19, and few women in contemporary society have more than two or three children. Contraceptives control conception, not instincts, and unless it were argued that women are forced to use contraceptives,[1] there is little scope to argue for such a thing as maternal instinct.

71

Consider further that women who conceive babies now when they are *not* married are not hailed as true followers of their natural instinct, but are considered as 'immoral', 'loose', 'whores', and so on. As Antonis (1981, p. 59) notes: 'maternal instinct is ascribed to *married women* only'. That women can conceive and bear children is a universal phenomenon; that they do so by instinct is a fallacy. So is the notion that they always raise them. From the moment of birth motherhood is a social construction.

[· · ·]

[GENDER]

Implicit in definitions of kinship is a way of perceiving the social organization of reproduction and mating, at the centre of which therefore is an organization of relations between the sexes. The organization of, and differentiation between, male and female takes many different forms, but all societies do have a social construction of the sexes into gender. Gender is an inherent part of the manner in which all societies are organized and is also a crucial part of the different ways in which kinship has been constructed and defined. The social, economic and political organization of societies has been initially at least based on kinship – and thus also on gender. Understanding society means understanding the ways in which a society organizes kinship and gender, and how these influence one another. Gender and kinship are universally present – as are mothers and children – but the content of them, and the meanings ascribed to them, [are] highly variable.

The most basic divisions of labour within any society . . . are based on age and sex. While age as a category can eventually be achieved, sex is ascribed, permanent and immutable. The biological differences between men and women are such that only women can conceive and lactate; only men can impregnate. In spite of these obvious differences, none of them is great enough to be adequate grounds for allocating one kind of work to women and another to men. Indeed, cross-culturally and historically there are very few jobs that can be claimed to be specifically and universally performed by either men or women. Women have ploughed and mined and still do; men have laundered, gathered fruit and minded children. Hunting and warfare have almost always been male activities, while care of the young and sick has usually been a female activity. But allocation of tasks is also strongly based on age, so it is important to remember that it may be *young* men who hunt and *old* men or women who care for children; old women may be responsible for cooking, while both young men and women may work in the fields or mines.

72

Age is an important factor to consider in trying to understand the organization of kinship and households. Nobody remains the same age – contrary to contemporary images in the media of the 'happy family' where the couple is permanently 30 and the children forever 8 and 6. As individuals age, so the composition and structure of the unit in which they live change. Consider the ways in which the household composition and resources of a couple change as, first, aged 20, they marry and both work; second, aged 25, they have had two children and the wife has left the labour market for a few years to rear the children until they attend school; third, at 30, one partner leaves or dies and one parent is left with total care of the children; fourth, at 35, one or both may remarry someone who perhaps has three children from an earlier marriage, or may take in an elderly parent to care for, and so on. The number of wage earners and dependants changes over a household's cycle, just as it changes for the individuals within the household.

Thinking in terms of 'the' family leads to a static vision of how people actually live and age together and what effects this process has on others within the household in which they live. Moreover, the environment and conditions in which any household is situated are always changing, and these changes can and often do have important repercussions on individuals and households. As Tamara Hareven (1982) points out, it is important when analysing families to differentiate between individual time, family time and historical time. Thus in considering the structure and meaning of 'family' in any society it is important to understand how definitions of dependency and individual time vary and change, how patterns of interaction between individuals and households change, and how historical developments affect all of these.

The notion of there being such a thing as 'the family' is thus highly controversial and full of ambiguities and contradictions. Childbearing, childrearing, the construction of gender, allocation of resources, mating and marriage, sexuality and ageing all loosely fit into our idea of family, and yet we have seen how all of them are variable over time, between cultures and between social sectors. The claim that 'the family' is universal has been especially problematic because of the failure by most to differentiate between how small groups of people live and work together, and what the ideology of appropriate behaviour for men, women and children within families has been.

Imbued in western patriarchal ideology, as discussed previously, are a number of important and culturally specific beliefs about sexuality, reproduction, parenting and the power relationships between age groups and between the sexes. The sum total of these beliefs make up a strong *symbol-system which is labelled as the family*. Now while it can be argued that all societies have beliefs and rules on mating, sexuality, gender and age relations, the content of rules is culturally and historically specific and variable, and in no way universal. Thus to claim that patriarchy is universal is as meaningless as claiming that the family is universal.

[· · ·]

Ideals of family relationships have become enshrined in our legal, social, religious and economic systems which, in turn, reinforce the ideology and penalize or ostracize those who transgress it. Thus there are very real pressures on people to behave in certain ways, to lead their lives according to acceptable norms and patterns. Patriarchal ideology is embedded in our socio-economic and political institutions, indeed, in the very language we use, and as such encourages, cajoles and pressurizes people to follow certain paths. Most of these are presented and defined in terms of 'the family', and the family is in turn seen as the bulwark of our culture. The pressures of patriarchal ideology are acted out – and reacted against – in our inter-personal relationships, in marriage and non-marriage, in love and hate, having children and not having children. In short, much of our social behaviour occurs in, and is judged on the basis of, the ideology of 'the family'.

Relationships are universal, so is some form of co-residence, of intimacy, sexuality and emotional bonds. But the *forms* these can take are infinitely variable and can be changed and challenged as well as embraced. By analysing the ways in which culture has prescribed certain, and proscribed other, forms of behaviour, it should be possible to begin to see the historical and cultural specificity of what is really meant when reference is made to 'the family'.

Note

1   For a full discussion of power relationships between men and women with regard to contraceptive practice, see Gittins (1982).

NARROW DEFINITIONS OF CULTURE: THE CASE OF EARLY MOTHERHOOD
Ann Phoenix

... A growing proportion of black adults in Britain have either been born here or have lived most of their lives here. They are not therefore faced with the task of settling in Britain and coping with the migration process. Rather, they are black people who have been through the British education system and are familiar with a range of British cultures and institutions.... These black adults are not 'between two cultures' (Watson, 1977) as has been commonly believed. Instead, they are situated in their social networks as well as in the wider society, and in that sense are clearly British.

This [article] argues that concentration on cultural differences between black people and white people has frequently obscured the fact that cultural beliefs, identities and practices necessarily embody the structural forces that affect people's lives, and that culture itself is dynamic rather than static. In particular, analyses of class, race[1] and gender are crucial to the understanding of British society and of individual behaviours, since the intersection of these structural forces serves to locate individuals in their social positions and also to produce social constructions of beliefs and identities....

The first part of the [article] is concerned with reasons why simplistic views of cultural influence are inadequate for the understanding of young black women's lives. The second part uses empirical material as a way of exploring how analyses which rely on such simplistic views of culture (referred to in this paper as narrow definitions of culture) obscure the similarities between black women and white women who become pregnant before they are twenty years of age.... Particular attention is given to class, race and gender as forces that simultaneously structure young women's lives. Although it is generally thought that race only influences black women, what it means to be 'white' can only be understood in contradistinction from what it means to be 'black'. White women's lives are thus as racially structured as black women's lives ..., although the effects are of course vastly different. The [article] concludes that young black women and young white women become pregnant for the same sorts of reasons, and that this is because they share the same socio-economic contexts. A more dynamic definition of culture would therefore necessarily include analyses of material factors.

CULTURAL INFLUENCE AND YOUNG BLACK WOMEN

Young black women have rarely been the subjects of academic study. The category 'youth' has tended to be applied almost exclusively to young men, both black and white. Similarly, the term 'black' has tended to be used as if it were either gender neutral or male. When 'women' have been written about it is almost exclusively white women that have been discussed, yet the term has been used as if it were colour neutral. The net effect of this is to render black women, and young black women in particular, invisible (Hooks, 1982).

There are some exceptions to this omission of black women. Over the last decade black women have increasingly documented and theorized their experiences themselves (see, for example, Parmar, 1982; Carby, 1982; *Feminist Review* 17; Hooks, 1984; Bryan *et al.*, 1985), and the experiences of young black women (Amos and Parmar, 1981). By way of contrast, white academics who have focused on young black women have tended to treat them as if they were pathological. Thus, while black women have frequently been omitted from work which has sought to gain an understanding of 'normal' women, black women have frequently been the focus of research which studies devalued groups.

Studies of 'teenage mothers' provide examples of this negative focus on young black women. These studies frequently either compare black mothers (of African descent in the USA, and of Afro-Caribbean origin in Britain) with white mothers, or concentrate only on black mothers. This focus on black women as 'teenage mothers' occurs within a context in which early motherhood is stigmatized and devalued. 'Young motherhood' has been associated with a variety of negative outcomes both for the women themselves and for their children. These poor outcomes include postnatal depression, poor educational qualifications, and 'welfare dependence' for the women and risks of perinatal mortality, child abuse, and developmental delay for their children (Scott *et al.*, 1981; Butler *et al.*, 1981).

[· · ·]

YOUNG BLACK WOMEN AND STUDIES OF 'TEENAGE MOTHERHOOD'

In literature on 'teenage mothers', black 'teenage mothers' are presumed to be different from white 'teenage mothers'. Phipps-Yonas in a 1980 review of American literature pointed out that psychological explanations, to do, for example, with problems in individual mother–daughter relationships, tend to be advanced for the incidence of early motherhood in white, middle-class women. For black, lower-class women, however, socio-cultural explanations, suggesting that early motherhood occurs for 'cultural reasons', tend to be invoked. Phipps-Yonas suggested that this common approach was unjustified because there was no evidence that black teenagers and white teenagers became pregnant for different reasons or that their families were more accepting of early motherhood than white mothers.

By comparison with the USA, Britain has produced little research on early motherhood. However, the north American model of black 'teenage mothers' and white 'teenage mothers' becoming pregnant for different reasons has been reproduced in British research. Examples of these different types of explanation for early motherhood in black women and in white women are provided by two recent British studies (Skinner, 1986; Ineichen, 1984/5). Both these papers start by considering whether 'West Indian' cultural patterns account for there being proportionally more black mothers of Afro-Caribbean origin who are under twenty years of age than of white mothers of British origin. To do this, both researchers discuss family patterns that have been observed in the Caribbean (in fact almost exclusively in Jamaica).

While Skinner states in her introduction that she found no evidence to support the hypothesis that young black women have children for cultural reasons, she none the less makes consistent reference to 'West Indian' family patterns as a means of explaining the behaviour of the black women in her study. Much of the material for the typologies she uses is drawn from Clarke's (1957) study done in Jamaica, and Fitzherbert's (1967) work on 'West Indian family patterns'. The implicit assumptions underlying this use of work which is thirty and twenty years old respectively are twofold. They are first, that the behaviour of British people of Afro-Caribbean origin can only be understood by making reference to behaviour in Jamaica (one of many Caribbean countries). This suggests that the British context in which black people live is irrelevant to an understanding of their behaviour. The second assumption is that 'the West Indian family' is timeless and remains unchanged over decades.

Skinner herself recognizes that problems are presented by the use of an explanatory framework that is derived from work which is geographically and historically removed from the black British sample whose behaviour she is trying to explain. She says, for example:

> It would be misleading to describe early pregnancies in the UK black teenagers as being attempts to prove fertility on the grounds that similar behaviour observed in the West Indies has, in the past, been interpreted in this way.
>
> (Skinner, 1986, p. 97)

The recognition of the problematic nature of such explanations does not prevent Skinner from drawing parallels between 'Jamaica and West Indian society in the UK' (ibid., p. 99). She does so because this is the usual way of understanding black British people's behaviour in academic writing. In the absence of equally long-established alternative discourses to draw upon, she reverts to these comparisons.

This readiness to draw parallels between the behaviour of black people in the Caribbean and that of black people in Britain is further illustrated by the study done by Ineichen (1984/5). In his study Ineichen claims that:

> the contrasts between these two groups of teenagers (white and black) can best be illustrated by prefacing a consideration of their situation by quoting from recent writers . . . on attitudes to and patterns of youthful fertility in the Caribbean.
>
> (Ineichen, 1984/5, p. 52)

Ineichen then lists eight Caribbean traits which he considers particularly relevant to 'West Indian patterns' of fertility. His black British samples are discussed under the headings provided by these eight traits. The Caribbean traits he identifies (from the literature) thus provide the framework for the analysis of the behaviour of his black British sample.

The first trait on which Ineichen compares his black British sample with Caribbean women is 'frequency of teenage motherhood'. He concludes that:

> This ['teenage motherhood'] appears to be commoner among Afro-Caribbean girls. They formed one-fifth of our sample, but a much smaller proportion of the teenage population of the Bristol Health District, although precise figures are not available.
>
> (Ibid., 1984/5)

It is in fact difficult to establish whether, and if so by how much, black British rates of early motherhood exceed white ones. . . . Britain does not produce national statistics broken according to the mother's colour. Very few studies of early motherhood have been done in Britain, and Ineichen and Skinner have so far conducted the only research which has shown a higher rate of early pregnancy in black women than white women. Since national figures are not available, the conclusion that early motherhood is more common among black women than among white women must be a tentative one. However, Ineichen draws this conclusion from a study of only eighteen women of Afro-Caribbean origin (with Afro-Caribbean partners). Why does he feel confident on the basis of such slight evidence?

One reason is probably to do with Ineichen's belief that Caribbean patterns of fertility behaviour are likely to be reproduced in black British women of Afro-Caribbean origin. Any evidence in the correct direction, however slight, is considered to provide confirmation of this hypothesis without it being felt necessary to discuss factors such as class, which influence the incidence of early motherhood (in both black women and white women) and provide the context in which it occurs. The absence of discussion of this sort makes it necessary to question Ineichen's analytical framework and his interpretations of his data.

PROBLEMS WITH EXPLANATIONS OF BLACK BRITISH BEHAVIOUR BASED ON COMPARISONS WITH THE CARIBBEAN

This emphasis on the Caribbean as providing the key to understanding young black British women's behaviour is inappropriate for the following . . . reasons.

1 *It excludes black people from the category 'British'*
A major implication of this concentration on the Caribbean is that black people of Afro-Caribbean origin are not really British. Their behaviour does not have its roots in Britain and can only be understood by reference back to the Caribbean as their place of origin.

2 *It oversimplifies Caribbean cultures*
The use of narrow cultural explanations implies that 'West Indian' culture is unitary and static. Class differences and urban/rural divisions in the Caribbean are not given serious consideration. . . . The description of Caribbean culture presented is extremely simplistic. Particular elements of behaviour (such as 'pro-fertility values') are singled out as if they were definitive of Caribbean society.

3 *It starts from the assumption that all black people are different from all white people*
Culture only becomes a primary focus when black women's behaviour is being explained. This helps maintain the social construction of white people as the norm and black people as deviations from that norm, because it emphasizes that only black people's behaviour needs justification. However, it also falsely implies that culture does not influence white people's lives as crucially as black people's. White people also have a diversity of cultural backgrounds. The focus on young black women as culturally influenced only by the Caribbean, and young white women as being acultural serves to exaggerate differences and underplay similarities.

4 *It confuses colour with culture while ignoring issues of power*
Work which is structured around the narrow definition of culture frequently confuses colour and culture. White people are treated as if they were culturally homogeneous and British whatever their ancestry or religion (although there is sometimes an ambivalence about the Irish!). Black people are treated as similar to other black people whose ancestry lies roughly in the same region, but not as British. It is colour not culture which is being represented in such instances (although vague notions of ancestry are included). This is done without any

reference being made to the differential social and power positions which black people and white people occupy.

This issue illustrates one way in which power relations permeate social relations. In this case people from the dominant social group (white British) infer the importance of cultural influences for a subordinate social group (black people), without ever asking them how *they* perceive culture to influence them. At the same time they fail to acknowledge cultural influences on their own group's behaviour. . . . Hence, in studies of 'teenage mothers', culture is implicitly accepted as an important influence on young black women, but not on young white women. Class is sometimes recognized as an important influence on white people, but in these cases, white working-class people have frequently been studied (in the sociology of community) as if they were deviant in comparison with white middle-class people.

5 *It oversimplifies the notion of culture*
Cultures are necessarily dynamic (Saifullah Khan, 1982). The culture (as shared systems of meaning) that young black adults now subscribe to has some roots in, but is not precisely that of their parents. Given that the young black women described in the above studies were either born in or have lived most of their lives in Britain, their cultural roots are likely to lie at least as much in British society as in the Caribbean (which most have never visited).

Furthermore, culture is not a discrete entity. It cannot be divorced from its socio-economic, political and historical contexts (Westwood, 1984). Since all societies have a plurality of socio-economic groupings, it is inaccurate to describe a country as having one culture. The non-unitary nature of culture is particularly relevant for the Caribbean which is composed of dozens of countries, extends 1,500 miles, contains a variety of languages, has a varied mix of ethnic groupings, different musical traditions and cuisine. To speak of 'West Indian culture' is thus rather inaccurate. This inaccuracy is compounded by the fact that many writers generalize from observations made only in Jamaica to people from the whole of the Caribbean.

[· · ·]

THE BROADER MEANING OF CULTURE

Work which perpetuates the narrow definition of culture has tended to be carried out in isolation from the theoretical advances in cultural studies made, for example, by those who have worked in the Centre for Contemporary Cultural Studies. Work of this kind has taken a dynamic, structural view of culture by theorizing it as lived experience, inextricably linked with race, sex and class, and only having meaning in the context of the society in which it occurs (in this case Britain). Hence everyday features of society and of behaviour like the media, styles of dress and music, as well as what these mean to and for, the groups under study, are closely examined. In this way the notion of culture is broadened to include the idea of 'cultures of resistance', rather than being narrow versions of cultural influence. (See, for example, Hall and Jefferson, 1976; McRobbie, 1984; Centre for Contemporary Cultural Studies, 1978 and 1982).

It seems likely that white children and young adults from the working classes share more cultural features with their black peers than either do with white children and young adults from the middle classes. Inner city London schools in which white working-class children interact with black peers allow the sharing of cultural knowledge and practices. Evidence for this is provided by the pattern of language use in such schools which tend to incorporate elements of both black Afro-Caribbean and white Cockney styles of talk (Hewitt, 1986). The cultures that working-class young people share are therefore new, combining features from many groups. This does not mean that they do not also have cultural patterns and identifications that are not shared across black–white groupings, but it does mean that explanations of similar behaviour in young people (early motherhood, for example) should not automatically presume different aetiologies.

THE CASE OF EARLY MOTHERHOOD

The second part of this [article] will use data from a longitudinal study, done at the Thomas Coram Research Unit, of women who were between sixteen and nineteen years of age when they gave birth (between 1983 and 1984).[2] Interviews done when the women were heavily pregnant will be used to illustrate how the presumption that early motherhood in black women is the result of narrowly defined cultural influences obscures the similarities between black women's and white women's reasons for becoming pregnant. It will also explore whether, as would be suggested by narrowly defined cultural explanations, relationships with mothers are different for young black women and young white women. . . . About a quarter of the women in this study were black.

This study was originally designed to compare 'West Indian' women with white women. It quickly became evident during piloting and the early stages of data collection, however, that black women and white women responded similarly to questions other than those which expressly dealt with racial discrimination. Partly for this reason it was decided to analyse the data from everyone in the study together rather than dividing the sample into a black 'West Indian' group and a white group. There were two additional reasons for analysing the sample in this way.

First, comparisons between black people and white people tend to construct white people as the norm, and black people as deviant by comparison (see discussion above) but, second, because it is difficult to operationalize satisfactorily the categories 'West Indian' and 'white' as analytical constructs. This is partly because 'West Indian' and 'white' are not equivalent terms in that one describes certain countries of origin, and is used as a shorthand for cultural heritage, while the other describes colour. It is also partly because many people do not in reality fit neatly into these categories. Most of the women in our sample (black and white), for example, were British born (as are most of their age peers), but their parents came from a variety of places, had been in Britain for varied amounts of time, and had different religions. Several respondents had parents who came from different places and/or were different colours.

[· · ·]

The aim of the analysis section is to give some indication of whether similar factors influence black women's and white women's behaviour.

WHY BECOME A MOTHER BEFORE TWENTY?

Current dominant reproductive ideologies would suggest that women who are under twenty years of age should not become pregnant. This is partly because mothers are meant to be indisputably adult, and it is not clear whether or not teenage women are adult (Murcott, 1980). It is also partly because marriage is expected to precede motherhood (Busfield, 1974), and women who are under twenty years of age are more likely to be single than married when they give birth (63 per cent of mothers under twenty years of age who gave birth in 1985 were single: (Office of Population Censuses and Surveys, 1986)). A third reason is that parents are meant to be economically independent of the state, with mothers and children being dependent on the economic provision fathers make for them. Increasing unemployment has, however, meant that young people from the working classes are more likely to be reliant on state provision of money and housing than they were in the past. Young women's position as dependants is not therefore new since they have long been expected to be dependent on their male partners. However, as their dependence has been increasingly transferred from male partners to the state, mothers who are under twenty years of age have received more public attention as deviants from social norms.

Given this negative social construction it is important to attempt to understand the reasons why about 3 per cent of women in this age group have become mothers each year of this decade. If simple 'perpetuation of cultural norms' hypotheses are to be confirmed, then black women and white women should become pregnant for different reasons, with black women having more 'pro-natalist tendencies' and being more desirous of having children early in their life course (Ineichen, 1984/5). However, black women and white women give remarkably similar accounts of reasons for and responses to early pregnancy. The socio-economic contexts within which they live crucially influence these reasons and responses. These contexts are largely similar for black women and white women who become mothers early in their lives in that the majority come from the working classes.

Pregnant women's orientations to motherhood at the point of conception are usually treated as if they were bipolar. Either they were 'trying' to become pregnant – that is, they intended to conceive – or they became pregnant accidentally. However, orientations to motherhood are rather more complex than this. Nearly half of the women in the Thomas Coram study either did not mind whether or not they became pregnant, or had not thought about pregnancy as something that might affect them. This challenges two widely held assumptions about the conception of children: first that there is a clear dichotomy between wanting and not wanting a child, and second, that women always make clear and conscious decisions about whether or not to conceive. Asked whether it had been important to them not to become pregnant, this group commonly replied, 'I wasn't bothered'. Those who had no conscious thoughts about conception had just started their sexual careers. They illustrate the clear separation that some women (and no doubt some men) make between sexual intercourse and pregnancy, and motherhood.

Women's feelings about motherhood were influenced by how they thought pregnancy and motherhood would affect their lives. Thus employment and education prospects, relationships with parents as well as with male partners, whether or not they had previously been pregnant, their orientations to contraception, when other people in their social networks tended to give birth, as well as their perception of the ideal time to give birth, all affected how they felt about motherhood. While women in the study reported here could not be dichotomized into a group which 'planned' its pregnancies and a group for whom pregnancy was 'accidental', they did none the less have general views about the best time to have children. The following section will consider this sample's views about the ideal time to conceive.

IDEAL TIME TO CONCEIVE

Within the narrow version of cultural influence (that it is separable from structural factors so that 'West Indians' can be picked out as automatically different from 'whites'), it is expected that black women of Afro-Caribbean origin believe it to be acceptable and ideal to have children early in life, while white women do not share these beliefs.

However, most of the women in this study, whether black or white, reported that they thought it better to have children earlier rather than later in life. This is aptly illustrated by considering some quotations from white women:

> If you have a baby when you're older you're tied down . . . I'll still be able to do what I want to.
>
> *(Jan, seventeen years old)*

> I think they look down on women who don't have a child by 30 but there's no set time for anybody to have a baby by. (*What do you think is the ideal age to have a baby?*) I think about now is all right . . . I don't want to get too old and have children.
>
> *(Mary, nineteen years old)*

> Yeah I think I'm young and people say I'm young but I don't think it makes any difference how old you are . . . whether you're thirty or sixteen you can still give it as much love . . . She's twenty-six [R's sister] but she's getting on to have a baby when you think of it. The younger you are the more likely that it's going to be healthier.
>
> *(Alice, seventeen years old)*

[· · ·]

Not . . . all the women in the study considered that theirs was the ideal age at which to reproduce. However, only one fifth considered that the ideal age was over twenty-one years. The general feeling was that women should start to have children early in their life course. It could be argued that since the interviews were conducted in late pregnancy, these women's responses about ideal ages are simply *post hoc* justifications of a situation which is inevitable. However, they illuminate the differences between 'insider' and 'outsider' perceptions of early motherhood.

It is also important to note that early motherhood was common rather than unusual in the women's social networks. Nearly half of the sample's mothers had themselves had their first child before they were twenty. . . .

In this study it was not the case that attachment to early motherhood was culturally specific to young black women. White women were similar to black women in wanting to have children early in life, and knowing many other women (including their own mothers) who had done similarly. In addition, the mothers in this study, both black and white, generally considered that motherhood conferred high status on women and so felt that having a child would improve their social status.

THE EXPERIENCE OF (UN)EMPLOYMENT

Women's feelings about the timing of motherhood were influenced by how they anticipated that it would affect other aspects of their lives. Dominant reproductive ideologies suggest a conflictual model of employment and motherhood in which motherhood should be deferred until the employment career is well established. The rationale for this is that mothers ought not to be employed while their children are young. Therefore, unless they are well established in their careers, they will be unable to return to the same occupational position.

This deferment of motherhood makes sense only if women have managed to obtain and keep employment which has built-in career progression, and for many women this is not the case. The jobs which women commonly do, in factories, shops, catering, and the health service, give few opportunities for career progression. Less than one quarter of women in this study had at least one 'O' level or equivalent. Their lack of formal qualifications meant that they were not well placed to obtain employment with career prospects. Indeed, only 39 per cent of our sample were employed when they became pregnant. A further 6 per cent were on MSC schemes, and 16 per cent were in full-time education. This means that 39 per cent were unemployed at the start of pregnancy.

For women who are unemployed, childbearing does not threaten the current employment career, and may well appear a welcome alternative to unemployment. More than a third of the sample had done more than one job since they started working (one woman had done eight jobs since leaving school). This was either due to redundancy (which some women in the study had experienced more than once in their short employment careers) or because they hoped to get more money or better working conditions in another job. Many women (black and white) had experienced difficulty finding work. This means that for the majority of the sample it was not possible to be continually employed for the necessary two years in order to qualify for statutory maternity leave. . . . The following examples vividly illustrate how hard it has been for this cohort of women to get established in employment:

> When I was looking for work after I left my job, in the job centre it was all 'eighteen' or 'sixteen with experience', and I couldn't understand that. I know my boyfriend is finding it really hard to get a job.
> *(Linda, a white seventeen-year-old)*

> I don't know. If you go to the job centre they want people with 'O' levels and CSEs and things like that and you have to be a certain age . . .
> *(Ruth, a white seventeen-year-old)*

> First of all they say that you need education to get a job and then when – I think you just got to be lucky really … When you go they say you haven't got enough – or they want someone with at least two years' experience.
>
> *(Fay, a black nineteen-year-old)*

[···]

White women and black women alike had difficulty getting jobs because of the general unavailability, coupled with their lack of qualifications and youth (which partly signalled lack of experience). However, while prospects were poor for the majority of this group, racial discrimination made the situation worse for black women. This was mostly mentioned by black women, but some white women also commented on it.

> It was only when I got to the interviews and I didn't used to get the job I used to think I was unfairly treated because when I'd leave and they'd turn me down I used to hear that a white person got it and that she didn't have as much going for her like what I did.
>
> *(Joyce, a black nineteen-year-old)*

> I think they would rather take on a white person than a black person. I don't know why that is. They just would.
>
> *(Tracey, a white eighteen-year-old)*

> They [friends' siblings] say like how it's harder … you could have the same qualifications as a white person and you could go in an office and get all their little exams and everything like that and you get a higher score than a white person but because you're black, you just don't get the job.
>
> *(Hayley, a black sixteen-year-old)*

These accounts illustrate the intersection of race and class in that, while all the sample found it difficult to get jobs because of their class position, black women were less likely than white women to get jobs.

[···]

In summary, the women in this study were clearly not in occupations which had career progression. Their difficulty in finding (and keeping) jobs meant that few were eligible for maternity leave in late pregnancy. Deferring motherhood would have made little difference to this since the types of employment they were eligible for tended not to be ones which provided career prospects. For these women the intersection of the motherhood career and the employment career does not fit a conflictual model in that childbearing would make little difference to their employment prospects. In the late pregnancy interview it remained to be seen how many women in this group would actually participate in the labour market post birth. Black women's and white women's experiences of the employment market were largely similar. Differences could more readily be attributed to racial discrimination than narrowly defined cultural differences.

[· · ·]

This does not mean that culture is irrelevant to the study of young people's behaviour or that it is never legitimate either to focus solely on black people or to compare black people and white people. However, complex (rather than simple) representations of culture need to be used. Such complex definitions encompass structural influences of class, gender and race, which influence white people's as well as black people's lives. This sort of approach allows the representation of differences in style among young black women and young white women. It also takes account of the common experiences that young black women and young white women share as the result of being of the same sex and of similar class positions. However, it also recognizes that racism divides white people from black people and stops them from being aware of their similarities. The narrow representations of cultural influence discussed in this [article] cannot portray these complexities, and are therefore inadequate for the explanation of human behaviour.

Notes

1   'Race' is used here to refer to the social construction of black people and white people as belonging to different races. This [article] concentrates on black women of Afro-Caribbean origin, and white women, most of whom have been born and brought up in Britain. The term as used here connotes the differential treatment that black people and white people in British society receive. As such it refers to racial discrimination on the basis of colour rather than to cultural differences on the basis of ethnicity.

2   The sample was recruited from the ante-natal clinics of two large, inner-city London hospitals. Apart from the age criterion, women had to be having the first child they intended to rear themselves. Any woman who met these criteria and agreed to participate was included in the study. Seventy-nine women were given in-depth interviews, and the other 101 women were given shorter interviews. The quotations used here all come from the longer interviews, but some of the percentages given refer to the whole sample. All names used are pseudonyms.

Article 2.4
BOCAS: A DAUGHTER'S GEOGRAPHY
Ntozake Shange

i have a daughter/ mozambique
i have a son/ angola
our twins
salvador & johannesburg/ cannot speak
the same language
but we fight the same old men/ in the new world

we are so hungry for the morning
we're trying to feed our children the sun
but a long time ago/ we boarded ships/ locked in
depths of seas our spirits/ kisst the earth
on the atlantic side of nicaragua costa rica
our lips traced the edges of cuba puerto rico
charleston & savannah/ in haiti
we embraced &
made children of the new world
but old men spit on us/ shackled our limbs
but for a minute
our cries are the panama canal/ the yucatan
we poured thru more sea/ more ships/ to manila
ah ha we're back again
everybody in manila awready speaks spanish

the old men sent for the archbishop of canterbury
"can whole continents be excommunicated?"
"what wd happen to the children?"
"wd their allegiance slip over the edge?"
"dont worry bout lumumba/ don't even think bout
ho chi minh/ the dead cant procreate"
so say the old men
but i have a daughter/ la habana
i have a son/ guyana
our twins
santiago & brixton/ cannot speak

the same language
yet we fight the same old men

the ones who think helicopters rhyme with hunger
who think patrol boats can confiscate a people
the ones whose dreams are full of none of our
children
they see mae west & harlow in whittled white cafes
near managua/ listening to primitive rhythms in
jungles near pétionville
with bejeweled benign natives
ice skating in abidjan
unaware of the rest of us in chicago
all the dark urchins
rounding out the globe/ primitively whispering
the earth is not flat old men

there is no edge
no end to the new world
cuz i have a daughter/ trinidad
i have a son/ san juan
our twins
capetown & palestine/ cannot speak the same
language/ but we fight the same old men
the same men who thought the earth waz flat
go on over the edge/ go on over the edge old men
you'll see us in luanda, or the rest of us
in chicago
rounding out the morning/
we are feeding our children the sun

3
CLASS, RACE AND GENDER

CLASS DIVISIONS

In her poem, Shange mentions a wide range of countries. The differences in women's living standards and their material circumstances vary enormously between and within these countries. In Chapter 3 we examine some of the differences between women in terms of their income, employment, educational attainment and overall living standards: a set of differences often summarized in the term 'social class'. The focus here, however, is not on international variations but on women's different class positions in the UK over the last century.

Allocating women to a social class is not always straightforward, as social class is usually based on some measure of an individual's occupation. For women, many of whom have interrupted working lives or are not in waged employment at all, it is not self-evident how to classify them. Many women still leave the labour market on the birth of their first child, re-entering it at a later date after the birth of their final child. In addition, women frequently experience downward social mobility on re-entry, often taking a part-time job in which their previous experience is not utilized to the full. This creates a problem for studies of the changing social structure of contemporary Britain, particularly for those studies investigating the extent of social mobility, whether between generations or over a single lifetime. Because women's employment patterns are more complicated than those of men, social scientists tended, at least until recently, to cut women out of their analyses of social mobility altogether. Thus the whole range of sociological studies that found evidence for considerable social mobility in the UK, most notably during the 1950s and 1960s, based this conclusion solely on the experience of men!

Certain social scientists have argued that it is, in fact, unnecessary to resolve these problems and to allocate women to their own class category, if living standards are the focus of attention and analysis. They suggest that as overall living standards, and possibly the attitudes and values of family members, are related to the male head of household's occupation, it is this that should be used as the basis of that household's class position. In most circumstances it is, after all, the male partner's occupation that is usually financially the better rewarded job. (Patterns of gender segregation in the labour market and the reasons for pay differentials between men and women are discussed in Part III.) However, such a practice hides inequalities within households. Feminist social scientists, have, for example, documented the often unequal division of total family income between different household members. And, of course, not all women live for all of their lives in a household headed by a man. For women living alone, or with other women, it is their own occupation, pension or income-generating ability that determines their class position and their standard of living.

So, all in all, comparisons of the class position and living standards of women raise considerable methodological problems for social scientists. But more than methodological questions are raised. The sameness/difference dichotomy is also important here. The meaning of waged work, and hence the experience of class, may not be the same for a woman as for a man. For men, definitions of masculinity and of their sense of personal worth are bound up with their occupation in ways that are not the same as for women, although as we shall demonstrate in Part III, femininity is also defined in the labour market. But it seems that women's sense of self is seldom bound up with their waged work in quite the same way as men's sense of identity is; for women, expectations of social mobility, for example, may be through marriage rather than, or as well as, through waged work. Here too, however, there are important differences between women as well as between women and men.

Article 3.1 gives a broad brush summary of the nature and importance of class differences between women in the UK in the late nineteenth and the twentieth centuries. The extract is from Anne Phillips' book *Divided Loyalties* (1987). In the book, Phillips shows how the significance of gender and class, as bases for uniting or dividing women, has varied over the last hundred years. At certain periods, the differences between women who are in waged work and those who are not have been so great that it is hard to see where their common interests as women lay. At other times, and Phillips suggests that the current period is one of them, women are united by their common experiences of gender rather than divided by class.

DIVISIONS OF RACE AND ETHNICITY

Phillips also raises the question of race or ethnic origin as she shows that white women are often in different types of jobs and occupations to women from other ethnic backgrounds. The differences between women on nationalist, racial and ethnic grounds raise complex questions for feminism. In Article 3.2, Floya Anthias and Nira Yuval-Davis address the way in which these differences became important in the politics of race in the UK. Their argument is related to the issue of language and terminology that was raised in the Introduction to Part II. Many members of minority groups, other than those from the Afro-Caribbean population, argue that the generic use in the UK of the term 'black' as an umbrella term to include most of the non-white population, disguises the significance of differences between groups, especially between people of Asian origin and Afro-Caribbean people. Here, Anthias and Yuval-Davis argue strongly for a more disaggregated definition of divisions between women, based on ethnicity rather than on the bipolar distinction between black and white women. However, other feminists argue that the black/white distinction is useful as it describes a *racist* polarity in the UK. Thus Michèle Barrett and Mary McIntosh suggest that the position taken by Anthias and Yuval-Davis, that of recognizing multiple differences and divisions, may be 'completely disabling of political mobilisation' (Barrett and McIntosh, 1985, p. 28).

However, a debate between advocates of recognizing difference and political pluralism and those who regard such recognition as a slide into relativism, became both more significant and more fiercely contested as the 1980s progressed. By the end of the decade, the notion of a politics of identity, based on the recognition of difference between women and between minority peoples, often the victims of colonial oppression, had become an essential part of the new post-modern discourse that swept the social sciences. It has been argued that so-called universal truths in fact reflect the experience of white western men and that structures of knowledge must become more diverse and partial in order to include the multiple 'others' – women among them – who were previously excluded as subjects and objects of academic analysis. At the political level, the notion of a 'politics of identity', rather than politics based on gender and class, gained credence. Thus the idea that there is a clear homogeneity of (class or gender) interests is challenged, and difference rather than commonality is placed at the centre. Such a politics of *difference* also assists in the rejection of the notion that there is a *hierarchy* of oppressions – that certain oppressions are more salient than others, or that oppressions are additive. Rather than the abstract ranking of relations of power inherent in class, race, gender and sexual orientation, the focus shifted to the ways in which each of these relations intertwine, reinforce and contradict each other in historically specific contexts. Thus a more complex view of feminist politics arose, in which women from different class positions and from different ethnic backgrounds unite on specific issues where their interests are in common, but divide on others. We return to the implications of this diversity in Part IV on politics.

Article 3.1
CLASSING THE WOMEN AND GENDERING THE CLASS

Anne Phillips

Class has undoubtedly defined the experience of women; the female experience has in turn defined the meaning of class. But the way this has happened has altered through time, and if we look at how class has been perceived by women we can identify some significant shifts and turns. Three voices should alert us to what we can expect: middle-class feminists speaking from the 1850s, the 1930s and today.

The first one speaks with confidence of her distress; she makes no apology for her station; she has neither the money of those above her nor the freedom of those below. The dictates of gentility made her a lady but they prepared her for nothing more . . . . She was trained in the butterfly role of idle lady, denied her chances of paid employment, forced to depend for her future on meeting a suitable man. The victim of circumstances beyond her control, her fate was all too easily dictated by the failure of a father's business, the foolish speculation of a brother, the unexpected death of a husband. At any moment she could be thrown onto an inhospitable job market which had little time for her genteel skills. Few enough trades were open to women in the nineteenth century and of these only two were respectable enough for her – the wretched . . . existence of the lady's companion or governess.

The middle-class feminist of the mid-nineteenth century felt anything but privileged: if at the poorer end of her class, she was exposed to poverty and degradation; if at the richer end, to passivity and humiliation. Far from apologizing for her advantages, she could feel herself the most downtrodden of her sex. It was not that she ignored the sufferings of poorer women – if she had the time and money she might devote years of an otherwise empty existence to philanthropic activities in the city slums – but she felt the closure of opportunities to women of her own class an outrageous example of woman's oppression. Working-class women were at least free to earn their bread; the middle-class woman was condemned to nothing.

To today's listener, this early predecessor can sound unbearably self-obsessed, wrapped up in her own concerns, oblivious to the harsher drudgery of the working-class woman, convinced in her ignorance that no one was worse off than she. Eighty years on, the second voice sounds more gently on our ears: it is Virginia Woolf reflecting on her attendance at a conference of the Women's Co-operative Guild. Deeply committed to feminism, she was also a wealthy woman influenced by socialist ideals, perennially disturbed by the implications of class. The conference had been an uncomfortable experience for her, for however hard she tried, she felt her sympathy with the co-operative women could only be fictitious: . . .

> All these questions – perhaps this was at the bottom of it – which matter so intensely to the people here, questions of sanitation and education and wages, this demand for an extra shilling, for another year at school, for eight hours instead of nine behind a counter or in a mill, leave me, in my own blood and bones, untouched. If every reform they demand was granted this very instant it would not touch one hair of my comfortable capitalistic head. . . .
>
> *(Virginia Woolf, in Davies, 1977, p. xxxi)*

. . . Sitting there listening to the talk of money and baths, she wanted to shout out that these were not everything, that literature and art and science mattered too. She knew it was money that had bought her the luxury of such concerns – she recognized and questioned her privilege – but she was not to be silenced by this. . . .

A third speaker, who is our contemporary though by no means our only voice, seems to have travelled a long way on. In a marked reversal of the first perspective she will accept without question that working-class women are the most oppressed; in her guilty relationship to their sufferings, she is hard put to it to assert her own oppression at all. She goes down the list of demands drawn up at successive women's conferences. Women want equal pay and equal opportunities; well, that's so much easier in a middle-class job. Women want free abortion and nurseries: perhaps not such a priority if you have the money to pay. Women want to be legally and financially independent: with the right qualifications and the right sort of job, it's not such a distant dream. Women want an end to discrimination against lesbians: their chances against employers at least may prove more favourable in a professional job. Women want freedom from male violence: it helps a lot if you drive home in a car. The speaker is considerably less privileged than Virginia Woolf – probably not rich at all – and yet unlike her predecessors she has talked herself into silence. All the oppressions she associates with womanhood seem so much alleviated by the privileges of class.

What do these three moments tell us? Not that feminists have grown in self-awareness, from complacency to consciousness to guilt, for though all three characters can be described as 'middle class', they are markedly different in position and status. The real lesson is that what working class and middle class mean has constantly changed, and that what they mean for women has perhaps changed most of all.

UPPER, MIDDLE AND WORKING: THE TRIPARTITE DISTINCTION

The language of class is a novel one – widely spoken only in the last 150 years – yet it has already undergone major transformation. E.P. Thompson has said that class is a relationship, something that happens when the people in one group claim an identity with each other and assert their opposition to those outside (Thompson, 1968, p. 9). This is undoubtedly true, and one thing it implies is that 'class' alters with whom it relates. In British politics the categories of working and middle class developed initially in an opposition to the *upper* class; only later did they come to be used in opposition to each other. The divisions people have seen as the most pertinent have not been static over the last two centuries.

[· · ·]

[The] boundaries [between classes] were . . . insecure . . . because the original distinction was with that upper class. . . . Apart from this, both middle and working class embraced . . . disparate and divided groups. The middle classes included manufacturers and bankers, farmers and traders, doctors and lawyers, curates and clerks. The working classes included shopkeepers and costermongers, artisans and factory hands, teachers and domestic servants. . . .

FEMININITY AS A CLASS IDEAL

Class began and continued as a muddle, but as 'middle' and 'working' came into sharper focus in the course of the century, they did so partly through the roles they allotted their women. Boundaries were redrawn . . . and as the new classes were made, gender roles proved to be crucial.

   This was particularly true of the middle class, for as Catherine Hall has put it, 'the new bourgeois way of life involved a recodification of ideas about women' (Hall, 1979, p. 15). Wives who once participated in the family business now withdrew to domestic seclusion; daughters who once helped in the home now devoted themselves to their feminine accomplishments; women developed what feminists later derided as their parasite role. Their separation was noted, for example, among farmers, for as the enclosure movement speeded up in the second half of the eighteenth century and smaller farmers and cottagers lost their tenuous grip on the land, those more successful increased their property and 'gentrified' their lives. Women were allowed to free themselves from household or farming activities, to abandon the kitchen for the parlour, the dairy for the boarding school.

[· · ·]

Over much the same period successful entrepreneurs were beginning to stake out a new division between work and home, a distinction they made visible by building brand new mansions at a decent distance from the factory or shop. Wives who had previously taken their share in management now lost contact with the business; women who had worked in the household now relied on servants; they were no longer supposed to bother their heads with business, but to decline gracefully into their decorative role.

. . . If aristocrats could afford to keep their women in elegance, so too could the bourgeoisie – with the difference that the bourgeois woman would be chaste as well as idle. Women were not to work, either in the business or the home; wealth would be made prominent by female inactivity.

It was gender differentiation writ large, and though the examples above are taken from the upper end of the new middle class, the ideals they represented pervaded all the lower sub-divisions. Whatever the income, whatever the cost, middle-class existence was to be guaranteed by the status of its women, and though respectable artisans also hoped to keep their wives from working, it was in the middle class that female passivity established its sway. The result . . . was that in this class women were *uniquely* separated from men.

[· · ·]

The irony, of course, is that just as the ideal of the leisured lady was spreading, so the women from the *working class* were being called out of their homes into the fields, mines and factories, and away from their homes into domestic service for the rich. In agriculture, the gentrification of the farmer's wife had coincided precisely with the increased employment of women as day labourers. Larger farmers consolidated their wealth and smaller farmers lost their independence; men, women and children alike were reduced to the status of agricultural labourers, with women and children doing much of the heavier forms of seasonal work. In textiles too, the leisured elegance of the mill-owner's wife coexisted with increased employment of women as mill-hands, a phenomenon that developed so rapidly that contemporaries feared men might lose their jobs for ever. And in a more direct causal connection, as the number of middle-class households increased, so too did the demand for domestic servants, which soon reached such a level that domestic service became the largest single employer of women. The angel in the middle-class house demanded a servant from the working-class one. . . . The demand for dressmakers and milliners also increased, again in rhythm with the growth of the middle classes. Feminine inactivity was of necessity a class ideal.

Women in fact worked in large numbers, as the 1851 census

revealed: out of an adult population of six million women, more than half worked for their living; of these, two out of three were supporting themselves – and sometimes children – on their own. . . . Women went out to work as domestic servants, as dressmakers and milliners, as factory workers in the textile trades, as agricultural labourers. In less well documented numbers, they stayed in to work as laundresses, needlewomen, landladies, shopkeepers. And while the majority of those who went *out* to work were single, a substantial minority were married with children – anathema indeed to the new ideal.

The irony was not lost on all Victorians, and the nineteenth century was punctuated by periodic outbursts on the iniquities of female employment: the 'scandal' of women in the cotton mills in the 1840s; of women roaming the country in agricultural gangs in the 1860s; of women at the pit-brow in the 1880s. Scandal is the appropriate word, for the employment particularly of *married* women was considered shocking, and the conditions under which they worked a degradation to their feminine nature. The incidence of married women working was in fact much exaggerated by those who pressed for factory legislation (Hewitt, 1975), and the long hours of factory employment made it ill-suited to a woman with a young child. Yet throughout the nineteenth century a *quarter* of the women employed in Lancashire cotton mills were married, and the figure rose to 30 per cent in times of heavy labour recruitment (ibid., ch. 2). Infant mortality in Lancashire was appallingly high, with as many as one in five children dying before their first birthday, and *half* before the age of five (ibid., ch. 8).

Poverty was always just around the corner for working-class households, and historians have estimated that barely one in seven was permanently free of its shadow (Anderson, 1971; Foster, 1974). Only the wives of skilled artisans could live exclusively on their husbands' earnings, while others had to supplement the household income in some way or another. A small minority relied on factory jobs – which offered better wages than most for women – and in the mills of Lancashire and Yorkshire, the potteries of Staffordshire, the jute factories of Dundee, married women were a substantial part of the labour force. Some abandoned the job when they had a child, but the more the children the greater the need for money, and fear of losing their job forced many women back to work within two weeks of childbirth. Children were then cared for by grandmothers, young girls, lodgers or neighbours – if the worst came to the worst by the often disreputable paid child-minders (Anderson, 1971, ch. 6; Hewitt, 1975, ch. 9).

All this was shocking to Victorian sensibilities, as were the women toiling in the fields with their skirts tucked up above the knees (Kitteringham, 1975), the women at the pit-brow dragging heavy wagons of coal (John, 1980), or the women in the chain-making foundry wielding their heavy hammers. Less disturbing were those whose health was ruined in more typically feminine ways: the seamstresses and the washerwomen and the many, many domestic servants – though the plight of the seamstress (usually depicted as sad but refined) did arouse considerable sympathy (Walkley, 1981).[1] But least disturbing of all were those who managed to keep their work to the privacy of their own home – taking in washing, needlework, lodgers, running a small shop, all the everyday activities of a nineteenth-century married woman from the working class (Alexander, 1976; Davidoff, 1979). In contemporary convention, married women were not supposed to go *out* to work, but the ban on all forms of remunerative employment applied only to the ladies of the upper and middle class. And whatever objections were raised to the employment of *married* women, no one suggested that *single* working-class women should be maintained in idle luxury. Of course they should work, and if they got a place as a domestic servant (an ill-paid drudge), this would be excellent training for their future as wives.

Femininity was being reconstructed as a class ideal which served to distinguish one level from another, for even if working-class women were encouraged to imitate middle-class feminine norms, the cards were stacked against them. In these years, perhaps more than ever before or since, you could identify a class by the role it allotted its women: gender was not so much a separate structure as something incorporated into the meanings of class. The result for women was that their lot in life was dictated not by gender *or* class but by a complex combination of the two – a double causation which simultaneously inspired and troubled the emergent feminist movement.

[· · ·]

Of course marriage and motherhood remained the common lot of women, for while middle-class women in particular suffered from the 'surplus' of women over men, the majority from all classes got married and bore children. And as far as the debilitating years spent in pregnancy were concerned, the suffering in childbirth, the tragedies of infant mortality, there was little to choose between them. Though professional middle-class families began to restrict the numbers of their children from the 1860s onwards, it was not till the twentieth century that contraception made an appreciable difference to birth rates, and conditions of childbirth were comparable for all.[2]

But the experience of motherhood and marriage still varied across the classes. Middle-class women might be confined to the domestic sphere, but their job was to manage their households, not to do the work themselves. The daily details of domestic labour and childcare were not yet dignified into respectable life: homemaking as a 'career' entered popular ideology only in the later years of the nineteenth century, with the duties and responsibilities of motherhood coming into their own even later (Branca, 1975; Ehrenreich and English, 1979). Servants provided one of the keys to middle-class status. . . . But however close the margins between the lower end of the middle and the upper end of the working class, the life and expectations could widely diverge. While the poorer working-class mother had a hard battle to provide even the minimum of food and clothing for her children (after the superior claims of the father were met), the poor middle-class mother was caught in a different game: she had to preserve that veneer of respectability which concealed the relative poverty of her household; she could never admit a similarity with women lower down the scale.

[· · ·]

THE STRAINS OF THE FEMALE ROLE

Because gender roles had assumed such a decisively class character, women experienced their oppression differently according to their class, and inevitably it was in the middle and upper classes that the strains of femininity became most acute. For the upper-class woman cushioned by wealth the female ideal could still mean an unbearably empty life. No one should underestimate the intensity of her oppression nor seek to annihilate it with evidence that other women faced more materially biting conditions.

[· · ·]

As the middle class consolidated itself in size and power, it spawned a huge lower middle-class division – and here the pressures on women were even more acute. Middle class was coming to mean not so much those with businesses and property as those with 'white-collar' salaried jobs – commercial clerks, schoolteachers, managers, commercial travellers, sales assistants. . . . These were soon the majority in the Victorian middle classes, and while their fantasies of female dependence were much the same as those above them, their resources were far from equal to the task.

[· · ·]

WORK FIT FOR LADIES

By the middle of the nineteenth century the basic divide between working-class women who worked and middle-class women who did not was firmly established, and it was a source of suffering on virtually every side. A league table of oppression is beside the point: how do you compare the country girl forced by rural poverty out of her village to live-in as a servant, the seamstress ruining her health with excessive labour in one season and then starving through lack of work in another, the better paid cotton hand who has to abandon her children to the care of possible unscrupulous child-minders, the governess who has enough to eat as long as she works but will be turned out at forty with nowhere to go?

[· · ·]

At the turning point in the mid-nineteenth century, the problem of female employment still seemed intractable, for gentility marked the boundary between middle- and working-class jobs, and genteel jobs were few and far between.

But . . . a shift in the economic basis of class, a transformation . . . broke the old basis of class differentiation between women, . . . [and] reassemble[d] it in another form. *Lower* middle-class women began to go out to work, taking their place in a changing job market, with new jobs in teaching, nursing, sales and clerical work. . . . Class barriers cracked and threatened to break. The working woman lost her exclusively proletarian character as daughters of clerks and managers and teachers joined the daughters of shopkeepers and artisans and labourers in the search for work. [The expansion of education was very important here.] . . . The 1870 Education Act laid down the basis for free public education. Local authorities were required to provide elementary schooling for *all* children in their area, and rate-aided Board schools were set up to supplement the existing Church schools. Elementary education became first compulsory and then free, a development that inevitably increased the demand for teachers.

It was women who came forward to fill the gap. The number of women teachers went up from 79,980 in 1861 to 183,298 in 1911, and a job that in the 1850s was almost equally divided between men and women became by the First World War three-quarters female (Holcombe, 1973, appendix 1). Expansion had meant feminiz-ation, and simultaneously a process of reclassification. The first elementary teachers were recruited from the working class, with a few stray souls from the higher echelons of society. By 1914 elementary teaching had been upgraded and its recruits were much more likely to be from (lower) middle-class backgrounds.

[· · ·]

The teachers' story was repeated elsewhere with a parallel lower middle-class entry into nursing, saleswork and, as an indication of things to come, above all in clerical work. Nursing, like teaching, was upgraded into a potentially middle-class profession . . . As numbers went up so too did status, and though the hours were long and the wages pitiful, the job now attracted recruits from all over the social scale. In 1902 one matron noted that 'nurses are recruited from all classes . . . in the hospitals a housemaid may be found sitting next to a baronet's daughter, and all the gradations of rank between these two may be found at the same table' (Holcombe, 1973, p. 14).

Saleswork too was increasing, with department stores and chains of shops set up all over the country, and the lady shop assistant soon became a regular feature of life. To qualify for the work a woman had to be able to read, write and add, and was expected in addition to be reasonably well dressed and mannered. The expansion of elementary schooling meant in fact that most working-class girls could meet the literacy requirements, but the additional aura of respectability made the jobs just about suitable for a middle-class girl . . . . But the respectability of the job was tenuous – depending very much on the kind of shop you worked in – and its hours and pay were considerably worse than in a factory; 'the upper and middle classes considered shop workers to be about on a level with the servant class, while the working classes sneered at their pretensions to respectability, derisively calling them "counter-jumpers"' (Holcombe, 1973, appendix 3).

[· · ·]

As has become clear since, it was the identification of clerical work with women's work that was the crucial step, for work in this area continued to grow in leaps and bounds and the job became more and more exclusively female. Thousands upon thousands of women came forward to work as 'typewriters', a phenomenon that helped spawn a whole literature on the 'new woman' – that independent-minded female who had abandoned the boredom of the suburbs for her dingy bed-sit in the middle of town, who studied at a secretarial college and took it for granted that she would earn her own living.[3]

[· · ·]

So as it became more normal for middle-class women to have jobs, the major boundary of the previous century – between those women who had to work and those who could not – was seriously eroded. The idea that a lady should not work still lingered on in the more hidebound of middle-class households where daughters were discouraged from education and employment alike. But the idea that you could tell a woman's class by whether or not she had a job was on its way out, and the final death blow was delivered in the course of the First World War when going out to work became a woman's patriotic duty. In the nineteenth century, social class had dictated whether or not a woman went out to work; by the early twentieth century the key question was whether she was married and had children. By 1911 nearly three-quarters of single women had some form of paid employment compared with barely one in ten of women who were married. Marital status had apparently supplanted class as the key determinant of a woman's role.

WOMEN AS A SUBORDINATE CLASS?

So *that* class difference had been eroded and was not yet replaced by the difference that dominates us today, the variations in the kinds of jobs that women do. A mere handful of women had survived the obstacle race through the professions: as late as 1912 there were only 553 women physicians in Britain, and we can get some ideas of the struggles that took them there when we note that of these 518 were self-consciously feminist, supporters of one or other of the suffrage societies (Adam, 1975, p. 19). Some women were lecturers in the women's colleges, but these were very much the Cinderellas of the university system. . . . Women could not yet practise as lawyers, were excluded from accountancy, and kept out of the higher grades of the civil service. . . .

Women carried their subordination with them when they went out to work and in the job market their gender mostly overrode their class. The jobs that became available to *middle*-class women were upgraded 'working class' like teaching and nursing, or downgraded 'middle class' like sales assistant and clerk, both of which had a higher status before women appeared on the scene. The price of employment had been loss of status, and feminization had been accompanied by a marked de-skilling. Wages and conditions for middle-class women were not significantly different from the typically working-class jobs, and recruits to their work could come from virtually every section of society. There were no enclaves of exclusively middle-class work and no notable sectors of high paid employment.

[· · ·]

This is not to say that class had lost all pertinence for working women, or that as a subordinated sex they dissolved into a united classless whole. There were many jobs that a middle-class woman would not dream of doing – working in a factory, for example, as a general servant, at the pit-brow in the mines. . . . As a marginal group situated uneasily between the established middle class on the one side and the manual workers on the other, the lower middle class tended towards conservatism in its political and social values, plus a feverish insistence that it was miles better than the despised working class (Crossick, 1977, introduction). The paradox is that this deeply class-bound stratum was also what produced the 'new woman', whose experience of work necessarily reduced the sharpness of class distinctions. The interplay of gender and class was a complex one, but where middle-class women did work – in the schools, the hospitals, the shops and offices – they could not sever their links with the working class. Denied the chance of upward mobility, such women could tentatively explore their unity as a sex – and that they did so is indicated by the momentary classlessness of some of the early suffragette meetings.

But all this shifting of class and gender relations was deeply contradictory. On the one hand there was an undoubted convergence between women from the working and middle class. Whatever their origins, those who worked for a living were never far apart, for they were most of them condemned to a limited range of jobs at comparable rates of pay, and the contrast with more privileged men seemed the more stark. Yet almost because of these changes, the problems women faced began to look like a simple reflection of their class position, and less a product of their oppression as *women*.

[· · ·]

WOMEN IN CONTEMPORARY BRITAIN

After the Second World War, the similarities in women's lives became clearer, and 'by the early 1950s the extremes of difference between working- and middle-class women's experiences, which had been the result chiefly of poverty on the one hand, and a cloistered existence in a home where at least the heavy chores were performed by domestic servants on the other, had disappeared' (Lewis, 1984, p. 7). Domestic service plummeted after 1945; the typical number of children stabilized around the famous 2.4 mark; most importantly of all, growing opportunities for female employment meant that the majority of women came to continue work after marriage and even after children.

Most women still give up their jobs till their children reach school age, though a good number of mothers with small children have at least a part-time job, while large numbers of single mothers have no option but to continue full-time employment; by the time the children are five the overwhelming majority of women are back at work. . . . When the Second World War came to its end, women did not retreat permanently to the privacy of their homes – despite all those boisterous celebrations of their primary roles as wives and mothers. . . . Women had been 30 per cent of the labour force for so long that the proportion was regarded almost as natural fact, but through the 1960s and '70s male employment steadily fell and female employment steadily rose. Now women are up to 45 per cent of the total labour force and since the jobs they do – in services and semi-skilled assembly – are among the few growth areas of the economy, the proportion is set for further increase.

The change in working patterns has cut across class divides. What dictates whether a woman works or not is primarily her marital status and the age of her children; neither class nor income makes the same kind of difference. Women married to men in manual jobs may give up their job and have their first child slightly earlier than other women; along with professional women they may resume their jobs slightly earlier than women in routine non-manual employment.[4] But compared with previous periods, such differences are infinitesimal. For much of the nineteenth century a working woman was almost by definition working class; in today's popular mythology a working woman is a 'superwoman' ensconsed in a professional career. Neither could be further from contemporary reality. The housewife has all but disappeared, the working mother is now the norm, and as far as overall hours spent in paid employment are concerned, there is little to choose between the life of a middle-class and a working-class woman. Most women have children, most women go to work, most run their households without the help of servants. Compared with previous periods the lives of women are now amazingly homogeneous.

But as these similarities have strengthened, other distinctions have grown. As women are drawn more and more into paid employment, the gap between the kinds of jobs they do has inevitably grown. Not that women's jobs are anything like as sharply differentiated as men's; women are still bunched into a narrow range of occupations, excluded from society's 'top jobs', and whatever job they do, faced with lower pay and poorer prospects than men with a comparable training. With all these qualifications it is none the less true that in their working lives women can face markedly different conditions.

[· · ·]

Women's jobs are stratified into what can look like two different worlds: at one extreme, the growing army of part-time workers, disproportionately concentrated in 'women-only' jobs in saleswork and cleaning and canteens, earning wages that even hour for hour are appallingly low. At the other extreme, the women who have been through higher education, who have full-time and relatively powerful jobs, earning wages that are regarded as good – if not brilliant – even for a man. And somewhere in the middle, the fragile bridge of office workers.

The gaps are immense, and they are further reinforced by the racial segregation that has emerged as one of the key features of post-war employment and puts women of different ethnic origins in markedly different positions. The phenomenon of part-time employment, for example, is most marked among white women. The 1981 *Labour Force Survey* showed that, among women who are 'economically active' (have a job or are looking for one), 62.2 per cent of West Indian women, 61.9 per cent of Asian women, and a much smaller 49 per cent of white women have a full-time job; for part-time jobs the figures were 21.1 per cent of West Indian women, 12.5 per cent of Asian women, and a massive 36.9 per cent of white women (*Employment Gazette*, 1983, table 6). Part-time employment has continued to grow – by 1984 nearly 45 per cent of all women with jobs were in part-time work – and for white women it is the contrast between full- and part-time working that carries much of the burden of class distinction: part-time women workers are more likely to be in manual jobs; more likely to be in a workplace that is exclusively female; virtually guaranteed to earn less hour for hour than full-time workers (Martin and Roberts, 1984, ch. 3). For black women it is more a question of the kinds of *full-time* jobs they do. . . .

The jobs typically done by black women are not those typically done by white, and significantly fewer occupy the clerical and saleswork that is so much associated with female labour. . . . For Asian women the difference is the clothing trade; for West Indian women it is largely explained by their predominance in engineering and allied trades. Apart from this, West Indian women tend to be concentrated in work in the health service, and the two together account for the otherwise startling statistic that West Indian women earn more hour for hour than white women (Barrett and McIntosh, 1985, p. 31). But they are more at risk from unemployment . . . while being more dependent on full-time earnings (for so many of them have exclusive responsibility for the support of their children); their position is sufficiently distinctive for Annie Phizacklea to describe them as a separate 'class fraction' (Phizacklea, 1982).

The gulf in the female work experience is a yawning one, and we can see why the unities of class or race can often seem more pertinent than those of gender. Yet because women *are* women, they constantly cross over the boundaries between jobs. As they move in and out of paid employment, they may span a wide variety of different occupations. . . . Women who give up their full-time job to have children and later return to part-time work are more than likely to have to take a step down the occupational ladder: when asked in the 1980 Women and Employment survey if the job they went back to after having their first child was 'higher' or 'lower' than the one they left, 45 per cent of the women who went back to a *part*-time job said it was lower, and only 13 per cent could report that it was higher (Martin and Roberts, 1984, table 10.16). Downward mobility is one of the facts of life for women, and over the course of a lifetime it can erode once powerful social barriers. Women simply cannot afford the same sense of class as men, for the reality of their lives constantly contradicts it.

[· · ·]

Fulfilment through work ha[s] little resonance [for most women]; being able to cope [is] what matter[s].

[· · ·]

One of the peculiarities in women's position today [is] that the convergence in our needs coexists with a divergence in our sense of priorities. . . . For women . . . the division between working and middle class has become less substantial, but our daily experiences of work, of mothering, of entertainment, of life, still keep us apart. It would be nonsense to suggest that gender was the sole determinant of our lives, delusory to expect a 'women's politics' to reign supreme. We have to shuffle our way towards unity, marking en route the forces that divide. In the 1984–85 miners' strike, those involved in Women Against Pit Closures talked of their differences with men, their determination to retain an organization as women, their conviction that women's place in the home must change. But nobody could have driven a wedge between them and the men they supported; the unities of gender had to take their place alongside the unities of class. Black women have made their criticisms of black men, noting their assumption of leadership in the black communities, their opposition to women taking an equal role. But the place of black people in our society leaves no room for a simple politics of gender; the unity of women must find its place alongside the unities of race. As far as class is concerned, it is crucial to note how much it has changed, how far from obvious is the middle-versus working-class divide. But tracing its course through the last two hundred years we see differences dissolve and then recompose; what class means for women has altered almost beyond recognition; that it still means a lot is beyond our doubt.

Notes

1   Thomas Hood's 'Song of the shirt' was published in *Punch* in 1843, establishing a tradition of depicting the seamstress as sad but refined.

2   It is particularly notable that infant mortality rates could be as high and sometimes even higher in middle-class areas. See Branca 1975, ch. 6.

3   A later example of this genre is H.G. Wells' *Ann Veronica*, 1909 (published by Virago, 1980).

4   Gail Braybon has suggested that this divide was emerging even in the inter-war years.

Article 3.2
CONTEXTUALIZING FEMINISM: GENDER, ETHNIC AND CLASS DIVISIONS

Floya Anthias and Nira Yuval-Davis

'Sisterhood is powerful.' 'Sisterhood' can also be misleading unless contextualized. Black, minority and migrant women have been on the whole invisible within the feminist movement in Britain and within the literature on women's or feminist studies. . . . Our analysis serves to problematize the notion of 'sisterhood' and the implicit feminist assumption that there exists a commonality of interests and/or goals amongst all women. Rather, we argue that *every* feminist struggle has a specific *ethnic* (as well as class) context. Although the notion of the 'ethnic' will be considered later, . . . here . . . it primarily relates to the exclusionary/inclusionary boundaries of collectivities formed round the notion of a common origin.[1] The 'ethnic' context of feminist struggles has been systematically ignored (except in relation to various minorities, especially 'black'). . . . This has helped to perpetuate both political and theoretical inadequacies within feminist and socialist analyses.

The black feminist movement has grown partly as a response to the invisibility of black women and to the racism of the white feminist movement. . . . [Here] we want to broaden out the frame of reference of the existing debate. Within black feminism the most dominant approach defines black women as suffering from the 'triple oppression' of race, gender and class. This approach is inadequate, however, both theoretically and politically. Race, gender and class cannot be tagged on to each other mechanically for, as concrete social relations, they are enmeshed in each other and the particular intersections involved produce specific effects. The need for the study of the intersection of these divisions has been recognized recently by black feminists.[2]

We also suggest . . . that the issue of the interrelationship of the different social divisions cannot focus only on black versus white women's position. This has the theoretical effect of singling out 'racism' as applicable only to 'black' women and focuses then on the colour rather than on the structural location of ethnic groups as determinants of their social relations. . . . An exclusive focus on 'racism' fails to address the diversity of ethnic experiences which derive from other factors like economic or political position. The notion of 'black women' as delineating the boundaries of the alternative feminist movement to white feminism leaves non-British non-black women (like us – a Greek-Cypriot and an Israeli-Jew) unaccounted for politically. Although we recognize the impetus behind the black women's movement and the need for its autonomous organization, black feminism can be too wide or too narrow a category for specific feminist struggles. On the one hand, there are struggles which concern all migrant women, like those against immigration laws, and on the other hand there are struggles which might concern only Sikh Indian women, for instance.

For these reasons, our [article] will use the notion of ethnic divisions rather than the black/white division as a more comprehensive conceptual category for struggling against racism. One of our tasks will be to consider the links between the concepts of racism and ethnicity as well as attempting to relate ethnic divisions to those of gender and class.

[· · ·]

We . . . present an exploratory framework [then] for analysing the interrelationship of ethnic and gender divisions. We . . . briefly examine these divisions within two central areas of feminist analysis, employment and reproduction. The [article] . . . conclude[s] by considering some of the implications of the analysis presented for the western/Third World feminist debate.

[· · ·]

CLASS, GENDER AND ETHNIC DIVISIONS

As socialists working within a broadly Marxist-informed analysis, we see class divisions as grounded in the different relations of groups to the means of production which provides what has been called a group's class determination. However, class mobilization cannot be read from class determination for class goals are constructed through a variety of different mechanisms with ideological practices having a central role in this. Concrete class groupings may be composed of both men and women, of black and white and different cultures and ethnic identities. These concrete groupings are constructed historically. At times there may be a coincidence of class and gender or ethnic position (and at other times there may be cross cuttings). For example, some fractions of the working class may be primarily composed of women or black people. This may reflect economic, political and ideological processes but may also be structured through struggle and negotiation between the groups themselves and in relation to the state. Classes are not homogeneous ethnically, culturally or in terms of gender in most cases but class fractions may constitute some kind of homogeneity.

Gender divisions relate to the organization of sexual difference and biological reproduction and establish forms of representation around these, although their concrete contents will include notions of the appropriateness of wage-labour, education and so on to men and to women. Usually sexual difference and biological reproduction (the ontological basis of gender) are represented as having necessary social effects. . . . Gender divisions thus usually work with a notion of a 'natural' relationship between social effects and sexual differences/biological reproduction. We do not accept such a depiction nor that biological *reproduction* is an equivalent material basis for *gender* to that of *production* for *class*. Indeed, the attempt to discover a feminist materialism in the social relations of reproduction fails precisely in the attempt to superimpose a materialist project onto a different object and reproduce its terms of reference.[3] Finally, the end result is indeed to reduce these social relations to their material base (biology), just as within Marxist materialism the reduction is to 'mode of production'.

Rather, we reject both biological reductionism and class reductionism. We are suggesting that there is an *object* of discursive reference in the sphere of gender divisions which relates to groups of subjects *defined* by their sexual/biological difference as opposed to groups of subjects defined by their economic production difference as in class. Gender divisions are 'ideological' to the extent that they do not have a basis in reproduction, but reproduction is represented as their basis. However, the ideological nature of gender divisions does not mean they do not exist nor that they do not have social origins and social effects or involve material practices.

Unlike class and gender divisions, ethnic divisions are difficult to ground in some separate sphere of relations. This makes the various Marxist and sociological attempts to try to find systematic conceptual differences between national/ethnic and racial groupings even more problematic. . . .

The only general basis on which we can theorize what can broadly be conceived as 'ethnic' phenomena in all their diversity are as various forms of ideological construct which divide people into different collectivities or communities. This will involve exclusionary/inclusionary boundaries which form the collectivity. In other words, although the constructs are ideological, they involve real material practices and therefore origins and effects. Whether the boundaries are those of a tribe, a nation or a linguistic or cultural minority, they will tend to focus themselves around the myth of common origin (whether biological, cultural or historical). Although sometimes there will be other means of joining the collectivity than being born into it (like religious conversion or naturalization), group membership is considered as the 'natural' right of being *born* into it. The salience of the collectivity and the social relations involved can vary greatly.

Ethnicity is not only a question of ethnic identity. This latter does not exhaust the category of the 'ethnic' nor does it necessarily occur. Ethnicity may be constructed outside the group by the material conditions of the group and its social representation by other groups. However, in practice ethnic identity and . . . solidarity may occur either as a prerequisite for the group or as an effect of its material, political or ideological placement. . . . Ethnicity involves struggle, negotiation and the use of ethnic resources for the countering of disadvantages or perpetuation of advantages. Conditions of reproduction of the ethnic group as well as its transformation are related to the divisions of gender and class. For example, class homogeneity within the ethnic group will produce a greater cohesion of interests and goals.

. . . Our use of the term ethnicity has as a central element exclusion/inclusion practices and the relations of power of dominance/subordination that are aspects of these. Majority groups possess an ethnicity as well as minority groups. Ethnicity and racism share both the categories of exclusion and power but racism is a specific form of exclusion. Racist discourse posits an essential biological determination to culture but its referent may be any group that has been 'socially' constructed as having a different 'origin', whether cultural, biological or historical. It can be 'Jewish', 'black', 'foreign', 'migrant', 'minority'. In other words, any group that has been located in ethnic terms can be subjected to 'racism' as a form of exclusion. The 'Racist' category is more deterministic than the mere 'ethnic' category.

[· · ·]

In patriarchal white societies it is perceived as 'natural' that men will occupy a higher economic position in the labour market than women, and white people than black people. . . . Racism and ethnicity also have a role in justifying the economic/class subordination of black people. For example, arguments about the cultural choices of ethnic groups – and racial stereotypes about Asian men (money-seeking) and Afro-Caribbean men (work idle) – are used to account for their economic position. . . . [In addition] the 'natural' elements of gender and ethnic divisions are used as rallying points for political struggle against class inequality as well as gender and ethnic inequalities. This is the case in most anti-imperialist struggles where notions of national identity are used. The black power movement has often used racial–ethnic identification partly as a counter to existing racial stereotypes and oppressions (for example, in black nationalism the identification with Africa, and in black power the 'black is beautiful' rhetoric, and more recently, culturalist and religious revivals such as Rastafarianism). As regards gender, feminists have used women's 'nature' as a rallying point, particularly with reference to the positive values of women's culture and 'nature'. However, using ethnic and gender categories in this way as rallying points for political mobilization in class-related struggles can present a problem for class unity.

[···]

THE RELATIONS BETWEEN GENDER AND ETHNIC DIVISIONS

We suggested above that all three divisions are intermeshed in such a way that we cannot see them as additive or prioritize abstractly any one of them. Each division presents ideological and organizational principles within which the others operate, although in different historical contexts and different social arenas their role will differ. The fusion of gender and class and ethnicity and class will also operate in the relationship between gender and ethnic divisions.

For example, if we consider the household we will find gender divisions will differ according to ethnicity. Ethnically specific definitions of women's and men's roles underlie the sexual division of labour in the family. Such aspects as mothering, housework, sexual obligations, obedience and submissiveness to male commands (and indeed to other members of the family) will differ according to ethnicity (as well as class, of course). . . .

If we consider the sphere of employment, . . . this will be affected particularly by the gender divisions of the majority ethnic group. Values and institutionalized practices about women's 'nature' and 'role' present constraints to men and women from minority/subordinate ethnic groups despite their own gender ideologies.

Another link between ethnic and gender divisions is found in the way in which the *boundary* of ethnicity depends on gender. The definition of membership within the ethnic group often depends on performing gender attributes correctly. Both identity and institutional arrangements of ethnic groups incorporate gender roles and specify appropriate relations between sexes such as, for example, who can marry them. A Greek-Cypriot girl of the second generation is regarded as 'Kypraia' usually when she conforms to rules about sexually appropriate behaviour – otherwise she becomes excluded. The definition of boundaries is far from being an internal practice alone. If we consider racial stereotypes we can see the centrality of gender roles; for example, stereotypes about the 'dominant' Asian father and the 'dominant' black mother, or stereotypes about black men and women as sexual 'studs'. These all indicate the reliance on gender attributes for specifying ethnic difference. We want to suggest briefly some more specific links between ethnic and gender divisions in employment and reproduction.

Employment

The internal gender divisions of an ethnic group ... affect the participation of men and women of the group in the labour market. Men and women of a specific ethnic group will tend to hold particular but different positions in the labour market; for example, Afro-Caribbean men in the construction industry and on the buses, Afro-Caribbean women as service workers in manufacturing and as nurses, Asian men in textile firms and Asian women as outworkers in small-scale dress-making factories. A sexually differentiated labour market will structure the placement of subjects according to sex but ethnic divisions will determine their subordination with them – so, for example, black and white women may both be subordinate within a sexually differentiated labour market but black women will be subordinated to white women within this.

We would suggest that within western societies, gender divisions are more important for women than ethnic divisions in terms of labour market subordination. In employment terms, migrant or ethnic women are usually closer to the female population as a whole than to ethnic men in the type of wage-labour performed. Black and migrant women are already so disadvantaged by their gender in employment that it is difficult to show the effects of ethnic discrimination for them. When examining the position of ethnic minority men in the labour market, the effect of their ethnic position is much more visible. This may lead to a situation where, for example, Afro-Caribbean or Asian women have at times had greater ease in finding employment – as cheap labour in 'women's work', whether it be nursing, assembly-line or clerical work – than the men.

But the interrelationship between ethnic and gender divisions in employment goes beyond the mere differentiation in employment of ethnic subjects according to their gender. . . . The economic and social advancement of a migrant group may depend partly on the possibility of using the *household*, and in particular the women within it, as a labour resource. The extent to which migrant ethnic men have become incorporated into wider social production and the form this takes may also depend on the use of *migrant* women's labour *overall*. Men from different migrant/ethnic groups have been incorporated differently economically. Afro-Caribbean men, for example, are in the 'vanguard' of British industry in large-scale production (Hall *et al.*, 1978, p. 349). Asian and Cypriot men, on the other hand, have had a greater tendency to go into small-scale entrepreneurial concerns and into the service sector of the economy. In particular, entrepreneurial concerns both within the formal and hidden economy depend on the exploitation of female wage-labour and in particular on kinship and migrant labour. Ethnic and familial bonds serve to allow the even greater exploitation of female labour (Anthias, 1983). The different form of the family and gender ideologies may partly explain the differences between Afro-Caribbean employment patterns and those of Asians and Cypriots.

Reproduction

We want now to turn to the area of reproduction and briefly consider it as a focus for the interrelation of gender, ethnic and class divisions.

[· · ·]

Women not only reproduce the future human and labour power and the future citizens of the state but also ethnic and national collectivities. As in other aspects of the gender division of labour, the ethnic and class position of women will affect their role in the reproduction process. Questions concerning who can actually reproduce the collectivity and under what conditions are often important here. Such things as the legitimacy of marriage, the appropriate religious conviction and so on are often preconditions for the legitimate reproduction of the nation or collectivity. The actual degree and form of control exercised by men of ethnic collectivities over their women can vary. In the Muslim world, for example, and in Britain under the old nationality law, the ethnic, religious or national position of women was immaterial. In other cases, like in the Jewish case, the mother's origin is the most important one in delineating the boundaries of the collectivity, and this determined the reproduction of the Jewish 'nation' (Yuval-Davis, 1980). This clearly does not mean such women have greater freedom but only that they are subject to a different set of controls.

As in other areas, the links between gender divisions and ethnic divisions can be and often are subject to the intervention of the state. For example, in Israel even secular people have to marry with a religious ceremony and according to traditional religious rules, in order for their marriage to be recognized by law. In the most extreme cases, the way the collectivity is constituted by state legislation virtually prevents inter-marriage between collectivities. In Egypt, for instance, while a Christian man can convert to Islam, Muslim women are prevented from marrying Christian Copts – if they do, they are no longer part of the Muslim community nor are they recognized as part of the Christian community and they virtually lose their legal status. The state may treat women from dominant and subordinate ethnic collectivities differently. For example, the new nationality law in Britain has given autonomous national reproduction rights to white British women, while totally withholding them from many others, mostly black women.

This differential treatment does not relate only to ideological or legal control of reproduction. The infamous contraceptive injection Depo-Provera has been given in Britain and elsewhere virtually exclusively to black and very poor women, and a study found more birth control leaflets in family planning clinics in Asian languages than in English (see Brent Community Council, 1981). In Israel, Jewish families (under the label of being 'relatives of Israeli soldiers') receive higher child allowances than Arab ones, as part of an elaborate policy of encouraging Jewish population growth and discouraging that of Arabs. Indeed the Beveridge Report in Britain justified the establishment of child allowances in order to combat the danger of the disappearance of the British race (Beveridge Report, 1942, p. 154).

On the other hand, reproduction can become a political tool at the hand of oppressed ethnic minorities. A common Palestinian saying is that 'The Israelis beat us at the borders and we beat them at the bedrooms' – Palestinian women, like Jewish ones (and with a higher rate of success due to various material and ideological factors) are under pressure by their collectivity, although not by the state, to reproduce and enlarge it. It is a fact, for example, that no Palestinian children in Lebanon were allowed . . . to be adopted by non-Palestinians – all the children are looked on as future Palestinian liberation fighters. In other words, the control of reproduction can be used both as a subordinating strategy – by dominant groups against minority groups – as well as a 'management' strategy by ethnic collectivities themselves.

. . . The process of reproduction of human subjects, as well as of collectivities, is never unitary. We want to emphasize that this is the case also concerning the participation of women themselves in the control of reproduction. . . . Virtually everywhere, the interests of the nation or the ethnic group are seen as those of its male subjects, and the interests of 'the state' are endowed with those of a male ethnic class and not just a class which is 'neutral' in terms of ethnicity and gender. However, very often women participate directly in the power struggle between their ethnic collectivity and other collectivities and the state, including by voluntarily engaging in an intensive reproductive 'demographic' race. At the same time, women of dominant ethnic groups are often in a position to control the reproductive role of women of other ethnic groups by state welfare and legal policies, as well as to use them as servants and child minders in order to ease part of their own reproductive burden.

[· · ·]

114

POLITICAL IMPLICATIONS

. . . Our interest in the subject is far from being merely academic. It originates from our own frustration in trying to find a political milieu in which ethnic divisions will be seen as an essential consideration, rather than as non-existent or as an immovable block to feminist politics. . . . As we pointed out, there can be no unitary category of 'women'. The subordination of women to men, collectivities and the state, operates in many different ways in different historical contexts. Moreover, very often women themselves participate in the process of subordinating and exploiting other women.

One major form of women's oppression in history has been their invisibility, their being 'hidden from history'. The invisibility of women other than those who belong to the dominant ethnic collectivity in Britain within feminist analysis has been as oppressive. Except for black feminists who fought their own case in isolation, minority women have been virtually absent in all feminist analysis. Anthropological and historical differences in the situation of women have been explored, but only in order to highlight the social basis of gender relations in contemporary Britain. The heterogeneous ethnic character of the latter has never been fully considered.

[· · ·]

When we talk about the need of white feminists in Britain to recognize their own ethnicity, we are relating to questions as basic as what we actually mean when we talk about 'feminist issues'. Can we automatically assume, as has been done by western feminist movements, that issues like abortion, the depiction of the family as the site of female oppression, the fight for legal equality with men and against sex discrimination and so on are *the* feminist issues?

. . . Feminist goals cannot be the same in different historical contexts. For instance, the family may *not* be the major site for women's oppression when families are kept apart by occupying or colonizing forces (as in Lebanon or South Africa), abortion may *not* be the major issue when forced sterilizations are carried out, nor is legal equality for women the first priority in polygamic societies where there is no independent autonomous mode of existence open to women whose husbands marry other younger and more fertile women. . . . Once we stop perceiving western white feminism as providing the ultimate criteria for defining the contents of feminism, we are faced with the problem of how to evaluate politically various women's struggles.

The beginning of a possible approach might be found in an article by Gail Omvedt (1978) in which she suggests that there is a differentiation between 'women' struggles and 'feminist' struggles, in as much as the latter are those that *challenge* rather than *use* traditional gender divisions within the context of national or ethnic struggles. We would add . . . that the challenge has to be . . . directed to both women's and men's work. All too often, in national liberation struggles, as in other periods of social crisis, women are called upon to fulfil men's jobs, as men are otherwise engaged at the front (as in war). This expansion in women's roles is seen too often as an act of women's liberation rather than as another facet of women's work. When the crisis is over, women are often assigned again to the more exclusively feminine spheres of women, to the surprise, as well as disappointment, of all those who have seen in the mere participation of women in the 'struggle' (whether in the Israeli Kibbutz, Algiers or Vietnam), a feminist achievement. We claim therefore that the challenge has to be to the actual notion of the sexual division of labour rather than only to its specific boundaries. This is far from being simple, because . . . many, if not all, ethnic cultures . . . have as central the construction of a specific form of gender division. It is too easy to pose the question, as many anti-imperialist and anti-racist feminists do, as if the origin and site of their oppression is only constructed from above, by white male sexism.

Ethnic and gender liberation struggles and solidarities can cut across each other and be divisive. We do not believe that there is one 'right' line to be taken in all circumstances. The focus or project of each struggle ought to decide which of the divisions we prioritize and the extent to which separate, as opposed to unified, struggle is necessary. Political struggles . . . which are formulated on an ethnic or sexual essence, we see as reactionary. Nor do we see it as a viable political option for women of subordinate collectivities to focus all their struggle against the sexism of dominant majority men.

The direct conclusion from our analysis . . . is that any political struggle in relation to any of the divisions considered in this [article] – that is, class, ethnic and gender – has to be waged in the context of the others. Feminist struggle in Britain today cannot be perceived as a homogeneous struggle, for the participation and oppression of women, both in the family and at the work site, are not homogeneous. White middle-class feminists have to recognize the particularity of their own experiences, not only in relation to the Third World but also in relation to different ethnic and class groupings in Britain, and integrate this recognition into their daily politics and struggles. Only on this basis can a valid sisterhood be constructed among women in Britain.

Notes

1   The terms 'ethnic' and 'ethnicity' have come under a great deal of attack recently for mystifying racist social relations. However, as we argue later, we do not use these concepts within a mainstream sociological tradition. For a critique of these terms see, for example, Lawrence (1982).

2   In a series of seminars organized by the Thames Polytechnic Sociology Division on Gender and Ethnic Divisions, Valerie Amos, Pratibha Parmar and Amina Mama all presented analyses that stressed the importance of studying the way in which the fusion of ethnic, gender and class divisions of black women gave a specificity to their oppression.

3   This approach is found, for example, in Eisenstein (1979).

PART III
ON WORK

INTRODUCTION: THE PUBLIC AND PRIVATE IN WORK AND POLITICS

In this second half of the book, our focus shifts to two particular substantive areas of analysis. In Part III we are concerned with work, in particular focusing on the commonplace economic distinction between paid work in the labour market and unpaid labour in the home and community – commonplace, that is, in industrial societies. In less industrialized societies, the separation of waged work from the home is not so marked. However, there are clear gender divisions associated with the allocation of tasks, albeit varying across space and time. In Part IV we turn to the role of the welfare state and women's political struggles. In the articles for Parts III and IV, the interconnections between the 'public' (waged work, welfare policies, political action) and the 'private' (in particular, familial relations of caring and dependency) areas of women's lives are demonstrated. Unlike the conventional social sciences – economics, politics and sociology – feminist analyses have demonstrated that the analytical separation of the public and private – of home, work and politics – leads to an incomplete understanding of the structural inequalities in contemporary societies.

4
DEFINING WORK

In Chapters 4 and 5 the meaning of 'work', the history of the development of distinct areas of men's and women's work, and theories of gender inequality in the labour market are considered. We discuss the gendered nature of domestic work and wage labour, and the diversity of women's experience of work, primarily within the UK. Unfortunately, we have insufficient space to examine the range of differences that exist in women's participation in wage labour throughout the world, or to examine the reasons why women in the Third World, as well as in the First, are becoming an increasingly important part of the labour force.

Work of various forms, but especially wage labour, constitutes a large part of most people's sense of self. Conventionally, work is regarded as an area that is clearly demarcated from domestic or social lives, as something people are paid to do, usually for set hours each week. Work is often experienced as the opposite of home; it constitutes the 'public' side of our everyday life, as distinct from the more 'private' or intimate side shared with family and friends. Work is associated with production, with the manufacture of some sort of goods or services for exchange in a market, in presumed opposition to consumption, which is defined as 'non-work', or as leisure-time activity. While 'at work' we exchange our time and labour power for a monetary reward – at least, in advanced industrial societies. In consumption activities or leisure, the monetary exchange is either reversed or the cash nexus is irrelevant. And, of course, work is represented as a masculine domain, both as the arena in which men are dominant, numerically and in terms of power, and as the arena in which masculinity is constructed. The feminine domain is the household and family. This does not mean that women are absent from the workplace or men from the home; rather, it stipulates that work is primary to masculine identity and home and family are primary to the construction of femininity. Men thus relate to their families as 'breadwinners', while women's paid work is often interpreted as an extension of their roles as wives and mothers, as a secondary activity in their lives.

These structural distinctions, work and home, public and private, are made so routinely that they seem to be self-evident: 'how things are'. But is it inevitable that we see things in this way?

Where do our contemporary ideas about work come from? Has work always been associated with payment? What about unpaid work? Have work and home always been physically separate? Are they really opposites or are they merely talked about in this way? Once these questions are raised it becomes difficult to draw a clear line between what is work and what is not. As sociologist Ray Pahl points out in Article 4.1, it is only since the nineteenth century that work has become synonymous with paid employment.

Feminist sociologists and historians have also been active in questioning the meaning of work. They have pointed to the ways in which it seems to privilege men's experience over women's; to the ways in which women have been denied access on equal terms to paid work, and to the ways in which definitions of work exclude women's contribution. Historically, home and work have not always been separate. It was only with the emergence of industrial capitalist production that they became spatially separated and even now the separation is not complete. Women have always been part of the informal cash economy that co-existed with the development of formal production in factories and other specialized workplaces. Women have always worked – taking in lodgers, doing washing and ironing, running small shops, producing clothes and food for sale. Their gradual incorporation into the formal economy in the UK, and so their appearance in the official statistics of employees, has in part been through the movement of many productive activities previously undertaken in the home or within the community, whether or not for financial reward, into the factory. The significant shift was not from leisure to work but from intra-familial to employer–employee working relations.

The separation of men's work and women's work between the labour market and the home, but also within wage labour, has evolved historically. Chris Middleton (1988) has demonstrated that patriarchal forms of divisions of labour long pre-date industrial capitalism, findings which he suggests 'will no doubt be received as meat and drink by those who believe in the existence of an autonomous system of patriarchy and wish to assert its independence of the mode of production and class structure'. Middleton himself rejects the idea that patriarchy is an autonomous structure and emphasizes the ways in which both gender and class relations are historically constituted and interrelated in particular places at certain times. It is clear that the construction of the category 'women's work' in the nineteenth and twentieth centuries is linked with the categorization of women as dependants, and the obscuring of their contribution to family enterprises. For example, behind the ideology of separate spheres for men and women in Victorian England, a great deal of work continued to be carried out by women in the home. And, of course, large numbers of working-class women were

123

in various types of paid employment, as the article by Anne Phillips in Part II has shown.

WOMEN'S WORK IN THE HOME: HOUSEWORK AND OTHER FORMS OF UNPAID LABOUR

Feminists interested in work have been concerned with what they refer to as the sexual division of labour, the allocation of tasks on the basis of sex. This structures women's and men's work both at home and in the paid workforce, as well as situating 'home' as subordinate to 'work'. The sexual division of labour cannot be understood in purely economic terms. It has sexual and symbolic dimensions as well. It is not just imposed on people but comes as part of a social package in which it is presented as right, natural and desirable. Our identities as masculine or feminine beings are bound up with it.

In the 1970s and 1980s feminists broadened the definition of work to include housework, sexual and emotional servicing of men, the caring for children, the elderly and the sick. They stressed that women's activities in the home constitute work, albeit financially unrewarded, and criticized definitions that are narrowly based on employment or productivity. Alongside the production of goods and services for exchange in a market, we must consider the tasks of reproduction, as part of work. These include the reproduction of children, the reproduction of human beings in the sense of their daily physical and emotional welfare, and the reproduction of existing social relations, including class and gender relations. This type of work is essential in producing socialized individuals and current and future wage labourers. It is work in another sense, too, in that women's domestic labour is exchanged for a share in the financial remuneration received by other members of the household who go 'out to work' – usually a male 'breadwinner'.

Domestic labour can have a timeless quality about it, as work that women have always done. But obviously it has changed dramatically, even in the last decade or so in a society like that of the UK, and when women's unpaid work is compared cross-culturally the differences are enormous. The concept of 'the housewife' who stays at home and cares for house, husband and children is essentially a modern one – few women before the twentieth century had that option, other than the affluent who had domestic servants. The arrival of running water, gas and electricity, refrigerators and washing machines, dishwashers and microwave ovens, and the decline of domestic service, have obviously affected the nature of housework,[1] which, like much factory work, is now lighter than it used to be. But whether it is less time consuming, or has become more widely shared, is debatable. The one thing that seems not to change is that women do most of it, even if the contributions of other members of the household have changed. Even that most biological function of childbirth has been affected by technology; while shifts in decisions about the number, timing and spacing of children have affected child care responsibilities. Women have fewer children now than they used to, but it can be argued that they are expected to give more attention to the child's mental and emotional welfare than they did in the past. While the technology is now there to do away with much domestic labour, expectations of home as the dimension of personal fulfilment have given it a new set of meanings. Instead of being just 'hard work', it has a set of sexual, emotional and symbolic significances. Nevertheless, there are indications that the time spent on housework by women in the paid workforce is falling; husbands and children do not seem to be picking up more, but women are doing less (Hartmann, 1981).

Here we take up two main themes. First, there is the relationship between domestic work and the 'caring' capacities associated with femininity. Second, there is the question of what has remained constant and what has changed. How has domestic and caring labour changed over the generations? Are the theories developed to analyse work in the home appropriate to changing conditions in contemporary societies?

In Article 4.2 Ann Oakley outlines the complex ways in which the concept of 'housewife' in contemporary Britain is bound up with the social construction of femininity and womanhood. Oakley has written widely on the areas of housework, maternity and child care. She was one of the first British feminist writers to argue that housework has a sociology and to pinpoint the sexist biases of a sociology that ignored it. Her book *Housewife* was first published in 1974. Where Oakley perceives the housewife as a characteristic figure of contemporary capitalism, Christine Delphy, a French sociologist, suggests that domestic labour constitutes a separate mode of production in which the husband appropriates the labour of his wife and family. She argues, in Article 4.3, that the lack of value attached to domestic work derives from the marriage contract, which is in fact a work contract, and one which tends to persist even after divorce. This leaves open the question of how to analyse the domestic labour of single women.

Debates about the nature of housework began to crystallize in the late 1950s. At the point when women's role as 'home-makers' was most celebrated, there was an underlying ambivalence about the extent and the value of housework. There were question marks about whether women needed to be doing it full-time, and whether it was satisfying. Housework in the UK and the USA was not such heavy work as it had been and it was becoming de-skilled as many traditional 'feminine' skills such as baking and jam making were being replaced by commercial products. Emphasis began to be placed on the loneliness and isolation of the suburban housewife, which Betty Friedan in the USA summed up in *The Feminine Mystique* in 1963 as 'the problem that has no name' (Friedan, 1963). The factors that had created the ideology of domesticity and an enhanced possibility for self-respect on the part of the housewife were dissolving by mid-century. Thereafter it was left largely to conservatives to articulate the value of the housewife role.

Women in the UK had, in any case, been moving into the paid workforce in large numbers in the 1950s and 1960s as they had in other advanced industrial societies, and there was a mainstream literature and policy concern about how women combined their 'two roles' and the traumas of 'latch-key children'. Nevertheless, Veronica Beechey argues that:

> It is housework, rather than waged work, which preoccupied feminist writers in the early days of the new feminist movement. A central tenet of such thinking in the 1970s was the belief that the family lay at the heart of women's oppression, and a major theoretical breakthrough involved the recognition that housework, the 'labour of love' performed by women in the home, was a form of work. This insight made feminist analysis of the 1970s and 1980s substantially different from that of previous periods, which mainly disregarded women's work within the family.
>
> (Beechey, 1987, pp. 171–2)

Since 1970, numerous accounts of women's domestic activities have been produced from a variety of disciplinary perspectives. Some writers, like Selma James and Mariarosa dalla Costa (1972), attacked the left for focusing narrowly on the factory, and argued for wages for housework, while others argued that this would only confirm women's entrapment in the domestic sphere. Socialist feminists were more interested than radical feminists in women and employment, which is perhaps not surprising given the traditional socialist emphasis on the emancipation of women through their incorporation into socialized production. Feminists of all shades, liberal, socialist and radical, supported anti-discrimination legislation and equal opportunity programmes.

Feminist strategists attempted to analyse the interrelations of the family and production in capitalist societies. It was clear that inequalities at work were related to inequalities at home. Women's waged work was constructed as secondary, their wages seen as pin money; often their paid work was regarded as an extension of what they did at home – office wives, service and caring work. But equally obviously, inequality at home was linked to their employment options. Without equal access to jobs and child care provision, women had little choice but to locate themselves primarily as wives and mothers. The inevitable question was, which of these domains was to be given explanatory primacy. Here the debate between capitalism and patriarchy (introduced in Part I) became relevant. Initially, most feminists emphasized the domestic arena, as the 'home-base' as it were, of patriarchy, as distinct from capitalism. Debates about the relation between domestic and paid work took up the larger questions of the relation between gender and class, and between patriarchy and capitalism. Christine Delphy (1984) argued that patriarchy was a separate mode of production, while the North American economist, Heidi Hartmann (1981), referred to capitalism and patriarchy as 'dual systems'. She argued that, in the twentieth century, a partnership of patriarchy and capitalism has emerged in which the interests of both have been served by allowing women a secondary place in the wage labour market. For her, women's place in the labour market was primarily the result of patriarchal gender relations operating, in this case, in a capitalist production environment. These approaches marked a big step forward because they allowed gender relations to be treated in their own right, and not simply as a by-product of capitalism. They also had their problems, for, apart from attributing a timeless quality to patriarchy, the dual systems approach treated capitalism itself as essentially gender neutral. However, they helped to clarify a focus on the specific ways in which different relationships interact in particular historical and social contexts and circumstances.

In the UK in particular, feminism has been divided between 'radical feminists', who concentrated on patriarchy, and 'socialist feminists', who focused on capitalism, or at least on the relation between the two. But these labels have a characteristically 1970s flavour. Material conditions have changed significantly since that time and feminist theory and politics have not stood still. By the 1980s there was greater awareness of the problems of making theoretical statements at this level of abstraction. Feminists discouraged 'either/or' polarities and the distinction between radical and socialist feminism had less meaning.

Recent changes in the economy and in the welfare sector also raised the question of the extent to which contemporary capitalist societies are still based on the old model of an accommodation between capital and patriarchy. Socialist feminists tended to see the world as a bargain between men and capital, based on support for the traditional nuclear family in which a wage-earning male is serviced by the domestic labour of a home-based woman, and the institutions of the welfare state buttressed the bargain. But it now seems as if the model male worker of earlier eras, who worked solidly in a single job throughout his life, is no longer needed, and that capitalists can make greater profits from women's labour without society crumbling if the beds don't get made on time or men don't have hot dinners every day. Socialist feminists may have to re-evaluate their theories about the links between the family and the welfare state, between capitalism and domestic labour. As Barbara Ehrenreich argues in Article 4.4, we may have to devise new theories for the 1990s that are appropriate for a 'Life without father'. We will return to recent changes in 'women's work' in the final article in Chapter 5.

One of the most marked features of changes in the nature of domestic labour has been the decline of clearly *productive* work in the home (for example, making clothes or bottling fruit and making jam) and its replacement by a range of goods, commodities and services purchased in the market. Home cooking, for example, as Ehrenreich mentioned, is being displaced by meals purchased at fast food outlets or other types of restaurants, most clothes are now purchased off-the-peg rather than made by women at home, and other activities, such as cleaning and child care, may also be purchased. This 'commoditization' of domestic labour has been accelerated by women's entry into the labour market. Paradoxically, at the same time, other types of goods are being purchased and used at home to replace previously market-based commodities. Here music systems and video recorders are good examples, as are DIY prerequisites. Rosemary Pringle suggests that these home-based activities are regarded increasingly as 'leisure' rather than 'work' and whereas 'production' is perceived as a worthy activity, consumption tends to be trivialized. In Article 4.5, she suggests that we should break this identification of work with production and consider the labour processes of consumption. Nevertheless, it is clear that the home is still the locus of work for women and that an increasing part of this is so-called community care.

CARING AND SERVICING WORK: AT HOME AND IN THE COMMUNITY

A central element of the social construction of femininity is that women are 'naturally' equipped to love and care for others. One of the experiences that unites almost all women is their serving and caring function for men of their own class and race. This servicing work is also a central element of relations between mothers and their children while in turn it is considered 'natural' for daughters to care for their ageing parents. Increasingly, in an ageing society, women as daughters are shouldering a great deal of the responsibility for the care of their elderly parents. These lifelong obligations, to care for husbands or partners, for children and for elderly parents, have been dubbed the 'tricycle of care'. An additional set of relations of dependency and obligation for women and their relatives are being enforced by policies to encourage the community care of elderly people and people with disabilities. This was exemplified most clearly with the introduction of the invalid care allowance in the UK which provided cash benefits for people caring for others in their homes, with the exception of married women, whose labour was seen as one of love (the colloquial use of the term 'love' to mean free could not be more apt). It took an appeal to the European court by a married woman to get this legislation overturned and the allowance paid to wives.

Community care raises difficult questions for feminists. As conscious as other critics of the negative aspects of residential care, they challenge the orthodoxy of community care as a more humane alternative for the all too obvious reason that 'community' is a euphemism for women's unpaid care of their own family members. But as Janet Finch, a feminist known for her critique of community care policies, has argued, 'Women must have the right not to care and dependent people must have the right not to rely on their relatives' (Finch, 1988, p. 30). Gillian Dalley, in her book *Ideologies of Caring* (1988), has examined the development of community care and the implications for carers and cared for. In her definition of 'caring', she distinguishes between caring for and caring about. Whereas men are permitted to care without caring for, policy makers have assumed that for women these two are one and the same. This assumption operates to keep women at their unpaid labours or ensures feelings of guilt in those women who deny their 'obligations'.

At the same time as women's labour-force participation has increased, the welfare services of the central and local state have been cut. An increasing amount of the caring and servicing labour described by Dalley is needed to keep these services functioning and to compensate for the cuts. Thus women's unpaid labour is increasing at the very time when they are needed in greater numbers in the labour market, again adding to the workload of those women who cannot afford to purchase replacement goods and services in the market.

HOW TO COUNT 'WORK'

The practical and political implications of broadening the definition of work, to include both 'conventional' domestic work and women's caring labour, are still not clear. Marilyn Waring (1989) has attempted to follow these through by insisting that even if women's work is not waged, it should at least be 'imputed' (her word) or calculated as part of the gross national product (GNP) of an economy. Her arguments are particularly important for 'work' in non-industrialized countries where a much larger proportion of women's work is still outside the formal structures of the labour market and the economy as narrowly defined in a conventional sense. For example, gathering fuel and carrying water takes up a large part of women's everyday lives in many parts of the world. The arguments in Waring's book *If Women Counted* have met an enthusiastic response from some feminists, keen to turn the argument about the value of women's work into social and economic policy terms. On the other hand, some economists believe she misunderstands accounting categories, that domestic work takes the forms that it does precisely because it is not paid, and that it is counter-productive to assign a monetary value to all areas of human activity. If housework were waged, it would be more likely to be heavily supervised, subjected to time-and-motion studies and reduced in hours. And, as Ehrenreich points out in Article 4.4, drawing the boundaries between 'housework' and all the types of loving and caring 'work' that constitute unpaid labour would be impossible. Is reading a bedtime story to children, for example, work, leisure or pleasure?

THE MEANING OF WORK

While feminists have not often directly applied post-structuralist ideas to the world of work, their historical and empirical studies, and their concerns with meanings and definitions, have led them in rather similar directions. The notion of work as a conceptually distinct, clear-cut area has been destabilized. It is through discourse that certain material practices are interpreted as work while others are excluded. 'Work', rather than being fixed or given, is subject to a variety of meanings, in a variety of discourses. Feminist interventions might be understood as interventions into debates about meaning. Rather than simply asserting a different reality, or reality from a women's point of view, feminists have challenged the dominant discourses. It is not, for example, simply a matter of asserting that housework is work, but of dismantling the code which continues to deny it such a status.

Understandings of 'home' and 'work' derive from a larger symbolic system, a totality of social and cultural practices including language itself. Though home and private life may be romanticized, they are generally held to represent the 'feminine' world of the personal and the emotional, the specific, the domestic and the sexual. The public world of work sets itself up as the opposite of all these things: it is rational, abstract, ordered, concerned with general principles and, of course, masculine. In an alternative discourse, 'home' may represent an ordered and stable haven which contrasts with the anarchy of the business world. It is for men that 'home' is the domain of 'non-work', where they expect to relax, let their barriers down and be looked after. Home and work are not opposite for women, even if they are experienced as such by men. Much of their 'work' takes place at 'home'; wives might act as unpaid and unacknowledged secretaries to their husbands as well as taking on domestic responsibilities and 'supplementary' paid work. Home is not a respite from work but another workplace. For some women, work may actually be a respite from home, as the place where they relax and have their social time, away from the demands of husbands and children! Rather than taking it for granted that home and work are opposites, we therefore have to look at the historical processes that construct them as such and the ways in which men and women are differently placed as subjects and objects of these discourses. These arguments parallel those made by Linda Nicholson in Article 1.3.

Once we start thinking about the range of work that women actually do, it also becomes clear that the problem for women is not necessarily that they have been excluded from work but that they have too much work. The issue may be how to reduce or to spread it more equally rather than to continue trying to be super-woman. This raises questions about part-time work and shorter working hours, not only for women but also for men. At present, part-time work in the UK is inferior, in the sense that women working part-time are less well paid pro rata, and are excluded from many of the benefits of full-time employment, such as holidays, fringe benefits and security of employment. To a large extent, this is because part-time work is constructed as women's work and so seen as secondary. Until there is greater equality of employment conditions between full-time and part-time workers, this association will be difficult to change, although it may be that a shorter working week should become the norm for most people in order to create more balanced lives. The difficulty, of course, is that most employees need full-time pay, but recent technological advances, such as automation and computerization, do make the reorganization of work possible. But we are getting ahead of ourselves. We need first to understand the gender division of labour in paid work and the ways in which certain tasks and occupations have become defined as 'women's work'. We therefore turn to explanations of women's labour market position in Chapter 5.

Note

1   For a discussion of technological change, see the companion volume in this series, *Inventing Women: science, technology and gender* (Kirkup and Keller, 1992).

Article 4.1
WORK AND EMPLOYMENT
Ray E. Pahl

[· · ·]

Employment is simply one form of work. In the past, work was synonymous with toil: an agricultural worker might do some digging or ploughing as part of the collective household labour needed for that household to achieve a modest livelihood; other digging or ploughing could be done as wage labourer. The distinction between remunerated or non-remunerated labour did not prevent either being equally unpleasant on a cold, wet day.... Perhaps wage labour was perceived as more constraining in the sixteenth century, as work in the domestic dwelling is perceived as more constraining by some women today.

[· · ·]

The notion that one should obtain most, if not all, of one's material wants as a consumer by spending the money gained through employment, emerged for the first time in the nineteenth century. Whilst there has, indeed, been a market for labour for at least 800 years in England so that most households probably had some source of income, however erratic and irregular that might be, income generation was not an essential basis for livelihood.... To give all one's labour power in return for a wage was seen as a grievous loss of independence, security and liberty....

In pre-industrial times, then, most of an individual's work was done in and for the household. The viability of the household was the crucial priority in life and the work of all members of the household had to be co-ordinated to achieve that end.... There was no a priori assumption that wage labour was a superior form of work or that men were the natural wage earners. Very often women were the main money earners, either by selling produce at markets or by producing textile goods in their homes in the proto-industrial era of the eighteenth or early nineteenth centuries.

[· · ·]

For an untypical period of 100 years or so, households were dependent on a male chief earner, who was, in theory, paid a family wage to support his wife, children and possibly elderly dependants as well. How this curious shift to a single male breadwinner supporting his household of dependants took place is a complex matter to resolve and has given rise to considerable debate in recent years. . . . Some stress the advantages to capitalism as a system in having its workers cheaply and effectively 'reproduced'. Clearly, if workers are well fed and cared for and are kept in good health they will operate more efficiently. 'Providing for' a wife and children is likely to be a stabilizing factor on incipient rebels and is also likely to encourage commitment to employment and a willingness to work hard and long. Furthermore, if workers are individually cared for in individual homes their propensity to acquire and to consume goods and services may be enhanced. They may, further, be encouraged to pursue the advancement of their social status through styles of consumption, rather than the advancement of their collective position in relation to the means of production through collective class action. . . .

Such a view has been criticized for being cynical and for having an inflated and unrealistic view of the general wiliness and machiavellian nature of mid-nineteenth-century capitalists. An alternative approach stresses the humanitarian concern of individual employers, whose own wives were safely cocooned in bourgeois domesticity and who, not unreasonably perhaps, imagined that such a goal was equally appropriate for their workers. Such people may have come to understand something of the impact of the harsh conditions of employment on disease and mortality rates, particularly for women and children. At the same time, the shift to heavy manufacturing in what are now called the 'smoke-stack' industries generated what was taken to be more appropriately male employ-ment. As the captains of industry began to equip their factories with new and expensive machinery, they extrapolated their own views about who should do what work on to their workforce. . . .

Such a position, in its turn, was attacked by those who claimed that there was an unholy alliance between male employers and male workers. The former did not wish to encourage an alternative value system allowing women more economic equality: that might open the way to social and political equality, which could endanger their own privileged position. Their workers, on the other hand, feared the competition of effective, efficient and potentially lower-paid workers: reducing the role of married women employees might enhance their own labour market position and have the further advantage of providing a cosy, caring home to which they could retreat for comfort and material sustenance and support. This argument has been adduced by those writing from a feminist perspective, who have adopted what might be called a 'patriarchy first' position. A collusion between men, whether bourgeois or proletarian, may be expected in a tacit conspiracy to encourage and to enhance the subordination of women.

. . . A fourth position, also put forward by those who . . . assert that they [also] write from a feminist perspective, . . . refutes the 'patriarchy first' perspective. Jane Humphries (1988) . . . claims that, in the case of the 1842 Mines Regulation Act, men were not acting primarily out of gender-based self-interest. Coal miners needed the extra income provided by their wives and children and family teams were a convenient and efficient means of getting the work done, given the technology of the time. . . . It was not clear that there was much demand amongst miners for a cosy home in which they could dominate in private when the tradition was for collective and communal social life based on the pub or the chapel. . . . More plausibly, the men may have been genuinely concerned for the health of their wives and children and were thus prepared to work harder and, later, to organize collectively in order to be paid wages sufficient to support their dependants.

Evidently, the shift to the model of a male breadwinner was a long and complex process and, in many places and industries, it was never fully achieved. Nevertheless, the system of social security outlined by Sir William Beveridge in his report, first published in 1942 . . ., was based on a fundamental assumption of a wage earner and his dependent family.

[· · ·]

After the Second World War the domination of the male wage earner ensured that the confusion arising from the elision of work with employment continued for a further two or three decades. Thus in 1958, in a widely used American textbook *The World of Work* by Robert Dubin, work was defined as 'continuous employment in the production of goods and services, for remuneration'. Professor Dubin asserted that 'from the standpoint of the life history of the individual, the significant work he performs is done continuously by him'. Dubin then goes on to claim that 'in a sociological sense, only those expenditures of human energy producing goods or services are defined as work'. However, that definition does not include housework, solely because, even though the housewife certainly produces goods and services, she does not get paid and hence 'falls outside the subject matter of our field'.

Some thirty years later, such an explicit focus on men's remunerated employment appears archaic. Throughout history most work has been done by women and most has not been remunerated . . . . Now, in the last years of the twentieth century, the participation rates of women in formal employment have never been higher and the growth of redundancy, unemployment and early retirement amongst men has led to a return to patterns of unremunerated work amongst men. They may no longer cut turf or timber for their fires or rear hogs in scrub woodland, but they may install their own storm windows or build on a patio with their own tools, with their own labour and in their own time. Most would see such work for themselves, or self-provisioning, as highly productive. . . .

If most people who equate work with employment are trapped in the concepts and ideology of a period now passed, how should the notion of work be appropriately conceptualized in order to illuminate current reality? What is it that analytically distinguishes work from 'all purposeful activity', and what is the special position of paid employment in the overall spectrum of work? How is unpaid domestic work and all the other forms of unpaid or informal work to be brought into a common analytical schema?

. . . Whilst the old stereotypes may be crumbling, old concepts still have an unexpected currency, largely perhaps because the social institutions of the age of male employment, such as trade unions and the social security system based on the male breadwinner, have not been superseded. Conceptual classification does not necessarily produce new and appropriate institutions: it is certainly hard to make new curtains without first locating and measuring the windows, and the need for conceptual clarification may be greater than is commonly realized.

[· · ·]

Article 4.2
WHAT IS A HOUSEWIFE?

Ann Oakley

A housewife is a woman: a housewife does housework. In the social structure of industrialized societies, these two statements offer an interesting and important contradiction. The synthesis of 'house' and 'wife' in a single term establishes the connections between womanhood, marriage and the dwelling place of family groups. The role of housewife is a family role: it is a feminine role. Yet it is also a work role. A housewife is 'the person, other than a domestic servant, who is responsible for most of the household duties (or for supervising a domestic servant who carries out these duties)' (Hunt, 1968, p. 5). A housewife is 'a woman who manages or directs the affairs of her household; the mistress of a family; the wife of a householder' (*Oxford English Dictionary*).

The characteristic features of the housewife role in modern industrialized society are (1) its *exclusive allocation to women*, rather than to adults of both sexes; (2) its association with *economic dependence*: that is, with the dependent role of the woman in modern marriage; (3) its *status as non-work* – or its opposition to 'real', that is, economically productive work; and (4) its *primacy* to women; that is, its priority over other roles.

A man cannot be a housewife. A man who says he is a housewife is an anomaly. On the level of fact his statement may be true: he may indeed do housework and assume the responsibility for it. But on another level his claim rings of absurdity, or deviation. It runs counter to the social customs of our culture.

[· · ·]

The social trivialization of housework (and of women) is in part responsible for the tendency to underestimate or ignore the amount of time women spend doing it. But other features of the housewife role also conspire to conceal it. Housework differs from most other work in three significant ways: it is private, it is self-defined and its outlines are blurred by its integration in a whole complex of domestic, family-based roles which define the situation of women as well as the situation of the housewife. Housework is an activity performed by housewives within their own homes. The home is the workplace, and its boundaries are also the boundaries of family life.

In modern society, the family and the home are private places, refuges from an increasingly impersonal public world. . . .

The physical isolation of housework – each housewife in her own home – ensures that it is totally self-defined. There are no public rules dictating what the housewife should do, or how and when she should do it. Beyond basic specifications – the provision of meals, the laundering of clothes, the care of the interior of the home – the housewife, in theory at least, defines the job as she likes. Meals can be cooked or cold; clothes can be washed when they have been worn for a few hours or a few weeks; the home can be cleaned once a month or twice a day. Who is to establish the rules, who is to set the limits of normality, if it is not the housewife herself?

Housewives belong to no trade unions; they have no professional associations to define criteria of performance, establish standards of excellence, and develop sanctions for those whose performance is inadequate or inefficient in some way. No single organization exists to defend their interests and represent them on issues and in areas which affect the performance of their role.[1] These facts confirm the diagnosis of self-definition in housework behaviour.

[· · ·]

In the social image of a woman, the roles of wife and mother are not distinct from the role of housewife. . . . 'Housewife' can be an umbrella term for 'wife' and 'mother'. Women's expected role in society is to strive after perfection in all three roles.

A study of housework is consequently a study of women's situation. How did the present position of women as housewives come about? Has housewifery always been a feminine role? Housewives are neither endemic to the structure of the family, nor endemic to the organization of human society. . . . Other people in different cultures may live in families, but they do not necessarily have housewives.

Note

1 Organizations like the Housewives' Register meet certain needs, especially the need for social contact, but they are neither professional organizations nor trade unions.

Article 4.3
A THEORY OF MARRIAGE
Christine Delphy

[· · ·]

My proposition is that marriage is the institution by which unpaid work is extorted from a particular category of the population, women-wives. This work is unpaid for it does not give rise to a wage but simply to upkeep. These very peculiar relations of production in a society that is defined by the sale of work (wage labour) and products, are not determined by the type of work accomplished. Indeed, they are not even limited to the production of household work and the raising of children, but extend to include *all* the things women (and also children) produce within the home, and in small-scale manufacturing, shopkeeping, or farming, if the husband is a craftsman, tradesman, or farmer or various professional services if the husband is a doctor or lawyer etc. The fact that domestic work is unpaid is not inherent to the particular type of work done, since when the same tasks are done *outside the family* they are paid for. The work acquires value – is remunerated – as long as the woman furnishes it to people to whom she *is not related or married*.

The valuelessness of domestic work performed by married women derives institutionally from the marriage contract, which is in fact a work contract. To be more precise, it is a contract by which the head of the family – the husband – appropriates all the work done in the family by his children, his younger siblings, and especially by his wife, since he can sell it on the market as his own if he is, for example, a craftsman or farmer or doctor. Conversely, the wife's labour has no value because it cannot be put on the market, and it cannot be put on the market because of the contract by which her labour power is appropriated by her husband. Since the production intended for exchange – on the market – is accomplished outside the family in the wage-earning system, and since a married man sells his work and not a product in this system, the unpaid work of women cannot be incorporated in the production intended for exchange. It has therefore become limited to producing things which are intended for the family's internal use: domestic services and the raising of children.

Of course, with the increase of industrial production (and hence the number of wage-earners) and the decrease in family production, many women-wives now work for money, largely outside the home. They are none the less expected to do the household work. It would appear that their labour power is not totally appropriated since they divert a part of it into their paid work. Yet since they earn wages they provide their own upkeep. While one could, with a touch of bad faith, consider the marriage contract as an *exchange* contract when women work only within the household, with married women providing domestic work in exchange for upkeep, when married women earn their own living that illusion disappears altogether. It is clear then that their domestic work is given for nothing and the feature of appropriation is even more conspicuous.

[· · ·]

A large number of women who are divorced or about to be divorced come on the labour market in the worst possible conditions (as do widows), with no qualifications, no experience and no seniority. They find themselves relegated to the most poorly paid jobs. This situation is often in contrast with the level of their education and the careers they envisaged, or could have envisaged, before their marriage, the social rank of their parents, and not only the initial social rank of their husband but, more pertinently, the rank he has attained when they divorce, some five, ten, or twenty years after the beginning of their marriage. In addition, those with dependent children have to look after them financially, and this new responsibility is added to the domestic work which they were already providing before divorce. For the majority of women, the contrast between the standard of living that they enjoy while married and that which they can expect after divorce simply redoubles the pressures in favour of marriage or remarriage depending on the circumstances.

[· · ·]

The fact that the material responsibility for children is assumed by the woman after divorce confirms the hypothesis concerning the appropriation by the husband of his wife's work, but it suggests as well that the appropriation which is a characteristic of marriage persists even after the marriage has been dissolved. This leads me to contend that divorce is not the opposite of marriage, or even its end, but simply a change or a transformation of marriage.

[· · ·]

Article 4.4
LIFE WITHOUT FATHER: RECONSIDERING SOCIALIST-FEMINIST THEORY

Barbara Ehrenreich

By the late 1970s, most socialist feminists accepted as 'theory' a certain description of the world: 'the system' we confronted was actually composed of two systems or structures, capitalism and patriarchy. These two systems or structures were of roughly equal weight (never mind that capitalism was a mere infant compared with patriarchy or, on the other hand, that patriarchy had no visible corporate headquarters). And capitalism and patriarchy were remarkably congenial and reinforced each other in thousands of ways (which it was the task of socialist feminists to enumerate). As Zillah Eisenstein wrote in her 1979 anthology *Capitalist Patriarchy and the Case for Socialist Feminism*, patriarchy and capitalism meshed so neatly that they had become 'an *integral process*: specific elements of each system are necessitated by the other'. Capitalism plus patriarchy described the whole world – or nearly: racism usually required extensive addenda – and that world was as orderly and smoothly functioning as the Newtonian universe.

It was a brave idea. Today, few people venture vast theoretical syntheses. . . . If 'capitalism plus patriarchy' was too easy an answer, at least we (the socialist feminists of the 1970s) asked the hard questions. In a practical sense, too, it was a good theory, because it served to validate the existence of socialist feminism. . . .

The capitalism-plus-patriarchy paradigm was an ingenious defensive stance. If the world was really made up of two systems that were distinct and could not be reduced to each other, it was never enough to be just a socialist or just a feminist. If patriarchy was not only distinct but truly a 'system' and not an attitude (like sexism) or a structure of the unconscious (as Juliet Mitchell saw it), those who opposed patriarchy were not just jousting with superstructural windmills; they were doing something real and 'material'. Finally, if patriarchy and capitalism were mutually reinforcing, it didn't make any sense to take on one without the other. If 'the system' was capitalist-patriarchy, the only thoroughgoing oppositional politics was its mirror image, socialist feminism.

Not all socialist feminists were perfectly comfortable with the capitalism-plus-patriarchy formulation, however. For one thing, there always seemed to be something a little static and structuralist about it. Deirdre English and I argued, in our book *For Her Own Good*, that 'patriarchy' ought to be left where Marx last saw it – in pre-industrial European society – and that modern feminists should get on with the task of describing our own 'sex/gender system', to use Gayle Rubin's phrase, in all its historic specificity. In addition, we were not convinced that capitalism and patriarchy were on as good terms as socialist-feminist theory demanded. If the theory couldn't account for the clashes as well as the reinforcements, it couldn't account for change – such as the emergence of feminism itself in the late eighteenth-century ferment of bourgeois and *antipatriarchal* liberalism. The world of capitalism plus patriarchy, endlessly abetting each other to form a closed system with just one seam, was a world without change, a world without a subject.

There is another problem. Things *have* changed, and in ways that make capitalist-patriarchy (or, better, 'patriarchal capitalism') almost seem like a good deal. Socialist feminists – not to mention many plain feminists and socialists – went wrong in assuming that 'the system', whatever it was called, would, left to itself, reproduce itself.

WOMAN AS DOMESTIC WORKER

The linchpin of socialist-feminist theory . . . was domestic work. In theory, this work included everything women do in the home, from cooking and cleaning to reading bedtime stories and having sex. Radical feminists were quick to point out how women's efforts, whether serving coffee in a movement office or polishing the coffee table in a suburban home, served the interests of individual men. Socialist feminists, coming along a few years later, asserted that women's domestic work served not only men but capital. As Zillah Eisenstein put it:

> All the processes involved in domestic work help in the perpetuation of the existing society: (1) Women stabilize patriarchal structures (the family, housewife, mother, etc.) by fulfilling these roles. (2) Simultaneously, women are reproducing new workers, for both the paid and unpaid labor force. . . . (3) They work as well in the labor force for lesser wages. (4) They stabilize the economy through their role as consumers. . . . If the other side of production is consumption, the other side of capitalism is patriarchy.[1]

(Eisenstein, 1979, p. 29)

The discovery of the importance of women's domestic work put some flesh on the abstract union of capitalism and patriarchy. First, it gave patriarchy, which had otherwise had a somewhat ghostly quality (stretched as it was to include everything from rape to domestic slovenliness), a 'material base' in 'men's control over women's labor power'. Second, it revealed a vivid parallel between 'the private sphere', where patriarchy was still ensconced, and the 'public sphere', where capital called the shots. In the public sphere men laboured at production, and in the private sphere women laboured at 'reproduction' (not only physical reproduction but the reproduction of attitudes and capabilities required for all types of work). Finally, it showed how essential patriarchy was to capitalism: most capitalist institutions produced only things, but the quintessential patriarchal institution, the family, produced the men who produced things – thanks to the labour of women.

It was not altogether clear where one went with this insight into the centrality of women's domestic work. If what women did in the home was so critical to the reproduction of both capitalism and patriarchy, shouldn't women be advised to stop doing it? Perhaps to sabotage it? The 'wages for housework' position, which surfaced in . . . [the USA] in 1974, provided a strategic answer and an unintended caricature of American socialist-feminist theory. American socialist feminists had argued that women's work was 'necessary' to capitalism; the Italian feminists who launched wages-for-housework, insisted, with considerable eloquence, that domestic work actually produced surplus value for the capitalists, just as what we ordinarily thought of as 'productive' work in the public sphere did. If you were going to say that women's domestic work reproduced the labour power needed by capital, you might as well go all the way and say it was as much a part of the productive process as the extraction and preparation of raw materials for manufacturing. Thus the home was an adjunct to the factory; in fact it was part of the great 'social factory' (schools and all other sites of social reproduction) that kept the literal factories running. Women's domestic activities were no longer a shadowy contribution but a potentially quantifiable productive factor with the distinguished Marxist status of 'producing surplus value'. The only difference between the man labouring for Fiat or Ford and the woman labouring in her kitchen was that she was unpaid – a patriarchal oversight that wages-for-housework would correct.

This proposal and the accompanying theory sent shock waves through American and British socialist-feminist networks. There were debates over the practicality of the demand: who would pay the wages for housework, which would, after all, constitute an enormous redistribution of wealth? There were even more debates at the level of high theory: was it scientifically accurate to say that housework produced surplus value? (A debate which, in my opinion, produced almost nothing of value.) Unfortunately, there was much less attention to the bizarre but utterly logical extreme to which wages-for-housework theory took homegrown socialist-feminist

142

theory. Everything women did in the home was in the service of capital and indispensable to capital. When a mother kissed her children goodnight, she was 'reproducing labour power'. When a childless working woman brushed her teeth, she too was reproducing labour power (her own, in this case), as an American wages-for-housework advocate argued in an exchange I participated in. This was commodity fetishism with a vengeance, and even with the modification that kissing, for example, serves the miniature patriarchy of the family more directly than corporate capital, it all boiled down to the same thing, since patriarchy was firmly in league with capital.

THE OBSOLESCENCE OF CAPITALISM-PLUS-PATRIARCHY

From the vantage point of 1984, the debates of 1975 have an almost wistful quality. They (men, capitalists) needed us (women) to do all our traditional 'womanly' things, and, if theory were to be trusted, they would apparently go to great lengths to keep us at it. Well, they don't seem to need us anymore – at least not that way – and if this was not completely evident in 1975, it is inescapable today.

No matter how valuable the services of a full-time homemaker may be, fewer and fewer men earn enough to support one. The reasons for the disappearance of the male 'family wage' and the associated influx of married women into the workforce have been discussed at length. The relevant point here is that for all we say about the 'double day', employed women do far less housework than those who are full-time homemakers, twenty-six hours per week as compared with fifty-five hours per week (Vanek, 1974, p. 116). Other family members may be compensating in part (though most studies I have seen show little increase in husbands' contributions), but it is hard not to conclude that the net amount of housework done has decreased dramatically. (By as much as 29 million hours per week per year during the peak years of women's influx into the labour market. Of course, a certain amount of this work has been taken up by the commercial sector, especially by restaurants and fast food places.) If women's work were as essential to the status quo as socialist-feminist theory argued, capitalism would have been seriously weakened by this withdrawal of women's labour. Yet no one is arguing, for example, that the decline of American productivity is due to unironed shirts and cold breakfasts. Nor has any sector of capital come forth and offered to restore the male family wage so that women can get back to their housework.

If capital does not seem to need women's domestic work as much as theory predicted, what about individual men? Mid-1970s feminist theory tended to portray men as enthusiastic claimants of women's services and labour, eagerly enlisting us to provide them with clean laundry, homecooked meals, and heirs. If we have learned anything in the years since then, it is that men have an unexpected ability to survive on fast food and the emotional solace of short-term relationships. There are, as Marxists say, 'material' reasons for this. First, it is physically possible, thanks to laundromats, frozen food, and other conveniences, for even a poor man to live alone and without servants. Second, there have always been alternatives to spending a 'family wage' on an actual family, but in the last few decades these alternatives have become more numerous and alluring. Not only are there the classic temptations of drink, gambling and 'loose women' to choose from, but stereos, well-appointed bachelor apartments, Club Med, sports cars, and so forth. For these and other reasons, American men have been abdicating their traditional roles as husbands, breadwinners and the petty patriarchs of the capitalism-plus-patriarchy paradigm.[2]

In a larger sense, events and some belated realizations of the last few years should have undermined any faith we had in capital's willingness to promote the 'reproduction of labour power'. Capital, as well as labour, is internationally mobile, making US corporations relatively independent of a working class born and bred in this or any one country. Furthermore, capitalists are not required to be industrial capitalists; they can disinvest in production and reinvest in real estate, financial speculation, or, if it suits their fancy, antiques; and they have done so despite any number of exhortations and supply-side incentives. In their actual practices and policies, capitalists and their representatives display remarkable indifference to the 'reproduction of labour power', or, in less commoditized terms, the perpetuation of human life.

This is not to say that individual companies or industries do not maintain a detailed interest in our lives as consumers. They do, especially if we are lucky enough to be above 'the buying point' in personal resources. But it is no longer possible to discern a uniform patriarchal or even pronatalist bias to this concern. Capitalists have figured out that two-paycheque couples buy more than husband-plus-housewife units, and that a society of singles potentially buys more than a society in which households are shared by three or more people. In times of labour insurgency, far-seeing representatives of the capitalist class have taken a minute interest in how ordinary people organize their lives, raise their children, and so on. But this is not such a time, and it seems plain to me that the manufacturers of components for missile heads (a mile from where I sit) do not care whether my children are docile or cranky, and that the people who laced our drinking water with toxins (a mile the other way) could not much care whether I scrub the floors.

With hindsight, I am struck by what a *benevolent* system the capitalism-plus-patriarchy paradigm implied. In order to put women's hidden and private interests on the economic map, we had to assume that they reflected some much larger, systemic need. Since these efforts of women are in fact efforts to care and nurture, we had to project the functions of caring and nurturing onto the large, impersonal 'structures' governing our all-too-functional construct of the world. Capitalism, inscribed with the will to 'reproduce', became 'patriarchal capitalism'. This suggested that in a sense our theory was a family metaphor for the world: capitalists were 'fathers', male workers were 'sons', and all women were wives/daughters, both mediating the relations between fathers and sons[3] and producing more sons (and daughters) to keep the whole system going. The daughters had the worst deal, but at least they were members of the family, and this family, like actual ones, intended to keep on going – a motivation that is no longer so easy to attribute to the men who command our resources and our labour.

I think now that the capitalism-plus-patriarchy paradigm overpersonalized (and humanized) capitalism precisely because it depersonalized women. The paradigm granted 'the system' an undue benevolence because it had no room for motive or caring on the part of women. Once all the interactions and efforts of child raising have been reduced to 'reproducing labour power' (and children have been reduced to units of future labour power), there is no place for human aspiration or resistance. Once it has been determined that 'all the processes involved in domestic work help in the perpetuation of the existing society', the women who perform these 'processes' have lost all potential autonomy and human subjectivity. And once it is declared that all acts other than production are really 'reproduction' (of labour power and the same old system of domination), only one kind of resistance *is* possible. Suicide, or the wilful destruction of labour power.

Ironically, the intent of the capitalism-plus-patriarchy paradigm was to validate feminism and insert women, as actors, into the Marxist political calculus. The problem was that we were too deferential to Marxism. Socialist feminists tried to account for large areas of women's experience – actually everyone's experience – in the language of commodities and exchange as if that were the 'scientific' way to proceed. It would have been better perhaps to turn the tables: for example, instead of asking, 'How can we account for women's work in the home in Marxist terms?', we should have asked, 'How can we account for what *men* do *outside* the home in feminist terms, in women's terms?' Trying to fit all of women's experience into the terms of the market didn't work, and adding on patriarchy as an additional 'structure' didn't help.

So where do we go from here? Is it possible to be a socialist feminist without a 'socialist-feminist theory'? Yes, of course it is. After all, those who are plain socialists or feminists get along – with no evident embarrassment – on just half a theory at best. The socialist-feminist project has always been larger and more daring than that of either of our progenitors, so if we have fumbled, it is in part because we attempted more.

But we do need a better way to understand the world we seek to act in. I hesitate to say we need a new 'theory', because that word suggests a new set of structures and laws of mechanics to connect them. If not capitalism-plus-patriarchy, you are probably thinking, what is it? The point is that 'it' is changing, and in a more violent and cataclysmic fashion than we had any reason to expect. The statics of capitalism-plus-patriarchy help explain a world that is already receding from view – a world of relative affluence and apparent stability – where categories like 'the family', 'the state', and 'the economy' were fixed and solid anchor points for theory. Today, there is little we can take as fixed. 'The family', so long reified in theory, looks more like an improvisation than an institution. A new technological revolution, on the scale of the one that swept in industrial capitalism (and state socialism), is transforming not only production but perception. Whole industries collapse into obsolescence; entire classes face ruthless dislocation. At the same time, the gap between the races domestically, between the north and the south internationally, widens to obscene proportions. Everywhere, women are being proletarianized and impoverished, becoming migrants, refugees and inevitably 'cheap labour'. . . .

I still believe that if there is a vantage point from which to comprehend and change the world, our world today, it will be socialist and feminist. Socialist – or perhaps here I should say Marxist – because a Marxist way of thinking, at its best, helps us understand the cutting edge of change, the blind driving force of capital, the dislocations, innovations and global reshufflings. Feminist because feminism offers our best insight into that which is most ancient and intractable about our common situation: the gulf that divides the species by gender and, tragically, divides us all from nature and that which is most human in our nature. This is our intellectual heritage, and I do not think we have yet seen its full power – or our own.

Notes

1   I don't mean to pick on Zillah Eisenstein; many other writers could be quoted, especially if I were doing a thorough review of socialist-feminist theory and its nuances (which I clearly am not). Eisenstein is singled out here because her introduction to and chapter in *Capitalist Patriarchy and the Case for Socialist Feminism* (1979) seem to me to provide an excellent state-of-the-art summary of mid-1970s socialist-feminist theory.

2   One poignant indication of this shift in male values and expectations: when I was in my early twenties (in the early 1960s), it seemed to require a certain daring and resourcefulness to dodge the traditional female fate of becoming a full-time housewife and mother. Today, I hear over and over from young women that they would like to have a family or at least a child but do not expect ever to be in a stable enough relationship to carry this off.

3   In so far as the capitalists paid their workers enough to support a wife, thus buying off the workers with patriarchal privilege and ensuring labour peace – a crude summary of Heidi Hartmann's much more complex and interesting argument. The family metaphor was developed extensively by Batya Weinbaum in *The Curious Courtship of Women's Liberation and Socialism* (1980).

Article 4.5
WOMEN AND CONSUMER CAPITALISM
Rosemary Pringle

Consumption provides a fruitful starting point for reconceptualizing the relationship between 'patriarchy' and 'capitalism' and for understanding the specific forms of sexual oppression in advanced capitalist countries. . . . We live in a society that is conventionally labelled 'consumer capitalist' and we have long known that our oppression as women is tied to our role as consumers and the use of our bodies to sell commodities. Yet the connections remain obscure and consumption has rarely been the focus of theoretical debate. Its elements (economic, symbolic, emotional, sexual) are usually discussed separately or appear in the context of other debates. It is argued here that the changing relationship between consumption and production is of central importance for periodizing male domination and understanding the particular forms it takes under late capitalism.

[· · ·]

The taboo on discussing consumption is a result of some fundamental patriarchal biases, which have affected even feminist thinking on the subject. Consumption stands for destructiveness, waste, extravagance, triviality and insatiability – in fact for all the things that men traditionally hate or fear about women. It is only safe to talk about it in appropriately negative or *passive* terms. Accordingly, it must be subordinated to production, as women are to men, and reduced to a role in 'reproducing' labour power. Baudrillard (1975) . . . made the most thoroughgoing critique of this framework. He talks of the 'unbridled romanticism of productivity' which, even amongst anarchist thinkers, leaves no space outside itself. It is thus only through the 'mirror' of production that each and every moment of our lives becomes intelligible. This ignores the complexity of the *symbolic* exchange that takes place in consumption. It is not merely a matter of devouring or destroying an object but of communication and exchange. . . . Consumption activity makes stable and visible the categories of culture.

[· · ·]

This continuing preference for talking about production is part of the feminist tendency to see capitalism and patriarchy as separate and only loosely related systems. It was, of course, important to assert that male domination was not merely a function of capitalism.

But in avoiding this type of reductionism we saw the alternative danger of setting up 'patriarchy' as a universal and ahistorical category (Beechey, 1979; Barrett, 1980). In attempting to provide a materialist account, feminists have frequently treated patriarchy as a separate mode of production outside capitalism (Delphy, 1977), or as a subordinate mode within it (Rowbotham, 1973). Quite apart from the vagueness of definition, this makes it very difficult to account for historical changes in family form or the nature of housework or domestic production.

Alternately, those who want to link capitalism and patriarchy more tightly have merely echoed the notion that consumption is the sphere of reproduction. . . . In the midst of this, consumption *per se* seems to get lost.

Juliet Mitchell (1971) offered an interesting alternative framework in which patriarchy was treated as essentially ideological and capitalism as primarily economic. At least in this account they were part of the same social structure, functionally interconnected, even if they remained almost entirely separate. Mitchell (1971, p. 31) noted that 'Without a highly articulated, ramified ideological world, a consumer society could not exist' and went on to argue that 'in a consumer society, the role of ideology is so important that it is within the sphere of ideology that the oppressions of the whole system sometimes manifest themselves most apparently' (ibid., p. 35). However, she said little more about the system of consumption and left housework almost entirely out of account.

. . . If we are to understand the changing position of women under capitalism, we must understand the changing relation between production and consumption. The expansion of the consumption sphere has created new forms of work, largely performed by women, largely unpaid and ostensibly relegated to 'private' life. Despite the illusion of free choices, this world is as structured and controlled as that of production.

[· · ·]

As production was gradually removed from the home, the space was filled with *new* consumption activities. The development of capitalist markets depended on the promotion of consumption as a 'way of life' and the superiority (and relative cheapness) of the 'bought' over the homemade. The home itself was, of course, the commodity *par excellence*, a spur for male paid labour and the site of female unpaid labour. The wage labourer and the housewife became the typical figures of modern capitalism. The split between production and consumption was immediately paralleled by the split between public and personal life. Consumption assumed emotional, and later sexual, connotations as the arena of personal fulfilment and individual meaning.

149

Fairly obviously the expansion of production has implied the expansion also of consumption. But under monopoly capitalism the proportion of workers involved directly in production has declined and the proportion of consumption workers has accelerated. The nineteenth century had already seen the expansion of domestic servants, and particularly *female* domestic servants, to meet the growing consumption capacities of the new 'middle class'. By the twentieth century we have what Galbraith (1973) calls the transformation of women as a whole into a 'crypto-servant class'.

[· · ·]

In articulating women's position as that of unpaid personal servants, Galbraith is making important connections between gender and class. He is also aware that we have to move beyond economics for an explanation of how and why women are made to acquiesce in this situation and subordinate themselves to male authority. Though he plays down the class differences between women, he does draw attention to the importance of housework in *all* classes under monopoly capitalism. In a sense it is true that there *has* been a growing uniformity of women's experience. Women of *all* classes are substantially occupied with consumption activities centred around their own homes, and the associated relational skills have become a defining characteristic of femininity.

Consumption activities may be considered in terms of three different phases: acquisition or purchase; transformation and servicing; destroying, appropriating or 'using up'. These phases have undergone different types and rates of change. In practice, of course, it is not always easy to make this distinction, and they do not always follow in neat chronological order.

[· · ·]

In the first instance then, consumption 'is the work of acquiring goods and services' (Weinbaum and Bridges, 1979, p. 194). This takes up a much higher proportion of women's time – according to Vanek (1974, p. 116), one full day a week, compared with two hours in the 1920s, and it has undergone fundamental changes in structure and meaning. As capital removes production from households, it also expands market relations and increases the necessity of *purchasing* the means of life. . . . A woman's value as housewife and mother is reflected largely in her success as a *shopper*, which has replaced the older emphasis on such productive skills as food preservation and home sewing. In addition, the housewife now performs services which were once carried out by the retailer: searching the supermarket shelves, selecting items, filling the trolley, packing [etc.].

[· · ·]

The housewife is not simply buying 'goods and services'. She is operating a highly symbolic process. The goods that she buys have a social meaning which comes from the relation between goods and is not inherent in the individual goods themselves (Sahlins, 1976). The immediate point to make is that in this overall use of goods as a *code*, the actual *buying* process has become much more important.

[· · ·]

Shopping is work . . . . As it expanded to take up more time, shopping took on a sexual and symbolic significance, purporting to offer fulfilment and identity.

[· · ·]

It might be thought that with this growing emphasis on the purchase of commodities the work actually carried out within the home might have been reduced. This has not been the case, although there has been a shift from what might loosely be called 'productive' work to work associated more closely with the transformation of servicing of commodities.

[· · ·]

Most important of all, the emotionalization of housework (the phrase is Cowan's, 1976, p. 22) occurred to an extent apparently quite out of proportion to its own inherent value (Friedan, 1963).

[· · ·]

> Laundering was not just laundering but an expression of love. . . . Feeding the family was not just feeding the family but a way to express the housewife's artistic inclinations and a way to encourage feelings of family loyalty and affection. Diapering the baby was not just diapering, but a time to build the baby's sense of security and love for the mother. Cleaning the bathroom sink was not just cleaning, but an exercise of protective maternal instincts, providing a way for the housewife to keep her family safe from disease. Tasks of this emotional magnitude could not possibly be delegated to servants, even assuming that qualified servants could be found.
>
> *(Cowan, 1976, p. 18)*

'Emotionalization' thus provided a rationalization for the middle-class woman who was in most parts of the advanced capitalist world now doing her own housework. It also provided a justification for many working-class women to leave the workforce and do their own domestic work instead of someone else's. Women frequently had to work to be able to buy things, and the consumer economy provided increasing numbers of low-paying 'women's' jobs to juggle with their household duties as wives, mothers and consumers.

But, most importantly, the ideal of the non-working wife was consolidated. . . . Housework . . . became not just a job but an expression of love and warmth, performed by each woman for her own family.

. . . After World War II images of domesticity and maternal love were not sufficient settings for consumption and it became more directly sexualized. . . . Though there were big shifts in the overall structure of sexuality they did not threaten the domestic sphere. In fact, advertisers linked sexuality to the emotionalization of housework and the establishment of private life as the place where we 'find our real selves'. 'Subliminal promises of sexual fulfilment, love and a happy home life – all the prizes at stake in the marriage competition – were attached to anything from automobiles to toilet paper in the hope of engendering compulsive buying habits' (Ryan, 1975, p. 295).

[· · ·]

Consumption is directly sexual, for we are offered back a 'complete' masculine or feminine identity through consumption patterns. We are under pressure to 'produce' ourselves constantly through consuming commodities. . . . Does consumption always involve sexuality? It seems to us difficult to find an advertisement which does not refer to our sexual identity – in fact this is almost axiomatic since our society is organized so heavily around gender differences. Clearly though, the sexual attractions of some advertisements and some products are much more obvious than others. The attractions of clothes and make-up are of a different order from those of washing machines or vacuum cleaners. Yet both kinds of goods have a place in the construction of femininity: the first through self-adornment and the second through being a good wife and mother, taking care of home and family. And women are particularly vulnerable to all this because our 'lack' is supposedly made good by the approval of others, and particularly men.

[· · ·]

The specific forms of male domination and female oppression in our society are crucially linked to the development of the consumption sphere, which has a high degree of autonomy from production and an ability, in turn, to influence it. Once we reject the absolute dominance of production, the categories fall into place. The old dichotomies of economic/ideological, public/private, physical/mental and materialist/idealist have little applicability. If theoretical and political primacy were given to the consumption area, we might find that the analysis of capitalism and the analysis of male domination *could* proceed simultaneously as one and the same process, without any reductionism taking place.

[· · ·]

5
GENDER AND WAGE LABOUR

CHANGING PERSPECTIVES ON WORK

In this chapter we examine the ways in which feminists have challenged and reconstructed conventional theories about women's position in the labour market. Paid work was important to feminists long before the current women's movement. In the nineteenth century, when the UK ostensibly had a 'surplus' of women, and not all women could expect to marry, there was widespread concern with the predicament of single (especially middle-class) women, and their rights to support themselves. The nineteenth-century women's movement had been very much focused on the public sphere – not only on the vote but on civil rights and access to higher education and the professions. The first half of the twentieth century leaves a legacy of struggles to improve women's pay and working conditions. The contemporary movement initially resituated these issues in the context of a critique of marriage and the family. The right of married women to work outside the home in order to achieve economic independence was emphasized. Women need paid work in order to have the choice to leave the family if they want to do so, as well as to be in a position to renegotiate the terms on which they would live in households with men.

Early feminist writings stressed that women had a right to work and attempted to debunk the prevailing attitudes which presumed that women's work was marginal both to the economy and to individual households. A number of strikes for equal pay and improved working conditions occurred in the late 1960s and 1970s, including the strike of the sewing machinists at Ford's Dagenham factory, the London night cleaners' campaign for unionization, the occupation at the Fakenham shoe factory in Norfolk and the strike by Asian women at Imperial Typewriters in Leicester. The Working Women's Charter campaign was established nationally in 1974, demanding action by employers, unions and the state to ensure women's greater equality in the labour market. Waged work has continued to be the focus of campaigns by feminists. In the 1980s and 1990s issues about the *value* of women's work compared with men's are important (this issue of value is readdressed in Chapter 7), as are the implications of remedies to improve the position of low-paid workers, particularly notions of a national minimum wage. Women are a majority among the workers who will benefit if such a policy is introduced.

As well as being a focus for practical campaigning, work has also generated a large body of case studies of women's position in the labour market. These academic analyses of women's participation have identified three broad areas of concern. First there has been a focus on women's exclusion from the paid workforce – even when there, they have been treated as invisible, as invaders, whose 'proper' and primary place is at home. Secondly, the question of occupational segregation and wage differentials has been analysed. Women and men still work in very different types of jobs, with women clustered in a narrow range of occupations, particularly in the service sector. There are also differences between women, on race and class grounds, as Anne Phillips argued in Article 3.1. However, in this chapter we deal primarily with the differences between women and men. Thirdly, feminist scholars, as well as activists, have turned their attention to remedies, to notions of equality, equal pay, equal value or comparable worth and equal opportunities in the labour market.

ALTERNATIVE EXPLANATIONS OF THE GENDER DIVISION OF LABOUR

The main contribution of orthodox economics to explaining wage differentials between men and women has been human capital theory. This suggests that an individual makes an investment in him- or herself by devoting time to studying, gaining additional qualifications or by acquiring skills and work experience. The higher the initial investment in human capital, the higher future earnings are likely to be. Evidence of earning distributions broadly backs this up. However, the earnings differentials, particularly between women and men, are usually far larger than the theory would lead us to expect, so human capital theories at best offer only a partial explanation. They are also essentially sexist, since they only count as production those skills which the market rewards, and many skills which women possess go unrewarded and unrecognized.

Labour economists have developed theories of discrimination which either supplement or replace human capital theory. Two types of theory have been developed to explain gender divisions in the workforce: dual and segmented labour market theories which are also derived from economics, and labour process theories building on the work of Marxist social theory. The initial, and simplest dual labour market model, as its name indicates, distinguishes two labour markets, a primary and secondary sector. The former offers high wages, good working conditions, security of employment and opportunities for promotion. Jobs in the secondary sector, by contrast, tend to be low paid, heavily supervised, with poor working conditions and little chance of advancement. The majority of women are located in the secondary sector workforce and this is seen as, in large part, the explanation for their lower pay. However, this model does not offer much precision, since obviously there are large numbers of men on the periphery, while there are also many women – nurses, teachers and other professionals, for example – in the primary labour markets.

These models have been developed to be more complex and acknowledge a high degree of segmentation rather than a two-fold division. Radical economists have given a more dynamic account, emphasizing the processes which create a segmented labour market, suggesting that different labour markets arise as employers seek to divide, and rule, workers from one another. To counter working-class militancy, they suggest, employers turned to strategies designed to retain control. They achieve this by dividing the workforce into distinct segments, so that the actual experiences of workers would be different and the basis of their common opposition to capitalism would be undermined. Hence, labour markets are segmented by sex, age, race and ethnic origin. This account creates space for treating gender as central to the structuring of labour markets, and not simply as a reflection of men's and women's different relations to the family.

There was a renewed interest in the labour process with the publication, in the USA in 1974, of Harry Braverman's book, *Labor and Monopoly Capital*. His central thesis was that new technology was degrading the dignity of work, taking away old craft skills and drawing more and more workers into the ranks of an enlarged proletariat. The book was of particular interest to feminists because it paid attention to the 'proletarianization' of clerical work; that is, work done predominantly by women. Braverman argued that changes in the organization of work should not be treated simply as technological innovations based on capital's search for higher profits. They are, rather, the outcome of struggles for control between capitalists and workers. Feminists added a gender dimension to this, arguing that labour processes are also shaped by struggles between men and women. Braverman himself had little to say about gender, assuming it was women's position in the family that allowed them to be treated by employers as a reserve army of labour. But he did provide a springboard for feminist exploration of the labour process, and for sustained work investigating why women's jobs tend to be defined as unskilled regardless of the content of the job.

Feminist scholars interested in work began, from the mid-1960s onwards, by pointing to the absence of women from most studies. The first step was to fill this gap by making female workers more visible. Researchers initially concentrated on working-class women, particularly in manufacturing. Clerical work was looked at only in so far as it seemed to be becoming more like factory work, as a result of new technology and the imposition of new work disciplines. Ironically, this had the effect of reiterating the heroic myth of the 'real' worker as a factory worker. In so far as it kept to the existing contours for the study of work, fundamentally shaped by the labour/capital relation, this could be described as the 'add women and stir' approach.

As feminists began to accumulate detailed case studies, they moved away from the idea that the nature of the labour process is determined purely by struggles between labour and capital. Rather than simply making women 'visible', there has been a concern with gender as an organizing principle of work relations. Gender should not be seen as constructed at home and then taken out to work. It was becoming clear that gender is constructed in a number of sites and that work is a crucial one. Accounts of the construction and manipulation of masculinity and sexuality in the workplace were published in the 1980s (Cockburn, 1983, 1985; Hearn and Parkin, 1987). Cockburn (1983, 1985) and Game and Pringle (1984), among others, looked at the ways in which a segregated workforce was defended not only by managers but also by male workers. While new technology was constantly changing the content of men's and women's work, and threatening to break down the existing division of labour, in one way or another jobs were continually redefined in order to retain a distinction. Thus, while the sexual division of labour was always changing, what did not seem to change was a distinction between men's work and women's work, and power differentials between them.

The articles in this chapter trace some of this history and draw on a variety of disciplines to attempt to explain inequalities in the workplace. In Article 5.1, Veronica Beechey poses questions about the relationship between the family and the labour market by comparing women's rather different profiles in the UK and France. That French women are far more likely to work full-time must be attributed not to 'natural' choice but to very different social policies in the two countries. Despite working full-time, French women are, like British women, concentrated in a limited band of jobs. Beechey shows how employers' and trade union practices, state policies and cultural factors construct women as different kinds of workers.

Both orthodox and radical theories have made sexist assumptions about what constitutes skill and productivity. This has been pursued by a number of feminist theorists building on an influential paper by Anne Phillips and Barbara Taylor (1980). The classification of women's jobs as unskilled and men's jobs as skilled frequently bears little relation to the amount of training or the ability required for them. As Phillips and Taylor point out, 'far from being an objective fact, skill is often an ideological category imposed on certain types of work by virtue of the sex and power of the workers who perform it'. They link their discussion of skill directly to the labour process as it has been theorized by Braverman and his followers. As Braverman had pointed out, capitalists often tried to undercut men's power by introducing women workers. Men struggled to preserve their skills against capital, rather than uniting with women to prevent the latter being used as a cheap labour force.

The struggle to have women's skills acknowledged continues in more recent debates about flexible specialization. Current changes in the production process involve a move away from the special purpose machinery of mass production which relied on semi- and unskilled workers to make standardized goods for mass consumption. This change in the production process has been so significant that some theorists have distinguished between an earlier period of Fordist organization (from the 1930s to the mid-1970s) and a contemporary period dubbed 'post-Fordist'. New machinery enables skilled workers to make quick adjustments to changing markets and more differentiated tastes. While some theorists have rosy visions of a post-Fordist future in which skilled workers will control their labour process, others foresee a growing gulf between skilled and unskilled, in which women will fare very badly. Jenson points out that production is increasingly organized around small groups which may operate to shut other workers out. She concludes:

> Such groups are encouraged to develop ties among themselves and even to compete with other groups over meeting production norms, and improving efficiency. In such tightly knit work collectives, the topic of group composition comes to the fore. Thus questions of difference – whether to include and co-operate with workers who are ethnically, racially, or sexually 'different' – can appear in the workplace. Where the practices of Fordism de-emphasized differentiation among workers to some extent, uniting them by the moving line, stress on co-operation, in consultation, and on planning can make it seem compelling to find 'pals' with whom one feels comfortable. In this way, as a by-product of the new management form of work organization, internal lines of cleavage in the working class around visible differences may be accentuated ... Restructuring the labour process so as to privilege skilled work and workers will further marginalize women unless political actors challenge long-standing processes which isolate women from machinery and which define women's skills as talents ... Unions and other actors must also reject notions of 'difference' within the working class which can be the basis

for legitimation of a two-tier labour force in which the 'real workers' all seem to be skilled men, and women and others who have been historically without power fill the marginal categories.

(Jenson, 1989, pp. 154–5)

A number of case studies have analysed the relationship between gender and ethnic divisions and the fragmented labour process. Miriam Glucksmann, writing as Ruth Cavendish, noted that assembly work in a car components factory was done almost entirely by immigrant women – Irish, West Indian and Gujarati (Cavendish, 1982). She argued that women's labour is regarded as less valuable because of their responsibilities for child care and domestic labour, and that immigrant women sell their labour under less favourable conditions than white women. The division of labour thus presupposes the existence of different types of labour. In her later work she placed greater emphasis on the 'demand' side, on the role of employers in actively shaping gender relations at work (Glucksmann, 1990).

In Article 5.2, Angela Coyle, in her study of the clothing industry, also emphasizes the demand side. She shows how the concentration of women in unskilled and low-paid jobs results from management strategies designed to cheapen labour, and trade union practices in which skilled male workers have struggled to differentiate themselves from unskilled female labour and to preserve pay differentials. Following the collapse of the late 1970s and early 1980s, clothing production has not simply been shipped off to South East Asia or relegated to high technology automated factories. Instead, production has been shifted out of the factories and into the workers' own homes. Women from a variety of ethnic backgrounds in the UK are doing piecework at home for rates of pay that make them almost as cheap to employ as women in the Third World.

These accounts tend to stress, on the one hand, the importance of management strategies in dividing the workers, and on the other, the family and other factors that determine the supply of different sorts of labour. Accounts of both the demand for and supply of women's labour tended to take gender as given. Several recent studies have looked at work as one of a number of sites on which gender relations are actively constructed. Game and Pringle (1984), for example, argue that work is centrally organized around gender differences, and that gender is not just about difference but about power. The power relation is maintained by the distinction between male and female jobs. Male workers have a vested interest in maintaining the sexual division of labour, in maintaining a sense of themselves as superior to women. They have traditionally done

158

this by defining their work as skilled and women's as unskilled, thus setting up an association between masculinity and skill.

Game and Pringle consider the relationship between gender identities and technological change, and ask, what happens when mechanization takes place? They argue that men's skills are seen to be built into the machines, that there is a conscious association between machinery and masculinity. Thus any work that is associated with machinery, especially big machinery, is thought of as appropriate for men. There are some ironies in this. Their chapter on whitegoods manufacturing (washing machines, stoves and refrigerators) looks at a whole set of polarities that define the difference between men's work and women's. These include: skilled/unskilled, heavy/light, dirty/clean, dangerous/boring, mobile/sedentary. While new technology is making all the work more like 'women's work', new distinctions (technical/non-technical) are emerging to justify an ongoing sexual division of labour.

Miriam Glucksmann (1990) takes a similar approach in her account of women assembly workers in the new industries of inter-war Britain. Such industries included electrical engineering, synthetic fibres, food processing, motor vehicles, chemicals, rubber, glass and paper. These were set up using mass production techniques. Glucksmann argues that employers deliberately recruited women to operate the assembly lines and conveyor belts. The restructuring of industry involved a restructuring of the gender composition of the industrial workforce. A new sexual division of labour came into being whereby women were assigned almost exclusively to assembly work and men to everything else. This actually constituted new gender meanings. In one of the factories, 'being an assembler meant being a woman and being a woman meant being an assembler' (Glucksmann, 1990, p. 3).

Veronica Beechey and Tessa Perkins, in their research on part-time work, have also identified the labour process as a site of gender construction. They comment:

> We tried to identify features of the organization of the labour process which could account for the fact that certain jobs were part-time. But one thing which became absolutely clear is that these features only resulted in jobs being organized on a part-time basis when women were employed. When men were employed, managements used other mechanisms for attaining flexibility. Two examples illustrated this point. Within the hospital sector there was 100 per cent occupational segregation between portering, done exclusively by men, and other manual work, done by women. Yet portering was done by men working on a three-shift system, while women's manual work was all part-time. The second example is from baking. Both

bread and confectionery production required a lot of flexibility of labour. There were peaks and troughs over the working week, and since bread and cakes are perishable, work had to be organized in a concentrated way when demand was high. Yet bread production, done entirely by men, was organized on a full-time basis, and flexibility was attained by extensive use of overtime and by some use of casual labour. Flexibility within the predominantly female confectionery production, however, was attained by extensive use of part-time labour for which a complex variety of patterns of work has been devised.

It appears, then, that a crucial part of the explanation as to why certain jobs are part-time is that they are typically done by women, and that the demand for part-time labour is inextricably linked to the presence of occupational segregation.

(Beechey and Perkins, 1987, pp. 163–4)

Some recent writing on work has been influenced by post-structuralist ideas. It has moved away from the labour market and the labour process to focus on the discourses that structure workplace power relations. Occupations are not simply a given but embody sets of social and cultural meanings. In her study of secretaries, in Article 5.3, Rosemary Pringle emphasizes the multiplicity of con-tested meanings, the fragility of 'identity' and the importance of discourses about the sexual and the familial in defining women. These discourses are not simply imported from 'outside' the workplace but are actively produced within it. While organizations might appear to be sexless and gender neutral, sexuality and gender are actually central to the construction of workplace power relations. Marny Hall, in Article 5.4, considers some of the implications of this for the ways in which lesbian women negotiate the workplace. But all women are constructed as gendered subjects in the labour market and are always 'women workers' rather than just 'workers'. Even in the universities, supposedly liberal institutions, where entry to the teaching profession is on individual merit and the possession of the requisite credentials, women are discriminated against. As Caroline Ramazanoglu argues, based on her own experience as a lecturer in a sociology department, 'Thirteen years of teaching in universities has at last disclosed to me the secret that there is no second sex in academe. There is only one sex: male' (Ramazanoglu, 1987). Linda McDowell (1990) has investigated the nature of power between men and women in her own discipline of geography, revealing not only the ways in which men use verbal, vocal and visual power to oppress women, but also that the social organization of academia undervalues 'feminine' traits of caring, counselling and even teaching in comparison with 'hard' research. And, as we have argued throughout this book, the social construction of knowledge itself is gendered.

Finally, in Article 5.5, Linda McDowell returns to the impact of recent changes in the two areas of 'women's work' – the labour market and the home or community – and argues that women, although still depicted as 'secondary' workers, are an increasingly important part of the labour market in the UK. This increased centrality, however, runs counter to the greater demands being imposed on them as 'caring and servicing' workers in the home as the welfare state is restructured, and seems to be having the effect of increasing the overall workload for many women in the UK in the 1990s. Whether or not this will lead to wider changes in the structure of gender relations remains an open question.

Article 5.1
WOMEN'S EMPLOYMENT IN FRANCE AND BRITAIN: SOME PROBLEMS OF COMPARISON
Veronica Beechey

. . . The comparison between France and Britain is interesting and important politically. The differences between the two countries raise some important questions of interpretation, especially about the relationship between the family and the labour process in explaining the position of women in the workforce. Moreover, the comparison of how women have fared in two countries which have been similarly hit by recession in the 1970s and 1980s makes it possible to begin to isolate some of the factors involved in the construction of gender in the labour market.

[· · ·]

Despite the fact that French women have a history of having had higher levels of participation in the formal economy earlier this century because of the continuation of family farms and businesses and because of their ongoing economic importance in manufacturing industry, today women's activity rates are similar in the two countries. . . . Moreover, they have continued to rise in both countries, despite the recession. Women also comprise almost identical proportions of the economically active labour force in Britain and France. . . . However, there are two crucial respects in which women's activity rates are markedly different. . . . First, women in the two countries have very different work profiles. Work history data show that in France women participate in the labour market in a similar way to men, tending to leave the labour market only when they have three or more children or because they have been made redundant. In Britain, in contrast, women's work histories still tend to follow a bimodal pattern (although this is being modified among younger cohorts). Overall, British women tend to leave the labour market when they have children rather than taking maternity leave, returning subsequently to part-time work. It is the presence of dependent children and in particular the age of the youngest child which is the key determinant of women's participation in the labour market in Britain, whereas in France the critical variable is how many children a woman has: whether she has three or more, or two or less.

The second marked difference in women's activity rates is the presence in Britain of a high level of part-time working among women, white women especially. . . . One woman worker in two works part-time, whereas in France the figure is one in five. Part-time working has grown quite rapidly in France in recent years but it is not a structural principle of organization of the labour market there. Most women in the workforce in France work full-time.

Important questions are raised by an analysis of these differences in the patterns of women's economic activity. What happens to women's careers in the two countries? And in particular, what differences does being married and having children make? What do these differences suggest about the possibilities for women attaining economic independence? And do women in the two countries have different kinds of choices as to what kind of jobs they do? It is clear that marriage and having children have far more disadvantages for women in Britain than they do in France. French women tend to stay in the labour market when they have children and they also receive generous family allowances so that the state takes on economic responsibility for their well-being when they have large families. They are thus less dependent, economically speaking, on their husbands. Culturally, it seems, notions of femininity have been constructed differently in France. France also has much better systems of child care support, both in the form of services and cash benefits. In Britain, on the other hand, being a paid worker and being a mother have been constructed as being contradictory. Most women leave the labour market when they have children, and if they return to part-time jobs, as most do, they generally suffer downward mobility and a considerable loss of lifetime earnings (cf. Joshi, 1984).

[· · ·]

Several factors are important in explaining the different forms of women's participation in the labour market in France and Britain. State policies and cultural constructions are especially important variables on the 'supply' side. As Hilary Land (1987) has shown, cash benefits and services for children are . . . far more generous and extensive in France. Elizabeth Garnsey's comparative discussion of part-time work (Garnsey, 1984) points to child care provision as a crucial variable differentiating France from Britain. Family allowances too developed in quite different ways in the two countries and in France employers bear some responsibility for the costs of children. In Britain, child benefits are paid out of general taxation and are very low. There is certainly an underlying demographic difference in that France has been concerned about its falling birthrate in the post-war world whereas Britain has not. None the less, one still has to explain *why* the two countries developed such different patterns. Both countries were faced with a labour shortage in the post-war years, but this was coped with very differently in each. Britain recruited workers from the Commonwealth in the 1950s and 1960s, whereas France sought actively to keep women in the labour force. Thus, in France the issue for post-war social policy has been how to develop policies which would enable women to stay in the labour market *and* have children. In Britain, in contrast, social policies developed quite differently. Where mothers have been in paid employment this is often because they have had relatives who could provide child care or because employers constructed part-time jobs in order to recruit women. State family policies are thus a crucial part of the story of whether or not women enter into the labour market, and on what terms. In France the state has acted to facilitate women's entry into the labour market, when they have children. In Britain, in contrast, the state has done little or nothing to enable women to combine paid employment with children. Responsibility for children is seen as an essentially 'private' affair.

. . . Jenson (1986) points out that at the turn of the century both France and Britain were concerned with infant mortality, which was a real problem in both countries. However, she argues, the definitions of the problem and the solutions offered in each country differed markedly. In France, concern focused on maternal welfare rather than on maternal work. Policy makers didn't mind the fact that women were in paid employment. They objected to the lack of maternity leave and lack of adequate financial support to enable women to spend time out of the labour market when they had babies. In Britain, in contrast, working mothers were seized on as the single cause of maternal mortality (cf. Lewis, 1980). Social reformers and many feminists were therefore critical of women working when they had children, and the state did nothing to alleviate the problems they suffered. The 'solution' proposed was that mothers, and indeed, married women more generally, should not be in the labour market. . . . In the British literature, in particular, this has often had the effect of making the patterns of women's employment appear to be 'natural', a product of biological processes rather than social ones. The comparison with France, where women's participation in the labour market is connected to childbearing and rearing in a different way, illustrates the limitations of many of the conventional explanations. Instead of taking activity rates as given, we need to ask different, and more sociological, questions: In what conditions does the presence of young children and adult dependants lead to a two-phase working life for women? And what are the conditions in which marriage and the presence of dependent children lead to a return to part-time work?

[· · ·]

It would be wrong to conclude from the above discussion that women's activity rates can be explained solely in terms of labour supply. An analysis of the changing industrial structure and the changing demand for labour are also a crucially important part of the explanation. So too are education and training schemes.

[· · ·]

When one looks in more detail at women's position in the workforce and at women's unemployment in France and Britain, two extremely interesting facts stand out. First, despite the striking difference in the patterns of women's participation discussed above, the extent and nature of occupational segregation in the two countries is very similar. Moreover, women's unemployment is higher than men's in France, whereas the obverse is true of Britain. Both these findings challenge the view, commonplace in Britain, which attributes women's disadvantaged position in the occupational hierarchy to their position in the family and their interrupted work histories. The fact is that French women have work histories which are more like men's but they are none the less disadvantaged in the labour market. . . .

In both countries approximately three-quarters of women work in the tertiary or service sectors. . . . Secondly, in both countries the bulk of women are concentrated in a small range of predominantly female occupations – clerical work, 'professions intermédiaires' like teaching and nursing, and personal service jobs – whereas men are more widely spread throughout the occupational structure. Overall, women are over-represented in lower-graded occupations and under-represented in higher graded ones in both countries, but there is one important difference: French women appear to have made more advances in administrative and lower level managerial jobs in the 1970s than British women did. . . .

In terms of pay, too, the situation is not terribly different between the two countries. Although women generally get equal pay when they do exactly the same jobs as men, a gap of over 25 per cent remains between men's and women's earnings because of occupational segregation. The gap is larger in the private sector than the public one and it tends to be widest at the top of the occupational hierarchy. In both countries the gap is widest between men and women with the highest qualifications, and it also widens with age. . . .

A variety of different factors contribute to these similarities between the two countries, among them employers' and trade union policies and practices which have restricted women to lower paid and less-valued jobs, state policies (e.g. national insurance contributions, employment legislation), education and training programmes, and cultural factors which have resulted in women being constructed as distinctive kinds of workers.

[· · ·]

Article 5.2
SEX AND SKILL IN THE ORGANIZATION OF THE CLOTHING INDUSTRY

Angela Coyle

... In asking the questions, why are women still concentrated in unskilled and low paid work, and why hasn't anti-discrimination and equal pay legislation changed that, it would appear that some answers lie in the forms of organization of the labour process itself. To perceive women's marginalized relation to production as a consequence of their 'dual role' and a discriminatory labour market is not enough, and here the concentration of women in low-paid work is placed within the context of the de-skilling of the labour process. Such changes in the organization of the labour process have created the unskilled jobs which women undertake, but it does not explain why women's wages are so persistently lower than men's, nor the blanket categorization of women's work as always being of lower skill value than men's work. De-skilling is not an abstract formula, and in clothing, as elsewhere, the range of strategies available to management to effect the cheapening of production occur in the context of economic constraints and labour resistance. What is shown here is that strategies employed by management to exert a downward pressure on wages (and along the way to avoid equal pay), combine with union strategies to resist that, to have the effect of reinforcing sexual divisions within the labour process. So that, although the actions of management and male workers derive from quite different imperatives, they can have a short-term coincidence of interests in keeping female labour segregated in certain jobs. It does raise questions about traditional forms of trade union strategy, especially trade union sectionalism, and just how women can get out of the low-wage ghetto.

[· · ·]

Precisely how de-skilling occurs will depend on the specific conditions ... but, within a range of strategies available to management, there are two possible emphases. One is to exert pressure on labour itself and to maximize efficiency of effort through reorganizing work methods and extending the division of labour. Skilled work is broken down into a series of simplified routinized processes which can be undertaken by less skilled, and cheaper, labour. As a managerial strategy, this was developed by Frederick 'Speedy' Taylor whose 'scientific' approach to the division of labour

166

laid the basis of work study as it is employed today. The second possibility for management is to replace human labour by machines. . . . The use of machinery is governed by how much capital is available for such investment and whether it is adequately compensated by reduced labour costs. Where particularly cheap labour is available there may be no particular incentive to replace labour with expensive machines (Marx, 1976, pp. 515–16). De-skilling as a range of managerial strategies, occurs in an uneven and eclectic way, rather than as a pervasive and driving logic. Old methods will do for as long as they remain profitable.

This is certainly demonstrated in the clothing industry where a characteristically low capital investment contributes to the industry's hand-to-mouth existence, whilst, at the same time, narrow profit margins, a changing product and highly competitive markets often militate against further investment. It is still true that if wages can be kept at rock bottom levels, small producers can be very competitive and profitable (Roche, 1973, p. 203). Fashion and seasonal changes and an unstable market means that there are regular changes in production methods. The clothing industry needs a rapidly adaptable labour process and human labour is more adaptable than machinery. Technical change and rationalization first occurred in the inter-war period, and in the context of the relatively reduced availability of cheap labour, the streamlining of the product and market stability. The industry's reliance on cheap labour was upset both by the introduction of the Trades Boards which set minimum wage rates for the industry and by restrictions imposed on the early wave of immigration from Eastern Europe (Wray, 1957, p. 19). This forced changes in production methods, most notably in men's wear which employed a higher proportion of skilled male labour and which was far less subject to fashion changes.

[· · ·]

DE-SKILLING: A CHANGING LABOUR PROCESS AND A CHANGING LABOUR FORCE

[· · ·]

Men's skills were significantly attacked during the inter-war period with the transition from craft workshop to factory production. The extensive sub-division of processes, combined with technical change, not only attacked the skills of previously very highly skilled men but provided the basis for substitution. . . . The introduction of new machines has reduced both the skill level which the industry requires and the quantity of labour. . . . Most processes have now become mechanized and each has been broken down into operations of the simplest form and the shortest time. The assembly of a garment is now based on a series of short simple operations for which operators can be trained very quickly.

[···]

These technical changes and the rationalization of the labour process have occurred in the context of the relative availability of cheap labour, which in turn effects changes in the kind of labour required by the industry. In the post-war period many clothing factories were set up in government-designated Development Areas which had 'the only major source of relatively cheap female labour available to an industry where the prevailing trend was towards the creation of larger units, using less skilled and hence cheaper labour' (Hague and Newman, 1952, p. 58). Moreover, skilled workers are not just expensive, but resistant to change. So that one firm's labour policy was not just concerned with cost *per se* but with control as well:

> It was rather the impossibility of adapting a labour force from traditional methods to mass production line operation. For cost reasons such a system was becoming vital to our future well being. We had attempted to introduce it and had been forced to abandon it, partly because of our inadequate premises, but chiefly because of worker resistance. Our labour experience probably holds for the clothing industry in general; in traditional clothing centres it is very hard to break with traditional methods.
>
> *(Hague and Newman, 1952, p. 54)*

The industry's endemic labour shortage is actually a shortage of cheap labour, and a more or less permanent feature since the war. The war period actually created the conditions upon which the industry could stabilize and develop and yet after the war the industry faced acute labour shortages, particularly of female labour, who were reluctant to return to the industry when better work and pay was available elsewhere (*Garment Worker*, May, 1970).

The ideal labour recruit has always been a school-leaver: quick to learn, not resistant to new work methods and not eligible for an adult wage rate. The reliance on school-leavers has not been without problems, however, especially in terms of labour turnover. Many leave before they fully train or reach full pay rates.

[···]

Immigrant labour has always been important.... From the late nineteenth and early twentieth centuries, immigrants from Eastern Europe supplied the industry with a great deal of its skilled male labour, and Birnbaum suggests, were responsible for establishing the difference between men's and women's work as the difference

168

between skilled and unskilled work (Birnbaum, undated). Now it is female immigrant labour only which is significant as a distinctive labour force. West Indian, Filipino and Asian women are employed in a new kind of sweatshop that has grown up in the inner ring areas of large cities, and are a particularly vulnerable and cheap source of labour (Williams, 1972).

Finally, it is worth noting, in relation to the industry's labour force, that the use of homeworkers is a traditional resolution of the search for cheap labour. Technically self-employed, their wages are low and unprotected by either union organization or wages council orders (Brown, 1974). Economic recession and competition from foreign markets has once again made production based on the labour of homeworkers more economical than factory production. This is particularly true for London, the traditional site of women's wear production, where it is estimated that half the fashion trade's output is produced by homeworkers (Campbell, 1980). The number of homeworkers employed is difficult to estimate, but it is clear that rapid loss of jobs in the industry is not entirely due to increased efficiency and increased labour productivity, and some clothing firms have chosen to move out of manufacture and into the business of orchestrating the labour of homeworkers (Campbell, 1979).

Article 5.3
WHAT IS A SECRETARY?

Rosemary Pringle

> I think the word 'secretary' means a girl or a woman that works for another man in the company, no matter what she does.

> We have a problem as secretaries that nobody knows what to call us. A secretary could be a typist or it could be a full-blown personal assistant or administrative officer. No one can say that they are a secretary without doing certain tasks but even typists seem to say they do those tasks regardless of whether they have got a business qualification or whether they have done anything like the HSC . . .

There is nothing straightforward about defining secretaries or identifying them as a group. The first speaker, a senior executive, . . . gives a very broad definition which makes no reference at all to specific tasks or skills. Instead, he stresses that secretaries are *women*, and that they work *for* bosses (who are presumed to be men). In doing so he voices the conventional assumptions first, that 'secretary' is a gendered category and second, that it takes its meaning from its *relation* to another category, namely bosses. Pushed further, he said that a secretary is an 'appendage' of the boss's function. To understand the meaning of 'secretary' produced here it is helpful to consider the unconscious elements that underlie this man's conscious definition. If, as the psychoanalysts suggest, 'woman' is perceived as 'lacking' what it takes to be a 'man', so are secretaries defined as 'lacking' the qualities that make a successful boss. Our executive defines secretaries in negative terms as representing everything that bosses are not. His answer to the question 'what is a secretary' is effectively 'not a boss'. This understanding, widely shared by both men and women, goes some way to explaining the general 'vagueness' about what a secretary is, the trivialization of her work, and the reluctance to acknowledge secretarial skills as a path into management.

That these ideas are largely unconscious means that they are accepted as 'natural' and rarely articulated. The equation of secretary with woman or 'wife', and boss with man, is important in establishing the normative versions of what a secretary is. It creates problems, not only for female secretaries but for female bosses and male secretaries. Not only can a woman not have a wife, but the discourse casts doubt on whether any woman can fully be a 'boss'.

Can a boss take up the 'feminine' position and still be a boss? In our culture these unconscious meanings go deep. They are present in the reservations that secretaries have about working for women and, more openly, in the ridicule that male secretaries receive and the deep unease that they have with the title.

The second speaker, a representative of the Institute of Professional Secretaries (IPSA), indicates the kinds of problems secretaries have had in asserting the importance of skills in their self-definition. She is operating at a conscious, rational level and seeking to ignore or play down the deeper levels at which meanings are generated. It will not be sufficient merely to assert that secretaries have skills if the current sexual meanings are not acknowledged and challenged. An important part of the struggle to improve the conditions of secretaries is the deconstruction of existing meanings.

There is no single answer to the question, 'what is a secretary?'. There is not even agreement about what the question 'means'. Statisticians, work analysts and industrial sociologists answer it by attempting to describe what a secretary *does*. But secretary is one of the few employment categories for which there has never been a clear job description. Secretaries do a wide variety of things and there is not even one task which we can confidently say they all perform. We cannot simply point to a place in the labour process and say, *that* is occupied by secretaries. The meanings that derive from job definitions and the labour process offer only one kind of answer to the question of what a secretary is.

We come to know about secretaries, and to identify them as a group, through the ways in which they are represented. This is true of all groups but in most cases the emphasis is on the actual work and the social relations surrounding it. A plumber or, for that matter, a stenographer or typist does not have a particularly strong cultural presence. By contrast, the secretary is constructed in popular culture in a way that plays down the importance of what she *does*, in favour of a discussion of what she *is*. The ambiguity about what constitutes a secretary's work makes it easily 'available' for cultural redefinition. Secretaries are part of folklore and popular culture and are represented in stereotypical ways in advertising and the media, even in pornography.

[· · ·]

If secretaries are represented as women, they are also represented almost exclusively in familial or sexual terms: as wives, mothers, spinster aunts, mistresses and *femmes fatales*. The emphasis on the sexual has made it easy to treat the work itself as trivial or invisible. We experienced the inside of this when we visited workplaces to do our research. Everywhere people cracked jokes about whether we were going to harass them, whether we were perverts and what we had found out about their sex lives. They would often ask 'how's 'secs' going?' basing the joke on the phonetic identity of 'secs' and 'sex'. At every workplace at least some people assumed that studying secretaries meant unravelling sexual scandals. As sociologists we became aware that we too might be perceived as trivial or frivolous, not dealing with work in a 'serious' way. The interviews seemed to contrast with earlier ones we had done, in factories, banks and retail stores, where we had asked workers to describe in detail their place in a particular production process. It was impossible to talk to secretaries about what they do without the talk running fairly quickly onto questions about coffee-making, personal services, clothes, femininity and sexuality. These themes are central to their self-definition and their working relations.

Everybody has something to say about secretaries, makes jokes about their sexuality or their relationship with the boss. For secretaries, the boss is often supposed to be a highly sexualized being, representing a kind of sex-power that may be desired or repudiated or both. For him the sexual is presented as a piece of light relief, a diversion from his real business. The boss–secretary relationship is the subject of fantasy, both in a general way and in specific office situations.

[· · ·]

It is virtually impossible to talk about secretaries without making a set of sexual associations. Images of secretaries sitting around filing their nails or doing their knitting reinforce the idea that they do little work, that their work is of secondary importance or that their interests and priorities are in a sphere 'outside' work. If they are idle it is linked to their femininity and blamed on them rather than on poor management. They are [not] acknowledged as 'real' workers. Discussion of what a secretary *does* seems inseparable from popular images and expectations of what a secretary *is*.

'Secretary' has not one but a variety of meanings. These meanings are not fixed for they have to be continually produced and reproduced. Herein lie the possibilities for transformation and change. However, the alternative meanings are not infinite. The prevailing images and representations operate in the context of structures which, if not fixed, do have a certain longevity. Structures of patriarchy and capitalism, gender and class, the labour process and psycho-sexuality provide a context and a set of limitations to the transformations that are possible at any point in time. . . .

The question of 'what is a secretary' may be answered with reference to three discourses which have coexisted, at times peacefully and at others in open competition with each other. The first of these, the 'office wife', is strongly middle class and may be found in 'serious' journals, teaching manuals, the ideas and practices of a good many secretarial studies teachers as well as [in] the [ideas and practice of] more 'traditional' bosses and secretaries. The second, the 'sexy secretary', became the dominant one in the 1950s and 60s and is predominantly working class. It relates to folklore and popular culture, particularly the tabloids, as well as some soft-core pornography. It rests on stereotyping and caricature and its central theme is the mindless Dolly bird. Women who refuse this image may be lampooned as asexual spinsters or dragons who will never be attractive to men. The third discourse, the 'career woman', derives from a variety of approaches that may be described as 'modernist' in the sense that they seek to extend the principles of bureaucratic rationality and efficiency to all those parts of life that are still seen to be governed by the personal, the familial or the arbitrary. It is within the modernist context that attempts to measure secretarial skills become relevant. There is no place here for familial or sexual definitions. Nevertheless, it has not been at all easy to shake them off and a number of compromises have been reached.

[· · ·]

The two main requirements of the office wife were (and still are) that she be deferential and that she be ladylike. Marriage services still speak of a couple becoming, not husband and wife, but man and wife. Men are never referred to, even in secretaries' discourse, as 'office husbands', though secretaries will at times make comparisons between their husbands and bosses. Bosses do not take their identity primarily from their relationship with their secretaries but from relations with equals and superiors in their own and other organizations. As 'wives' secretaries are positioned as subordinates who are defined in relation to their bosses rather than having separate identities. . . .

The office wife is portrayed as the extension of her boss, loyal, trustworthy and devoted. She is expected to 'love, honour and obey', relieving him of the routine and the trivial, creating the conditions for his detachment from the mundane rituals of everyday life. She is the gatekeeper, protecting him from those who would waste his time or want to know his private business, mediating his relations with the outside world and even with himself. In folklore she may either rival the wife or liaise with her in order to 'organize' him. . . .

While thoroughly subordinate to her boss, as 'wife' the secretary is . . . [not without] power. She acts on his behalf, determines who gets to see him and, through having his ear, has considerable influence. Since in some sense she participates in his class position, she is expected to look, sound and behave like a lady.

[· · ·]

While it is open to different meanings, 'office wife' continues to structure work arrangements. Bosses and secretaries are still perceived as operating in 'pairs'. Although most secretaries work for more than one person, there is always a 'boss' with whom they have a special relation; bosses often do not admit to sharing a secretary; she is still 'their' secretary who happens to work for other people as well.

Debate about changes in secretarial work is frequently cast in terms of how far office marriages are changing. Are traditional marriages based on deference being transformed into more companionate and egalitarian relations, where the wife might have other interests or refuse to do certain aspects of the housework? 'Deference' and 'respect' have been replaced by 'friendship' and 'team-work'. . . . Informality in itself is no guarantee of a more reciprocal relationship. It may serve to disguise the operations of power.

[· · ·]

Since the 1950s a growing proportion of secretaries have been both younger and married. It became less feasible, even bigamous, to represent married women as 'office wives', but it was possible to represent them more openly as mature sexual beings. Both of these factors were significant in the moves to represent secretaries in sexual terms.

[· · ·]

The post-war period saw the rapid expansion of all sectors of the economy. As companies grew and diversified, their management structures became . . . more complex and the demand for different types of secretaries increased. There was an expansion of mass consumption and the mass media, the emergence of a sophisticated advertising industry, the commodification of sex and its use to sell a range of other commodities, the preoccupation with glamour and sex appeal and wider participation in clothes, fashion, make-up and so on. In the office, unlike the factory, women could dress in ways that evoked desire. So the growth of offices provided a central site for 'sexuality'. Secretaries were targeted for this treatment, becoming a metaphor or a euphemism for sex. They were a focal point in new discourses about 'sexuality' as identity, adventure, recreation, commodity.

[· · ·]

The earlier image of the secretary as a prim, bespectacled mousy-looking woman in her late thirties was now displaced by the blonde bombshell: not very smart but long-legged, big-bosomed and above all young. In the popular press she is usually perched on the boss's knee taking shorthand while he is winking back at the viewer. This

174

image was obsessionally reiterated in the 1950s and 60s and has since receded somewhat. But it is still the one most readily produced in casual conversation and in tabloids.

[· · ·]

In contrast to the office wife, the 'Dolly' is the 'bad girl', a potentially disruptive presence in the office. While clearly the object of male fantasy, she has a certain power of her own. Where the office wife is subservient, passive and reserved, the Dolly is cheeky and loud and is represented as having an active sexuality and a degree of sexual power over her boss. Where the office wife is a drudge, the Dolly is represented as not doing any serious work at all, as taking the boss for a ride. . . .

Stereotypes do not exist because of their truth functions and they cannot be removed simply by being shown to be an inaccurate account of 'reality'. Whether or not the Dolly Bird exists as a referent, the stereotype affects the ways in which people think about secretaries. The Dolly signifies that secretaries/women are ranked in terms of heterosexual attractiveness and their ability to please a man. Men are always the subjects in these discourses, entitled to comment on women's attractiveness in terms of their own choosing. As with much popular romance the only subject position available for the woman is in advice on how to catch a man or marry the boss.

[· · ·]

Struggling to emerge from the previous two identities is a third one, which emphasizes skill and experience, resists the sexual and familial definitions and plays down the 'special' relationship between boss and secretary in favour of being an autonomous part of the management *team*: this is the career woman. 'Career woman' remains a contradictory term, for it implies questions about whether it is possible both to be a woman and to have a career. Can a 'career woman' maintain her femininity or does she have to give up her gender and become an honorary man? Is it possible to create new understandings of the feminine that are not inconsistent with careers? And is 'femininity' so implicated in our ideas about secretaries that the term 'secretary' would have to be dropped?

The secretary as 'career woman' shares the same origins as the 'office wife': being a 'wife' was itself portrayed as a 'career' for women. It is only since the 1970s that the 'career' secretary, in a larger sense, has gained much public recognition. This is often conceptualized as a transition 'from office wife to office manager' (e.g. ACIBS, 1985). A variety of factors have brought the 'office manager' identity to the fore. They include the struggles of secretaries themselves, supported by the wider women's movement; the more sophisticated communications and decision-making requirements of large corporate structures; severe shortages of people with skills and qualifications; technological change with its implications for the transformation of jobs and skills; and the arrival, [in Australia] in the 1980s, of Equal Employment Opportunity (EEO) and Affirmative Action (AA) legislation which has created at least the potential for a proper recognition of secretarial skills and the opening up of career positions.

[· · ·]

'Professionalization' . . . comes into conflict with 'traditional' expectations. Is it professional to make the tea? There is a tendency to play this down as part of the job, part of the hostessing role, too trivial to make a fuss about. Yet it is of immense symbolic importance, to bosses no less than secretaries. How does a professional image sit with a continued requirement that they do 'office wife' duties? This dilemma is comparable to the one which nurses face. With professionalization, who does the general nursing care? This is part of the question of the relation between professionalization and femininity. How far does success for secretaries, or for that matter any woman, depend on the cultivation of a certain kind of femininity? And does this femininity in itself place limits on what they can achieve? . . .

While the secretaries' organizations were calling for professionalization, other secretaries were becoming more militant. The popularity of a film like *Nine to Five* was that it played with the fantasy of turning the tables on the bosses, allowing the audience vicariously to act out long-suppressed anger and frustration. The 'dolly' fights back in the person of Dolly Parton, making it clear that she is not to be fooled with: and secretaries are represented as skilled workers who are much more capable of running the office than their bosses.

[· · ·]

In the United States organizations like Nine to Five and Women Office Workers developed a national presence, and there has been considerable militancy amongst secretaries (Cassidy and Nusbaum, 1983; Carroll, 1983). In Australia . . . activists among secretaries have preferred to rely on the trade unions, with their strong institutional links and women's caucuses. While the main union covering secretaries in the private sector, the right-wing Federated Clerks' Union (FCU) has done little for its members, the public sector unions have been active in struggles for improved pay and working conditions. . . .

It is only in the context of struggles to improve the conditions of secretaries and to recognize them as skilled workers that it becomes feasible to answer the question 'what is a secretary' by developing a job description.

Article 5.4
PRIVATE EXPERIENCES IN THE PUBLIC DOMAIN: LESBIANS IN ORGANIZATIONS

Marny Hall

. . . Eroticism, not easily consigned to the margins of consciousness, violates the norms which rule that the organization must *appear* to be a sexless, rational realm.

An obvious and intense flirtation between two heterosexual colleagues may not elicit actual censure until the two are discovered *in flagrante delicto* in the staff lounge. In contrast, the person known to be homosexual must do nothing in particular in order to be perceived in terms of excessive eroticism. This role spillover or, more aptly, role suffusion, may bring into consciousness the previously subliminal homosexuality which threads certain apparently innocent homosocial exchanges. Newly self-conscious, the actors may be too inhibited to interact spontaneously. Within the shadowy world of organization sexuality, then, homosexuality must remain within the darkest penumbra, sealed away from any illuminating awareness.

[· · ·]

DOUBLE JEOPARDY: THE CASE OF LESBIANS

Lesbians in particular not only contribute as symbol to this transgression of organizational culture, but their presence also violates the precepts of the organization on a more personal level. . . . According to Chodorow (1978), it is the male's definition of differentness *vis-à-vis* his primary love object – the mother – that accounts for his firm sense of self. Women, for better or worse, forfeit this degree of self-definition, because for them mother represents not difference but similarity. If one considers the role of women in institutions – for example, the organization – it would seem that this process of male individuation, reputedly a stage-specific event, is, instead, a never-ending psycho-social process.

At the same time, women must prove their own credibility in organizations in which they are, in every sense, incredible; they must not overtly (by being too masculine in dress or behaviour) deny males the 'other' they require for their continuing process of self-definition. Rather than analysing the elements in this narrative-building dialogue – how much of it is erotic, where the erotic merges with or parts from particular signs and symbols, roles and statuses etc. – it is important to note how frequently the narrative

177

must, because of slight changes in context, switch tones or modalities. The boss interacts very differently with his secretary in the inner sanctum of his office than he does when she is the designated note taker at a board meeting. When he encounters her again, at lunch, on the company jogging track, there is yet another tonal shift.

The sheer weight of dominant cultural attributions lesbians must carry, if their orientation is known, renders them unavailable for the myriad and quickly shifting micro-projections necessary to maintain and elaborate the male narrative of self. Because her identity is dense with specific meaning, the lesbian cannot be the protean 'other' who can at one moment be perceived as coy, at another motherly, at another seductive and available, and at yet another moment self-contained and competent. Although women, to varying degrees, collude in, or refrain from, this male narrational process, they are forbidden to contradict it by citing an opposing reality. Except to those males who, by particularly strenuous imaginative exertions, can incorporate it into their personal narratives, lesbianism constitutes, *ipso facto*, an opposing reality – a defiance of the mandate to occupy the role of 'other'. The penalty for this mutiny is, within the organization, at the very least, a forfeiture of good will; at the most retaliation, harassment and the loss of one's job.

[· · ·]

[In] a survey distributed at a 1980 meeting of career-oriented lesbians in San Francisco, California, [it was] revealed that thirty-eight (78 per cent) of the fifty-one women responding to the questionnaire felt that disclosing their lesbianism would be a problem. . . . Accompanying the need for protective secrecy was a 'state-of-siege' mentality, a feeling of 'us and them'. Often the feeling associated with these states was anxiety or anger, or both, sometimes in the form of intellectual distance: 'I don't fit in, and I don't necessarily want to'; 'They're so ignorant'; 'You just have to see where they're coming from'.

Even if a subject's lesbianism continued to be a well-kept secret, it was perceived as a disadvantage that caused lesbians to receive 'unfair treatment'. No matter how long they had lived with their partners, lesbians couldn't tap corporate benefits, such as 'family' health insurance or travel bonuses which included spouses. . . . Nor could lesbians play the management game, because they would never have the requisite opposite-sexed spouse and a country club membership in the suburbs.

Being secretive created inner conflicts: 'I wanted to come out, but I just couldn't', as well as constant anxiety about discovery: 'If my bosses knew, they'd find a way to get rid of me'; 'In the case of my supervisees, sometimes it gets emotional, and they might hug me. What would go through their minds if they knew I was a lesbian?'

[· · ·]

Their lesbianism reinforced separation between work and leisure. Some respondents contended that this was congruent with their needs: 'I am a private person anyway. Even if I weren't gay, I wouldn't want to mix work with my life outside work.' For the others the discontinuity was a source of frustration and anger: 'These guys go home and their friends are the same people they see all day. For me, coming to work is bowing out of my world completely and going into theirs'.

The respondents felt conflict between the need or expectation to be open and friendly and their realization that if they were to share the ordinary events of their day-to-day lives they would show that they were different from everyone else. One way to avoid this was simply to avoid heterosexual co-workers. Several respondents said they tried to keep out of personal situations: 'I maintain a professional air and shy away from those issues. I never socialize with them'. Another common strategy to cope with this need for deceit was to dissociate oneself from part of one's behaviour. In the same interview, respondents would talk about ways of concealing their lesbianism while stating firmly, 'I don't hide my gayness'. The use of this form of dissociation spared respondents the knowledge – and attendant self-reproach – about their own deceptiveness and, at the same time, protected them from the anxiety and risks of revelation.

Several comments indicated that at times the respondents experienced their lesbianism as a source of strength. 'Because I am gay, I have more confidence'; and 'There's a feeling of camaraderie with other lesbians at work'.

[· · ·]

Even though the non-disclosure of their homosexuality was crucial, several respondents felt the secret was not always within their control. For example, one woman was showing a friend from work the plans of the new house she and her lover had bought. Pointing out the main bedroom, she accidentally said, 'This is where we sleep'. She was appalled to have revealed the intimate nature of her relationship. Other respondents felt they revealed their lesbianism through their physical appearance. A lesbian who wore jeans to a clerical job said, 'The way I dress I was in a way forcing it down their throats'. Another woman said, 'At the time they started suspecting, I made a mistake and cut my hair short. That was the tip-off'.

[· · ·]

179

Disclosure options

Certain respondents did choose to disclose their lesbianism. Friendship with a co-worker was the primary impetus: 'We'd gotten very close and she shared a lot about her personal life. She kept talking about some gay friends of hers who tended to keep to themselves and exclude her . . . how disappointed she felt. I thought she was trying to let me know it was OK to come out'. Another impetus for disclosure was feeling misunderstood, depersonalized or victimized. One woman said, 'They sit there every day and make cracks about gays. I don't say anything. One day I'm just going to yell "Surprise! I'm one of them"'.

[· · ·]

Disclosure had the paradoxical effect of magnifying the problem of concealment because now one or more others were included in keeping the secret. After an initial release, these women experienced increased tension because of the greater possibility of inadvertent disclosure. The new heterosexual confidante didn't have the same investment in secrecy as did the lesbian involved and had nothing to lose – and perhaps something to gain – by passing on the woman's secret. And respondents had the additional worry of implicating their friends. If their lesbianism became known widely, their lovers or friends who worked in the same company might also be labelled as lesbians.

[· · ·]

IMPLICATIONS AND CONCLUSIONS

Rather like a horse that finds itself simultaneously reined in and spurred on, corporate lesbians are caught in a crossfire of conflicting cultural and subcultural imperatives. The strategies lesbians used to manoeuvre their ways through this thicket of contradictions reveals that the old reductionist notion of 'coming out' is not an act, but rather a never-ending and labyrinthine process of decision and indecision, of nuanced and calculated presentations as well as impulsive and inadvertent revelations – a process, in short, as shifting as the contexts in which it occurs.

[· · ·]

The rare lesbian who reveals her orientation, and who survives the consequences of violating the gendered expectations which structure the organization, succumbs . . . to the organization in another way. Stylized out of existence, she forfeits her private mutinies, cannot mobilize the resistance necessary to shield her individuality from engulfment by the collective purpose of the organization. Homogenized, the token corporate lesbian becomes the consummate 'organization (wo)man'.

Article 5.5
GENDER DIVISIONS IN A POST-FORDIST ERA: NEW CONTRADICTIONS OR THE SAME OLD STORY?

Linda McDowell

... The scale and nature of economic change in advanced industrial societies in the last two decades has ... [made it] virtually axiomatic in a range of economic and geographic literature to distinguish two [highly] distinct economic regimes ... [Fordism and post-Fordism]. However, I shall argue that a marked continuity in the role of women in the labour market is a unifying, rather than distinguishing, feature of both regimes.

The Fordist regime that spanned the period of post-war reconstruction from the mid-1940s until the late 1960s was based on mass production and stable demand in mass markets. Rising public expenditure underpinned rising real incomes and led to a sustained period of economic growth with high aggregate spending on consumption. Women were drawn in increasing numbers into tight labour markets, in part to meet the costs of the mass consumption life style. Their entry was facilitated by the provision of a range of social welfare services that to a degree mitigated women's family responsibilities. These included state income support, care for the elderly and other dependants and limited child care provision. These services themselves created significant employment opportunities for women as they relied on a predominantly female labour force and the expansion of educational and training opportunities provided women with skills and training that also improved their labour market position.

Women's entry into wage labour in this period was not, however, on equal terms with men. Even in the newly expanding public sector, women were concentrated at the bottom of the occupational hierarchy, trapped in the ghettos of 'female' jobs where caring and servicing were seen as desirable but poorly rewarded attributes. In the manufacturing sector women also were concentrated in less skilled and low-paid jobs. In Britain, in particular, part-time employment with less security and fewer occupational rights and benefits was a key strategy in expanding female employment. Thus traditional ideas about gender roles combined with labour market regulation created a labour force that was highly segmented by gender.

The fundamental economic and political changes that occurred from the early 1970s [summarized by the term 'post-Fordism'] reinforced, rather than restructured, women's ambiguous place in the labour market. Faced by the internationalization of capital and increasing competition from newly industrializing countries, as well as competition between the advanced industrial economies, the link between mass production and stable domestic demand broke down. Keynesian economic and welfare policies proved ineffective in the face of recession, rising unemployment and inflation. . . . Neo-liberal ideologies that placed blame for the widespread recession in the early 1980s on state intervention in the market gained dominance. This new emphasis on market mechanisms lies behind the partial dismantling of the welfare state in Britain, with greater reliance on the rhetoric of consumer sovereignty and market provision. Increased diversification and the fragmentation of mass demand led to changes in the production process and in the composition and organization of the labour market. New methods of industrial organization, the development of just-in-time systems, a speed up in the rate of turnover and product innovation, the vertical and horizontal disaggregation of tasks, both the concentration and the deconcentration of ownership and the movement towards industrial decentralization have been associated with greater flexibility in the employment of labour and new forms of contracts. In this move towards flexibility, women have emerged as increasingly desirable employees. Their traditional attachment to the labour force developed in the Fordist era mirrors the new pattern of flexible working – viz. temporary work, discontinuous periods of employment, part-time contracts, less eligibility for 'fringe' benefits. It begins to appear as if women are the new model workers of the post-Fordist regime.

The continuity in women's labour market position under both regimes has not, however, been a feature that has been greatly emphasized by either the adherents or opponents of the post-Fordist thesis. Indeed, in a remarkably optimistic reading of current trends, Piore and Sabel, proponents of *The Second Industrial Divide* (1984) version of this thesis, have managed, by concentrating their attention on the new high-skill and high-wage sectors of the restructured economy, to argue that flexible specialization has an emancipatory potential for labour. The irony of this view for women whose increased penetration of the labour market is based on their disadvantaged position goes unremarked. Other versions of the flexible specialization/post-Fordist vision of the future have remarked on the increasing labour market divides, particularly the bifurcation into a skilled and permanent core and a temporary, exploited periphery. The recognition that workers are gendered, however, goes little further than attributing all women to the peripheral labour market, along with other 'marginal' groups such as immigrants and members of ethnic minority populations. . . .

. . . Not only . . . [is] women's labour . . . central to the current economic transformation but . . . they are being drawn into wage labour in ways that both deepen pre-existing patterns of exploitation and at the same time open up opportunities for certain women. . . . The changes are complex and contradictory. . . . In the particular context of women's position, I argue that new class divisions are opening up between women and between households who are differentially placed in the restructuring process.

[· ·]

WOMEN'S WORK IN THE POST-FORDIST REGIME: RESTRUCTURING THE GENDER DIVISION OF LABOUR

One of the central features of the labour market restructuring that characterizes the post-Fordist regime has been a shift to new types of labour, employed under different conditions. The changing nature of employment has been variously dubbed as flexible, contingent or peripheral – that is, for many workers there is no longer an expectation that their attachment to the labour market will be permanent. Full-time, life-long employment in a single industry working for the same employer increasingly is a pattern of the past for all but a core of privileged workers. This core consists in the main of professionals and an élite group of manufacturing workers. Part-time employment, especially in the service sector, has expanded considerably over the last two decades, as has casual and temporary work. This has led to the identification of a dual labour market that is a permanent feature of the overall structure of the post-Fordist regime rather than a declining or residual feature of industrial Fordism. The core of well-paid permanently employed workers, relatively well protected from the vicissitudes of economic recession or inflationary growth, are distinguished from a growing margin of poorly paid, casual and dispensable workers, many of whom are women. Apart from such fleeting references, however, the full significance of the growing numbers of women in the labour market, in both the core as well as in the periphery as will become apparent, has yet to be recognized. It is here, in the feminization of the labour force, that a potential crisis of reproduction has its origin.

WOMEN'S PARTICIPATION IN WAGED LABOUR

During the years of crisis and economic restructuring there has been an important alteration in the gender composition of the British labour market. In 1988, 70 per cent of British women of working age (15–59 years) were in paid employment or seeking work, compared with only 56 per cent in 1971. Between these dates, male employment as a whole in Britain fell by almost 1.8 million, whereas the employment of women increased by almost exactly the same number of jobs (1.7 m.). Several factors are important in explaining this change: the so-called deindustrialization of the economy, the restructuring strategies of capital, especially the flexible use of labour, the impact of the demographic 'time bomb', the labour market and family policies of the state and changing social norms about women's position.

Table 5.5.1 Trends in men and women's employment, 1971–1988 (Great Britain)

			Employees in employment (June)			
	Males	**Females**	**Females as % of total**	**% Female full-timers**	**% Female part-timers**	**% Share of part-timers of all females**
1971	13,424	8,224	38.0	25.3	12.6	33.5
1976	13,097	8,951	40.4	24.3	16.3	39.6
1981	12,278	9,108	42.6	24.7	17.8	41.9
1986	11,643	9,462	44.8	25.2	19.6	42.4
1988	11,978	10,096	45.7	26.2	19.5	42.8

(Source: Department of Employment, *Employment Gazette*, various dates)

Sectoral change in the economy and the greater use of types of flexible labour are among the most important factors affecting the demand for female labour. Despite an evident academic fascination with the labour process in manufacturing, it is the growth of service sector employment that has had the greatest effect on the gender division of labour in the British economy. The total number of workers in manufacturing has declined from its peak in 1955 and since that date the growth of employment has been in the service sector. The decline in manufacturing has, however, been particularly steep in the decade since 1979. By the end of the 1980s, 68 per cent of all workers were employed in the service sector. Although service sector employment has expanded for both women and for men, it is for women that the growth has been particularly significant. Whereas 56 per cent of all male workers are service employees, the sector employs 81 per cent of all women workers and no less than 91 per cent of female part-time workers.

The growth of part-time work for women has been a particularly marked feature of post-Fordist restructuring in Britain. Activity rates for full-time female employment actually fell in the 1970s (from 37 to 33 per cent) and remained static until 1986 when they began to rise. Over the same period, part-time employment rose steadily, even through the years of severe recession between 1979 and 1981. Because the increasing feminization of the British labour market has been achieved through the use of part-time labour, however, the figure of a 1.7 million increase in the total number of women workers exaggerates the opening up of opportunities for women in the tertiary sector. Rather, what the 1970s and 1980s restructuring has achieved is the *sharing out* of employment between larger numbers of women. The trend towards the 'flexible' use of labour through part-time employment contracts is exacerbated by the particular nature of the social insurance system in Great Britain in which both employer and employee contributions are less than for full-time workers. This brings with it severely restricted entitlement to a range of social benefits such as unemployment and sick pay as well as poorer provision of work-related entitlements such as holidays and security of employment.

Table 5.5.2 Ratio of hourly earnings of female to male full-time employees, Great Britain

1971–1989

1971	1972	1973	1974	1975	1976	1977
63.3	63.4	63.2	65.4	69.7	73.2	74.2
1978	**1979**	**1980**	**1981**	**1982**	**1983**	**1984**
72.9	71.3	72.4	72.6	72.4	75.0	74.2
1985	**1986**	**1987**	**1988**	**1989**		
74.7	74.1	73.4	74.9	76.0		

Until 1983 male adult employees were those aged twenty-one and over, female adults eighteen and over; from 1983 the figures are for all those on adult rates. The 1983 estimate on the former basis is 73.1. All figures exclude overtime payments.
(Source: *New Earnings Surveys*)

Married women's labour market participation

The majority of women who work part-time are married women. Indeed, one of the most noticeable effects of the expansion of part-time work in the 1970s and 1980s has been the rising activity rates among married women. The proportion of married women in paid employment in the late 1980s was barely lower than the proportion for single women (59 per cent and 60 per cent respectively). However, domestic and family responsibilities exert an important influence on the pattern and timing of women's waged work. The presence of children and, in particular, the age of the youngest child, is the most important factor in women's employment careers. Participation rates in Great Britain vary from 41 per cent for mothers with children under five, 70 per cent for mothers of children aged between five and nine, and 77 per cent for mothers of older children. Typically, women with children have a bimodal pattern of participation with peak rates prior to childbirth and after the youngest child reaches the age of nine. Whereas full-time employment is usual before having children, the majority of returning mothers re-enter the labour market on a part-time basis. In addition, many women experience downward social mobility on re-entry, taking employment that does not match their educational attainment or previous skill levels.

During the 1970s and 1980s these patterns of participation by mothers have begun to change. The time between leaving and re-entering the labour market declined over the two decades from over seven years to a little over three years by 1989 and increasing numbers of women work between births. Thus the conventional view that women's attachment to the labour market is temporary increasingly is incorrect. The majority of women now engage in waged labour for most of their 'working' lives and many women do not leave the labour force even after childbirth. The trend towards continuous employment is particularly marked among women working in family enterprises, especially shops and farms, and among women with professional qualifications. The women who are most likely to depart are unskilled workers in the manufacturing sector and service sector employees. These women's labour market attachment is less strong than either men's or their professional sisters' and their career patterns remain discontinuous. To a large degree employers have been able to base their labour market restructuring strategies on the availability of such a labour pool.

But it is a mistake to assume that the interests of women and employers coincide here. It is too often assumed that women with children prefer to work on a part-time basis. The Department of Employment in Britain clearly holds this view: as they explained to a House of Lords Select Committee (1988) investigation of part-time employment, 'while there are clearly disadvantages which part-timers suffer in relation to full-timers, it is possible to see this as a price which part-timers are prepared to pay for the opportunity to fit work into other commitments'. But a range of evidence makes it increasingly clear that part-time workers themselves find the price too high. Part-time, 'flexible' work has not been created in response to 'demand' on the part of workers, whether men or women. Rather, many have had part-time or temporary jobs imposed on them or have taken them for want of alternatives while continuing to seek full-time and stable work (Hakim, 1987, pp. 549–60).

[· · ·]

It seems clear that women's significance in the labour market will not decline in the near future. Whether the marginal status and low pay levels of the majority of women workers will improve is, however, a more open question. During the 1990s, married women with children will continue to be the most important element in recruitment to the labour market. In the UK, the Department of Employment estimated in 1989 that 80 per cent of the new entrants in the first three years of the 1990s would be exactly this group, partly as a consequence of the demographic 'time-bomb'. Between 1987 and 1995 the number of under 25-year-olds in the UK labour market is projected to fall by 1.2 million (approximately 20 per cent) (Department of Employment, 1988). The need to attract women into the labour market to retain its overall size at approximately the same level as in the early years of the decade led the Department to issue advice to employers:

> Employers must recognise that women can no longer be treated as second class workers. They will need women workers, and must recognise both their career ambitions and domestic responsibilities. This will involve broadening company training policies, much more flexibility of work and hours and job-sharing to facilitate the employment of women with families and help adapt to their needs.

(Department of Employment, 1988)

Whether the Department really intended to so freely admit the second class status of women workers in the past or not, its current advice seems to guarantee its continuance. It appears to be taken for granted that women's 'domestic responsibilities' are theirs and theirs alone. No vision here of a more equal division of domestic tasks and a corresponding need for flexible work practices for men to enable them to shoulder dual roles. It is assumed that employers' previous neglect of the flexible work practices needed to attract women in larger numbers into the labour market is the constraint on raising numbers and that this might easily be remedied by changing attitudes and methods of work organization. What is equally clear is that women's exploited position in the labour market is not seen as an issue to be tackled. Rather, the attributes associated with their gender – and particularly their continuing responsibility for domestic labour and child care – are seen as immutable. . . . Women continue to be constructed as marginal labour with particular characteristics that mean that their attachment to the labour market is temporary or flexible.

But as the Department of Employment has recognized, women workers will play an increasingly significant role in economic restructuring in the 1990s and their designation as 'marginal' or part of the 'peripheral' labour market both in the academic literature on economic change and also in practice through the newly recognized and recommended – but in fact for women long-standing

– forms of 'flexible' attachment to the labour market, disguises their *centrality* to the post-Fordist economy.

[· · ·]

GAINS OR LOSSES FOR WOMEN?

[· · ·]

There can be little doubt that for most women their increasing integration into the wage economy of post-Fordist Britain has reinforced rather than challenged existing structures of inequality in the labour market. Indeed, as Rubery and Tarling tartly remark: 'women's employment has been protected and expanded not because women are progressively overcoming their relative disadvantage in the labour market, but because of the continued existence of these disadvantages which causes them to be an attractive source of labour supply to employers for particular sorts of jobs' (Rubery and Tarling, 1988, p. 126). So for most women the notion of emancipatory forms of labour market organization or morally desirable new flexible working patterns 'predicated on collaboration' between employer and employees (Piore and Sabel, 1984, p. 278) remains a chimera. While there can be little doubt that the entry into waged work brings increased self-respect for most women, some greater degree of control over economic resources and may reduce subordination in the home, the real material gains for working-class women have not been significant. Low-paid work and continued domestic labour in the home based on traditional gender divisions is the lot of most women. When placed in the context of the extremely poor public provision of family support services in Britain, particularly child care, ... the net result is that women are shouldering a disproportionate share of the cost of economic restructuring.

New gender and household divisions

The economic restructuring of the last two decades has, however, also opened up new divisions between women and between households. While the particular effects for individual women and their households will depend on a complex set of social circumstances including age, race, family status and composition, housing market position and location within the country, it seems that one of the consequences has been a growing class division between women. A small minority of women, especially those who have acquired professional qualifications, have captured labour market opportunities and the rewards traditionally reserved for male labour. As the vast majority of women in Britain live with a male partner and as, despite cross-class marriages, women in professional occupations have a tendency to choose a partner in a similar social position, the divisions opening up between women as individuals also are

Table 5.5.3 Distribution of gross hourly earnings of full-time adult employees

	Ratios to median				Ratio of women's wages to men's	
	Men		Women		%s	
	'80	'89	'80	'89	'80	'89
Top decile	175	200	169	193	71	76
Top quartile	130	140	126	139	72	78
Median	100	100	100	100	73	78
Lowest quartile	81	76	81	78	76	80
Lowest decile	68	60	70	64	76	83
Mean					72	76

1980 sample: men twenty-one and over, women eighteen and over.
1989 sample: workers on adult rates.
(Source: *New Earnings Survey*, Table 26, overtime excluded)

reflected in a resorting of households and a greater degree of stratification between the 'winners' and the 'losers'.

... Although the 1970s had seen a lessening of the gender differential, the 1980s saw no diminution in the disparity between men and women's wage rates. Instead, the decade was marked by a widening differential between workers of the *same* sex: an 'upheaval, after a decade of stability, in the degree of inequality' (Ermisch *et al.*, 1990). Table 5.5.3 shows how the income distribution for men and for women in full-time employment opened out over the decade, increasing the share earned by the top decile and reducing that of the bottom 10 per cent. The distribution for women remained somewhat less unequal than that for men at the end of the decade, although women in the most highly paid occupations made clear gains. The final column reveals that *all* women in full-time work gained relative to men.

The most marked discrepancies for women, however, are between those who are employed on a full-time basis and those who work part-time. For this latter group the decade was not one of labour market gains. Part-timers' relative hourly pay fell during the 1980s from 81 per cent of female full-timers to 75 per cent in 1989 (New Earnings Survey, 1989). For these women labour market participation seldom brings with it the prospect of economic independence. Indeed, it might be argued that the expansion of low-wage part-time work for women over the 1980s in combination with the decline of well-paid work for working-class men has actually reduced working-class women's prospect of economic independence and, particularly in tight local housing markets, has made 'coupledom' almost an economic necessity.

[· · ·]

THE CHANGING RELATIONSHIP BETWEEN PRODUCTION AND REPRODUCTION IN THE POST-FORDIST ERA

[· · ·]

The declining need for domestic labour

Women's large-scale and permanent entry into the labour market poses a . . . challenge to orthodox arguments, whether from a post-Fordist or feminist perspective. The circumstances of the 1980s have cast doubt on the necessity of domestic labour, whether for capital or for individual men. The disappearance of the family wage in the economic transformation of recent years means that fewer and fewer men can afford to support the services of a full-time homemaker. And capital has discovered that the exploitation of women's cheap labour maintains profit levels. Overall, amounts of domestic labour in the economy can be reduced without disaster. Male workers seem able still to perform their tasks without a cooked breakfast and ironed clothes. Although it is women who continue to perform the vast majority of the tasks of domestic labour, . . . the total number of hours has declined. By definition, women who work for wages have less time for other tasks. But a larger scale change has also increased capital's indifference to what goes on in the home. The significance of labour power produced *in situ* has declined. Capital is now internationally mobile and relatively independent of a working class born and raised in a particular place. . . .

If capital does not seem to need domestic labour anymore, what of individual men? Barbara Ehrenreich's pithy comment is instructive: '. . . men have an unexpected ability to survive on fast food and the emotional solace of short-term relationships' (Ehrenreich, 1985, p. 273). Ehrenreich has suggested that, with hindsight, the model of capitalism implied by the capitalism-plus-patriarchy equation of socialist-feminist theory seems too benevolent. The caring and nurturing work of women was assumed to be a *systemic* need, projected on to the impersonal structures of advanced capitalist society. The world that this model explained is already receding from view:

> a world of relative affluence and apparent stability – where categories like 'the family', 'the state' and 'the economy' were fixed . . . Today there is little that we can take as fixed. 'The family' so long reified in theory, looks more like an improvisation than an institution. A new technological

190

revolution on the scale of the one that swept in industrial capitalism (and state socialism) is transforming not only production but perception. Whole industries collapse into obsolescence; entire classes face ruthless dislocation, everywhere women are being proletarianised and impoverished, becoming migrants, refugees, and inevitably 'cheap labour'.

(*Ehrenreich, 1985, p. 275*)

As well as changes in the relationship between women's wage labour and domestic labour, the collective institutions of social reproduction are being recast in the post-Fordist period, creating dislocations, innovations and crises.

[· · ·]

These [new forms] tend to be based on state withdrawal and consequently on private market provision and greater voluntary community effort.

In Britain, in justifying the cuts in the state provision of welfare in the 1980s, there has been a marked reliance in the official discourse of the state on an idealized version of the family and an appeal to 'Victorian' values. The juxtaposition of these two notions – the family and Victorian values – is significant, for the vision of the family that lies behind this rhetoric is that same reified one that has now receded into the past. It is a nuclear family headed by a male *paterfamilias* and breadwinner, and based on a strict gender division of labour. In this idealized vision the primary significance of motherhood is reasserted for women. Caring and serving in the home and in the community is presented as an ideal to aim for.

[· · ·]

The state, unlike capital, is increasingly reliant on women's unpaid labour in the sphere of reproduction. This is seen most clearly in the movement towards 'community care', rather than institutional provision, for the elderly, disabled and terminally ill. In the debates about community care there has been the familiar juxtaposition of moral responsibility and personal achievement *vis-à-vis* collective provision that saps initiative.

[· · ·]

A NEW CRISIS?

... The welfare state and the benefit system in Britain continue to depend on idealized gender divisions in a nuclear family that no longer exists. This dependence of women on men in the welfare sector has been strengthened in a decade when changes in the economy increasingly have challenged it. This contradiction between restructuring in the spheres of reproduction and production has, so far, been contained by greater inputs of female labour to both spheres. But the consequent 'social speed up' is not infinitely extendable.

The seeds of a crisis, but also of struggle and renegotiation, lie in this contradiction. The association between industrial organization and the institutions of social regulation is being recast in the post-Fordist era in a contradictory way that places gender relations at the centre. Women's labour power is an increasingly important element in both the arenas of production and reproduction. Capital has resolved the contradiction between the short-term needs of the economy for cheap female labour and the long-term needs for social reproduction in favour of the former requirement. At the same time the state is also withdrawing from the latter area. The resolution of this contradiction so far has been at the individual level, by the purchase of goods and services for reproduction in the market by an affluent minority and by an increased reliance on the labour of individual women in almost all households. It seems unlikely that the current UK government will resolve the contradiction inherent in the post-Fordist restructuring by re-introducing collective provision. Even in the area of child care, which is pitifully inadequate in Great Britain, responsibility is assumed to lie with the individual or with employers.

. . . The competing and contradictory needs and interests regarding women's role in the home and in the labour market create new cleavages and scope for new alliances. Any 'economic' analysis that ignores the centrality of the gender division of labour, and issues of housework, child care and the support of the expanding dependent population, is an inadequate explanation of the nature of contemporary industrial restructuring. Nor can such an analysis point the way to a political understanding of how such restructuring may be challenged.

[· · ·]

PART IV
WOMEN AND POLITICS

INTRODUCTION:
REDEFINING POLITICS

In the preceding parts of this book, we have shown how women, albeit divided by race and ethnic origin, by class, age and sexual orientation, have been defined in particular ways at certain times by the institutions and practices of the state, civil society and the economy. But women have never been passive agents in these definitions and have struggled to contest and renegotiate their position. Here in Part IV, we turn to an examination of certain instances of these struggles. The conventional literature of political science has had very little to say about women's political involvement and where it has addressed this issue it has tended to convey an erroneous image of women's political passivity or conservatism. For example, it has been widely assumed that, in the UK and elsewhere, women are more conservative, more moralistic and less interested in political questions than are men.

Since the 1970s, a feminist literature has emerged to redress many of these misconceptions and stereotypes. In the literature on voting alliances, for example, it has been found that in the UK and the USA, when women's age, education and occupation are taken into account, they are not as conservative as might appear at first sight. For example, in general elections in the UK during the 1980s, young women were more likely to vote for the central parties and for the Labour party than for Conservative candidates. And throughout the same decade, a 'gender gap' appeared in US politics in which women were more progressive on social issues than men. But feminists have not only 'added women' into political science, they have also challenged the definition of the subject itself, arguing that a range of 'informal' political campaigns, outside the structures of formal power, are a legitimate object of analysis. On this wider definition, women's actions – ranging from international co-operation, for example, between women in the clothing trade to challenge their exploitation, through issue-based campaigns such as women's peace camps to very local-scale mobilization, perhaps to improve a local school – all fall under the rubric of politics.

A number of important issues are raised by women's political participation. First, what are the sorts of issues around which women have mobilized and how have these evolved, historically and between countries? Secondly, how do these actions – around different issues at different times – fit into an overall campaign to challenge women's subordination? Thirdly, and related to the second point, are political campaigns around 'women's issues' necessarily feminist, or progressive, by their very nature? Because women come together as women to protest, do their activities therefore constitute a distinctive form of protest that should be analysed as such?

The last questions summarize what is perhaps *the* central issue of women's political participation: how can we organize 'as women', giving the meaning of womanhood or femininity, of so-called women's issues, a solid political meaning as a basis for struggle, while at the same time working to dismantle this very meaning, its long history and social construction on the basis of exclusion from power? This dilemma, or contradiction, lies at the heart of the history of women's political organization, around issues as varied as the campaign for suffrage, the peace movement, women's involvement in trade unions, in campaigns for equal pay, in women's diverse reactions to the increasing power of fundamental religious movements, and in struggles such as those by the Mothers of the Plaza de Mayo in Argentina from the late 1970s onwards to have their children returned to them. Some of these forms of political protest and action will be examined in Part IV.

6
WOMEN AND CITIZENSHIP

The two articles in Chapter 6 address the ways in which women have campaigned to become citizens – to enter the political arena as equals with men. However, as the articles show, equality in the formal or liberal sense has limitations for women. In Article 6.1, Anne Phillips, as a political scientist, unpacks the notions of equality, equal rights and sexual difference. In particular, she examines the parallels and differences between feminism and liberalism, as the latter developed in seventeenth- and eighteenth-century Europe and North America. She shows how the first stage of feminist organizing – the suffrage movement – seized on the notions of equality and civil rights to argue for formal equality and equal rights to citizenship with men. More recently, however, feminist political scientists, including Phillips and Carole Pateman, whose article about the welfare state is the other reading for this chapter, have argued that the central dimensions of citizenship, far from being gender neutral, actually construct men and women differently because of women's association with the family and the private sphere. This difference between women and men undermines notions of equality and citizenship and, as Pateman demonstrates, means that we have to analyse the patriarchal structure of the modern state.

In Part I, the ways in which women's position in advanced societies is constructed through various dimensions of state policy were indicated. Taxation policies, social welfare institutions, the role of the law, all play a central part in defining women as wives, mothers and workers, in constructing their dependence on men and in the definition of particular issues and domains as private. Thus central dimensions of the roles of women are constituted by their relationship to the state. Similarly, the central institutions of state policy, in particular those of the welfare state, embody and depend upon particular notions of femininity, motherhood and women's central role in the family.

There is a vast literature on the role of the state in advanced industrial nations, a great deal of it concerned with the extent to which the state reflects the interests of capital or of specific economic classes, or, alternatively, is relatively or totally autonomous from the economy and civil society, reflecting the outcome of struggles between diverse interest groups. While it is impossible to provide a detailed summary of these arguments here, it is pertinent to note briefly a number of influential developments in these debates. These will help to put into context the different conceptions of the state that have influenced feminist writing on the institutions of the welfare state in the UK, and also women's practical involvement in state institutions. The following short extract from Yuval-Davis' and Anthias' book *Woman-Nation-State* (1989) provides a useful introduction:

> Contemporary analyses of the state have tended to broaden out the conception of the state from seeing it purely as a managerial structure, on the one hand, or as centrally dedicated to repression, coercion, force and social control, on the other. First there has been a shift towards looking at the state as incorporating a number of institutions whose role appears strictly private and/or primarily 'ideological' (such as the church, the family, the school, the media etc.). Secondly there has been a tendency to see the state as the place where the global interests of capital are expressed, either in the sense of capital accumulation or in the sense of the state as co-ordinating the different interests and activities of fractions of capital. The main difficulty here lies in being able to specify the mechanisms or intentionality at work and the processes by which they are achieved, a particular problem faced by any form of functionalism. This approach is similar in form if not in content to seeing the state as an arena within which different social forces can articulate their interests and therefore as a kind of battleground where, however, for the functionalist the winner is always already known! Finally, partly as a result of some of the theoretical and empirical difficulties involved in specifying the state, a further tendency has been to reject the idea of a unitary state and focus on social policies, the law, institutional arrangements and discourses as heterogeneous elements which are not reducible to 'the state'. This work has rightly pointed out that the effects of these practices neither emanate from a given primary source nor do they have unitary effects.
>
> Having sketched out very briefly the terms of reference in some of the writings on the state, we can now turn first to the issue of the links between the state and civil society and second to the relationship specifically with gender divisions and women. We share the view that the state is neither unitary in its practices, its intentions nor its effects. Nonetheless, we feel it is useful to retain the concept of the state. The term refers to a particular 'machinery' for the exercise of 'government'

over a given population, usually territorially and nationally defined, although the definitions of what constitutes these boundaries etc. will shift and change depending on what it is government or power over and what is being managed or negotiated. Hence we can specify the state in terms of a body of institutions which are centrally organised around the intentionality of control with a given apparatus of enforcement at its command and basis. Coercion and repression are then to be seen both as forms of control and as a back-up. Different forms of the state will involve different relationships between the control/coercion twin which is the residing characteristic of the state. Using this formulation, the state can harness a number of different processes, including ideological ones, through juridical and repressive mechanisms at its command. Education and the media are the prime institutional forms for ideological production in the modern liberal-democratic state but they are not part of the state as such.

Civil society includes those institutions, collectivities, groupings and social agencies which lie outside the formal rubric of state parameters as outlined but which both informs and is informed by them. This includes the family, social strata, ethnic and national groupings to note some of the most significant, as well as institutions like those of education, trade unions and the means of communication like the media. These produce their own ideological contents as well as being subjected to those of the state. In this way ideology does not reside (in a privileged sense) in either civil society or the state nor is it monolithic in terms of its contents. There is a question regarding, however, the degree to which the state is able to tolerate those forms that conflict with its political project. Again, different forms of the state and different historical and regional differences exist worldwide in this respect. To avoid both a static essentialism and functionalism, it is important to consider the state both in terms of its intentions and in terms of its effects. This involves looking at the specific political projects of states and the economic and social context within which they are articulated as well as the social forces that both construct and oppose them.

(Yuval-Davis and Anthias, 1989, pp. 4–6)

Many 'women's' and/or feminist struggles have been involved with the specific political projects of the state. Here our focus is on the welfare state. In the next chapter we will look at the role of the legal system in addressing gender inequalities and at the institution of religion.

THE WELFARE STATE AND GENDER DIVISIONS

The increasing intervention of the institutions of the post-war welfare state in the UK in previously 'private' issues – child welfare, the regulation of sexuality, notions of the rights and responsibilities of different household members – has meant that the welfare state has been an arena of central concern to feminists in the second-wave women's movement. This is not to deny, of course, either earlier interventions in 'family' life by the state and by the church, for example, nor to ignore pre-Second World War campaigns to improve the welfare of women and children.

The changing relationship between public and private responsibilities – or more correctly between state and non-state responsibilities – has been an important area of interest among social scientists, including feminists, for many years. Debates about the role of the state in contemporary Britain intensified during the 1980s as the nature and philosophical basis of state intervention was questioned. This questioning came mainly, but not solely, from critics from the radical right of the political spectrum. During the Thatcher era it was argued that the state had become a 'nanny' state, sapping the moral fibre of the nation and interfering unnecessarily in what were essentially private matters between individuals. An ideological preference for the provision of goods and services through the market, rather than by the state, led to the introduction of welfare policies to 'roll back the boundaries of the state', to enhance individual responsibility for welfare, and to changes in the nature and structure of provision, especially the introduction of community care during the 1980s. But for others too, of different political persuasions, a critique of the institutions of the welfare state as insensitive, bureaucratic and remote from everyday concerns has been a continuing theme.

Feminist responses to the growth of state intervention and its consequent impact on women and 'the family' have also varied from a passionate belief in the positive benefits of legislation and state provision, through to analyses that emphasized the pervasive and oppressive nature of state intervention in women's lives. Critics of the state have argued that it sustains a particularly oppressive family form and women's continued economic dependence on men. More recently, feminist scholars have re-evaluated the nature and impact of state intervention, suggesting that it may have contradictory effects for women: neither completely positive nor completely negative.

For the feminists who wrote about the welfare state in the early years of the second-wave women's movement from the late 1960s onwards, the perspective shifted towards an emphasis on the patriarchal power of the state. There was a greater awareness of the ways in which welfare provisions were based upon a particular view of women's nature and their responsibilities in modern Britain. Thus, for example, the views of Beveridge, the architect of the 1940s' reforms, about the importance of the family as an economic unit and women's place within it, were frequently quoted:

> In any measure of social policy in which regard is had to facts, the great majority of married women must be regarded as occupied on work which is vital though unpaid, without which their husbands could not do their paid work and without which the nation could not continue.
>
> (Beveridge, 1942, p. 49)

This statement has a resonance with the views of socialist feminists about the necessity of domestic labour for capitalist production (see Ehrenreich, Article 4.4 in this volume). The institutional structure of the welfare state established in the 1940s was built on the assumption that men were the family breadwinners and that their wives and children were their economic dependants. Their crucial work in the home was seen as an essential component of the current social organization.

In her influential book *Women and the Welfare State* (1977), which is representative of feminists' view of the state as an oppressive institution common throughout the 1970s, Elizabeth Wilson argued that the institutions of the welfare state were not only based on a particular view of femininity but were themselves part of its very *construction*. Thus she suggested that:

> the manipulations of the Welfare State offer a unique demonstration of how the State can prescribe what women's consciousness should be . . . [F]eminism has made it possible for us to see how the State defines femininity and that this definition is not marginal but is central to the purposes of welfarism. Woman is above all Mother, and with this vocation go all the virtues of femininity; submission, nurturance, passivity.
>
> (Wilson, 1977, p. 7)

In other words, the same characteristics which, as we saw in Part III, are part of the social construction of women as waged workers are also embodied in and reinforced by the institutions and practices of the welfare state.

Thus in numerous ways, the welfare state relies on assumptions about femininity and about women's role in the family: women, and in particular mothers, are, in the main, the clients of the welfare state. Here is Wilson again:

> The 'feminine client' of the social services waits patiently at clinics, social security offices, and housing departments to be ministered to sometimes by the paternal authority figure,

sometimes by the nurturant yet firm model of femininity provided by the nurse or social worker; in either case she goes away to do as she has been told – to take the pills, to love the baby.

(Ibid., p. 8)

As this extract indicates, the welfare state relies on the unpaid labour of women to link the public and the private spheres. Although many goods and services previously provided in the family are now part of the public arena, somebody (and that somebody is usually a woman) has to ensure that the clients of the welfare state are in the right place at the right time – children need to be delivered to and collected from school, especially when young, and somebody has to ensure that patients and clients arrive to wait for their appointments at the appropriate places at the right times.

By providing welfare services that are dependent on women's unpaid work – for example, community care rather than residential care for elderly people and for people with disabilities, by limiting the provision of day nurseries, through the incorporation in a range of policies from housing to education of women as child carers – the policies and institutions of welfare result in nothing less than, according to Wilson 'the *State organisation of domestic life*' (original author's emphasis) (Wilson, 1977, p. 9).

In these accounts the relationship between the state and women is straightforwardly oppressive and repressive. The state itself is seen as patriarchal and as capitalist and policies are presented as uni-directional and non-contradictory. In more recent feminist analyses these assertions have been questioned and a more contradictory relationship between the aims and effects of welfare policies, the position of women and the links between the state and the nuclear family has been drawn out. There has also been some unpacking of the notion of the state itself and the assumption that it is a homogeneous entity. Over time it is clear that redefinitions of family relationships are embodied in state policies. The rights of women, men and children have not remained unchanged, nor has the assumption of an 'ideal' nuclear family gone unchallenged. The rights and obligations of spouses in marriage and divorce, for example, have been fundamentally altered by legislation throughout the nineteenth and twentieth centuries, from the Married Women's Property Acts in 1870 and 1882 to the Divorce Reform Act in 1969 (implemented in 1971) which for the first time introduced the notion of 'no fault' divorce. More recently, assumptions about the rights and obligations of parents are being reassessed as cases of violence against children, and child sexual abuse, influence notions of parental responsibility and notions of which issues are public and which are private.

Further, if it is assumed that the aim of state welfare policies is to reinforce a particular patriarchal family form – that of a male breadwinner and a dependent mother – current social trends are clearly proving these policies somewhat ineffective. For example, one in twelve recent marriages ends in divorce; unmarried cohabitation and births outside legal marriage are increasing (almost 30 per cent of all births at the end of the 1980s in Great Britain were outside legal marriage), and women, especially mothers of young children, are entering the labour market in ever greater numbers. So, the presumption that the state is reproducing a particular family form in the interests either of capital or of men now seems to be open to question. Capitalism does not appear to have been seriously weakened by the decline in the overall amount of domestic labour that has been consequent on women's entry into waged labour. Barbara Ehrenreich suggested in Article 4.4 that '... no-one is arguing ... that the decline of American productivity is due to unironed shirts and cold breakfasts' (p. 143) and that 'the statics of capitalism-plus-patriarchy help explain a world that is already receding from view' (p. 146).

Two additional criticisms of the capitalist/patriarchal model of the state may be made. First, as Yuval-Davis and Anthias argued, the state is not a homogeneous entity driven by a single logic. Rather, it is a set of institutions that operates at a variety of geographical scales, from the local to the international, embodying different aims, principles and practices that are often in contradiction with each other. In addition, the agents who implement state policies belong to a range of professional and other occupations with diverse histories and traditions and also often mutually contradictory aims. As Linda McDowell suggested in Article 5.5, the changes to welfare policies introduced by the Thatcher governments were in direct contradiction to the policies that drew women in increasing numbers into the labour market throughout the 1980s.

Secondly, conceptions of the state as inevitably patriarchal leave little room for struggles for and against particular policies by women. Rather, women tend to be portrayed as helpless victims, acted upon by the inexorable logic of the state. But, as Carole Pateman shows in Article 6.2, the welfare state, both by creating employment opportunities for women and by providing an (albeit limited) income for women in their own right, allows some prospect of their economic independence. Her article also raises the broader issues about equality and difference that we addressed in the Introduction. In particular, Pateman examines the basis of citizenship in contemporary capitalist societies, demonstrating the different ways in which women and men have been incorporated. She argues that the welfare state is a response to the challenge to full citizenship that is imposed by unemployment. Exclusion from the labour market robs individuals of the resources necessary to play a full part in civil society. However, Pateman demonstrates that this is a notion that applies only to men. Women have never been incorporated into civil society as individuals and citizens, but as members of a family: as part of the private sphere as opposed to the public world. As well as examining the links between employment and citizenship, Pateman assesses the problems for women of claiming full citizenship in the present meaning of the term, something which they can achieve only as 'lesser men'. But the alternative strategy of demanding proper support for women's responsibilities (the difference side of the dilemma) condemns them to incorporation into public life as 'women' and hence beings from another sphere. Pateman concludes that the current opposition between men's independence and women's dependence has to be broken down and a new definition and practice of citizenship developed.

Article 6.1
FEMINISM, EQUALITY AND DIFFERENCE
Anne Phillips

The words women have chosen to express their condition –
inequality, oppression, subordination – all have their implications,
for each carries its own version of the problem it describes.
Inequality notes that women are denied what is granted to men. It
focuses our attention on the injustices of letting men vote when
women could not, of giving men access to higher-paid jobs while
restricting women to low-status work. . . . Oppression, by contrast,
carries with it a sense of the weight pressing down on women;
alerting us not so much to the anomalies of female exclusion, as to
a complex of ideological, political and economic forces that combine
to keep women in their place. Subordination takes this one step
further, identifying the agents in the process. Women don't just
happen to have less than men; they are actively subordinated by
the holders of power.

The terms are not mutually exclusive, but the particular weight
attached to each in different periods is often a guide to the
preoccupations of the moment. In the period defined as the
contemporary women's movement (from the late 1960s to the present
day) the concepts of oppression and subordination have been . . .
favoured – a shift reflected also in the language of 'liberation' rather
than 'emancipation'. A hundred years ago one might have defined
feminism as a movement towards the equality of the sexes; by now
this is hardly apt. Equality remains of course central to feminist
discussion, but its recurrence in the writing signals as much
disagreement over its meaning as certainty over its goals.

A commitment to sexual equality does not of itself tell us what
shape that equality should take. Equal pay for the jobs women do
or equal shares in the jobs done by men? Equal opportunities to
compete with men or numerical equality in each sphere of
life? Equal responsibilities for housework and children or better
conditions for women at home? Those who describe themselves as
feminists have been almost as much at odds over such issues as
their opponents. . . . [Here I] concentrate on two broad sets of
issues: a constellation of arguments around the notion of equal
rights and equal opportunities, sometimes codified as the relationship between feminism and liberalism; and an ever-present tension
in feminist thinking between . . . equality and . . . sexual difference.

The first group of issues commands considerably more attention
today than it did fifteen years ago, perhaps because of the very
successes of the women's movement and the way these have

enhanced equal opportunities and equal rights; perhaps conversely because of the failures. In the late 1960s and early 1970s, feminists on both sides of the Atlantic split between those who argued a relatively traditional equal rights case and those who anticipated a radical future; the proportions in which they divided varied enormously from country to country, with liberal or equal rights feminism much more prominent in America than Britain, but in both cases there was some kind of 'reform versus revolution' axis. The 'revolutionary' camp subdivided further into radical and socialist feminism – and it was between these two that arguments became most intense. . . .

Subsequent gains and losses have altered the picture. In Britain – where liberal feminism was so weakly represented that one could hardly identify it as a force at all – the most lasting gains have been in areas that liberals might well claim as their own. This is most literally so with the legalization of abortion, where fifteen years of feminist campaigning did little more than hold onto an Act which had been introduced by a Liberal MP [David Steel in 1967]. But in the area of employment too, it was the rather conventional and unimaginative Equal Pay [1970] and Sex Discrimination [1975] Acts that edged the earnings of women at least marginally upwards. The more ambitiously transformative language (like building an alternative to the family, breaking the hold of patriarchal power) has tended to falter in a climate of economic and political retreat. And the most promising of recent developments fit quite easily with liberal ideals: local councils adopting equal opportunities policies for hiring and promotion; political parties bowing (at least a little!) to pressures for greater representation of women as councillors or MPs. In a final irony for those who once dismissed the inadequacies of liberal reform, a main lever of change in social policy in Britain has turned out to be the dauntingly respectable EEC (see Hoskins, 1986).

What British feminists saw across the Atlantic looked even odder. In the name of equal rights and equal opportunities, American women seemed to have scored extraordinary victories over at least some firms – and it is to the American experience of positive action that those involved in the fledgling equal opportunities industry in Britain have usually looked for their inspiration. At the same time America has been swept by a rising tide of New Right moralism, a politics that in its profoundly reactionary views on women and the family threatens to destroy the tentative gains around employment, abortion or nursery provision. In both Britain and America, feminists have had to ponder again the relationship with liberalism, not just as an academic interest in origins . . . but as a matter of urgent political concern. What exactly is the relationship between sexual equality and equal rights? Are equal rights and

206

opportunities what in the end feminism is about? . . . Is feminism essentially an extension of the liberal project? or something incomparably more?

The questions are further complicated by the second angle . . . pursued [here], that age-old dilemma of equality versus difference. When people first hear of feminism they often assume it denies sexual difference: 'anything he can do I can do too.' Yet as long as women bear children there is at least one inescapable difference between the sexes, and many recent writings have identified women's role in reproduction as the source and the mechanism of patriarchal power. What do such arguments imply? Do they mean we should aim to obliterate all difference, and if so, how far can we go? . . . In the course of the seventies, it became commonplace to talk of the distinction between sex and gender: to use the former when referring to an inescapable biological difference, and the latter for the construction society puts upon it. That women bear children, for example, is a biological fact. That they then have exclusive responsibility for caring for those children reflects a particular and inegalitarian pattern of gender relations, and one that is open to change. In the eighties, this approach too has been seen as rather glib, with feminism moving much more thoroughly towards the assertion of sexual difference.

Androgyny is not fashionable in the women's movement today. Fifteen years ago the aspiration to equality might well have been expressed in the longing to be a 'person' instead of a 'woman', in a desire to escape the stereotypes and definitions of sex. Today the emphasis would be different, and partly, of course, because of the very existence of a movement that has helped women assert themselves with pride. Adrienne Rich, for example, gave theoretical expression to the politics of lesbian separatism when she argued that women have a fundamental attachment to one another, and that they are only wrenched into relationships with men through a complex of power relations that impose heterosexuality as the norm (Rich, 1980). . . . Dale Spender has rewritten the feminist project as the assertion of women's experience and values over and against the different values of men (Spender, 1982). These and other writings combine in a popular rendering that treats women as not only different from, but superior to, men, bearers of essentially 'female' qualities that sometimes replicate too closely for comfort the very stereotypes feminists once tried to avoid: emotional rather than rational; peace-loving rather than destructive; caring about people rather than things.[1] The kind of 'woman-centred culture' that is promised in such visions leaves little space for the petty politics of equal rights and opportunities. . . .

Parallel to this assertion of women's power and women's difference – if theoretically worlds apart – are the arguments of psychoanalytic theory, which have entered into American and British debate largely through translations of French feminist writing (e.g. Marks and de Courtivron, 1980). Here there is less obviously an essential woman and essential man: the emphasis . . . is often on the very fragile and precarious nature of woman's sexual identity. But if sexual identity is precarious and shifting, it is still grounded in difference: to be a woman is not to be a man. We are brought back to the perennial and difficult question: if the sexes are different, in what sense and how can they be equal?

The meaning and implications of sexual equality are almost as much contested within feminism as they are by feminism's detractors, and indeed it is part of my project . . . to make this clear. On equality, as on many crucial issues, there is no single 'feminist' line, for feminism is a tradition rich in debate. My own comments are organized under three headings: first, I explore the scope and limitations of the concepts of equality and equal rights; second, I develop what has emerged as a specifically feminist critique of the liberal tradition, centring most commonly on the separation liberalism makes between the public and private; third, I examine the vexed area of equality versus difference . . . .

EQUALITY AND EQUAL RIGHTS

Sexual oppression shares with racial oppression the tendency to operate on two different levels. In both cases there have been long periods of history when the oppressed were denied their very place in humanity; in both cases the successful negotiation of this major hurdle (as, for example, when women and black people are admitted to the category of those who can vote) seems to leave the structures of oppression intact. In the case of women's oppression it is the first aspect that has given liberal feminism its power and resonance, for the extraordinary denial of women as citizens is a gross expression of arbitrary power. The second aspect is what leads so many to view liberalism as inadequate, for while few societies today will dare to contest the legal equality of women with men, it still remains the case (in the . . . [words] of the United Nations) that 'women constitute one half of the world's population, perform nearly two-thirds of its work hours, receive one-tenth of the world's income, and own less than one-hundredth of the world's property'. Liberalism typically focuses its attention on formal equalities; what relevance can it have for women today?

The question-mark is not, as it happens, just a matter of past versus present. The equal rights project has shifted its focus with the victory of the suffrage campaigns, the removal (in most countries) of legal barriers to female participation in the labour force, the concession of women's right to hold property in their own name. But it would be too simple to say that nineteenth-century feminists took the law as their target, while with hindsight we transcend the naïveties of their view. As the so far unsuccessful campaign for an Equal Rights Amendment in America warns us, equal rights in a broader sense are still much contested. The relationship between equal rights and women's liberation is an issue that must concern us today.

That liberalism and feminism share some common history is widely agreed in the literature. . . . As liberalism developed through the seventeenth and eighteenth centuries in Europe and America, it rejected the 'natural' order of things; it refused the divinely ordained right of monarchs to govern; it challenged the patriarchal basis of political power. Introducing a 'conception of individuals as free and equal beings, emancipated from the ascribed, hierarchical bonds of tradition', it seemed to cry out for application to women (Mill, 1869, p. 103). And while early liberals hardly rushed to make this connection, their principles seemed a basis for feminist ideals. . . .

. . . Women . . . seized on the language of equality and made out a case of their own. The notion that people had rights rather than just duties or responsibilities was so apposite to women, while the attack on tyranny and arbitrary power had an all too obvious bearing on the privileges of men. And in the republican version that was to emerge in America there was a further link, for republicanism emphasized the responsibilities of citizenship, regarding virtue as participation in public life. Here it clashed with what was to become the main apologia for women's position: that doctrine of 'separate but equal' which legitimated women's exclusion from politics in terms of their supposedly superior qualities for domestic life (women were too good to soil their hands on a vote). . . .

. . . There are limits to the liberal perspective, and a century and a half of debate with socialist critics have already alerted us to some of the problems. . . . Liberalism gave us a version of equality that was fundamentally bounded by the forms of the law. This . . . is the best that capitalism can offer: that whatever rights society enshrines within its laws, then these should apply equally to all. The fact that people occupy different positions in society is, and should be, irrelevant: indeed it is essential to the argument that 'there are differences, but these should not count' (Marx, 1875). This is of course the strength of liberalism – that we are all of us citizens regardless of our status. But when the implication is that the differences no longer matter, then we have a concept of equality that abstracts from the sources and relations of power.

The tension between political equality on the one hand and social and economic equality on the other is . . . a familiar one, and it is part of what has been at stake in assessments of liberal feminism. Is it enough to talk of equal opportunities and rights, or does the obsession with formality obscure the realities of power?

The question would be relatively straightforward if it were a matter of liberalism being fine as far as it goes, but simply not going far enough. The case for giving at least partial support to liberal campaigns would then be psychologically compelling, for you have to be confident indeed in your longer-term projects to sniff at more limited gains. And to say that the struggle for equal rights is important, even if insufficient, is to voice an opinion on which many would agree: the equal right to a vote has not guaranteed women equal access to power, but this is not to say we'd be better off without it; the equal right to employment does not give women equal jobs or equal pay, but it was (and still is!) worth fighting against discriminatory laws. Can feminists not co-operate on the basics of equality, even if some pursue in addition their wider concerns?

The question is not that simple, for part of the accusation against liberalism is that it is counter-productive, that it mystifies and blocks any longer-term goals.

[· · ·]

Right can only mean applying an equal standard to all – but what if we are different and unequal? What if I have a child to support and you have none? What if I am weak and you are strong? What if I need more than you?

The argument has particular pertinence to sexual equality, for the tension between calling for equal treatment or insisting on women's special needs is one that remains at the heart of feminist dilemmas. For women to have an 'equal right' to work, for example, they may actually need *more* than the men. They need maternity leave; they need workplace nurseries; they need extra safety conditions when pregnant; they may need time off for menstruation. Such arguments, of course, can be a hostage to fortune, for once you admit that women are different from men, you may diminish their chances at work. In the late nineteenth and early twentieth centuries the difficulty surfaced in the question of protective legislation: should women support the laws which 'protected' them from especially arduous labour (preventing them in Britain from working in the mines, and restricting their employment at night); or should they challenge women's exclusion from certain categories of often higher-paid work?[2] The dilemma proved an intractable one, with positions shifting over the years, and the general tension of equality versus difference is one to which I shall return. In this case as in many, principles alone did not settle this matter. As Marx, I think rightly, pointed out, if your treatment is equal in one respect, you will be unequally treated in another.

There is a further dimension that is crucial here. When feminists talk of inequalities between women and men, they seem to imply that there is a unity of women: all women this, all men the other. This is most convincing when women are denied their rights under law: when, for example, they are deprived by virtue of their sex from the right to vote; when they are denied *as women* the right to certain kinds of employment; when regardless of their age, class, race, they are all in law subordinate to their husbands. Wherever the law employs sex to deny women rights, then all women are unequal to all men. What remains of this unity once women get their rights in law?

Again this is not a simple matter of past simplicities versus present sophistication, for even in the nineteenth century the unity of women was complex and troubled. While voting for men was on a ratepayers' basis, women's campaign for the vote seemed likely to enfranchise certain women before others; their campaign around the right of women to retain property on marriage had different consequences for those who owned capital and those who earnt a wage; their campaigns around the right of women to train as doctors or lawyers in practice only benefited middle-class women. All these gave cause for concern and the unity of women was not taken for granted (Phillips, 1987). But while the law could deny all women as women it gave a necessary cohesion to feminist demands.

The subsequent dismantling of overtly discriminatory laws did not destroy the only unity in women's condition, but it did shift the emphasis elsewhere. And while the first phase of the contemporary women's movement involved excited rediscovery of what women had in common, in recent years it is difference that has dominated debate. Contemporary statistics on the distribution of income reveal gross inequality between the sexes, but still women themselves vary in their incomes and power. And while as mothers, wives and daughters women may face similar patterns of oppression, it would be naïve to pretend that all the problems are the same. A feminism that focuses too exclusively on what seem to be similarities between women can pass over in silence the divisions by race and by class; its preoccupations may then express only minority concerns.

Black women and working-class women have long argued that under cover of a unitary female experience, the women's movement has spoken for the white middle class, in a politics that reflects this constituency alone. . . . Bell Hooks . . . [has] suggest[ed] that the language of equality is simplistic and glib. 'Since men are not equals in white supremacist, capitalist, patriarchal class structure which men do women want to be equal to?' (Hooks, 1987, p. 62). When feminism defines itself as a movement to gain social equality with men, it fudges the crucial questions: relying on the abstractions of equal opportunities, it obscures the real problems that beset women's lives.

Bell Hooks proposes an alternative definition: feminism as a struggle to end sexist oppression. Such a formulation, she argues, will focus attention more directly on the other forms of oppression, and thus link up the politics around sex, class and race. A partial feminism, she is suggesting, simply will not do. The ways in which women are discriminated against, exploited and oppressed, rest on combinations of all three of these factors, so unless the politics of socialism and anti-racism can be integrated into women's struggle, the movement will still speak to the middle class alone. You cannot say that feminism is about women and then just leave it at that, as if class or race are problems for others to take up. If you do, you end up with the kind of liberal or 'bourgeois' feminism that dominates the American movement – and for Bell Hooks this is not really feminism at all.

In thinking through some of these problems we can see that they share common ground with the socialist critique of liberalism: the notion that equality is only equality under the law; the idea that formal equality legitimizes real inequalities; the idea that it abstracts from differences of race and of class. But the feminist debate on liberalism has not just divided into socialist and liberal camps. Partly of course because radical feminism . . . stands outside either tradition. But also because the different contexts in which arguments have developed have shaped the political concerns. As already noted, equal rights/liberal feminism had few adherents in the emergence of the Women's Liberation Movement in Britain, which had little time for what it saw as a 'women into boardrooms' approach, and placed itself more definitively within a radical or socialist tradition. At the risk of gross oversimplification, I would say that because British feminism was so much engaged in debate with the socialist tradition, it had to challenge the tendency to regard *any* feminism as 'bourgeois'. Operating in a field where equality was too often prefaced by the denigratory 'mere', it moved towards a greater accommodation with the basic ideas of equality or equal rights.

Thus when Juliet Mitchell wrote her essay on 'Women and Equality' in 1976, she was simultaneously criticizing equality and defending its relevance for today. She made no bones about the link between feminism and 'bourgeois' thought, and while she explored the limits, she saw equality as fundamental to feminist thought. Part of her project was to rescue equal rights as worthy and far from complete: if equal rights could never be more than rights before the law, still they 'have by no means been won yet nor their possible extent envisaged' (Mitchell and Oakley, 1986, p. 42). Her final plea is definite, if carefully circumscribed. 'A new society that is built on an old society that, within its limits, has reached a certain level of equality clearly is a better starting point than one that must build on a society predicated on privilege and unchallenged oppression' (ibid.).

In similar vein, Michèle Barrett explores with sympathy Marx's critique of liberalism, yet refuses to dismiss the equal rights approach. With all the criticisms that can be levelled at 'mere' political emancipation, who, she asks, 'would care to argue against a systematic political project of eliminating racism and sexism from the working class on the grounds that such inequalities were not of prime significance?' (ibid., p. 50). The point is as much to query Marx in the light of feminism as it is to query feminism in the light of Marx. And to this extent it reflects what became an important characteristic of feminist thinking in Britain: a more sceptical questioning of socialism's claims.

The idea that capitalism is totally, or even primarily, responsible for women's condition has taken a battering in recent debates; the associated idea that feminism finds its natural home inside the socialist camp has likewise been held up to question. Socialist, and more specifically Marxist, theory has been criticized for the way it can subsume all forms of oppression under a more 'primary' class exploitation, leaving issues of either sexual or racial equality as subsidiary concerns. Equal rights or liberal feminism may smooth over and deny class differences between women, but socialism smooths over conflicts between women and men. In noting and criticizing this, British feminists became more resistant to the complaint that the women's movement was 'bourgeois', more reluctant to condemn an equal rights line.

[· · ·]

It is . . . important to bear in mind the political contexts. If liberal feminism was a bystander in Britain, in America it often dominated the stage. There was, and is, a powerful and active liberal-feminist lobby, organized largely under the umbrella of the National Organization for Women (NOW) which was launched in 1966, and focusing recently upon the campaign for the ERA. It is harder to tolerate what is a dominant position, and for those American feminists outside this mainstream the impulse has been much more to explode the tradition – either from without or else from within. One consequence of this is that where liberalism has been more politically important, the engagement has provoked a fuller feminist response. Juliet Mitchell and Michèle Barrett explore what is in a sense a universal critique of liberalism: arguments that could apply equally whether we were looking at the relationship between rich and poor, white and black, male and female, Christian and Jew. In the writings of Carole Pateman or Zillah Eisenstein [in the USA] what emerges is a more specifically feminist critique.

FEMINIST CRITIQUES OF LIBERALISM

With all the uncertainties as to what the terms mean, it is when feminists talk of equality and equal rights that they most closely approximate the liberal tradition. When they talk instead of the personal as political, they are profoundly at odds with liberal ideas. The relationship between public and private has become the real bone of contention between liberal and feminist thinking, and it is the focus of most feminist critiques.

Like all abbreviated statements, 'the personal is political' has had to carry a wide range of meanings. Partly a rebuttal of those who dismissed as trivial questions like who does the housework or who sleeps with whom; partly a reminder that in the most private corners of our existence the state and economy still hold sway. Partly saying that the kind of 'consciousness-raising' activities that became associated with recent feminism were as politically crucial as anything else; partly saying that change does not come from personal lives alone. The basic point is clear. If all aspects of our lives are up for question, then nothing is outside the political sphere.

For liberals this is anathema, for to make no distinction between private life and public affairs is the very antithesis of their thinking. Liberalism is that doctrine *par excellence* that tries to keep things separate, to demarcate the personal from the political sphere. For most liberals, the state is a necessary evil. Individuals cannot be trusted to regulate themselves, and the state must therefore play a referee role. But since governments and laws are by their very nature a restraint on our freedom, the question is when they can justly intervene. . . . Liberalism is not anarchism; it does not aspire to eliminate the state. But it guards jealously the autonomy of the individual, watching out for encroachments on the private sphere.

When this translates into police officers refusing to protect a woman beaten by her husband on the grounds that domestic quarrels are a private affair – or indeed into employers refusing a woman time off work to look after her sick child on the grounds that personal problems should not intrude on her work – we can see why feminists get worried. The private is very often taken to mean the family, and in the family men and women are unequal. In the name of freedom, liberalism can exempt from political interference the arena in which women are most subordinate and controlled. In its desire to keep separate the worlds of public and private, it offers us 'equality' in the former while hypocritically ignoring our real difference in the latter. The split between public

214

and private may present itself as a neutral, 'sex-free' distinction, but its effects are unequal between women and men.

Feminists have not argued that liberalism alone makes this distinction. In her book *Public Man, Private Woman* Jean Bethke Elshtain traces the split from Plato to the present day, and argues that the distinctions between public and private are 'fundamental . . . ordering principles of all known societies, save, perhaps, the most simple' (Elshtain, 1981, p. 6). . . . The notion that there are separate spheres of public and private existence – and the sleight of hand through which one becomes male and the other female – has a much longer history than the 300 odd years through which liberalism has been with us. What is disturbing about liberalism is that on the face of it, it should have been so different. Liberalism, as Carole Pateman notes, 'is an individualist, egalitarian, conventionalist doctrine; patriarchalism claims that hierarchical relations of subordination necessarily follow from the natural characteristics of women and men' (Pateman, 1987, p. 105). How did liberalism then end up so badly?

Denied entry by the front door, patriarchy crept in at the back. Instead of rejecting all forms of natural authority, early liberals restricted themselves to saying that government and the family were separate realms. John Locke, for example, fully accepted that fathers had a natural authority over their children, and indeed that husbands had a natural authority over wives. Where he broke with more obviously patriarchal theorists was in refusing the relevance of this to the state. Political authority, he argued, was conventional: free and equal beings had created a ruler to regulate their lives, and what they had created they had some right to control. But in a malignant failure of imagination, he then drew on this contrast to exclude women from any role in the state. If they were 'naturally' subordinate in the family, they could not be included among consenting adults; it was men who had created, and should monitor, their government, men who were the citizens of John Locke's state.

Locke here was perhaps breaking his own rules, for having suggested that the principles of the family should not be extended to the state, he then excluded women from the latter precisely because of their role in the former. Later liberals (and to the shame of the tradition this was very much later) queried this anomaly, arguing that women too should share in political life. But as a number of feminists have argued, . . . liberalism then got caught in another dilemma. John Stuart Mill, for example, rejected the idea that women's position as wives and mothers should exclude them from participation in public affairs, but he hoped and expected that women would still stay in their sphere. Arguing that legal equality need not prevent women from 'choosing' to be wives and mothers, and conversely that their continuing as wives and mothers need

215

not unfit them for public concerns, nineteenth-century liberals turned a blind eye to the fact that women and men occupied separate spheres. Yet as Carole Pateman notes, 'Mill's acceptance of a sexually ascribed division of labour, or the separation of domestic from public life, cuts the ground from under his argument for enfranchisement . . . How can wives who have "chosen" private life develop a public spirit?' (Pateman, 1987, p. 116). Locke, after all, had a point.

The issue connects with socialist complaints against the liberal tradition. How can we be politically equal despite all our difference, when the differences undermine the formality and make it pretence? Feminist writers, however, have picked up on another dimension; . . . Carole Pateman shows why this is so. Liberals make not one, but two, distinctions between the private and public: the prior distinction between family and the public, and then a subsequent one within the public itself. Much of the discussion (either among liberals or between liberals and socialists) has focused on the latter, the connection between what Marx called civil society and the state. What is the appropriate relationship between private enterprise and public regulation? Do inequalities in the private sphere (between, say, landlord and tenant, employer and employee) matter as long as we are equal in political rights? 'Private' in this sense is not about the family; abstracting entirely from the domestic sphere, it refers to the market, to the economy, to our 'social' as opposed to our 'political' life. And because the family is now completely out of the picture, liberalism can more plausibly pretend that we are indeed the private and isolated individuals on which its theories rest. In seemingly universal concern over the limits of the state and the freedoms of the individual, liberalism talks in effect of a world occupied by men.

There are two kinds of point here. Liberalism pretends we can be equal in the public sphere when our differences are overwhelming in the private: it exhorts women to apply for good jobs while treating the babies as their private affair; it offers them equality with one hand and takes it away with the other. This is damning enough, but feminists have more up their sleeves. Having pushed the familial into the background, liberalism creates a fictional world of autonomous atoms, each propelled by his (sic) own interests and desires, each potentially threatened by the others.

This kind of radical individualism is not of course without its attractions to feminists. Zillah Eisenstein argues that 'all feminism is liberal at its root in that the universal feminist claim that woman is an independent being (from man) is premised on the eighteenth-century liberal conception of the independent and autonomous self' (Eisenstein, 1981, p. 4). When nineteenth-century feminists insisted that women had rights of their own, they were refusing to be

216

subsumed under fathers or husbands. When twentieth-century feminists said that women had needs and desires of their own, they were refusing to be sacrificed to children or lovers. Asserting the self is part of the politics, and it is this – as much as the common language of equal rights – that provides the link between liberal and feminist traditions. The question Zillah Eisenstein poses is, how far can this go? Women straddle public and private worlds in different ways from men, and they cannot so readily conceive of themselves in public terms alone. Could feminism really throw in its lot with the market mentality of the liberal tradition? Can it consistently adhere to the individualist view?

The way Eisenstein herself puts this is somewhat formalistic: that because feminism is about women as a 'sex-class', it cannot express its politics in terms of individuals alone. When it tries none the less to keep within the contours of the liberal tradition it keeps posing questions it cannot resolve. . . .

'Liberal feminism, by dint of speaking of women as a group, is in contradiction with "the principles of liberalism," which do not see people as groups, only individuals' (Eisenstein, 1981, p. 191). Put like this, the argument is over-strained, for not all liberals are as radically individualist as this comment suggests, nor is it so obviously contradictory to say that women are oppressed as a group, but should be freed in the future to compete as individuals with men. The real power of the argument lies behind the formal contrast between liberal individualism and feminist groupiness, and rests on the idea that feminism has its own and different conception of individuality. 'Connection and relatedness,' Zillah Eisenstein suggests, are what characterize feminism, 'between people, between politics and economics, between ideology and actual social conditions' (ibid.). A politics based upon female experience must surely eschew the extremer versions of atomistic individualism, pointing instead towards a new relationship of public to private, and recognizing collectivity even as it claims independence.

The argument is plausible, but it leads us back to the question 'which feminism?'. Does the nature of women's politics point in a specific direction, or are there many feminisms, of which some at least may remain resolutely allied to their liberal friends? In *Public Man, Private Woman* Jean Bethke Elshtain criticizes liberal feminists for doing just what Eisenstein suggests they could not, for swallowing the 'market' perspective on life. And while she too notes the contradictory elements in their thinking, she criticizes them for trying to have it both ways, trying:

> to condemn woman's second-class status and the damaging effects of her privatization and, simultaneously, to extol or celebrate the qualities that have emerged within the sphere

women are to be 'freed' from. The result of all this is a confused admixture: a tough-minded market language of self-interest coupled with evocations to softer virtues, precisely the combination which plagued the Suffragists. Because the only politics liberal feminists know is the rather crass utilitarianism they implicitly or explicitly adopt, they have thus far failed to articulate a transformative feminist vision of public and private.

(Elshtain, 1981, pp. 248–9)

[· · ·]

Elshtain's account of liberal feminism is much less sympathetic than that of Eisenstein – if we were to try to fit them into pre-feminist categories, then the former is arguing from a conservative perspective, the latter from a socialist one. Their differences in respect to liberalism hinge on contrasting approaches to the public/private split, for as already noted, Zillah Eisenstein sees this as a function of patriarchal rule, while Jean Bethke Elshtain regards it as necessary to life. The private for her is the site of caring and concern; the pity is that the public has not reflected these values. The kind of reconstruction she proposes is one that would create an 'ethical polity': public life informed by social and moral responsibilities; private life lending of its values, but still keeping its autonomy clear.

There is a major dispute here, and it is one that leads on to the question of equality and difference. What Elshtain most objects to in the present version of the public/private split is not so much that it keeps women out of public affairs, as that it keeps out the values that women express. Largely because of their role as mothers, women have become the guarantors of a deeper humanity, carrying a sense of community, of belonging, of selflessness and care. Feminism should be building on this, not capitulating to a narrower self-interest. Yet as Elshtain sees it – and here she echoes what many *anti*-feminists would also say – the contemporary women's movement often took the second, more damaging road. Stridently asserting their own individual needs, women sacrificed the most helpless among them. They brought up their children outside the family, condemning them to the insecurities of a casual collectivity; pushed them prematurely into nurseries in order to further the mothers' careers. 'The feminist political thinker must ... ask at what price she would gain the world for herself or other women', and she must utterly reject 'those victories that come at the cost of the bodies and spirits of human infants' (Elshtain, 1981, p. 331). 'The reflective feminist must be as concerned with the concrete existences and self-understandings of children as she is with female subjects' (ibid., p. 333). '*As* concerned' is an interesting emphasis:

why is this particularly the challenge to feminists, as opposed to socialists or liberals or anyone else?

. . .[3] If we give up on the case for improved social provision for children, if we end up just glorying in our creativity as mothers, we retreat from the challenge feminism sets. The new celebration of motherhood that is becoming commonplace among feminists 'tells us what we already know: that there are passions and surprises bound up with child-care as well as the exhaustion and isolation dwelt on by women's liberation. But it tells us . . . so at the expense of thought about practical needs' (Phillips, 1987, pp. 180–1). Elshtain's emphasis on children leads her towards the status quo: children need the family, and while she sometimes seems to go along with the current ideas of shared parenting, she does not clarify the mechanisms that would bring this about. . . .

EQUALITY AND DIFFERENCE

It is one of the oddities in the tension between equality and difference that representatives from each end of the spectrum can make their case for being the more radical. Advocates of stricter equality have argued – with considerable force – that once feminists admit the mildest degree of sexual difference, they open up a gap through which the currents of reaction will flow. Once let slip that pre-menstrual tension interferes with concentration, that pregnancy can be exhausting, that motherhood is absorbing, and you are off down the slope to separate spheres. It was with good reason that prominent suffragists (like Millicent Garrett Fawcett) argued against emphasizing women's maternal role: the whole point of the movement was to get women out of their stereotyped domesticity, to assert their claims in the public sphere.

But those who have argued for a feminism grounded in sexual difference have their own very plausible case. The politics of equality directs energies to the spheres that are occupied by men, while the predominantly female activities around housework or child care remain obscured as always from view. Women are called on to fit themselves into slots devised for the men, and their own needs are in the process ignored. Why should equality mean women shaping themselves to a world made for men? Why shouldn't the world be made to change its tune?

. . . From the standpoint of today, it seems extraordinary that nineteenth-century feminists had no strategy for the family: that they uncritically accepted women's role as mothers and wives and concentrated on getting the vote. How could they not see that women's oppression was based in the family? How could they accept their domestic role? . . . The suffragists confronted and discredited the notion that being a mother and wife disqualified you from having a vote. 'Leave the family out of it', they said;

'accept us as individuals in our own right'. Arguing for full citizenship regardless of their familial status ('there are differences but these should not count!'), they refused to be defined in the traditional way. And if to twentieth-century ears this can sound like capitulation to domestic drudgery, it was dramatically contested at the time.

In the history of the women's movement there has usually been a class dimension to equality versus difference. In the nineteenth century, for example, it was middle-class women who felt themselves most acutely victimized by the doctrine of separate spheres, for they were the ones whose femininity was most explicitly defined through denying them useful work. The feminism this generated was primarily about challenging exclusion, claiming access to public life, the right to vote and to study and to work. And in Britain at least, it was left to the organizations of working-class women (like the Women's Co-operative Guild) to take up more domestic concerns: issues like contraception, divorce, provision for mothers and children. When in the 1920s British feminists were asked to choose between the older tradition of 'equal rights' and a 'new feminism' centred on motherhood, the case for the latter was very often put in terms of class. 'What rights had the working-class mother?' asked Dora Russell.[4] Those feminists who previously refused to engage with issues of maternity on the grounds that this would help push women back into the home were now identified as the voice of middle-class women. In the name of the working-class mother the emphasis was then reversed.

The example typifies the problems, for in effect neither position was satisfactory. The equality end of the feminist spectrum had tended to highlight women as workers, while the difference end has highlighted women as mothers. Since most women in practice are both, stressing either aspect to the exclusion of the other is usually a dangerous choice. Thus if the call for better contraceptive advice, more midwives, improved ante-natal care, 'family endow-ment' and so on, marked an important and welcome emphasis on the problems women faced as mothers, it also ran the risk of denying women's need for paid work. When the working mother came under threat in the 1940s and 1950s – with wartime nurseries shut down and women encouraged to see their place in the home – feminists by and large were ill prepared in her defence. Campaigns for paid employment had become too closely identified with the limited needs of better-off women, and feminism had temporarily lost the language in which to assert women's equal right to work (see Riley, 1983). Equality and difference had become too counter-posed in the politics, with, in this instance, unfortunate results.

The main thrust of the debate in contemporary feminism has come from the influence of psychoanalytic theory on the one hand

220

and the celebration of a woman-identified woman on the other. Here the discussion moves on to a new level. The earlier arguments were usually put in terms of which aspects of women's lives feminists should concentrate their activities upon: those where women were claiming an equality with men? or those that were traditionally the woman's concern? The argument was not so much about whether men and women were in principle different, for while this was continually discussed, it was not really the issue at stake. Today's arguments, by contrast, do imply a more essentialist line on sexual difference.

Anything stronger than 'imply' would expose me too roughly to critical complaint. Most exponents of a woman-identified politics remain officially agnostic over the extent to which women are essentially and ineradicably different from men, though in practice the differences are treated as enduring facts of life. Those influenced by psychoanalysis are much more likely to come clean about sexual difference being inevitable, but the content of this difference is shifting and obscure. . . . Jean Bethke Elshtain argues that the 'sex distinction is ineliminable and important' (Elshtain, 1987, p. 148), but her analysis of this only tells us that boys and girls learn who they are by noting that they have different bodies. A *'sexual difference'*, she suggests, 'is neither an affront, nor an outrage, not a narcissistic injury. A *sexual division*, on the other hand, one that separates the sexes and locks each into a vector of isolated, alienated activity *is* both a deep wound to the psycho-sexual identity of the human subject as well as a specific damage of an overly rigidified system of stratification and specialization' (ibid., p. 155). I am inclined to agree, but until we see more clearly what is entailed by this sexual difference it is hard to decide whether it matters.

Sally Alexander sees subjectivity and sexual identity as 'constructed through a process of differentiation, division and splitting, and best understood as a process which is always in the making, is never finished or complete' (Alexander, 1987, p. 171). The process is none the less fundamentally different for the little girl/woman and the little boy/man. Her main concern . . . is with how the unconscious enters politics, and in particular with the way our understanding of self and sexual identity changes our understanding of class. Thought-provoking as this is, its implications for feminism still need to be spelt out: what – other than *a* difference – does this sexual difference imply? The more content that feminist writers put into the notion of difference, the more worried I become; but the less content, the more confused!

In its various forms . . . the renewed interest in difference has become one of the central preoccupations of contemporary thought. . . . It seems . . . likely to set the terms of future debate, for it is a tension built into the feminist project. Men and women are different; they are also unequal; feminists will continue to debate and disagree over how far the inequality stems from the difference, and how far the difference can or should be eliminated.

[···]

Notes

1   For a critical discussion of this school of thought, see Eisenstein (1984) and Segal (1987).

2   See Phillips (1987) for a fuller discussion.

3   [Part of what has been cut here is from Denise Riley's essay on 'The Serious Burdens of Love' (Riley, 1983).]

4   For a fuller discussion see Phillips (1987, pp. 98–106). Olive Banks (1981, ch. 9) covers similar ground in relation to both American and British movements.

Article 6.2
THE PATRIARCHAL WELFARE STATE
Carole Pateman

According to Raymond Williams's *Keywords*, 'the Welfare State, in distinction from the Warfare State, was first named in 1939' (Williams, 1985, p. 333). The welfare state was set apart from the fascist warfare state, defeated in the Second World War, and so the welfare state was identified with democracy at the christening. In the 1980s most western welfare states are also warfare states, but this is not ordinarily seen as compromising their democratic character. Rather, the extent of democracy is usually taken to hinge on the *class* structure. Welfare provides a social wage for the working class, and the positive, social democratic view is that the welfare state gives social meaning and equal worth to the formal juridical and political rights of all citizens. A less positive view of the welfare state is that it provides governments with new means of exercising power over and controlling working-class citizens. But proponents of both views usually fail to acknowledge the sexually divided way in which the welfare state has been constructed. Nor do most democratic theorists recognize the *patriarchal* structure of the welfare state; the very different way that women and men have been incorporated as citizens is rarely seen to be of significance for democracy.[1] Even the fact that the earliest development of the welfare state took place when women were still denied, or had only just won, citizenship in the national state is usually overlooked.[2]

I do not want to dispute the crucial importance of class in understanding the welfare state and democracy. To write about the welfare state is, in large part, to write about the working class. However, my discussion treats class in a manner unfamiliar to most democratic theorists, who usually assume that the welfare state, democracy and class can be discussed theoretically without any attention to the character of the relation between the sexes. I shall suggest some reasons why and how the patriarchal structure of the welfare state has been repressed from theoretical consciousness. I shall also consider the connection between employment and citizenship in the patriarchal welfare state, the manner in which 'women' have been opposed to the 'worker' and the 'citizen', and a central paradox surrounding women, welfare and citizenship. By 'the welfare state' here, I refer to the states of Britain (from which I shall draw a number of my empirical and historical examples), Australia and the United States. In the more developed welfare states of Scandinavia, women have moved nearer to, but have not yet achieved, full citizenship.[3]

For the past century, many welfare policies have been concerned with what are now called 'women's issues'. Moreover, much of the controversy about the welfare state has revolved and continues to revolve around the question of the respective social places and tasks of women and men, the structure of marriage and the power relationship between husband and wife.... The difficulties of understanding the welfare state and citizenship today without taking the position of women into account are not hard to illustrate, because contemporary feminists have produced a large body of evidencé and argument that reveals the importance of women in the welfare state and the importance of the welfare state for women.

Women are now the majority of recipients of many welfare benefits.... A major reason why women are so prominent as welfare recipients is that women are more likely than men to be poor (a fact that has come to be known as the 'feminization of poverty'). In the United States, between 1969 and 1979, there was a decline in the proportion of families headed by men that fell below the official poverty line while the proportion headed by women grew rapidly (Erie *et al.*, 1983, p. 100). By 1982 about one-fifth of families with minor children were headed by women, but they constituted 53 per cent of all poor families (Kamerman, 1984, p. 250), and female heads were over three times as likely as male heads to have incomes below the poverty line (Smith, 1984, p. 291)....

The welfare state is now a major source of employment for women. For instance, in Britain the National Health Service is the biggest single employer of women in the country; about three-quarters of NHS employees, and 90 per cent of NHS nurses, are women (Doyal, 1985, pp. 237, 253). In 1981 there were more than five million jobs in the public health, education and welfare sector in Britain (an increase of two million from 1961) and three-fifths of these jobs were held by women (Land, 1985, p. 8)....

Women are also involved in the welfare state in less obvious ways. Negotiations (and confrontations) with welfare state officials on a day-to-day basis are usually conducted by women; and it is mothers, not fathers, who typically pay the rent, deal with social workers, take children to welfare clinics and so forth. Women are also frequently in the forefront of political campaigns and actions to improve welfare services or the treatment of welfare claimants. The services and benefits provided by the welfare state are far from comprehensive and, in the absence of public provision, much of the work involved, for example, in caring for the aged in all three countries is undertaken by women in their homes (something to which I shall return).

Finally, to put the previous points into perspective, there is one area of the welfare state from which women have been largely excluded. The legislation, policy-making and higher-level administration of the welfare state have been and remain predominantly in men's hands. Some progress has been made; in Australia the Office of the Status of Women within the (Commonwealth) Department of Prime Minister and Cabinet monitors cabinet submissions, and the Women's Budget Program requires all departments to make a detailed assessment of the impact of their policies on women.

HEGEL'S TWO DILEMMAS

To gain some insight into why the welfare state can still be discussed without taking account of these factors, it is useful to begin by looking at Donald Moon's account of the welfare state as a response to 'Hegel's dilemma' (Moon, 1988). Hegel was the first political theorist to set out the moral dilemma that arises when citizenship is undermined by the operation of the capitalist market. The market leaves some citizens bereft of the resources for social participation and so, as Moon states, as 'undeserved exiles from society'. Citizens thrown into poverty lack both the means for self-respect and the means to be recognized by fellow citizens as of equal worth to themselves, a recognition basic to democracy. Poverty-stricken individuals are not and – unless the outcome of participation in the market is offset in some way – cannot be full citizens. The moral basis of the welfare state lies in the provision of resources for what T.H. Marshall called the 'social rights' of democratic citizenship. For Moon, then, Hegel's dilemma is concerned with the manner in which the participation of some individuals as workers in the capitalist economy . . . can make a mockery of their formal status as equal citizens. In contemporary terms, it is a problem of class or, more exactly, now that mass unemployment could well be a permanent feature of capitalist economies, a problem of an underclass of unemployed social exiles. There is no doubt that this is an important problem, but Moon's reading of Hegel focuses on only *part* of the dilemma with which Hegel was faced.

In addition to the category of citizens who become social exiles through the accident that they can find no one to buy their labour-power at a living wage, Hegel also had to deal with a category of beings who are exiles because they are *incapable* of being incorporated into civil society and citizenship. According to Hegel – and to almost all the modern theorists who are admitted to the 'tradition of western political philosophy' – women naturally lack the attributes and capacities of the 'individuals' who can enter civil society, sell their labour-power and become citizens (for examples see Brennan and Pateman, 1979). Women, Hegel held, are natural social exiles. Hegel therefore had to find an answer to *two* dilemmas, and his theory gives a moral basis to both class division and sexual division.

The welfare state could not provide a solution to the problem of women. Hegel's response was simultaneously to reaffirm the necessity of women's exile and to incorporate them into the state. Women are not incorporated as citizens like men, but as members of the family, a sphere separate from (or in social exile from) civil society and the state. The family is essential to civil society and the state, but it is constituted on a different basis from the rest of conventional social life, having its own ascriptive principles of association.

Women have now won the formal status of citizens, and their contemporary social position may seem a long way removed from that prescribed by Hegel. But Hegel's theory is still very relevant to the problem of patriarchy and the welfare state, although most contemporary political theorists usually look only at the relation between civil society and the state, or the intervention that the public power (state) may make in the private sphere (economy or class system). This view of 'public' and 'private' assumes that two of Hegel's categories (civil society and state) can be understood in the absence of the third (family). Yet Hegel's theory presupposes that family/civil society/state are comprehensible only in *relation* to each other – and then civil society and the state become 'public' in contrast to the 'private' family.

Hegel's social order contains a double separation of the private and public: the *class* division between civil society and the state (between economic man and citizen, between private enterprise and the public power); and the *patriarchal* separation between the private family and the public world of civil society/state. Moreover, the public character of the sphere of civil society/state is constructed and gains its meaning through what it excludes – the private association of the family. The patriarchal division between public and private *is also a sexual division*. Women, naturally lacking the capacities for public participation, remain within an association constituted by love, ties of blood, natural subjection and particularity, and in which they are governed by men. The public world of universal citizenship is an association of free and equal individuals, a sphere of property, rights and contract – and of men, who interact as formally equal citizens.

The widely held belief that the basic structure of our society rests on the separation of the private, familial sphere from the public world of the state and its policies is both true and false. It is true that the private sphere has been seen as women's proper place. Women have never in reality been completely excluded from the public world, but the policies of the welfare state have helped ensure that women's day-to-day experience confirms the separation of private and public existence. The belief is false in that, since the early twentieth century, welfare policies have reached across from public to private and helped uphold a patriarchal structure of familial life. Moreover, the two spheres are linked because men have always had a legitimate place in both. Men have been seen both as heads of families – and as husbands and fathers they have had a socially and legally sanctioned power over their wives and children – and as participants in public life. Indeed, the 'natural' masculine capacities that enable them, but not their wives, to be heads of families are the same capacities that enable them, but not their wives, to take their place in civil life.

Moon's interpretation of Hegel illustrates the continuing strength of Hegel's patriarchal construction of citizenship, which is assumed to be universal or democratic citizenship. The exiles from society who need the welfare state to give moral worth to their citizenship are male workers. Hegel showed deep insight here. Paid employment has become the key to citizenship, and the recognition of an individual as a citizen of equal worth to other citizens is lacking when a worker is unemployed. The history of the welfare state and citizenship (and the manner in which they have been theorized) is bound up with the history of the development of 'employment societies'.[4] In the early part of the nineteenth century, most workers were still not fully incorporated into the labour market; they typically worked at a variety of occupations, worked on a seasonal basis, gained part of their subsistence outside the capitalist market and enjoyed 'Saint Monday'. By the 1880s full employment had become an ideal, unemployment a major social issue, and loud demands were heard for state-supported social reform (and arguments were made against state action to promote welfare) (Keane and Owens, 1986, pp. 15–18, 89–90). But who was included under the banner of 'full employment'? What was the status of those 'natural' social exiles seen as properly having no part in the employment society? Despite many changes in the social standing of women, we are not so far as we might like to think from Hegel's statement that the husband, as head, 'has the prerogative to go out and work for [the family's] living, to attend to its needs, and to control and administer its capital' (Hegel, 1952).

The political significance of the sexual division of labour is ignored by most democratic theorists. They treat the public world of paid employment and citizenship as if it can be divorced from its connection with the private sphere, and so the masculine character of the public sphere has been repressed. For example, T.H. Marshall first presented his influential account of citizenship in 1949, at the height of the optimism in Britain about the contribution of the new welfare state policies to social change – but also at the time (as I shall show) when women were being confirmed as lesser citizens in the welfare state. Marshall states that 'citizenship is a status bestowed on those who are full members of a community'

(Marshall, 1983, p. 253), and most contemporary academic discussions of citizenship do not question this statement. But, as shown graphically and brutally by the history of blacks in the United States, this is not the case. The formal status of citizen can be bestowed on, or won by, a category of people who are still denied full social membership.

Marshall noted that the Factory Acts in the nineteenth century 'protected' women workers, and he attributes the protection to their lack of citizenship. But he does not consider 'protection' – the polite way to refer to subordination – of women in the private sphere or ask how it is related to the sexual division of labour in the capitalist economy and citizenship. Nor does the 'in some important respects peculiar' civil status of married women in the nineteenth century inhibit his confidence in maintaining, despite the limited franchise, 'that in the nineteenth century citizenship in the form of civil rights was universal', and that, in economic life, 'the basic civil right is the right to work'. Marshall sees the aim of the 'social rights' of the welfare state as 'class-abatement': this is 'no longer merely an attempt to abate the obvious nuisance of destitution in the lowest ranks of society. . . . It is no longer content to raise the floor-level in the basement of the social edifice, . . . it has begun to remodel the whole building' (ibid., pp. 250–1, 257). But the question that has to be asked is, are women in the building or in a separate annex?

CITIZENSHIP AND EMPLOYMENT

Theoretically and historically, the central criterion for citizenship has been 'independence', and the elements encompassed under the heading of independence have been based on masculine attributes and abilities. Men, but not women, have been seen as possessing the capacities required of 'individuals', 'workers' and 'citizens'. As a corollary, the meaning of 'dependence' is associated with all that is womanly – and women's citizenship in the welfare state is full of paradoxes and contradictions.

[· · ·]

The dichotomy breadwinner/housewife, and the masculine meaning of independence, were established in Britain by the middle of the last century; in the earlier period of capitalist development, women (and children) were wage-labourers. A 'worker' became a man who has an economically dependent wife to take care of his daily needs and look after his home and children. Moreover, 'class', too, is constructed as a patriarchal category. 'The working class' is the class of working *men*, who are also full citizens in the welfare state.

[· · ·]

The position of men as breadwinner-workers has been built into the welfare state. The sexual divisions in the welfare state have received . . . [little] attention . . . [but] feminist analyses have shown how many welfare provisions have been established within a two-tier system. First, there are the benefits available to individuals as 'public' persons by virtue of their participation, and accidents of fortune, in the capitalist market. Benefits in this tier of the system are usually claimed by men. Second, benefits are available to the 'dependants' of individuals in the first category, or to 'private' persons, usually women. In the United States, for example, men are the majority of 'deserving' workers who receive benefits through the insurance system to which they have 'contributed' out of their earnings. On the other hand, the majority of claimants in means-tested programmes are women – women who are usually making their claims as wives or mothers. . . .

. . . As dependants, married women . . . [are assured to] derive their subsistence from their husbands, so that wives are placed in the position of all dependent people before the establishment of the welfare state; they are reliant on the benevolence of another for their livelihood. The assumption is generally made that all husbands are benevolent. Wives are assumed to share equally in the standard of living of their husbands. The distribution of income *within* households has not usually been a subject of interest to economists, political theorists or protagonists in arguments about class and the welfare state – even though William Thompson drew attention to its importance as long ago as 1825[5] – but past and present evidence indicates that the belief that all husbands are benevolent is mistaken.[6] Nevertheless, women are likely to be better off married than if their marriage fails. One reason why women figure so prominently among the poor is that after divorce, as recent evidence from the United States reveals, a woman's standard of living can fall by nearly 75 per cent, whereas a man's can rise by nearly half (Weitzman, 1985, ch. 10, esp. pp. 337–40).

The conventional understanding of the 'wage' also suggests that there is no need to investigate women's standard of living independently from men's. The concept of the wage has expressed and encapsulated the patriarchal separation and integration of the public world of employment and the private sphere of conjugal relations. In arguments about the welfare state and the social wage, the wage is usually treated as a return for the sale of *individuals'* labour-power. However, once the opposition breadwinner/house-wife was consolidated, a 'wage' had to provide subsistence for several people. The struggle between capital and labour and the controversy about the welfare state have been about the *family wage*. A 'living wage' has been defined as what is required for a worker as breadwinner to support a wife and family, rather than what is needed to support himself; the wage is not what is sufficient to reproduce the worker's own labour-power, but what is sufficient, in combination with the unpaid work of the housewife, to reproduce the labour-power of the present and future labour force.

[· · ·]

Of course, a great deal has changed . . . [in recent decades]. Structural changes in capitalism have made it possible for large numbers of married women to enter paid employment, and equal-pay legislation in the 1970s, which in principle recognizes the wage as payment to an individual, may make it seem that the family wage has had its day. And it was always a myth for many, perhaps most, working-class families (see Barrett and McIntosh, 1980, pp. 56–9). Despite the strength of the social ideal of the dependent wife, many working-class wives have always been engaged in paid work out of necessity. The family could not survive on the husband's wage, and the wife had to earn money, too, whether as a wage-worker, or at home doing outwork, or taking in laundry or lodgers or participating in other ways in the 'informal' economy. In 1976 in Britain the wages and salaries of 'heads of household' (not all of whom are men) formed only 51 per cent of household income (ibid., p. 58). The decline of manufacturing and the expansion of the service sector of capitalist economies since the Second World War have created jobs seen as 'suitable' for women. Between 1970 and 1980 in the United States over thirteen million women entered the paid labour force (Smith, 1984, p. 300). In Britain, if present trends in male and female employment continue, women employees will outnumber men . . . [by the end of the century] (Phillips, 1983). Nevertheless, even these dramatic shifts have not been sufficient to make women full members of the employment society. The civil right to 'work' is still only half-heartedly acknowledged for women. Women in the workplace are still perceived primarily as wives and mothers, not workers.[7] The view is also widespread that women's wages are a 'supplement' to those of the breadwinner. Women, it is held, do not need wages in the same way that men do – so they may legitimately be paid less than men.

[· · ·]

Women are prominent as welfare claimants because, today, it is usually women who are poor – and perhaps the major reason why women are poor is that it is very hard for most women to find a job that will pay a living wage. Equal-pay legislation cannot overcome the barrier of a sexually segregated occupational structure. [As Part III demonstrated] capitalist economies are patriarchal, divided into men's and women's occupations; the sexes do not usually work together, nor are they paid at the same rates for similar work. . . . The segregation is very stable: in Britain, for example, 84 per cent of women worked in occupations dominated by women in 1971, the same percentage as in 1951, and in 1901 the figure was 88 per cent (Bruegel, 1983, p. 133 and table 7.4).

[· · ·]

WOMEN'S WORK AND WELFARE

Although so many women, including married women, are now in paid employment, women's standing as 'workers' is still of precarious legitimacy. So, therefore, is their standing as democratic citizens. If an individual can gain recognition from other citizens as an equally worthy citizen only through participation in the capitalist market, if self-respect and respect as a citizen are 'achieved' in the public world of the employment society, then women still lack the means to be recognized as worthy citizens. Nor have the policies of the welfare state provided women with many of the resources to gain respect as citizens. Marshall's social rights of citizenship in the welfare state could be extended to men without difficulty. As participants in the market, men could be seen as making a public contribution, and were in a position to be levied by the state to make a contribution more directly, that *entitled* them to the benefits of the welfare state. But how could women, dependants of men, whose legitimate 'work' is held to be located in the private sphere, be citizens of the welfare state? What could, or did, women contribute? The paradoxical answer is that women contributed – welfare.

The development of the welfare state has presupposed that certain aspects of welfare could and should continue to be provided by women (wives) in the home, and not primarily through public provision. The 'work' of a housewife can include the care of an invalid husband and elderly, perhaps infirm, relatives. Welfare-state policies have ensured in various ways that wives/women provide welfare services gratis, disguised as part of their responsibility for the private sphere. A good deal has been written about the fiscal crisis of the welfare state, but it would have been more acute if certain areas of welfare had not been seen as a private, women's matter. It is not surprising that the attack on public spending in the welfare state by the Thatcher and Reagan governments goes hand-in-hand with praise for loving care within families; that is, with an attempt to obtain ever more unpaid welfare from (house)wives. The Invalid Care Allowance in Britain has been a particularly blatant example of the way in which the welfare state ensures that wives provide private welfare. The allowance was introduced in 1975 – when the Sex Discrimination Act was also passed – and it was paid to men or to single women who relinquished paid employment to look after a sick, disabled or elderly person (not necessarily a relative). Married women (or those cohabiting) were ineligible for the allowance [although this has now changed].

The evidence indicates that it is likely to be married women who provide such care. In 1976 in Britain it was estimated that two million women were caring for adult relatives, and one survey in the north of England found that there were more people caring for adult relatives than mothers looking after children under 16 (Dale and Foster, 1986, p. 112). A corollary of the assumption that women, but not men, care for others is that women must also care for themselves. Investigations show that women living by themselves in Britain have to be more infirm than men to obtain the services of home helps, and a study of an old people's home found that frail, elderly women admitted with their husbands faced hostility from the staff because they had failed in their job (Land, 1978, pp. 268–9).[8]Again, women's citizenship is full of contradictions and paradoxes. Women must provide welfare, and care for themselves, and so must be assumed to have the capacities necessary for these tasks. Yet the development of the welfare state has also presupposed that women necessarily are in need of protection by and are dependent on men.

The welfare state has reinforced women's identity as men's dependants both directly and indirectly, and so confirmed rather than ameliorated our social exile. For example, in Britain and Australia the cohabitation rule explicitly expresses the presumption that women necessarily must be economically dependent on men if they live with them as sexual partners. If cohabitation is ruled to take place, the woman loses her entitlement to welfare benefits. The consequence of the cohabitation rule is not only sexually divided control of citizens, but an exacerbation of the poverty and other problems that the welfare state is designed to alleviate. In Britain today:

> when a man lives in, a woman's independence – her own name on the weekly giro [welfare cheque] is automatically surrendered. The men become the claimants and the women their dependents [sic]. They lose control over both the revenue and the expenditure, often with catastrophic results: rent not paid, fuel bills missed, arrears mounting.
>
> (Campbell, 1984, p. 76)

It is important to ask what counts as part of the welfare state. In Australia and Britain the taxation system and transfer payments together form a tax-transfer system in the welfare state. In Australia a tax rebate is available for a dependent spouse (usually, of course, a wife), and in Britain the taxation system has always treated a wife's income as her husband's for taxation purposes. It is only relatively recently that it ceased to be the husband's prerogative to correspond with the Inland Revenue about his wife's earnings, or that he ceased to receive rebates due on her tax payments. Married men can still claim a tax allowance, based on the assumption that they support a dependent wife. Women's dependence is also enforced through the extremely limited public provision of child care facilities in Australia, Britain and the United States, which creates a severe obstacle to women's full participation in the employment society. In all three countries, unlike Scandinavia, child care outside the home is a very controversial issue.

Welfare-state legislation has also been framed on the assumption that women make their 'contribution' by providing private welfare, and, from the beginning, women were denied full citizenship in the welfare state. . . . In Britain the first national insurance, or contributory, scheme was set up in 1911, and one of its chief architects wrote later that women should have been completely excluded because 'they want insurance for others, not themselves' (Land, 1980, p. 72). Two years before the scheme was introduced, William Beveridge, the father of the contemporary British welfare state, stated in a book on unemployment that the 'ideal [social] unit is the household of man, wife and children maintained by the earnings of the first alone. . . . Reasonable security of employment for the breadwinner is the basis of all private duties and all sound social action' (Land, 1980, p. 72). Nor had Beveridge changed his mind on this matter by the Second World War; his report, *Social Insurance and Allied Services*, appeared in 1942 and laid a major part of the foundation for the great reforms of the 1940s. In a passage now (in)famous among feminists, Beveridge wrote that 'the great majority of married women must be regarded as occupied on work which is vital though unpaid, without which their husbands could not do their paid work and without which the nation could not continue' (Dale and Foster, 1986, p. 17). In the National Insurance Act of 1946 wives were separated from their husbands for insurance purposes. (The significance of this procedure, along with Beveridge's statement, clearly was lost on T.H. Marshall when he was writing his essay on citizenship and the welfare state.) Under the act, married women paid lesser contributions for reduced benefits, but they could also opt out of the scheme, and so from sickness, unemployment and maternity benefits, and they also lost entitlement to an old-age pension in their own right, being eligible only as their husband's dependant. By the time the legislation was amended in 1975, about three-quarters of married women workers had opted out (Land, 1983, p. 70).

A different standard for men and women has also been applied in the operation of the insurance scheme. In 1911 some married women were insured in their own right. The scheme provided benefits in case of 'incapacity to work', but, given that wives had already been identified as 'incapacitated' for the 'work' in question, for paid employment, problems over the criteria for entitlement to sickness benefits were almost inevitable. In 1913 an inquiry was held to discover why married women were claiming benefits at a much greater rate than expected. One obvious reason was that the health of many working-class women was extremely poor. The extent of their ill health was revealed in 1915 when letters written by working women in 1913–14 to the Women's Co-operative Guild were published (Davies, 1978). The national insurance scheme meant that for the first time women could afford to take time off work when ill – but from which 'work'? Could they take time off from housework? What were the implications for the embryonic welfare state if they ceased to provide free welfare? From 1913 a dual standard of eligibility for benefits was established. For men the criterion was fitness for work. But the committee of inquiry decided that, if a woman could do her housework, she was not ill. So the criterion for eligibility for women was also fitness for work – but unpaid work in the private home, not paid work in the public market that was the basis for the contributory scheme under which the women were insured! This criterion for women was still being laid down in instructions issued by the Department of Health and Social Security in the 1970s.[9] The dual standard was further reinforced in 1975 when a non-contributory invalidity pension was introduced for those incapable of work but not qualified for the contributory scheme. Men and single women were entitled to the pension if they could not engage in paid employment; the criterion for married women was ability to perform 'normal household duties' (Land, 1983, p. 70).

WOLLSTONECRAFT'S DILEMMA

So far, I have looked at the patriarchal structure of the welfare state, but this is only part of the picture; the development of the welfare state has also brought challenges to patriarchal power and helped provide a basis for women's autonomous citizenship. Women have seen the welfare state as one of their major means of support. Well before women won formal citizenship, they campaigned for the state to make provision for welfare, especially for the welfare of women and their children; and women's organizations and women activists have continued their political activities around welfare issues, not least in opposition to their status as 'dependants'. In 1953 the British feminist Vera Brittain wrote of the welfare state established through the legislation of the 1940s that 'in it women have become ends in themselves and not merely means to the ends of men', and their 'unique value as women was recognised' (Brittain, in Dale and Foster, 1986, p. 3). In hindsight, Brittain was clearly over-optimistic in her assessment, but perhaps the opportunity now exists to begin to dismantle the patriarchal structure of the welfare state. In the 1980s the large changes in women's social position, technological and structural transformations within capitalism, and mass unemployment mean that much of the basis for the breadwinner/dependant dichotomy and for the employment society itself is being eroded (although both are still widely seen as social ideals). The social context of Hegel's two dilemmas is disappearing. As the current concern about the 'feminization of poverty' reveals, there is now a very visible underclass of women who are directly connected to the state as claimants, rather than indirectly as men's dependants. Their social exile is as apparent as that of poor male workers was to Hegel. Social change has now made it much harder to gloss over the paradoxes and contradictions of women's status as citizens.

However, the question of how women might become full citizens of a democratic welfare state is more complex than may appear at first sight, because it is only in the current wave of the organized feminist movement that the division between the private and public spheres of social life has become seen as a major *political* problem. From the 1860s to the 1960s women were active in the public sphere: women fought not only for welfare measures and for measures to secure the private and public safety of women and girls, but for the vote and civil equality; middle-class women fought for entry into higher education, and the professions and women trade unionists fought for decent working conditions and wages and maternity leave. But the contemporary liberal-feminist view, particularly prominent in the United States, that what is required above all is 'gender-neutral' laws and policies, was not widely shared.[10] In general, until the 1960s the focus of attention in the welfare state was on measures to ensure that women had proper social support, and hence proper social respect, in carrying out their responsibilities in the private sphere. The problem is whether and how such measures could assist women in their fight for full citizenship. In 1942 in Britain, for example, many women welcomed the passage in the Beveridge Report that I have cited because, it was argued, it gave official recognition to the value of women's unpaid work. However, an official nod of recognition to women's work as 'vital' to 'the nation' is easily given; *in practice*, the value of the work in bringing women in to full membership in the welfare state was negligible. The equal worth of citizenship and the respect of fellow citizens still depended on participation as paid employees. 'Citizenship' and 'work' stood then and still stand opposed to 'women'.

The extremely difficult problem faced by women in their attempt to win full citizenship I shall call 'Wollstonecraft's dilemma'. The dilemma is that the two routes toward citizenship that women have pursued are mutually incompatible within the confines of the patriarchal welfare state, and, within that context, they are impossible to achieve. For three centuries, since universal citizenship first appeared as a political ideal, women have continued to challenge their alleged natural subordination within private life. From at least the 1790s they have also struggled with the task of trying to become citizens within an ideal and practice that have gained universal meaning through their exclusion. Women's response has been complex. On the one hand, they have demanded that the ideal of citizenship be extended to them,[11] and the liberal-feminist agenda for a 'gender-neutral' social world is the logical conclusion of one form of this demand. On the other hand, women have also insisted, often simultaneously, as did Mary Wollstonecraft, that *as women* they have specific capacities, talents, needs and concerns, so that the expression of their citizenship will be differentiated from that of men. Their unpaid work providing welfare could be seen, as Wollstonecraft saw women's tasks as mothers, as women's work *as citizens*, just as their husbands' paid work is central to men's citizenship.[12]

The patriarchal understanding of citizenship means that the two demands are incompatible because it allows two alternatives only: either women become (like) men, and so full citizens; or they continue at women's work, which is of no value for citizenship. Moreover, within a patriarchal welfare state neither demand can be met. To demand that citizenship, as it now exists, should be fully extended to women accepts the patriarchal meaning of 'citizen', which is constructed from men's attributes, capacities and activities. Women cannot be full citizens in the present meaning of the term; at best, citizenship can be extended to women only as lesser men. At the same time, within the patriarchal welfare state, to demand proper social recognition and support for women's responsibilities is to condemn women to less than full citizenship and to continued incorporation into public life as 'women'; that is, as members of another sphere who cannot, therefore, earn the respect of fellow (male) citizens.

The example of ... family allowances in ... Britain is instructive as a practical illustration of Wollstonecraft's dilemma. It reveals the great difficulties in trying to implement a policy that both aids women in their work and challenges patriarchal power while enhancing women's citizenship. ... There was opposition from the right and from *laissez-faire* economists on the ground that family allowances would undermine the father's obligation to support his children and undermine his 'incentive' to sell his labour-power in the market. The feminist advocates of family allowances in the 1920s, most notably Eleanor Rathbone in Britain, saw the alleviation of poverty in families where the breadwinner's wage was inadequate to meet the family's basic needs as only one argument for this form of state provision. They were also greatly concerned with the questions of the wife's economic dependence and equal pay for men and women workers. If the upkeep of children (or a substantial contribution toward it) was met by the state outside of wage bargaining in the market, then there was no reason why men and women doing the same work should not receive the same pay. Rathbone wrote in 1924 that 'nothing can justify the subordination of one group of producers – the mothers – to the rest and their deprivation of a share of their own in the wealth of a community' (Rathbone, in Land, 1980, p. 63). She argued that family allowances would, 'once and for all, cut away the maintenance of children and the reproduction of the race from the question of wages' (cited in Cass, 1983, p. 57).[13]

But not all the advocates of child endowment were feminists – so that the policy could very easily be divorced from the public issue of wages and dependence and be seen only as a return for and recognition of women's private contributions. Supporters included the eugenicists and pronatalists, and family allowances appealed to capital and the state as a means of keeping wages down. Family allowances had many opponents in the British union movement, fearful that the consequence, were the measure introduced, would be to undermine the power of unions in wage bargaining. The opponents included women trade unionists who were suspicious of a policy that could be used to try to persuade women to leave paid employment. Some unionists also argued that social services, such as housing, education and health, should be developed first, and the TUC adopted this view in 1930. But were the men concerned, too, with their private, patriarchal privileges? Rathbone claimed that 'the leaders of working men are themselves subconsciously biased by prejudice of sex. . . . Are they not influenced by a secret reluctance to see their wives and children recognised as separate personalities?' (Rathbone, in Cass, 1983, p. 59).

By 1941 the supporters of family allowances in the union movement had won the day, and family allowances were introduced in 1946, as part of the government's wartime plans for post-war reconstruction. The legislation proposed that the allowance would be paid to the father as 'normal household head', but after lobbying by women's organizations, this was overturned in a free vote, and the allowance was paid directly to mothers. . . . In the 1970s, . . . women's organizations again had to defend family allowances and the principle of redistribution from the 'wallet to the purse'.

The hope of Eleanor Rathbone and other feminists that family allowances would form part of a democratic restructuring of the wage system was not realized. Nevertheless, family allowances are paid to women as a benefit in their own right; in that sense they are an important (albeit financially very small) mark of recognition of married women as independent members of the welfare state. Yet the allowance is paid to women as *mothers*, and the key question is thus whether the payment to a mother – a private person – negates her standing as an independent citizen of the welfare state. More generally, the question is whether there can be a welfare policy that gives substantial assistance to women in their daily lives *and* helps create the conditions for a genuine democracy in which women are autonomous citizens, in which we can act *as women* and not as 'woman' (protected/dependent/subordinate) constructed as the opposite to all that is meant by 'man'. That is to say, a resolution of Wollstonecraft's dilemma is necessary and, perhaps, possible.

The structure of the welfare state presupposes that women are men's dependants, but the benefits help to make it possible for women to be economically independent of men. In the countries with which I am concerned, women reliant on state benefits live poorly, but it is no longer so essential as it once was to marry or to cohabit with a man. A considerable moral panic has developed in recent years around 'welfare mothers', a panic that obscures significant features of their position, not least the extent to which the social basis for the ideal of breadwinner/dependant has crumbled. Large numbers of young working-class women have little or no hope of finding employment (or of finding a young man who is employed). But there is a source of social identity available to them that is out of the reach of their male counterparts. The socially secure and acknowledged identity for women is still that of a mother, and for many young women, motherhood, supported by state benefits, provides 'an alternative to aimless adolescence on the dole' and 'gives the appearance of self-determination'. The price of independence and 'a rebellious motherhood that is not an uncritical retreat into femininity' (Campbell, 1984, pp. 66, 78, 71) is high, however; the welfare state provides a minimal income and perhaps housing (often substandard), but child care services and other support are lacking, so that the young women are often isolated, with no way out of their social exile. Moreover, even if welfare state policies in Britain, Australia and the United States were reformed so that generous benefits, adequate housing, health care, child care and other services were available to mothers, reliance on the state could reinforce women's lesser citizenship in a new way.

Some feminists have enthusiastically endorsed the welfare state as 'the main recourse of women' and as the generator of 'political resources which, it seems fair to say, are mainly women's resources'

(Fox Piven, 1984, pp. 14, 17). They can point, in Australia for example, to 'the creation over the decade [1975–85] of a range of women's policy machinery and government subsidized women's services (delivered by women for women) which is unrivalled elsewhere' (Sawer, 1986, p. 1). However, the enthusiasm is met with the rejoinder from other feminists that for women to look to the welfare state is merely to exchange dependence on individual men for dependence on the state. The power and capriciousness of husbands is being replaced by the arbitrariness, bureaucracy and power of the state, the very state that has upheld patriarchal power. The objection is cogent: to make women directly dependent on the state will not in itself do anything to challenge patriarchal power relations. The direct dependence of male workers on the welfare state and their indirect dependence when their standard of living is derived from the vast system of state regulation of and subsidy to capitalism – and in Australia a national arbitration court – have done little to undermine class power. However, the objection also misses an important point. There is one crucial difference between the construction of women as men's dependants and dependence on the welfare state. In the former case, each woman lives with the man on whose benevolence she depends; each woman is (in J.S. Mill's extraordinarily apt phrase) in a 'chronic state of bribery and intimidation combined' (Mill, 1970, p. 137). In the welfare state, each woman receives what is hers by right, and she can, potentially, combine with other citizens to enforce her rightful claim. The state has enormous powers of intimidation, but political action takes place collectively in the public terrain and not behind the closed door of the home, where each woman has to rely on her own strength and resources.

[WOMEN AND WELFARE]

Another new factor is that women are now involved in the welfare state on a large scale as employees, so that new possibilities for political action by women also exist. Women have been criticizing the welfare state in recent years not just as academics, as activists, or as beneficiaries and users of welfare services, but as the people on whom the daily operation of the welfare state to a large extent depends. The criticisms range from its patriarchal structure (and, on occasions, especially in health care, misogynist practices), to its bureaucratic and undemocratic policy-making processes and administration, to social work practices and education policy. Small beginnings have been made on changing the welfare state from within; for example, women have succeeded in establishing Well Women Clinics within the NHS in Britain and special units to deal with rape victims in public hospitals in Australia. Furthermore, the potential is now there for united action by women employees, women claimants and women citizens already politically active in the welfare state – not just to protect services against government cuts and efforts at 'privatization' (which has absorbed much energy recently), but to transform the welfare state. Still, it is hard to see how women alone could succeed in the attempt. One necessary condition for the creation of a genuine democracy in which the welfare of *all* citizens is served is an alliance between a labour movement that acknowledges the problem of patriarchal power and an autonomous women's movement that recognizes the problem of class power. Whether such an alliance can be forged is an open question.

Despite the debates and the rethinking brought about by mass unemployment and attack on the union movement and welfare state by the Reagan and Thatcher governments, there are many barriers to be overcome. In Britain and Australia, with stronger welfare states, the women's movement has had a much closer relationship with working-class movements than in the United States, where the individualism of the predominant liberal feminism is an inhibiting factor, and where only about 17 per cent of the work force is now unionized. The major locus of criticism of authoritarian, hierarchical, undemocratic forms of organization for the last twenty years has been the women's movement. The practical example of democratic, decentralized organization provided by the women's movement has been largely ignored by the labour movement, as well as in academic discussions of democracy. After Marx defeated Bakunin in the First International, the prevailing form of organization in the labour movement, the nationalized industries in Britain and in the left sects has mimicked the hierarchy of the state – both the welfare and the warfare state. To be sure, there is a movement for industrial democracy and workers' control, but it has, by and large, accepted that the 'worker' is a masculine figure and failed to question the separation of (public) industry and economic production from private life. The women's movement has rescued and put into practice the long-submerged idea that movements for, and experiments in, social change must 'prefigure' the future form of social organization.[14]

If prefigurative forms of organization, such as the 'alternative' women's welfare services set up by the women's movement, are not to remain isolated examples, or if attempts to set them up on a wider scale are not to be defeated, as in the past, very many accepted conceptions and practices have to be questioned. . . . Debates over left alternatives to Thatcherite economics policies in Britain [during the 1980s], and over the Accord between the state, capital and labour in Australia, suggest that the arguments and demands of the women's movement are still often unrecognized by labour's political spokesmen. For instance, one response to unemployment from male workers is to argue for a shorter working week and more leisure, or more time but the same money. However, in women's lives, time and money are not interchangeable in the same way.[15] Women, unlike men, do not have leisure after 'work', but do unpaid work. Many women are arguing, rather, for a shorter working day. The point of the argument is to challenge the separation of part- and full-time paid employment and paid and unpaid 'work'. But the conception of citizenship needs thorough questioning, too, if Wollstonecraft's dilemma is to be resolved; neither the labour movement nor the women's movement (nor democratic theorists) has paid much attention to this. The patriarchal opposition between the private and public, women and citizen, dependant and breadwinner is less firmly based than it once was, and feminists have named it as a political problem. The ideal of full employment so central to the welfare state is also crumbling, so that some of the main props of the patriarchal understanding of citizenship are being undermined. The ideal of full employment appeared to have been achieved in the 1960s only because half the citizen body (and black men?) was denied legitimate membership in the employment society. Now that millions of men are excluded from the ideal (and the exclusion seems permanent), one possibility is that the ideal of universal citizenship will be abandoned, too, and full citizenship become the prerogative of capitalist, employed and armed men. Or can a genuine democracy be created?

The perception of democracy as a class problem and the influence of liberal feminism have combined to keep alive Engels' old solution to 'the woman question' – to 'bring the whole female sex back into public industry' (Engels, 1942, p. 66). But the economy has a patriarchal structure. The Marxist hope that capitalism would create a labour force where ascriptive characteristics were irrelevant, and the liberal-feminist hope that anti-discrimination legislation will create a 'gender-neutral' workforce, look utopian even without the collapse of the ideal of full employment. Engels' solution is out of reach – and so, too, is the generalization of masculine citizenship to women. In turn, the argument that the equal worth of citizenship, and the self-respect and mutual respect of citizens, depend upon sale of labour-power in the market and the provisions of the patriarchal welfare state is also undercut. The way is opening up for formulation of conceptions of respect and equal worth adequate for democratic citizenship. Women could not 'earn' respect or gain the self-respect that men obtain as workers; but what kind of respect do men 'achieve' by selling their labour-power and becoming wage-slaves? Here the movement for workplace democracy and the feminist movement could join hands, but only if the conventional understanding of 'work' is rethought. If women as well as men are to be full citizens, the separation of the welfare state and employment from the free welfare work contributed by women has to be broken down and new meanings and practices of 'independence', 'work' and 'welfare' created.

For example, consider the implications were a broad, popular political movement to press for welfare policy to include a guaranteed social income to all adults, which would provide adequately for subsistence and also participation in social life.[16] For such a demand to be made, the old dichotomies must already have started to break down – the opposition between paid and unpaid work (for the first time all individuals could have a genuine choice whether to engage in paid work), between full- and part-time work, between public and private work, between independence and dependence, between work and welfare – which is to say, between men and women. If implemented, such a policy would at last recognize women as equal members of the welfare state, although it would not in itself ensure women's full citizenship. If a genuine democracy is to be created, the problem of the content and value of women's contribution as citizens and the meaning of citizenship has to be confronted.

To analyse the welfare state through the lens of Hegel's dilemma is to rule out such problems. But the history of the past 150 years and the contemporary record show that the welfare of all members of society cannot be represented by men, whether workers or capitalists. Welfare is, after all, the welfare of all living generations of citizens and their children. If the welfare state is seen as a response to Hegel's dilemma, the appropriate question about women's citizenship is: how can women become workers and citizens like men, and so members of the welfare state like men? If, instead, the starting point is Wollstonecraft's dilemma, then the question might run: what form must democratic citizenship take if a primary task of all citizens is to ensure that the welfare of each living generation of citizens is secured?

The welfare state has been fought for and supported by the labour movement and the women's movement because only public or collective provision can maintain a proper standard of living and the means for meaningful social participation for all citizens in a democracy. The implication of this claim is that democratic citizens are both autonomous and interdependent; they are autonomous in that each enjoys the means to be an active citizen, but they are interdependent in that the welfare of each is the collective responsibility of all citizens. Critics of the class structure of the welfare state have often counterposed the fraternal interdependence (solidarity) signified by the welfare state to the bleak independence of isolated individuals in the market, but they have rarely noticed that both have been predicated upon the dependence (subordination) of women. In the patriarchal welfare state, independence has been constructed as a masculine prerogative. Men's 'independence' as workers and citizens is their freedom from responsibility for welfare (except in so far as they 'contribute' to the welfare state). Women have been seen as responsible for (private) welfare work, for relationships of dependence and interdependence. The paradox that welfare relies so largely on women, on dependants and social exiles whose 'contribution' is not politically relevant to their citizenship in the welfare state, is heightened now that women's paid employment is also vital to the operation of the welfare state itself.

If women's knowledge of and expertise in welfare are to become part of their contribution as citizens, as women have demanded during the twentieth century, the opposition between men's independence and women's dependence has to be broken down, and a new understanding and practice of citizenship developed. The patriarchal dichotomy between women and independence–work–citizenship is under political challenge, and the social basis for the ideal of the full (male) employment society is crumbling. An opportunity has become visible to create a genuine democracy, to move from the welfare state to a welfare society without involuntary social exiles, in which women as well as men enjoy full social membership. Whether the opportunity can be realized is not easy to tell now that the warfare state is overshadowing the welfare state.

Notes

1   I have presented a theoretical elaboration of a modern conception of 'patriarchy' as the systematic exercise by men of power over women in *The Sexual Contract* (Pateman, 1988) – for a brief discussion of some of the issues, see chapter 2.

2   Women were formally enfranchised as citizens in 1902 in Australia, 1920 in the USA and 1928 in Britain (womanhood franchise in 1918 was limited to women over 30 years old).

3   On Scandinavia see, for example, *Patriarchy in a Welfare Society* (Holter, 1984), especially H. Hernes, 'Women and the welfare state: the transition from private to public dependence'; and *Unfinished Democracy: women in Nordic politics* (Haavio-Mannila et al., 1985).

4   I have taken the term from Keane and Owens (1986, p. 11).

5   Thompson was a utilitarian, but also a feminist, co-operative socialist, so that he took his individualism more seriously than most utilitarians. In *Appeal of One Half the Human Race, Women, against the Pretensions of the Other Half, Men, to Retain Them in Political, and then in Civil and Domestic Slavery* (1970, first published 1825), Thompson, writing of the importance of looking at the distribution of interests, or 'the means of happiness', argues that the 'division of interests' must proceed 'until it is brought home to every

individual of every family'. Instead, under the despotism of husbands and fathers, 'the interest of each of them is promoted, in as far only as it is coincident with, or subservient to, the master's interest' (pp. 46–7, 49).

6   As Beatrix Campbell has reminded us, 'we protect men from the shame of their participation in women's poverty by keeping the secret. Family budgets are seen to be a *private* settlement of accounts between men and women, men's unequal distribution of working-class incomes within their households is a right they fought for within the working-class movement and it is not yet susceptible to *public* political pressure within the movement' (Campbell, 1984, p. 57). Wives are usually responsible for making sure that the children are fed, the rent paid and so on, but this does not mean that they always decide how much money is allocated to take care of these basic needs. Moreover, in times of economic hardship women are often short of food as well as money; wives will make sure that the 'breadwinner' and the children are fed before they are.

7   The perception is common to both women and men. (I would argue that women's perception of themselves is not, as is often suggested, a consequence of 'socialization', but a realistic appraisal of their structural position at home and in the workplace.) For empirical evidence on this view of women workers, see, for example, Pollert (1981) and Wacjman (1983).

8   Land notes that even under the old Poor Law twice as many women as men received outdoor relief, and there were many more old men than women in the workhouse wards for the ill or infirm; the women were deemed fit for the wards for the able-bodied.

9   Information taken from Land (1978, pp. 263–4).

10   There was considerable controversy within the women's movement between the wars over the question of protective legislation for women in industry. Did equal citizenship require the removal of such protection, so that women worked under the same conditions as men; or did the legislation benefit women, and the real issue become proper health and safety protection for both men and women workers?

11   I have discussed the earlier arguments in more detail in 'Women and democratic citizenship' (Pateman, 1985).

12   For example, Wollstonecraft writes, 'speaking of women at large, their first duty is to themselves as rational creatures, and the next, in point of importance, as citizens, is that, which includes so many, of a mother'. She hopes that a time will come when a 'man must necessarily fulfil the duties of a citizen, or be despised, and that while he was employed in any of the departments of civil life,

his wife, also an active citizen, should be equally intent to manage her family, educate her children, and assist her neighbours' (Wollstonecraft, 1975, pp. 145, 146).

13   My discussion draws on Land and Cass. In the USA during the same period, feminists supported the movement for mothers' pensions. Unlike mothers eligible for family allowances, mothers eligible for pensions were without male breadwinners. The complexities of mothers' pensions are discussed by Sarvesy (1986).

14   See Rowbotham *et al. Beyond the Fragments: feminism and the making of socialism* (1979), a book that was instrumental in opening debate on the left and in the labour movement in Britain on this question.

15   See Hernes (1987, ch. 5) for a discussion of the political implications of the different time-frames of men's and women's lives.

16   See also the discussion in Keane and Owens (1986, pp. 175–7).

7

WOMEN'S STRUGGLES: UNITY AND DIVERSITY

CAMPAIGNING WOMEN

In this chapter, we analyse two variants of women's political struggle. The first example is based on women's formal engagement with the institutions of the state (the law). The second is a challenge to the power of organized religion, examining the actions undertaken by a small group of women in London at the end of the 1980s against the growing power of fundamentalist Islamic religion within Britain's Muslim community.

The first example is one of formal political action, revolving around pressure to improve women's position in the labour market, which, as Pateman has argued, is of fundamental importance for women's rights as citizens. It is an example of legislative change. In the UK and the USA laws have been introduced to enable women as individuals or as groups to challenge pay discrimination on the grounds of sex. One of the problems that women face in taking such actions, however, is the extent of segregation in the labour market, making the concept of equal pay *per se* unworkable. As we saw in Chapter 5, women and men in the vast majority of cases are not employed in the same jobs. For this reason the concept of equal pay for jobs of 'equal value' (in the UK) and of 'comparable worth' (in the USA) was introduced. Women, when bringing a case before an industrial tribunal in the UK or before the courts in the USA, compare their work with that of men doing comparable tasks but receiving greater financial rewards. Thus, for example, in a well-known case in the UK, a cook working for Cammell Lairds, a firm of shipbuilders, compared her work with that of a male painter.

In Article 7.1, Joan Scott unpacks the arguments in a sex discrimination case which was taken to court in the USA in 1985. In that year, women who were sales workers for the Sears-Roebuck retail group took their case against Sears to the Equal Opportunities Commission. Scott outlines the arguments that were made for each side – the women and the employers – and shows how, by allowing the debate to be polarized, along equality-or-difference lines, the women workers were badly outmanoeuvred in court. As Scott suggests, the debate should not have been about equality and difference at all, but rather about the need for special treatment to

246

allow for the particular circumstances of women workers at the time. Thus Scott argues that, in general, equality and difference should be seen as interdependent concepts, connected rather than opposites; and which is emphasized in feminist political struggles at any time should depend on the context rather than on universal claims or on a pre-given reality. This suggests that it is important to recognize the contingent and specific nature of feminist political claims at any one time and to avoid being manoeuvred into positions that seem to depend upon the assertion of grand statements of principle. In the first part of her article she outlines the utility of deconstructionist approaches in her challenge to the over-simple dichotomy of equality and difference, thus providing an empirical example of more recent post-structuralist analysis.

Action in court, of course, is not the only way to improve women's position in the labour market. Women's involvement in the trade union movement also plays an important part here. Through both local action and national change, instituted through the mechanism of the Trades Union Congress, women have long argued that their *particular needs* in the labour market should be taken into account. However, women activists have not always found it easy to work within the union movement. Traditionally, trade unions have been extremely male-dominated organizations – from their language of brotherhood, through to their membership and, particularly, in their mode of operation based on formal meetings (often held after working hours) and rigid procedures. Thus trade union 'culture' has been alien and off-putting to many women workers. In addition, for many years pay issues, and particularly the maintenance of differentials between skilled and unskilled workers, were the main concern of the union movement in the UK. As we have seen from Part III, these differentials often reflect gender differences in pay. Unions in the UK generally have been less involved with social issues, from holidays, through working hours to housing provision than have some of their counterparts in Western Europe. And these are often the issues of most interest to women.

In recent years, however, matters have changed. Economic restructuring and the decline of the heavy, male-employing industries, particularly in the north of Britain, have hit union membership rates. Increasingly, with the growth of service sector occupations, new members are being sought from among the ranks of the expanding numbers of women in the labour market. Issues such as part-time employment have become more important, both as an organizational question for union meetings and as an issue for political pressure. Women's increasing involvement in unions is raising new questions – about child care, for example, often dubbed a 'woman's issue' but which actually is a concern of both women and men who want to achieve a more satisfactory reconciliation of the demands of parenthood and waged work than seems possible at present.

Women's involvement in unions is challenging the sameness/difference dichotomy by suggesting that both women and men may gain by a new look at issues such as the length of the working day and parental leave entitlement. Women in unions are not organizing to replicate the conditions under which men live, nor even to modify them at the margins, but to raise and address more fundamental questions about the significance of wage labour in our lives and gender divisions of labour in the home as well as in the workplace. Wilson (1989) has suggested in her book *Hallucinations: Life in the Post Modern City* that women's and men's interests in the sphere of work increasingly are coinciding with the opening up of new divisions in the labour market between low-paid workers, both women and men, on the one hand, and a well-paid élite, also of women and men, on the other:

> ... what is happening today, and not only in Britain, is that women are set up as the advance guard of a *general* attack on workers with the intention of creating a low-wage economy in which the vast majority of workers, regardless of sex, are employed on 'female' terms. Both sexes will suffer from deregulation, de-unionization, so-called 'flexible' work practices, and men are already beginning to take part-time work in some areas.
>
> Simultaneously, there is a small but (slowly) growing group of much better-paid professional or managerial women workers, and a growing gap between their experience and that of their exploited and underpaid sisters. The interests of low-paid workers of both sexes are therefore likely to draw closer together, while on the other hand it may be increasingly difficult to create a unity of 'all women', although there will continue to be areas such as health care and violence where their interests are more likely to coincide. But, in general, the vulnerable position of the vast majority of women in the workforce should be a reason to support trades unionism rather than to engage in the union-bashing which is such an unpleasant and reactionary aspect of the general retreat of the '1970s Left', and which reappears in the debate on postmodernism as an iconoclastic and therefore radical view, when in fact it is neither.

(Wilson, 1989, pp. 198–9)

So, a woman's place is in her union as well as in the law courts. And increasingly, the interests of low-paid women *and men* may coincide in campaigns such as those to support a minimum wage for *all* low-paid workers.

Women and the peace movement

Women are also politically active in a whole range of other areas. One of the most important recent examples of women's informal or direct political action, rather than of struggles through the formal institutions of the state and the labour market, has been the women's peace movement camps. During the 1980s, women's peace camps were established at Greenham Common in the UK, at Seneca in the USA and at a number of other places in Western Europe. The origins of the Greenham camp lie in a march by thirty-four women, four men and a handful of children from Cardiff to Newbury in Berkshire in August 1981. As the news of their action spread these women and others decided to set up a permanent picket at Greenham Common – the site of a US nuclear missile base. The camp was organized in an open and non-hierarchical fashion and the women involved resisted the efforts of the media, the police and the courts to focus on individual spokeswomen. Men were excluded as there was a fear that they would be more willing to engage in violent confrontations with the authorities. Rather, the Greenham women developed strategies of non-violent direct action, from decorating the perimeter fence to invading the base.

As Anna Coote and Polly Patullo (1990) explain in the extract below, Greenham drew thousands of women into politics, both directly and indirectly. Many women who would not classify themselves as feminists visited Greenham or were involved in fundraising and, over the decade, links were built between this issue and others that affect women – whether as wives and mothers, as members of a particular class or working-class community, or as members of minority populations. Here, the motherist/feminist, the essentialist/socialist dichotomies became blurred and many women were involved as women rather than as feminists:

> Greenham was far more than a pressure group or a single-issue campaign. It was a mass movement which drew thousands of women into political awareness and activity during the early 1980s. It introduced many of them to feminism; those who had missed the high tide of discovery and invention that launched women's liberation in the seventies made similar connections through working with other women for peace. It also propelled many who were already feminists towards a new range of political concerns – and thus revitalized the women's movement, which drew energy and inspiration from Greenham, as did CND.
>
> It was never a working-class movement; indeed it was, like the Women's Liberation Movement, predominantly white

and middle-class. To leave home and family, to live (even temporarily) in a peace camp, to put oneself in the way of arrest and imprisonment was extremely hard, involving great risk and sacrifice. It was not lightly undertaken even by the most independent and fancy-free of women. For a working-class woman with husband and children, a paid job on which the family depended and heavy responsibilities at home, it was unimaginable. But the emphasis of Greenham shifted as women became increasingly aware of these limitations. 'The early simplicity of "women give life/men build death" could not sustain a movement for ever,' Barbara Norden commented in *Spare Rib.* 'The sort of feminism that saw the nuclear arms race as a direct expression of patriarchy has tended to give way to a more diverse brand of socialist feminism which has enabled Greenham to make links.'

(*Coote and Patullo, 1990, p. 126*)

However, we should take care not to underestimate the importance of the impetus behind the peace movement. What may seem at first sight to be a classic case of women organizing on the basis of their *difference* from men, and so open to the charge of essentialism, is too simple a view. Women who denounce violence and domination and its ultimate expression, war, are *political* thinkers making *political* decisions and choices. It denigrates these decisions to see them as the 'natural' consequence of a specifically female disposition.

Women and religious ideologies

In the second reading for this chapter, we turn to a different element in the oppression of women – the impact of religious ideologies. We address the implications of and reactions to the rise of religious and other fundamentalist movements during the 1980s. In a whole range of guises in different societies – including the resurgence of Islam in both First and Third World countries, the increased voice of the 'moral majority' in the USA, of evangelic Christians, Orthodox Jews, and Catholics in a range of societies – religious and nationalist politics have become more important. Here, in Article 7.2, Ruth Pearson, who identifies herself as 'a white non-religious socialist feminist with internationalist pretensions', addresses the response by a group of Islamic women, the Southall Black Sisters, to the increased policing and control of Islamic women by religious leaders in Britain's Muslim communities.

The rise of religious fundamentalism, the rights and responsibilities of 'minority' communities, the diversities and differences between women, and their differential placement with respect to the structures of power and control of the state and in civil society raise challenging issues for feminists in their theory and practice, as Pearson outlines. Questions of ethnicity and nationalism, about immigration controls, about eugenicist social and population policies, about alternative family structures and about the basis of 'nationhood' for minority groups, such as the Kurds or the Palestinians, living across the boundaries of several nation states, raise difficult questions that feminist political analysis is beginning to address.

FEMINIST POLITICS: UNITY IN DIVERSITY?

The issues addressed in the two preceding articles, and raised by us, indicate the wide variety of issues on which feminists have organized in the USA, the UK and elsewhere. And, as we have shown in the other parts of this book, women are divided on many issues: their age, their class position, their race and ethnic origin, their sexual orientation and many other differences influence their material circumstances and the nature of their political allegiances. Thus, as the conclusion to both Part IV and to the book as a whole, we return to our central theme: *What is the significance for the future of feminism as a united political movement of the recognition of diversity among women?* For some women the recognition of substantial differences between us has led to a denial of the possibility of feminist politics based around the assumption of the unitary interests of women. The strength of the post-modern critique of a unitary conception of 'woman', itself, and the recognition of the fractured and contradictory nature of subjectivity has also led to despair about the possibilities for feminist political action and change. Indeed, the term 'post-feminism' has been coined as the corollary of post-modernism.

However, post-feminism also seems to be composed of contradictory trends. As well as those who deny the possibility of a radical progressive feminist politics, others using this term seem to suggest that women have already achieved equality, citing as evidence figures for the increase in the number of women in positions of power. The term 'post-feminism' is also used as a label to summarize a more conservative strand in the women's movement, even perhaps stretching to embrace the anti-feminist position held by the pro-family lobby who have reasserted the significance of women's role as mothers and carers. For example, two of the influential authors from the 1960s second-wave feminist resurgence, Betty Friedan and Germaine Greer, have placed greater emphasis in their more recent books, *The Second Stage* (1981) and *Sex and Destiny* (1985), respectively, on the positive values of home-making and child-rearing than they did in their earlier work. Other feminists have also emphasized the 'private' sphere, seeing little prospect of improvements in women's position in the labour market in current circumstances. Thus Tery Apter has argued that 'women's rights and women's hopes' have been 'a casualty of the recession' (Apter, 1985, p. 150). She considers that positive discrimination on behalf of women who interrupt their working lives to have children is highly unlikely and yet without it, they will be held back. Her solution parallels that of the conservative 'feminists' – women should concentrate on their 'special suitability as mothers'. She sees this reassertion of 'difference' between men and women as 'feminism's only hope of salvation' (ibid.).

Other feminist scholars and activists are not so despairing and suggest that we should see our diversity as strength – in Harding's words we should 'embrace as a fruitful grounding for enquiry the fractured identities modern life creates – Black-feminist, socialist-feminist, women-of-colour and so on' (Harding, 1986, p. 28). And later in the same book, *The Science Question in Feminism*, she suggests that 'Even the infamous "hyphenization" of feminist political and theoretical stances – Socialist-Feminism, Radical-Feminism, Lesbian-Feminism, Black-Marxist-Feminism, Black-Lesbian-Socialist-Feminism, Radical-Women-of-Colour bespeaks an exhilaration felt in the differences in women's perceptions of who we are and of the appropriate politics for navigating through our daily social relations' (ibid., p. 163).

As women from different backgrounds and class positions, we have multiple political identities and overlapping sets of priorities. The 'Declaration of an independence' (Article 7.3) by June Jordan, a black-African-American-socialist-feminist, raises questions that she personally feels about trying to reconcile her political commitment to three movements: a First World, a Third World and a feminist struggle. Other writers are also optimistic about the possibility of reconciling the contradiction between recognizing the diverse experiences of women with a political ideology that is based on the commonalities between women and see that a stronger movement might emerge. Chela Sandoval (quoted in Haraway, 1990, p. 197) has argued for a politics based on 'oppositional consciousness' – the recognition of multiple 'otherness' as women, as ethnic minorities, as lesbian or bisexuals. Out of this sort of politics a unity rather than relativism or pluralism might appear. Caroline Ramazanoglu, in Article 7.4, assesses the future prospects for unity in diversity and for concerted feminist political action to transform the world. Although she frankly admits that the prospects are limited, she suggests that perhaps as western feminists we should be looking to the liberation struggles in Third World countries for inspiration. In societies such as South Africa, which is facing a fundamental transformation in the 1990s, perhaps we might see women's liberation as part of the overall change. But wherever we live, the prospect of redefining woman's place in the world is too important to relinquish now.

Article 7.1

DECONSTRUCTING EQUALITY-VERSUS-DIFFERENCE: OR, THE USES OF POST-STRUCTURALIST THEORY FOR FEMINISM

Joan W. Scott

That feminism needs theory goes without saying (perhaps because it has been said so often). What is not always clear is what that theory will do, although there are certain common assumptions I think we can find in a wide range of feminist writings. We need theory that can analyse the workings of patriarchy in all its manifestations – ideological, institutional, organizational, subjective – accounting not only for continuities but also for change over time. We need theory that will let us think in terms of pluralities and diversities rather than of unities and universals. We need theory that will break the conceptual hold, at least, of those long traditions of (western) philosophy that have systematically and repeatedly construed the world hierarchically in terms of masculine universals and feminine specificities. We need theory that will enable us to articulate alternative ways of thinking about (and thus acting upon) gender without either simply reversing the old hierarchies or confirming them. And we need theory that will be useful and relevant for political practice.

It seems to me that the body of theory referred to as post-structuralism best meets all these requirements. It is not by any means the only theory nor are its positions and formulations unique. In my own case, however, it was reading post-structuralist theory and arguing with literary scholars that provided the elements of clarification for which I was looking. I found a new way of analysing constructions of meaning and relationships of power that called unitary, universal categories into question and historicized concepts otherwise treated as natural (such as man/woman) or absolute (such as equality or justice). In addition, what attracted me was the historical connection between the two movements. Post-structuralism and contemporary feminism are late twentieth-century movements that share a certain self-conscious critical relationship to established philosophical and political traditions. It thus seemed worthwhile for feminist scholars to exploit that relationship for their own ends.

. . . The first part of this article is a brief discussion of concepts used by post-structuralists that are also useful for feminists. The second part applies some of these concepts to one of the hotly contested issues among contemporary (US) feminists – the 'equality-versus-difference' debate.

Among the useful terms feminists have appropriated from post-structuralism are language, discourse, difference and deconstruction.

Language. Following the work of structuralist linguistics and anthropology, the term is used to mean not simply words or even a vocabulary and set of grammatical rules, but, rather, a meaning-constituting system: that is, any system – strictly verbal or other – through which meaning is constructed and cultural practices organized and by which, accordingly, people represent and understand their world, including who they are and how they relate to others. 'Language', so conceived, is a central focus of post-structuralist analysis.

Language is not assumed to be a representation of ideas that either cause material relations or from which such relations follow; indeed, the idealist/materialist opposition is a false one to impose on this approach. Rather, the analysis of language provides a crucial point of entry, a starting point for understanding how social relations are conceived, and, therefore – because understanding how they are conceived means understanding how they work – how institutions are organized, how relations of production are experienced, and how collective identity is established. Without attention to language and the processes by which meanings and categories are constituted, one only imposes over-simplified models on the world, models that perpetuate conventional understandings rather than open up new interpretive possibilities.

. . . Post-structuralists insist that words and texts have no fixed or intrinsic meanings, that there is no transparent or self-evident relationship between them and either ideas or things, no basic or ultimate correspondence between language and the world. The questions that must be answered in such an analysis, then, are how, in what specific contexts, among which specific communities of people, and by what textual and social processes has meaning been acquired? More generally, the questions are: How do meanings change? How have some meanings emerged as normative and others have been eclipsed or disappeared? What do these processes reveal about how power is constituted and operates?

Discourse. Some of the answers to these questions are offered in the concept of discourse, especially as it has been developed in the work of Michel Foucault. A discourse is not a language or a text but a historically, socially and institutionally specific structure of statements, terms, categories and beliefs. Foucault suggests that the elaboration of meaning involves conflict and power, that meanings are locally contested within discursive 'fields of force', that (at least since the Enlightenment) the power to control a particular field resides in claims to (scientific) knowledge embodied not only in writing but also in disciplinary and professional organizations, in institutions (hospitals, prisons, schools, factories), and in social relationships (doctor/patient, teacher/student, employer/worker, parent/child, husband/wife). Discourse is thus contained or expressed in organizations and institutions as well as in words; all of these constitute texts or documents to be read.

Discursive fields overlap, influence and compete with one another; they appeal to one another's 'truths' for authority and legitimation. These truths are assumed to be outside human invention, either already known and self-evident or discoverable through scientific inquiry. Precisely because they are assigned the status of objective knowledge, they seem to be beyond dispute and thus serve a powerful legitimating function. Darwinian theories of natural selection are one example of such legitimating truths; biological theories about sexual difference are another. The power of these 'truths' comes from the way they function as givens or first premises for both sides in an argument, so that conflicts within discursive fields are framed to follow from, rather than question, them. The brilliance of so much of Foucault's work has been to illuminate the shared assumptions of what seemed to be sharply different arguments, thus exposing the limits of radical criticism and the extent of the power of dominant ideologies or epistemologies.

. . . Foucault has shown how badly . . . challenges to fundamental assumptions often fared. They have been marginalized or silenced, forced to underplay their most radical claims in order to win a short-term goal, or completely absorbed into an existing framework. . . . Although some have read Foucault as an argument about the futility of human agency in the struggle for social change, I think that he is more appropriately taken as warning against simple solutions to difficult problems, as advising human actors to think strategically and more self-consciously about the philosophical and political implications and meanings of the programmes they endorse. From this perspective, Foucault's work provides an important way of thinking differently (and perhaps more creatively) about the politics of the contextual construction of social meanings, about such organizing principles for political action as 'equality' and 'difference'.

Difference. An important dimension of post-structuralist analyses of language has to do with the concept of difference, the notion (following Ferdinand de Saussure's structuralist linguistics) that meaning is made through implicit or explicit contrast, that a positive definition rests on the negation or repression of something represented as antithetical to it. Thus, any unitary concept in fact contains repressed or negated material; it is established in explicit

255

opposition to another term. Any analysis of meaning involves teasing out these negations and oppositions, figuring out how (and whether) they are operating in specific contexts. Oppositions rest on metaphors and cross-references, and often in patriarchal discourse, sexual difference (the contrast masculine/feminine) serves to encode or establish meanings that are literally unrelated to gender or the body. In that way, the meanings of gender become tied to many kinds of cultural representations, and these in turn establish terms by which relations between women and men are organized and understood. The possibilities of this kind of analysis have, for obvious reasons, drawn the interest and attention of feminist scholars.

Fixed oppositions conceal the extent to which things presented as oppositional are, in fact, interdependent – that is, they derive their meaning from a particularly established contrast rather than from some inherent or pure antithesis. Furthermore, according to Jacques Derrida, the interdependence is hierarchical with one term dominant or prior, the opposite term subordinate, and secondary. The western philosophical tradition, he argues, rests on binary oppositions: unity/diversity, identity/difference, presence/absence and universality/specificity. The leading terms are accorded primacy; their partners are represented as weaker or derivative. Yet the first terms depend on and derive their meaning from the second to such an extent that the secondary terms can be seen as generative of the definition of the first terms. If binary oppositions provide insight into the way meaning is constructed, and if they operate as Derrida suggests, then analyses of meaning cannot take binary oppositions at face value but rather must 'deconstruct' them for the processes they embody.

Deconstruction. Although this term is used loosely among scholars – often to refer to a dismantling or destructive enterprise – it also has a precise definition in the work of Derrida and his followers. Deconstruction involves analysing the operations of difference in texts, the ways in which meanings are made to work. The method consists of two related steps: the reversal and displacement of binary oppositions. This double process reveals the interdependence of seemingly dichotomous terms and their meaning relative to a particular history. It shows them to be not natural but constructed oppositions, constructed for particular purposes in particular contexts. The literary critic Barbara Johnson describes deconstruction as crucially dependent on difference:

> The starting point is often a binary difference that is sub-sequently shown to be an illusion created by the working of differences much harder to pin down. The differences *between* entities . . . are shown to be based on a repression of differences

256

within entities, ways in which an entity differs from itself. . . .
The 'deconstruction' of a binary opposition is thus not an
annihilation of all values or differences; it is an attempt to
follow the subtle, powerful effects of differences already at
work within the illusion of a binary opposition.

(Johnson, 1980, pp. x–xi)

Deconstruction is, then, an important exercise, for it allows us to
be critical of the way in which ideas we want to use are ordinarily
expressed, exhibited in patterns of meaning that may undercut the
ends we seek to attain. A case in point – of meaning expressed in
a politically self-defeating way – is the 'equality-versus-difference'
debate among feminists. Here a binary opposition has been created
to offer a choice to feminists, of either endorsing 'equality' or its
presumed antithesis 'difference'. In fact, the antithesis itself hides
the interdependence of the two terms, for equality is not the
elimination of difference, and difference does not preclude equality.

In the past few years, 'equality-versus-difference' has been used as
a shorthand to characterize conflicting feminist positions and
political strategies. Those who argue that sexual difference ought to
be an irrelevant consideration in schools, employment, the courts
and the legislature are put in the equality category. Those who
insist that appeals on behalf of women ought to be made in terms
of the needs, interests and characteristics common to women as a
group are placed in the difference category. In the clashes over the
superiority of one or another of these strategies, feminists have
invoked history, philosophy and morality and have devised new
classificatory labels: cultural feminism, liberal feminism, feminist
separatism, and so on.[1] Most recently, the debate about equality
and difference has been used to analyse the Sears case, the sex
discrimination suit brought against the retailing giant by the Equal
Employment Opportunities Commission (EEOC) in 1979, in which
historians Alice Kessler-Harris and Rosalind Rosenberg testified on
opposite sides.

There have been many articles written on the Sears case,
among them a recent one by Ruth Milkman. Milkman insists that
we attend to the political context of seemingly timeless principles:
'We ignore the political dimensions of the equality-versus-difference
debate at our peril, especially in a period of conservative resurgence
like the present'. She concludes:

As long as this is the political context in which we find
ourselves, feminist scholars must be aware of the real danger
that arguments about 'difference' or 'women's culture' will be
put to uses other than those for which they were originally
developed. That does not mean we must abandon these

arguments or the intellectual terrain they have opened up; it does mean that we must be self-conscious in our formulations, keeping firmly in view the ways in which our work can be exploited politically.

(*Milkman, 1986, pp. 394–5*)

Milkman's carefully nuanced formulation implies that equality is our safest course, but she is also reluctant to reject difference entirely. She feels a need to choose a side, but which side is the problem. . . . What is required . . . is a new way of thinking about difference, and this involves rejecting the idea that equality-versus-difference constitutes an opposition. Instead of framing analyses and strategies as if such binary pairs were timeless and true, we need to ask how the dichotomous pairing of equality and difference itself works. Instead of remaining within the terms of existing political discourse, we need to subject those terms to critical examination. Until we understand how the concepts work to constrain and construct specific meanings, we cannot make them work for us.

A close look at the evidence in the Sears case suggests that equality-versus-difference may not accurately depict the opposing sides in the Sears case. During testimony, most of the arguments against equality and for difference were, in fact, made by the Sears lawyers or by Rosalind Rosenberg. They constructed an opponent against whom they asserted that women and men differed, that 'fundamental differences' – the result of culture or long-standing patterns of socialization – led to women's presumed lack of interest in commission sales jobs. In order to make their own claim that sexual difference and not discrimination could explain the hiring patterns of Sears, the Sears defence attributed to EEOC an assumption that no one had made in those terms – that women and men had identical interests. Alice Kessler-Harris did not argue that women were the same as men; instead, she used a variety of strategies to challenge Rosenberg's assertions. First, she argued that historical evidence suggested far more variety in the jobs women actually took than Rosenberg assumed. Second, she maintained that economic considerations usually offset the effects of socialization in women's attitudes to employment. And, third, she pointed out that, historically, job segregation by sex was the consequence of employer preferences, not employee choices. The question of women's choices could not be resolved, Kessler-Harris maintained, when the hiring process itself predetermined the outcome, imposing generalized gendered criteria that were not necessarily relevant to the work at hand. The debate joined then not around equality-versus-difference but around the relevance of general ideas of sexual difference in a specific context.[2]

... Kessler-Harris and the EEOC called into question the relevance for hiring decisions of generalizations about the necessarily antithetical behaviours of women and men. EEOC argued that Sears's hiring practices reflected inaccurate and inapplicable notions of sexual difference; Sears argued that 'fundamental' differences between the sexes (and not its own actions) explained the gender imbalances in its labour force.

The Sears case was complicated by the fact that almost all the evidence offered was statistical. The testimony of the historians therefore, could only be inferential at best. Each of them sought to explain small statistical disparities by reference to gross generalizations about the entire history of working women; furthermore, neither historian had much information about what had actually happened at Sears. They were forced, instead, to swear to the truth or falsehood of interpretive generalizations developed for purposes other than legal contestation, and they were forced to treat their interpretive premises as matters of fact. Reading the cross-examination of Kessler-Harris is revealing in this respect. Each of her carefully nuanced explanations of women's work history was forced into a reductive assertion by the Sears lawyers' insistence that she answer questions only by saying yes or no. Similarly, Rosalind Rosenberg's rebuttal to Alice Kessler-Harris eschewed the historian's subtle contextual reading of evidence and sought instead to impose a test of absolute consistency. She juxtaposed Kessler-Harris's testimony in the trial to her earlier published work (in which Kessler-Harris stressed differences between female and male workers in their approaches to work, arguing that women were more domestically oriented and less individualistic than men) in an effort to show that Kessler-Harris had misled the court.[3] Outside the courtroom, however, the disparities of the Kessler-Harris argument could also be explained in other ways. In relationship to a labour history that had typically excluded women, it might make sense to overgeneralize about women's experience, emphasizing difference in order to demonstrate that the universal term 'worker' was really a male reference that could not account for all aspects of women's job experiences. In relationship to an employer who sought to justify discrimination by reference to sexual difference, it made more sense to deny the totalizing effects of difference by stressing instead the diversity and complexity of women's behaviour and motivation. In the first case, difference served a positive function, unveiling the inequity hidden in a presumably neutral term; in the second case, difference served a negative purpose, justifying what Kessler-Harris believed to be unequal treatment. ...

The exacting demands of the courtroom for consistency and 'truth' also point out the profound difficulties of arguing about difference. Although the testimony of the historians had to explain only a relatively small statistical disparity in the numbers of women and men hired for full-time commission sales jobs, the explanations that were preferred were totalizing and categorical.[4] In cross-examination, Kessler-Harris's multiple interpretations were found to be contradictory and confusing, although the judge praised Rosenberg for her coherence and lucidity.[5] In part, that was because Rosenberg held to a tight model that unproblematically linked socialization to individual choice; in part it was because her descriptions of gender differences accorded with prevailing normative views. In contrast, Kessler-Harris had trouble finding a simple model that would at once acknowledge difference *and* refuse it as an acceptable explanation for the employment pattern of Sears. So she fell into great difficulty maintaining her case in the face of hostile questioning. . . . Caught within the framework of Rosenberg's use of historical evidence, Kessler-Harris and her lawyers relied on an essentially negative strategy, offering details designed to complicate and undercut Rosenberg's assertions. Kessler-Harris did not directly challenge the theoretical shortcomings of Rosenberg's socialization model, nor did she offer an alternative model of her own. That would have required, I think, either fully developing the case for employer discrimination or insisting more completely on the 'differences' line of argument by exposing the 'equality-versus-difference' formulation as an illusion.

In the end, the most nuanced arguments of Kessler-Harris were rejected as contradictory or inapplicable, and the judge decided in Sears's favour, repeating the defence argument that an assumption of equal interest was 'unfounded' because of the differences between women and men (Milkman, 1986, p. 391). Not only was EEOC's position rejected, but the hiring policies of Sears were implicitly endorsed. According to the judge, because difference was real and fundamental, it could explain statistical variations in Sears's hiring. . . . Difference was substituted for inequality, the appropriate antithesis of equality, becoming inequality's explanation and legitimation. . . .

The Sears case offers a sobering lesson in the operation of a discursive, that is a political field. Analysis of language here provides insight not only into the manipulation of concepts and definitions but also into the implementation and justification of institutional and political power. . . .

When equality and difference are paired dichotomously, they structure an impossible choice. If one opts for equality, one is forced to accept the notion that difference is antithetical to it. If one opts for difference, one admits that equality is unattainable. That, in a sense, is the dilemma apparent in Milkman's conclusion cited above. Feminists cannot give up 'difference'; it has been our most creative analytic tool. We cannot give up equality, at least as long as we want to speak to the principles and values of our political system. But it makes no sense for the feminist movement to let its arguments be forced into pre-existing categories and its political disputes to be characterized by a dichotomy we did not invent. How then do we recognize and use notions of sexual difference and yet make arguments for equality? The only response is a double one: the unmasking of the power relationship constructed by posing equality as the antithesis of difference and the refusal of its consequent dichotomous construction of political choices.

Equality-versus-difference cannot structure choices for feminist politics; the oppositional pairing misrepresents the relationship of both terms. Equality, in the political theory of rights that lies behind the claims of excluded groups for justice, means the ignoring of differences between individuals for a particular purpose or in a particular context. . . . The political notion of equality thus includes, indeed depends on, an acknowledgement of the existence of difference. Demands for equality have rested on implicit and usually unrecognized arguments from difference; if individuals or groups were identical or the same there would be no need to ask for equality. Equality might well be defined as deliberate indifference to specified differences.

The antithesis of difference in most usages is sameness or identity. But even here the contrast and the context must be specified. There is nothing self-evident or transcendent about difference, even if the fact of difference – sexual difference, for example – seems apparent to the naked eye. The questions always ought to be, what qualities or aspects are being compared? What is the nature of the comparison? How is the meaning of difference being constructed? Yet in the Sears testimony and in some debates among feminists (sexual) difference is assumed to be an immutable fact, its meaning inherent in the categories female and male. The lawyers for Sears put it this way: 'the reasonableness of the EEOC's a priori assumptions of male/female sameness with respect to preferences, interests, and qualifications is . . . the crux of the issue' (Milkman, 1986, p. 384). The point of the EEOC challenge, however, was never sameness but the irrelevance of categorical differences.

The opposition men/women, as Rosenberg employed it, asserted the incomparability of the sexes, and although history and socialization were the explanatory factors, these resonated with categorical distinctions inferred from the facts of bodily difference. When the opposition men/women is invoked, as it was in the Sears case, it refers a specific issue (the small statistical discrepancy between women and men hired for commission sales jobs) back to a general principle (the 'fundamental' differences between women and men). The differences within each group that might apply to this particular situation – the fact, for example, that some women might choose 'aggressive' or 'risk-taking' jobs or that some women might prefer high- to low-paying positions – were excluded by definition in the antithesis between the groups. The irony is, of course, that the statistical case required only a small percentage of women's behaviours to be explained. Yet the historical testimony argued categorically about 'women'. . . . To make the argument would have required a direct attack on categorical thinking about gender. For the generalized opposition male/female serves to obscure the differences among women in behaviour, character, desire, subjectivity, sexuality, gender identification and historical experience.

[· · ·]

The only alternative, it seems to me, is to refuse to oppose equality to difference and insist continually on differences – differences as the condition of individual and collective identities, differences as the constant challenge to the fixing of those identities, history as the repeated illustration of the play of differences, differences as the very meaning of equality itself.

. . . What is required in addition is an analysis of fixed gender categories as normative statements that organize cultural understandings of sexual difference. This means that we must open to scrutiny the terms women and men as they are used to define one another in particular contexts – workplaces, for example. The history of women's work needs to be retold from this perspective as part of the story of the creation of a gendered workforce. In the nineteenth century, for example, certain concepts of male skill rested on a contrast with female labour (by definition unskilled). The organization and reorganization of work processes was accomplished by reference to the gender attributes of workers, rather than to issues of training, education, or social class. And wage differentials between the sexes were attributed to fundamentally different family roles that preceded (rather than followed from) employment arrangements. In all these processes the meaning of 'worker' was established through a contrast between the presumably natural qualities of women and men. If we write the history of women's work by gathering data that describes the activities, needs, interests and culture of 'women workers', we leave in place the naturalized contrast and reify a fixed categorical difference between women and men. We start the story, in other words, too late, by uncritically accepting a gendered category (the 'woman worker') that itself needs investigation because its meaning is relative to its history.

If in our histories we relativize the categories woman and man, it means, of course, that we must also recognize the contingent and specific nature of our political claims. Political strategies then will rest on analyses of the utility of certain arguments in certain

262

discursive contexts, without, however, invoking absolute qualities for women or men. There are moments when it makes sense for mothers to demand consideration for their social role, and contexts within which motherhood is irrelevant to women's behaviour; but to maintain that womanhood is motherhood is to obscure the differences that make choice possible. There are moments when it makes sense to demand a re-evaluation of the status of what has been socially constructed as women's work ('comparable worth' strategies are the current example) and contexts within which it makes much more sense to prepare women for entry into 'non-traditional' jobs. But to maintain that femininity predisposes women to certain (nurturing) jobs or (collaborative) styles of work is to naturalize complex economic and social processes and, once again, to obscure the differences that have characterized women's occupational histories. An insistence on differences undercuts the tendency to absolutist, and in the case of sexual difference, essentialist categories. It does not deny the existence of gender difference, but it does suggest that its meanings are always relative to particular constructions in specified contexts. . . .

It is surely not easy to formulate a 'deconstructive' political strategy in the face of powerful tendencies that construct the world in binary terms. Yet there seems to me no other choice. Perhaps as we learn to think this way solutions will become more readily apparent. Perhaps the theoretical and historical work we do can prepare the ground.

[· · ·]

Notes

1   Recently, historians have begun to cast feminist history in terms of the equality-versus-difference debate. Rather than accept it as an accurate characterization of antithetical positions, however, I think we need to look more closely at how feminists used these arguments. A close reading of nineteenth-century French feminist texts, for example, leads me to conclude that they are far less easily categorized into difference or equality positions than one would have supposed. I think it is a mistake for feminist historians to write this debate uncritically into history for it reifies an 'antithesis' that may not actually have existed. We need instead to 'deconstruct' feminist arguments and read them in their discursive contexts, all as explorations of 'the difference dilemma'.

2   Rosenberg's 'Offer of Proof' and Kessler-Harris's 'Written Testimony' appeared in *Signs* 11 (Summer 1986), pp. 757–79. The 'Written Rebuttal Testimony of Dr. Rosalind Rosenberg' is part of the official transcript of the case, US District Court for the Northern

District of Illinois, Eastern Division, *EEOC vs Sears*, Civil Action No. 79-C-4373. (I am grateful to Sanford Levinson for sharing the trial documents with me and for our many conversations about them.)

3   Appendix to the 'Written Rebuttal Testimony of Dr. Rosalind Rosenberg', 1–12.

4   On this point, Taub asks a useful question: 'Is there a danger in discrimination cases that historical or other expert testimony not grounded in the particular facts of the case will reinforce the idea that it is acceptable to make generalizations about particular groups?' (Taub, 1986, pp. 10–11).

5   See the cross-examination of Kessler-Harris, *EEOC vs Sears*, 16376–619.

Article 7.2
FEMINISM AND FUNDAMENTALISM IN BRITAIN

Ruth Pearson

CONFLICTING POSITIONS IN THE RUSHDIE AFFAIR

Feminist theory and feminist politics have been stretched over the past decade and a half to grapple with the complexities and contradictions of race and ethnicity in a society increasingly cleaved by different identities born of class, religion and culture. Critiques of ethnocentricity in feminist writings and of white supremacy within the various groups making up 'the women's movement' (the term 'liberation' disappeared in the early 1970s) have resulted in a retreat into a relativist position in which hierarchies of oppression – black, working class, lesbian etc. – formed the landscape against which autonomous groups pursued their own politics and priorities, respecting the rights of self-definition and cultural practice of women of various persuasions and traditions.

This lack of a coherent framework on which to formulate progressive feminist strategies in response to the conflicting ideologies of competing patriarchal value systems nearly caught out feminists in Britain when the Rushdie affair broke in February 1989. The various positions taken by groups and individuals from all parts of the political spectrum to the furore which followed the publication [in 1988] of *The Satanic Verses* revealed the political vacuum which occupied the space where such a framework was needed. Here was a book which the Muslim community, backed by the right-wing Islamic state of Iran, claimed deeply offended both the values of Islam and of those who in Britain and elsewhere embraced such values. The debate quickly coalesced around fault lines demarking those who upheld western values and those who supported the rights of minorities to public respect for their religious beliefs and practices. The liberal and left intelligentsia, apparently steeped in centuries of 'rational' and 'civilized' values, defended the inalienable rights of free speech. . . .

CONTROL OF WOMEN'S SEXUALITY

So – in what sense was this an issue for feminists, and a challenge to the relativist position of 'live and let organize' which paralleled the multi-culturalist position in the race relations and education sector which also supported the autonomy and promotion of different cultural and religious practices.

[· · ·]

Both the fundamentalism of religions, and the left critique of them are centred around rules and controls of women's sexuality and the transgression of these rules. For the left the issue is only to explain how imperialism and racism give rise to religious fundamentalism. . . . It is left to feminism to 'explain' why control of women and women's sexuality is not an issue to be abandoned to the religious form of reaction of groups who are socially and economically dispossessed; it is an issue which has to be extracted from its embedded place in the discourse about imperialism and racism and has to be analysed in its own right. A feminist political strategy based on such an analysis has to foreground and contest the control of women and their sexuality as an accepted and understandable reaction to a social and economic change; it has to provide a strategy for contesting this control and for allowing women in all cultures and religions to pursue autonomy for themselves and all aspects of their lives.

OPPOSING FUNDAMENTALISM – THE SOUTHALL BLACK SISTERS

Fortunately for feminism and for the left in Britain the groundwork for such an analysis had been prepared. Not by . . . academic feminists; not by the lifestyle feminists within their own identity groups; not by the women's interest groups lobbying to get more women into politics or on the management boards of large corporations. The political and analytical basis for the feminist response to both the fundamentalist opposition to *The Satanic Verses*, and the liberal and ultra-left support of it came from a small activist black women's group in West London, called the Southall Black Sisters (SBS).[1]

SBS was founded in November 1979 when a small group of Asian and Afro-Caribbean women came together to organize around the issue of domestic violence in their community. At that time, such an organization was a brave and risky venture, within a political climate of black politics which sought (and still seek) to insist on the unity of the black community against the racist native society. SBS has continued to be attacked for divisive politics and for giving racists ammunition to attack black people. . . . With funding from the now abolished socialist Greater London Council (GLC), SBS developed into the Southall Black Women's Centre, and extended its services to cover employment and immigration rights, response to racial harassment and general support to black women in the community struggling with homelessness, unemployment and sexual harassment within a racist society and state. But from

266

the beginning SBS's political analysis was clear. Amongst its stated aims of protecting women from oppression and discrimination over the wide range of social and economic issues listed above, it had an additional aim of struggling against aspects of tradition and culture which impeded women achieving autonomy over their lives.

Before the Rushdie affair broke, SBS were already concerned about the rise of religious fundamentalism of various kinds within Britain and how it was affecting women. Various successes of the black women's movement – such as establishing refuges for black women who are the victims of domestic violence, so that their place of refuge did not become also the site of racial harassment and discrimination from white women – were being undermined by the growing political strength of fundamentalist 'community leaders', who were insisting with some success that the refuges should be taken out of the control of women's groups and be placed under the 'protection' of the community. The insistence of such leaders on separate schools for Muslim children was observed as a strategy for keeping Muslim girls out of mainstream education and restricting their life options.

CAMPAIGNS AGAINST RACISM AND SEXISM

SBS from the start had a political strategy which forged links with other groups and which forced other feminists to confront racism and separatism on a practical basis. In campaigns against the sexism of Britain's immigration laws SBS worked with a forum which campaigned with some limited success against clauses which allowed British men to bring in their immigrant wives or fiancés, but did not grant the same rights to British women; they were involved in campaigns to reverse racist and arbitrary deportation orders against black immigrants – both men and women. They were active in campaigns to limit cuts in health service provision within their local area; they participated in solidarity work with Women against Pit Closures during the Miner's Strike in 1984/5 and in delegations to Sinn Fein in Ireland.

Domestic violence continued to be the issue around which SBS's wider campaigns developed. Between 1984 and 1986 three women died as a result of domestic violence, two of them murdered by their husbands and other male relatives whilst living in women's refuges. In July 1986 SBS organized a demonstration and rally against domestic violence under the auspices of a broad umbrella group called the National Network of Women Against Violence Against Women, mobilizing radical feminists already organized around issues of sexual violence and socialist feminists anxious to seek political alliances with black women – both groups initially uneasy about being seen to 'interfere' with what was seen as black women's issues. But, in the words of an SBS speaker at a socialist-feminist conference in 1985:

> Why is it if a white woman is killed as the result of domestic violence, it is an issue for all feminists; if a black woman is killed it is an issue for black women only. It is as feminists, not as white women that we ask you to participate in this action. Until you see the struggles of black women against oppression as your struggles, there can be no basis of solidarity between black and white women.

SBS continued to attract further deprecation from local community groups as they insisted on raising as issues for political struggle aspects of 'community' life which oppressed women within their communities. In spite of the opposition of the Southall Youth Movement, formed in the wake of the riots in Southall, in which a young New Zealand teacher, Blair Peach, was killed by riot police, SBS have publicized the activities of male youth gangs which criminalize younger children, sexually harass young women and victimize single mothers who live outside the norms of the community regulated sexual roles. The Youth Movement saw as predominant the very real problems of police harassment of young Asian men on the streets; they argued that to denounce street gangs publicly would give the police justification for the 'Stop and Search' policy of controlling black youths. SBS saw the dangers, but also sees the dangers of not organizing to protect the interests of women in the name of unity against racism.

And so it was with fundamentalism and the Rushdie affair. SBS perceived not only the rising tide of fundamentalism within their own communities, but also within other religious groups including Irish Catholics, Orthodox Jews, Rastafarians, Evangelical Christians, as fundamentalism exerted not only religious power but political power. What linked these diverse tides was the stress placed by each in controlling women's lives – what they could wear, where they could go, whom they could associate with, whom they could marry, where they could live, what education was appropriate, what employment was attainable, and what control they could exercise over their own fertility became not a matter for individual conscience but for diktat by religious leaders policing and controlling the women of 'their' communities.

So, before the *fatwah* was declared on Rushdie on 14 February 1989, SBS had already organized a meeting to be held on 9 March to celebrate International Women's Day on the theme of 'The Resurgence of Religion: What price are women paying?'.

Attending that meeting at a community centre in the middle of Southall was for me, a white non-religious socialist feminist with internationalist pretensions, like reaching an oasis in the desert. As the left and right were occupying their various moral highgrounds of anti-racism and liberal freedoms, the discussion at this meeting was the one that got to the heart of the matter; for at the heart of religious fundamentalism is the necessity to control women. Without controlling women, the community has no boundaries, the religious authorities have no means with which to reproduce their faithful or police their moral codes. Without controlling women, authority within the family is broken, and it is through the model of patriarchal authority within the family that religious leaders impose their autocratic rule of terror on their subject citizens. Fundamentalism transfers the patriarchal power men have over the women within their households or kin networks to all women within the community it controls.

What presents itself as a religious tradition or a cultural form of community life hides a hierarchical political system in which self-appointed community leaders impose their undemocratic rule on the population which is their power base. And, like military regimes in which the rule of terror is maintained by legitimizing brutality and outrage by the soldiers of the state on the civil population, the authority of fundamentalist leaders is maintained by conferring on men the power to subjugate and control the lives and actions of women. . . . Fundamentalism requires the oppression of women for its own reproduction, and. . . , by speaking for women in the name of 'community', it denies women the possibility of contesting this oppression within the community, and forbids the possibility of organizing against this oppression within the wider society.

The analytical and political links made at this meeting were not lost. Speakers sketched out the meaning of religious fundamentalism in terms of Iranian women's struggle against a state that arbitrarily regulates every aspect of their dress and their activities, and sanctions the rape of 'virgins' by prison guards to ensure that they do not enter heaven after they have been executed; of Hindu women who are coerced into marriages against their will, bartered for a dowry which can ultimately lead to their death by burning if it does not meet the demands of the husbands' families; of protestant fundamentalism which sanctions the bombing of abortion clinics and risks the injury, distress and worse of pregnant women in the name of an unborn foetus. In spite of the gravity of these religiously sanctioned crimes against women, the meeting, attended by local women, with their daughters and granddaughters as well as interested 'feminist' outsiders, provided the basis for a future strategy which has developed apace ever since.

[· · ·]

WOMEN AGAINST FUNDAMENTALISM

This meeting gave birth to a new group called Women against Fundamentalism (WAF), which provides a forum to organize against separate religious schools for girls, state aid for religious education and the imposition of Christian worship in schools, and the blasphemy laws. It continues to organize meetings to exchange international experiences of women fighting fundamentalist and religious oppression, bringing together groups and individuals from North America, West Africa, Bangladesh, Pakistan, Israel, Eastern Europe, India, South America, Ireland and Britain. Its practice, both in terms of public actions and campaigning, continues to occupy the vanguard in feminist and socialist practice concerning religious fundamentalism and women's oppression.

[· · ·]

WAF have started to campaign to introduce the category of political persecution of women within the meaning of international asylum laws in order to give women who are the objects of state persecution on the grounds of their gender the same status as other political refugees. What started off in a community centre in West London may well change international law in human rights as part of a politics which seeks to secure for women inalienable rights regardless of religion, culture or any other code which oppresses us.

For, as one of SBS/WAF's best street slogans says:

'Women's tradition: struggle not submission.'

Note

1   'Black' is a political term used in Britain to signify non-white members of ethnic minorities; it includes both the largest ethnic minority populations of Asian and Afro-Caribbean origin. For a comprehensive account of the politics and history of Southall Black Sisters see *Against the Grain: A Celebration of Survival and Struggle: Southall Black Sisters 1979–1989*. Available from SBS, 52 Norwood Road, Southall, Middlesex. £7.50 for institutions and £4.50 for individuals, plus postage.

Article 7.3
DECLARATION OF AN INDEPENDENCE I WOULD JUST AS SOON NOT HAVE

June Jordan

If it is not apparent from the text, then let me make it clear that I wrote this from the inside. As a Black woman, and as a human being within the First World Movement, and as a woman who loves women as well as she loves men. *Ms.* magazine published this essay under their title, 'Second Thoughts of a Black Feminist'. My question at the end of this piece was answered by Black women who wrote to me, care of *Ms.*, from all over the country. Yes, they said, you are not alone!

I know I am not alone. There must be hundreds of other women, maybe thousands, who feel as I do. There may be hundreds of men who want the same drastic things to happen. But how do you hook up with them? How can you interlink your own struggle and goals with these myriad, hypothetical people who are hidden entirely or else concealed by stereotype and/or generalities of 'platform' such as any movement seems to spawn? I don't know. And I don't like it, this being alone when it is clear that there will have to be multitudes working together, around the world, if radical and positive change can be forced upon the heinous status quo I despise in all its overwhelming power.

For example, suppose the hunger and the famine afflicting some 800 million lives on earth is a fact that leaves you nauseous, jumpy and chronically enraged. No matter how intense your wrath may be, no matter how personally knowledgeable you may be about the cause and the conceivable remedies for this monstrous and unnecessary curse upon innocent human beings, you, by yourself, can do damned little, if anything, to destroy these facts of abject experience. But what can you join? Where can you sign up, sign in?

Or suppose you consider children, as I do, the only blameless people alive. And suppose you possess all the eyeball evidence, all the statistics, that indicate a majority of Black youngsters doomed to semi-illiteracy and/or obsolete vocational training for jobs, livelihoods, that disappeared from the real life marketplace at least five years ago. Or suppose you love children and you cannot forget that there are entire countries, even in this same hemisphere, where four- and five-year-olds, where nine- and ten-year-olds, have been abandoned, kicked out of their homes, or worse, where so-called packs of these little people must scavenge the garbage cans and the very streets for something to eat before they finally lie down to sleep in gutters and doorways, under the soiled newspapers that consistently fail to report the degrading fact that the children will probably not survive. What do you do? Where are the hands you can clasp in dedication against such enormous reasons for shame?

Or what about the poor, the dispossessed, families of America? Once you realize that Welfare supports have steadily declined, for instance, in the face of unprecedented, inflationary increases in the cost of living, once you understand what this particular disequilibrium implies for a family of five children and their mother who must, nevertheless, manage to secure food, heat, warm enough clothing, carfare, moneys for medical care, and the rent, where can you turn, effectively, to end this death-dealing disgrace? If you happen to be a Black woman, as I am, and a so-called female head of household, then, in an unlimited number of ways, you undoubtedly recognize that you are simply another unacknowledged single mother represented solely by official figures that bespeak a relentlessly rising percentage of Black people, *per se*: you are damned as Black, damned as a woman, and damned as a quote female head of household unquote. Can you point me toward the movement directly addressing the special, inexorable hardships borne by me and my sisters in like, involuntary circumstances?

Well, for a long time I thought it was perfectly fine to be alone, as far as political cause was concerned. You wrote poems, free-lance exposé articles, essays proposing remedies, even novels demonstrating the feasibility of solutions that you ardently trusted as possibilities for activist commitment. Or you hitched onto *ad hoc* committees against this or that nightmare and, when and if you had the bucks, you made tax-deductible donations of endorsement for whatever public fight seemed to you among the most urgent to be won. What did this yield? I felt pretty good, yes, and comfortable with my conscience. But nothing changed, nothing ever really changed as the result of such loner activity.

So now I am no longer as silly, as vaingloriously innocent, as I was. It is plainly the truth that, whatever its vast and various dimensions, human misery is the predicted, aforethought consequence of deliberate, deliberated arrangements of power that would distort the whole planet into miserly, personal rights of property belonging to extremely few men and their egotistical and/or avaricious interests. *Ad hoc*, loner protests will not make the difference, will not impose the revolutionary changes such undue suffering demands. I think it is necessary to form or join a well-defined organization that can and will work to destroy the status quo as ruthlessly, as zealously, as non-stop in its momentum, as are the enemy forces surely arrayed against our goals. Accordingly, since the bloody close of the Civil Rights era I have sought, repeatedly, just such a body of intelligently inclusive feelings and aims. I have found that there are three movements that compel my willing respect and hopes. But I have also learned that there exists, in each of these movements, a ranking of priorities, a peculiarity of perspective, that conflicts with the other two, in an apparently irreconcilable manner. Furthermore, since every one of these movements calls for liberation of some kind, it has become necessary to try and define what liberation apparently signifies to the Black Movement, the Third World Movement, and the Women's Movement, respectively. In this effort, I have encountered a woeful magnitude of internecine, unfortunate, and basically untenable conflicts of analysis. Let me break down what I mean, exactly:

1   The Black Movement: This is the battle I have attempted to help define, and forward, as though my own life depended on its success. In truth, my life does depend on the outcome of our Black struggles for freedom to be ourselves, in self-respecting self-sufficiency. But where can you find serious Black spokesmen, or women, for the impoverished, hungry, state-dependent Black peoples among us who still amount to more than a third of our total population? And why does it continue to be the case that, when our ostensible leadership talks about the 'liberation of the Black man' that is precisely, and only, what they mean? How is it even imaginable that Black men would presume to formulate the Black Movement and the Women's Movement as either/or, antithetical alternatives of focus? As a Black woman, I view such a formulation with a mixture of incredulity and grief: the irreducible majority of Black people continues to be composed of Black women. And, whereas many Black sons and daughters have never known our Black fathers, or a nurturing, supportive Black man in our daily lives, all Black people have most certainly been raised, and cared for, by Black women: mothers, grandmothers, aunts. In addition, and despite the prevalent bullshit to the contrary, Black women continue to occupy the absolutely lowest rungs of the labour force in the United States, we continue to receive the lowest pay of any group of workers, and we endure the highest rate of unemployment. If that status does not cry out for liberation, specifically as Black women, then I am hopelessly out of touch with my own pre-ordained reality.

On another front, I have difficulty comprehending our alleged Black leaders who postulate an antithetical relationship between the destinies of Afro-Americans and the fate of the First World – which is too commonly, and mistakenly, termed the 'Third World'. I cannot understand how we, Afro-Americans, have contended with racism, with life-denying exploitation, with brute-powerful despising of our culture, our languages, our gods, our children – how we have grappled with such a bedevilled history for more than four centuries and yet, today, cannot grasp the identical stakes, the identical sources of evil and oppression, that obtain in the lives of our First World brothers and sisters. Moreover, I cannot understand how any of us can fail to perceive the necessarily international nature of our oppression and, hence, our need for international unity and planned rebellion.

2   The First World Movements: The multimillion-fold majority of the peoples on earth are neither white, nor powerful, nor exempt from terrifying syndromes of disease, hunger, poverty that defies description, and prospects for worse privation or demeaning subsistence. With all my heart and mind I would strive in any way I could to eradicate the origins of such colossal exploitation and abuse. But, except for the inspired exceptions of China, Cuba and Tanzania, it appears that class divisions still suffocate the clearly legitimate aspirations of most First World Peoples, and that the status enjoined upon women is that of a serf, at best. Consequently, one can contribute to African liberation campaigns or to anti-famine collections, yes, but one must also wrestle with sober misgivings. Will these funds reach the afflicted peoples of your concern, or will the dollar bills merely fill the pockets of neo-colonial bourgeoisie who travel through the countryside in Mercedes-Benz limousines, air-conditioned and bullet-proofed against the men and women they have been empowered to serve? And how will the eventual victory be celebrated? Will the women cook the feast and then fear to share it with their menfolk at the same table, at the same time, on a basis of mutual regard and cherishing? What will victory mean for the traditional outcasts, the traditional lowest of the low: the poor, and women, generally? Will the changing of the colour of the guards bring about a verifiable change of policy and objectives? Do we have to expect that formerly colonized, newly independent, nation states will mistakenly pursue paths that verily imitate the powers that enslaved them? Will none of the newly emerging leaders reject, for example, industrialization and their ongoing dependence upon outside, hostile corporations and military allies, and concentrate, instead, upon land reform and intensive agrarian development that will determine the actuality of their independence?

3   The Women's Movement: I remain determined to fight for equal rights of fulfilment and exploration, as a person who is female. And for a while, and with exhilaration, I immersed myself in primer readings about the nature of women's subjugation, and about the legislative and social and economic proposals for corrective action. But then I began to falter in my excitement, in my sense of overdue confirmation, and sisterhood. The Women's Movement did not seem as large, in its avowed concerns, or as complicated, as I believe the world is large and complicated. Exceedingly little attention was granted to the problems of working-class or poor people, to the

victimization of Black women who head families, by themselves. Nowhere did I see an espousal of the struggles to end the predicament of children everywhere – a cause that seemed natural to me, as a woman. Nor did I detect a feeling awareness that you cannot aid half a people; you have to seek to assist the men as well as the women of any oppressed group. Nor have I discovered a political breadth of response that would certainly include, for example, the CIA murder of Patrice Lumumba, Martin Luther King, Jr. and President Allende of Chile, in a disastrous triumph of imperialistic will.

Finally, there is the question of the liberation of women. Will we liberate ourselves so that the caring for children, the teaching, the loving, healing, person-oriented values that have always distinguished us will be revered and honoured at least commensurate to the honours accorded bank managers, lieutenant colonels and the executive corporate élite? Or will we liberate ourselves so that we can militantly abandon those attributes and functions, so that we can despise our own warmth and generosity even as men have done, for ages?

And if women loving other women and/or women in love with women will be part and parcel of the manifest revolution we want to win, does that mean that we should condone lecherous, exploitative, shallow, acting out, and pathological behaviour by women who term themselves lesbians – in much the same way that we, Black people, once voluntarily called ourselves *niggas* out of a convoluted mood of defiance, a mood that proved to be heavily penetrated by unconscious, continuing self-hatred? That is behaviour, after all, that is the use of, that is submission to, an enemy concept such as we would never condone, or welcome, in interracial or heterosexual relationships of any sort.

I would hope that the sum total of the liberation struggles I have attempted to sketch, and briefly criticize, would mean this: that I will be free to be who I am, Black and female, without fear, without pain, without humiliation. That I will be free to become whatever my life requires of me, without posturing, without compromise, without terror. That I will soon be able, realistically, to assume the dignified fulfilment of the dreams and needs and potentialities of most of the men, women and children alive, today. That I can count upon a sisterhood and a brotherhood that will let me give my life to its consecration, without equivocating, without sorrow. That my son, who is a Black man, and that I, a Black woman, may keep faith with each other, and with those others whom we may have the privilege to serve, and to join.

Toward these ends, I have written this account of one woman's declaration of an independence I would just as soon not have. I believe I am not alone. Please verify.

275

Article 7.4
FEMINISM AND LIBERATION
Caroline Ramazanoglu

Divisions between women constitute both the theoretical and the political contradictions of feminism. If we are to avoid becoming trapped into contradictory strategies by our contradictory interests, then feminist politics has somehow to take these contradictions into account, and to offer some hope of resolution. This task is so daunting that it tends to be dealt with piecemeal and pragmatically. Around the world, and in many different ways, groups of women get on with what they see as the most immediate job at hand. This may be helping to set up a women's refuge, deciding to leave a violent husband, confronting a rapacious landlord alongside male peasants, defying apartheid, initiating a network, learning to read, setting up women's health groups, campaigning for more women politicians and engineers, fighting for a clean water supply, challenging sexism in a trade union, starting a women's co-operative, claiming land rights, picketing sex shops, or many, many other struggles. These diverse practical strategies have achieved many improvements in the quality of women's lives, and indeed have saved many women's lives, but they are improvements which can leave the divisions between women largely untouched.

We cannot afford wholly to abandon a sense of sisterhood. Without it there can be no basis for a feminist politics. But if feminism is to be more than a series of piecemeal reforms within the boundaries of our differences, we need to be able to develop feminist strategies for achieving women's liberation which connect women's struggles together.

CAN THE MEANS OF ACHIEVING WOMEN'S LIBERATION BE SPECIFIED?

While the goal of feminism is still women's liberation from oppression by men, few feminist texts address the practical problems of exactly how to liberate divided women. Since feminism deliberately has no hierarchical political organization, there is no authoritative source of political strategy. There cannot be a feminist 'party line' specifying the correct action to be taken in achieving liberation, because there is no 'party' which could lay down such specifications. Once the notion of universal sisterhood is challenged, there is no obvious basis on which a feminist political line could be drawn without encountering divisions between women. This means that there are no agreed principles for deciding what will or will not achieve liberation.

Maria Mies (1986, p. 217ff.), untypically, does follow her analysis of women's oppression in the context of world capitalism by a careful attempt to specify practical actions to be taken, particularly by western women, to transform the bases of oppression. These include a women's consumer boycott of luxury goods, goods which promote sexism, and goods made by exploited Third-World women, and demands to return the control of their production to the underdeveloped countries. The consequent reduction of standards of living in the west would relieve women of their economic dependence on men, since all women and men would have to work for survival. Mies recognizes the considerable problems with these strategies: those of the Third-World women who would be likely to die of starvation during the economic and political upheavals involved and the competition for survival between exploited women workers in different parts of the world. There would also be the problems of child care that would remain wherever home and work are separated. Most western women would have little incentive to comply with these strategies, since they have so much to lose.

If, on the other hand, we start politically from the contradictory ways in which women are oppressed, and leave different groups of women to define their own political priorities, then political fragmentation and divergence follow, which again leaves feminism without any clear political strategy. The consequent dilemmas are outlined by Anne Phillips (1987, p. 149ff.) when she indicates the problems for feminist politics in situations where gender and class pull women towards different strategies for change. She says:

> I would love to end with a long list of imperatives: to set out, for example, how feminists should relate to a labour movement under stress; what they should say when they call for higher wages for nursery workers and are reminded that some men are low paid too; what they should do when resource constraints seem to impose a choice between more aid to the Third World and more money to social services; how they should respond to women's desire to stay at home with their children without sacrificing the demands of a woman's right to work. But on these and all the other choices that confront us, easy answers are not the solution – confusion may be the reality we have to force ourselves to face.

(Phillips, 1987, p. 161)

It seems to be the case that neither prescribing specific political strategies nor simply acknowledging our contradictions in oppression provides a clearly feminist political programme. It is hardly surprising that so many feminists have been cautious about specifying the exact means to achieve liberation when the relationship between feminist analyses of oppression and feminist political practices is so contradictory. Feminists have expressed quite different political positions, ranging from Marlene Dixon's expulsion of 'lesbian chauvinists' from the Democratic Workers Party (Dixon 1983, p. 196) to Andrea Dworkin's view (1983, p. 35) that women's common struggle 'has the power to transform women who are enemies against one another into allies'. Barbara Omolade, writing as a black woman in America, has said (1980, p. 256), 'no other group can demand liberation for us, because in doing so they take away our own capacity to organise and speak for ourselves'.

Feminism can only develop means of evaluating possible political strategies when women develop shared conceptions of liberation. It is this absence of shared visions of liberation which separates Dixon's political strategy from Dworkin's, and which leaves Omolade separated from white American feminists. It is the absence of a theory of liberation which leaves feminism without common political principles. Mies acknowledges (1986, p. 232) that her proposals do not overcome all the divisions of interest between western and Third-World women which she documents, while Phillips's acknowledgement of divisions leads her to a regretful acceptance of the lack of common goals. Once we turn to asking what it is that women are to be liberated *to*, our present lack of shared conceptions of liberation becomes clear.

LIBERATION AND WOMEN'S POWER

The liberation of women, however it is defined, has to rest upon some notion of the empowerment of women. By empowerment I do not mean simply making individual women more confident and assertive, or more at peace with themselves. The goal of allowing women to exercise collective power entails a critical questioning of the nature of power and of how it is held by some rather than others. This means questioning and struggling against women's power over women as well as men's general domination.

Political divisions between feminists are not then matters of consciousness or language which can be resolved by the adoption of a correct sexual politics or a different discourse. Feminism has raised more broadly than before the problem of how people can live together in complex societies, without oppressing one another. Starting from the politics of gender, the development of new-wave feminism has made it clear that the domination of men over women cannot be altogether separated from other forms of domination. The disunity of interests between women cannot be resolved without also resolving more general antagonisms which divide people. Women cannot develop common political strategies while they have contradictory interests in class, race and culture.

The notion of women having contradictory interests is a means of indicating sets of interests which cannot both or all be met within the forms of social organization which give rise to them. Societies dominated by racist ideologies and with discriminatory practices cannot meet the needs of subordinate races or ethnic groups for freedom from domination while also meeting the needs of the dominating groups to dominate. Societies which legitimate men's power over women cannot satisfy women's interest in freedom from men and also men's interest in continued domination. In any resolution of such contradictions of interest, the dominant group will lose power and its associated benefits.

This assumption that women's liberation entails tackling not just men's domination of women but also other forms of power has caused political divisions among feminists. The alternative is to go back to the idea that as women we do have some interests in common. It was these interests to which new-wave feminism was originally addressed. The problem here is that feminist analyses of oppression have made it clear that women's liberation cannot be confined to women's common interests as women. If feminists turn from the immense task of tackling all sources of oppression, and refocus their sights on the narrower task of the transformation of sexual politics, then the divisions between women could worsen as relationships between women and men begin to improve. For example, changing white, male captains of industry into more caring, sharing parents, sexual partners and househusbands could just result in more of their wives and daughters joining them as captains of industry. Changing sexual relationships between women and men will not address racism between women, or the imbalance of political and economic power between western and Third-World women. More young men in Britain today 'help' their wives in the home and share in child care than did their fathers and especially their grandfathers, but this noticeable shift in behaviour has not affected relations between women of different races or classes.

Feminism is not a total social theory that can explain the connections between different forms of oppression. But the problem remains that the oppression of women is, in complex and contradictory ways, enmeshed in all the other forms of oppression that people have created. The conclusion that feminists should then address all forms of oppression, as many have suggested, however, comes up against the problem that feminism has no clear theory of other forms of oppression from which practical strategies could be drawn. Feminism is a partial social theory, but to exercise power women need a total political practice. Feminist energy needs to go into making the connections between gender and other forms of oppression.

Since women themselves hold power over other women, empowering women in general will mean some women losing their power over others. Power is not a zero sum game in which one person's gain has to be another person's loss, but where women are divided by class, by race, or by global inequalities, then the empowerment of subordinate women will mean that, for example, dominant, white, heterosexual, middle-class women will lose their superiority in relation to other categories of women. Putting the strategy of empowerment into practice raises uncomfortable problems for feminists.

THE PROBLEMS OF CONNECTING FEMINIST THEORY AND PRACTICE

The aim of empowering women indicates the need for feminism to address all forms of oppression, but it does not indicate how this may be done. There are a number of problems in linking feminist theory and practice, of which three are particularly problematic. First, the material divisions between us ... mean that women develop views of liberation from different standpoints. We do not only have standpoints as women, but also as members of different classes. Peasant women, black women, black working-class women, and lesbian middle-class women, do not have identical interests in liberation. As long as women have different class standpoints on these critical issues, and remain divided by race, culture and sexuality, there can be no agreement on what constitutes liberation.

Second, conceptions of liberation also depend on what views we take of the relations between different sources of power, such as those between modes of production and patriarchal sex/gender systems. The development of feminism has shown that 'women' cannot be treated as a unitary category, and so the interrelations of the sources of divisions between women must be identified. But feminism has shown the difficulty of disentangling the connections between different sources of power. We also need to identify and to clarify the ideologies which legitimate different forms of power. The ways in which modes of production interact with systems of patriarchal and racial domination are exceedingly complex and considerably mystified. As long as these connections remain confused, it is difficult for women to organize their political priorities.

Third, there is a split running right through the feminist movement over whether or not women and men in a transformed society will still be essentially different from each other. This split is at root a disagreement over the social and political significance of our biological natures as women and men. This is not simply a theoretical problem on which we can agree to differ. The question of whether women and men are essentially different by nature raises practical problems for how relations between women and men can be changed. Although biological reductionism has been extensively criticized within feminism, the problem of biological difference refuses to go away.

The problem of standpoint

In this [article] I cannot lay down a collective blueprint for a liberated humanity which can resolve feminism's contradictions, although it is tempting to try. Feminist politics will necessarily be constrained by the limits of women's experiences and the power of patriarchal ideology, and by women's affection, caring and guilt felt towards those they live with. Women with different experiences will not give all aspects of transformation equal priority, so it is impossible to transcend completely the limitations of my class and racial standpoints. I can only try to clarify the obstacles which still lie between feminist theory and liberatory political practice. While our standpoints certainly limit our visions of liberation, this does not mean that we cannot have useful visions.

If we were to shift the focus of feminism away from the dead end of our divisions towards our diverse visions of liberation, we would have more positive goals to struggle for. Our separate standpoints could then become the bases of alliances created between divided women (Cain, 1986). We need to make the bases of our differing standpoints clear, so that we can look beneath patriarchal, capitalist and religious ideologies to see the standpoints of other women.

A consequence of building alliances between women, however, is that tackling oppression on many fronts means also struggling against women; for example, against right-wing western women who collude with men in trying to drive women back into the family and out of public life, except as cheap labour (Dworkin, 1983), but also against Muslim fundamentalists and others who have defined their own version of liberation in serving men and God (Salman, 1978). Feminists who define political aims for women have been put in the position of telling women things they do not wish to hear, and pronouncing judgement on women's definitions of their own experience and needs (McArthur, 1984).

The alternative, of allowing women to define their own political aims from separated standpoints, however, undermines any general feminist politics. If different groups of women define their own versions of liberation without reference to each other, then no feminist evaluation can be made of the incompatible visions of liberation proposed. Loach (1987, p. 32) has pointed to the danger of aiming at popular democratic alliances across our differences which could end up as a 'bland political pluralism'. Feminism loses its political force if it is dissipated into an uncritical acceptance of women's experiences.

Feminists have stressed the importance of silenced women

being able to express their own experience which patriarchal cultures ignore or devalue. But women may value their own experience without realizing where the ideas on which their beliefs and values rest come from (Sassoon, 1987, p. 19). To adapt Gramsci's terms, men can dominate women by both leading and dominating. Women consent to marry men, indeed are eager to do so, and to some extent they have their interests met within marriage. They can gain fulfilment as mothers, considerable control over children and the domestic economy, and an assured position in society as married women (Campbell, 1987; Koonz, 1987).

Patriarchy need not, then, be a wholly negative experience for women. It only becomes perceived as negative by women when the concealed power relations between men and women become apparent; that is, when women take a critical stance towards patriarchy by standing back and seeing how the whole system works, and in whose interests. It is only when women think coherently and critically about the organization of society that they can see how patriarchy constrains their lives and divides them from each other, and they can choose to resist. Such critical understanding is particularly difficult to develop collectively when women have been personally successful in public life, or when women are excluded from public life and have little social value except as wives and mothers.

Most women do not recognize or resist patriarchal ideology, although they may organize around specific issues in their own interests. Resistance to feminist demystification of patriarchal ideology is, therefore, likely in a number of situations. First, resistance can be entrenched where the clear gains that women draw from male dominance are taken to outweigh their perceptions of the disadvantages. This can be the case, for example, where affluent housewives have their own incomes, cars, time and resources to pursue leisure and pleasurable activities and control their time, or to take up careers. At the other end of the social scale, women are unlikely to be critical of patriarchal ideas and arrangements where men are so socially and economically disadvantaged that women feel little if any worse off than men. Resistance to the feminist demystification of patriarchal ideology also occurs where feminism is seen as the imposition of a dominant culture threatening to the traditions and customs of subordinate groups. This has been the basis for much Third-World resistance to western feminism as a form of cultural colonialism.

The standpoints from which women understand the future, then, are not easily brought together. Depending on how far women develop a critical consciousness of their political interests, some feminist issues will be urgent, some may be of low priority, some will come up against barriers of class or racial interest, religion, or culture. In some cases it will seem more urgent to struggle with men than against them. Nevertheless, feminism *can* perhaps specify general areas of transformation without which women cannot be liberated. The boundaries of the transformation necessary to women's liberation can be defined. These boundaries are shaped, first, by the goal of ultimate liberation which is implicit in feminism; that is, by the notion that women can potentially live as sexual, productive and reproductive beings without being oppressed by men. Second, given this general notion of liberation, boundaries are shaped by the connections in actual societies between systems of sex/gender, production and reproduction; that is, by the ways in which people develop sexual, social, economic and political relationships.

The problem of interconnected sources of power

If women are to live in societies where men do not in general have power over them and, conversely, in which women do not in general have power over others, or particular categories of others (such as servants, or ethnic minorities), then the interconnected bases of power have to be changed. Power lies:

1   in the way in which systems of production are organized;
2   in the ways in which sexuality and gender are socially constructed;
3   in the way in which reproduction is organized;
4   in the ways in which social differences (such as those of race or caste) become ranked;
5   in the ideological legitimation of the relationships to which these forms of power give rise.

The question of how far these are independent systems of power, and how far power in any given society can be reduced to production or patriarchy, has been reviewed . . . [elsewhere], but remains unclear because of the complexity and social diversity of human history.

The institutions of marriage, kinship and family, which are central to social organization and so to the oppression of women, are conditioned in complex ways by all these sources of power. Families, households and kinship structures are integrated into the organization of production, of sexuality, of gendered work and of reproduction. They are notable locations of ideologies which confirm women's specialized inferiority to men, and which legitimate male violence to women. Ideas of social difference are recreated through restrictions on intermarriage and the social definition of kinship ties. Marriage and the family cannot then be changed without taking into account the interconnections of different forms of oppression in any given society. It is not family life as such that gives rise to women's oppression, but the oppressive features of production systems, patriarchal sexuality, men's control of reproduction, and patriarchal ideologies which give rise to male-dominated families. Women who value themselves as mothers, and who identify themselves by their place in the family, would be less threatened by feminism if these connections were made clear. Feminism needs to offer women more than the abolition of the only place in society which is theirs.

The processes by which different sources of power help to shape social institutions are not simple one-way processes in which material conditions determine everything else. Families may be sites of women's oppression, but they are also sites of resistance and struggle, where women can promote changes, as current divorce rates in Britain and the United States show. The rise in divorce in Britain in recent years has been facilitated by changes in the law, but cannot be fully explained by changes in legal or economic conditions. Women have become active agents in ending marriages largely because of their resistance to patriarchal ideology. They no longer feel that they have to accept their lot as wives. Lack of corresponding changes in the organization of sexuality, gender, employment, domestic labour and child care, however, mean that very many of these divorced women suffer emotionally, and are compelled to live in poverty when their marriages end. The rate of remarriage is high.

Impoverished Indian peasant women, however, have shown that struggles against men in the domestic sphere can be linked to economic struggles shared with men (Kishwar and Vanita, 1984, p. 41; Mies, 1986, p. 231). When, on the other hand, women have limited opportunities to exercise choice, and have no other space of their own except family and domestic life, they can become very vulnerable to subordination through the acceptance of right-wing, patriarchal practices which grant them this space (Afshar, 1984).

Changes in power relationships within families will depend on challenges to systems of production, notably capitalism, but also to socialist systems which are organized into male-dominated hierarchies (Bengelsdorf, 1985). Transformation of production would have wide-reaching implications for women. Changes in production would mean changes in the nature of ownership, and in the economic dependence of women on men. These changes would affect the organization of domestic labour and child care. Ultimately the social organization of kinship and household structures would have to be transformed, limiting male power over women and ending the legitimacy of male violence. Changes in production would need to be linked with changes in the power relationships between races and ethnic groups which are enmeshed in both capitalism and socialism.

To be effective, transformation of production would need to be accompanied by more direct transformation of power relationships between women and men. This would be a sexual revolution in which male and female sexuality and gender would have to be reconstructed. Transformation of sex and gender would lead to changes in control of reproduction, and so to the reconstruction of parenthood and child-rearing and to the transformation of kinship and household structures. These changes would transform the place of emotion in social life, and also conceptions of what is social and what is personal. Rethinking our notions of collective harm and benefit (Alderson, 1988) would also help to undermine the present legitimation of male violence towards women.

The problem of difference

Feminists have become divided on the problem of whether or not women and men are essentially different, and so will remain different in classless, post-patriarchal societies. The alternative is that women and men could be merged into a single transformed humanity, comprising both sexes, with either one androgynous, shared sexual identity or several different sexual identities. Carolyn Heilbrun (1980, p. 265) has argued that androgyny is 'a necessary stopping place on the road to feminism. We must not claim more for it . . .'. This makes androgyny a way of conceiving that people could break out of the 'prison of gender' (ibid., p. 258), with a transitional period in which differences are reconstructed. In some final state of sexual indifference, men would no longer dominate, exploit, or oppress women.

Underlying this conflict of opinion is the unresolved problem of how far the biological differences between women and men are socially significant. This is an issue which has split feminists more fundamentally than perhaps any other, and one which has immediate implications for feminist political strategies. If men are biologically determined to dominate women, then the political prospects for women's liberation are not of an active process of struggle for change but of a passive retreat into separate enclaves within unchangeable patriarchal societies. The affinity between sociobiology and right-wing politics should make feminists sensitive to the political dangers of biological determinism (Rose with Rose, 1987). If men are natural rapists, are women no more than natural wombs?

Few feminists defend biologically determinist arguments explicitly, but there is some political divergence between strands of radical feminism which would avoid engaging men in common struggles with women and other strands of feminism which take co-operation with men as essential to women's liberation. It is important for the future of feminism that these arguments are not

used to exclude either biological determinists or socialist feminists
from women's struggles. Nor should the painful processes of living
in patriarchal societies which lead women to adopt separatist
strategies be underestimated. But I would suggest that challenging
the idea of an unchanging, essential femininity and an essential
masculinity creates an active prospect for women's liberation which
is otherwise lacking.

The problem with this challenge, though, is that while
biological determinism has been extensively criticized at the
level of feminist theory, when women come to consider what a
reconstructed sexuality might be like in practice, the loss of
femininity through the abolition of essential difference begins to
appear unattractive. Naomi Schor (1987) argues that we really have
very little idea of what might replace the sexual differences between
men and women which exist now. The danger of having no
difference between men and women would be that this might allow
men to define the single or plural sexualities that would emerge.
Schor suggests (1987, p. 110) that women's position in western
society is somehow connected through 'a tangled skein of mediation'
to our anatomical differences. These connections remain obscure,
but she comments (ibid., p. 109) that 'some of the most sophisticated
feminist theoreticians' who are writing today are showing a growing
resistance to the idea of a world without male/female sexual
difference. Women's valuing of at least some aspects of femininity,
then, shows some common ground between today's 'sophisticated
theoreticians' and the biologically determinist, radical feminists of
the 1970s. This convergence is as contradictory as any other aspect
of the connections between feminist theory and practice.

It is not at all clear where this debate over essential sexual
difference leaves feminist political strategy. If rejecting biological
determinism means rejecting the positive aspects of womanhood
which feminists have identified, then women's liberation has much
to lose. Women then have no special claim to nurturance, co-
operation, caring, creativity and closeness to nature. But if these
characteristics can all be incorporated into new sexual identities,
learned and shared with men, then there is little to be lost.
The contradictions of femininity which have been revealed by
psychoanalysis indicate the difficulties of generalizing about difference. Again it is difficult to develop connected strategies for
liberation when this issue of biology remains unresolved. It does
seem much more hopeful, though, to expand the positive aspects
of what is now feminine into new feminine and masculine identities,
rather than to preserve our present femininity through separation
from men. The political problem for the future is how to safeguard
as much difference as women need from men, rather than to treat
femininity and masculinity as unchanging.

IMAGINING THE FUTURE

The problem with developing safeguards to deal with difference is that it is not very clear what sort of societies feminist transformation would give rise to. Any attempt to specify exactly what should be done encounters both serious disagreements and the danger of utopianism. It is clear that there cannot be one view of what women would like or indeed of what they would need. It is also clear that any form of liberation will be enormously difficult to achieve. Nor can minimum rights be specified as a solution, such as the right to a source of income, health, education, or civil rights, because such a list does not challenge the power base of the male-dominated hierarchies within which such needs are now met. Transformation of production, particularly in advanced capitalist societies, has quite clearly revolutionary implications, since it entails the overthrow of capitalism. Feminism needs, then, to develop some relationship to socialist transformation, which is very far from the intentions of many feminists, let alone from the mass of women who are not feminists.

More than a hundred years of socialist endeavour have produced adaptations of patriarchy rather than liberation for women. The post-revolutionary societies which now exist are far from ideal communist societies, but they do demonstrate some of the contradictions for women that remain after a revolution. Maxine Molyneux has argued (1981, p. 175) that socialist societies, in spite of their many differences, have adopted very similar policies towards women. In the USSR, China and Cuba, the labour of child care and domestic tasks remains largely in the hands of women or is taken over by the state. There is little evidence of the freedom of choice hoped for by Marx and Engels (1968, p. 45). The state has early access to children for purposes of political socialization and to women's labour for purposes of national development. Although most women are far better off than in their pre-revolutionary situations, the reproduction of social life and the social relations between men and women have been adjusted rather than trans-formed (Wolf, 1985).

One way of approaching the problem is to abandon Marx's conception of socialism in favour of a broader, humanist conception of liberation. This version of social democratic socialism might appear to show some way out of feminism's dilemma. If liberation from oppression can be equally addressed by all, regardless of class or material interests, then women do not so clearly have to struggle with men and against other women. They can struggle at an ideological level to win people round to their vision of more equal, just and democratic societies. The divisions between women which now exist, however, indicate that this let-out is less than satisfactory

287

as the basis for effective feminist political strategy. Ellen Meiksins Wood's attack on the new 'true' socialism of the 1980s (Wood, 1986, p. 1) characterizes social democratic socialism as having lost its revolutionary zeal by excising 'class and class struggle from the socialist project'. Class and work relations between people still need to be transformed and still divide women. 'True' socialism does not provide the new 'fundamental and enduring bonds' (ibid., p. 198) which social transformation requires.

Feminists have given very little attention to alternatives to male-view socialism. Women's liberation requires something very different from existing forms of socialism, since socialism accepts considerable harm to its opponents in the course of a revolution and afterwards. Ideally, women's liberation is not aimed at men as a class enemy, but at the economic, social and sexual structures which allow men to dominate women and to legitimate this domination. Men are to be reconstructed through the empowering of women rather than to be rendered helpless or destroyed.

Feminism's relationship to socialism also raises the problem of how to deal with the conflict between personal liberty and collective freedom. The divisions in feminism over pornography and lesbian sado-masochism show this conflict in acute forms. It would be naïve to suppose that we can expect opposing factions always to reach sisterly agreement. Socialism offers no guidance on the avoidance of factionalism. Women's liberation needs, then, to connect a range of related goals and political priorities, rather than to impose a specific or western view of individual women's autonomy. We need many more practical ideas on how to balance these oppositions, and how to make alliances.

Having a range of related goals, rather than one goal which every woman can agree on, is not intended as another way of saying that liberation can be achieved by leaving different groups of women to define their own goals. I have argued above that the sum of separated actions cannot achieve liberation spontaneously. A range of related goals does not specify exactly what women should be doing to achieve liberatory change, and does not provide agreed principles by which women can judge between the competing claims of some women against other women or between privileged women and oppressed men. Looking towards liberation is a shift in the emphasis of feminist effort rather than a resolution of irreconcilable contradictions.

CAN WOMEN'S LIBERATION BE ACHIEVED?

Realistically, the prospects of concerted political action by women in general to transform the world are limited. The extent to which the power of men has become entrenched at every level, including that of women's consciousness, is formidable. The way in which capitalist labour markets have developed, together with landholding and property rights more generally, has left the great majority of women in the most powerless sectors and also separated from each other. While workers in factories or on plantations might well be able to see their common interests both against capital and against men, women in service industries and caring professions, in clerical work, in part-time work, in sweatshops and brothels, as housewives, or workers for their households on the land, will have their interests considerably mystified.

Being realistic, though, need not discourage us from trying. Any evaluation of feminist theory should leave us clearer as to how we take action against women's oppression and for women's liberation. While the personal is political, the politics of gender are limited by the divisions between women. Practical consideration of how women can be liberated can encourage us to think through the connections between gender and other forms of oppression. Since feminism does not provide a political manifesto to guide individual actions, we are left with the task of connecting our actions with those of others, in the light of our views on liberation.

I have tried to explore the contradictions within feminism as a social theory and as a political practice to show more clearly the range of problems that women have to deal with, and to think around ways in which divided women can look towards liberation. If we take feminism personally, we can clarify for each other our visions of liberation, and compare them with those of other women. Until the convergence and divergence of our views of liberation are made clear, we cannot connect our practical political struggles together in ways that will achieve liberation. These visions of liberation will not be personal idiosyncrasies if they emerge from collectivities of women, and from women's critical consciousness of their experience. Building collectivities and clarifying the goals of liberation will also clarify the major divisions between women, such as those between separatist activists and those who feel they need to work with men.

The position of men in relation to women's liberation remains contradictory. But the interrelations of men's and women's interests should not mean that all women have to engage in all forms of struggle. It does mean that separatist and non-separatist struggles need to be connected, rather than either of them being declared outside feminism. It is these connections that we need to work on, rather than devaluing each other in efforts to decide whose version of feminism is the purest. Separatism will continue to be politically necessary for some women and for some of the time. Given that women are living in patriarchal societies, and that the choices open to them at present may be very limited, then living and working separately and taking political action separately from men may be the only way in which some women feel they can practise feminism. What is needed is a political connection between women who choose separation and women who make other choices. It is only in this way that effective political links can be established between radical and Marxist feminists, and between reforming and revolutionary activists.

If women's lives cannot be liberated without simultaneous transformation of gendered production systems, then men cannot sensibly be left out of women's struggles. This does not mean that women who want to lead separate lives should have to work with men. The contradictions of feminist theory show quite clearly the need to struggle with men while simultaneously struggling against them. Men have to be engaged in struggle against patriarchy as well as against other forms of oppression. This means men becoming conscious of the parts they play, through their normal and legitimate behaviour, in oppressing women. Since men have a great deal of power to lose, they also need to be educated in what benefits they could gain from the liberation of women.

The difficulties of getting men to change and to engage in struggle make it imperative that women forge some basis of unity between each other which men can recognize. Otherwise men will continue to exploit the differences between women, and women's emotional involvement with men. Robin Morgan (1983, p. 303) has warned that women fear and mistrust each other, as a consequence of men's contempt for women. In societies which encourage misogyny, women can project their self-contempt on to other women. Feminists need to make women's fears explicit in order to dispel them.

If we look towards liberation in our various ways, we should all be addressing the need to change the way power is organized in production, reproduction, sexuality and domestic and family life, and to connect these struggles. We cannot expect to overcome altogether the contradictions of feminism, but we need not be downhearted if we can accept them and, in particular, if we can accept the many situations in which women clearly share interests with men. Feminists should not be depressed because the concept of 'woman' has been shown to be fragmented. This theoretical development simply shows that feminist theory is catching up with the 'reality' of women's diverse and contradictory interests.

Western middle-class feminists can build bridges to working-class and impoverished western women who are engaged in their own struggles. Women can connect the struggles of different racial and ethnic groups, as well as making links between western and other women. We have to be careful not to develop a feminist politics that can appeal to middle-class women in Calcutta, but can offer nothing to women who are trying to raise their children on a strip of pavement. Feminist consciousness has also to come from the pavements. Third-world women have to consider how far their strategies for change should differ from those developed in the west, while taking the divisions of class, ethnicity, culture and sexuality into account. It is quite possible to have an international movement which has a shared goal of liberation but which tackles the obstacles in different ways in different situations. Third-World women can make their varied needs known, and make alliances with other women. We have to find new ways of making connections which avoid the 'power relationship of the "helper/helped dyad" that has characterised white women's relations with black women' (Sykes, 1984, p. 64). We have to find new ways of redistributing resources through changes in economic power relations. Liberal women can become aware of the political limitations of attempts to rectify inequalities which do nothing to change power relationships. Marxist feminists can become aware of the perils of party hierarchies and of factionalism. Western radical feminists can make connections with Third-World women's economic needs. Every politically active group of women can seek understandings and alliances with others, rather than develop exclusionary practices.

Alliances need not be permanent or formally organized (Wood, 1986, p. 198), but women can put their efforts into networking and connecting with each other as a way of counteracting the moral prescriptivism and fragmentation which currently endangers feminist politics. We have to listen ever more carefully to other women, and to broaden our awareness of other women's lives.

Philosophical discussions of human liberation have tended to pay too little attention to the problem of how the work of cleaning toilets, collecting food, preparing and clearing up after meals, sick nursing, laundry and child care can best be organized in transformed societies. When standards of living are low, the work of fetching water, collecting fuel, finding and preparing food, and controlling dirt and faeces can be arduous, time-consuming and socially unvalued. Even where standards of living are high, and domestic labour is less demanding, these essential and time-consuming tasks will remain. As these are the most basic tasks of any society, women's liberation demands some critical attention to who shall perform them and why. Limited demands for men to share in domestic labour and parenting do nothing to connect domestic labour and child care to changes in work outside the home, to racial difference, or to the emotional implications of change.

Struggles for liberation will continue to be painful. Miller (1976, p. 129) comments, 'it is clear that as women now seek real power, they face serious conflict'. Liberation entails transformation of women's most intimate experiences, of sexuality, motherhood and family life. The prospect of such changes can make liberation

291

seem fearful and dangerous. Feminism needs to be much more sensitive than socialism to the emotional harm of change, to people's fears of loneliness (Rosenfelt and Stacey, 1987), and to the enormous emotional difficulties of living in complex societies.

The prospects for women's liberation in the short term may be limited because of the scale of the changes that are required, but the short term may be all that we have left. We cannot afford to be utopian about the prospects for women's liberation when we live in a precarious world system dominated by private greed, competitive individualism, economic crises, sectional and inter-national violence, the growing poverty and indebtedness of much of the Third World, environmental disaster, and the prospect of nuclear pollution and war. But women's potential power to make changes, once a feminist consciousness has emerged, has no historical precedent.

Major changes which do something to resolve women's conflicting interests are probably least likely in the stable states of the west, where capitalism, individualism and male domination are entrenched, and the population is ageing. It is more likely that feminist politics can succeed in some of the more volatile parts of the Third World, where war and economic deprivation have forged new values, and new forms of collective consciousness, in young populations. We should perhaps be looking for feminist successes in Eritrea and Nicaragua rather than in Europe or America. This is not to argue that feminist work should stop elsewhere, or that western feminists should instruct others on how to achieve what we have failed to achieve ourselves. Feminist resistance and struggle will continue wherever women develop feminist political consciousness. By looking towards liberation, by connecting struggles against oppression, by imagining a less oppressive future for all women, and by making connections between women, we can perhaps avoid getting bogged down in our differences and begin to deal more effectively with the problems of living together.

REFERENCES

ACIBS (1985) *From Office Wife to Office Manager – new roles for tomorrow's secretaries*, report of a seminar, Sydney, Australian Council of Independent Business Schools, April.

ACKER, J. (1989) 'The problem with patriarchy', *Sociology*, 23, pp. 235–40.

ADAM, R. (1975) *A Woman's Place 1910–1975*, London, Chatto and Windus.

AFSHAR, H. (1984) 'Muslim women and the burden of ideology', *Women's Studies International Forum*, vol. 7, no. 4, pp. 247–50.

ALDERSON, P. (1988) 'Informed consent: problems of parental consent to paediatric cardiac surgery', unpublished PhD thesis, London, Goldsmiths' College.

ALEXANDER, S. (1976) 'Women's work in nineteenth century London', in Mitchell, J. and Oakley, A. (eds) *The Rights and Wrongs of Women*, London, Penguin.

ALEXANDER, S. (1987) 'Women, class and sexual differences', in Phillips, A. (ed.) *Feminism and Equality*, Oxford, Basil Blackwell, ch. 8, pp. 160–77.

ALLEN, J. (1990) 'Does feminism need a theory of "the state"?', in Watson, S. (ed.) *Playing the State: Australian feminist interventions*, Verso, pp. 21–36.

AMOS, V. and PARMAR, P. (1981) 'Resistance and responses: the experience of black girls in Britain', in McRobbie, A. and McCabe, T. (eds) *Feminism for Girls: an adventure story*, London, Routledge and Kegan Paul.

ANDERSON, M. (1971) *Family Structure in Nineteenth Century Lancashire*, Cambridge, Cambridge University Press.

ANTHIAS, F. (1983) 'Sexual divisions and ethnic adaptation', in Phizacklea, A. (ed.) (1983) *One Way Ticket: migration and female labour*, London, Routledge and Kegan Paul.

ANTONIS, B. (1981) 'Motherhood and mothering', in Cambridge Women's Study Group *Women in Society*, London, Virago.

APTER, T. (1985) *Why Women Don't Have Wives: professional success and motherhood*, London, Macmillan.

ARENDT, H. (1958) *The Human Condition*, Chicago, IL, University of Chicago Press.

ARTHUR, M. (1977) '"Liberated" women in the classical era', in Bridenthal, R. and Koonz, C. (eds) *Becoming Visible*, Boston, MA, Houghton Mifflin, p. 67.

BALDOCK, C. and CASS, B. (eds) (1983) *Women, Social Welfare and the State*, Sydney, Allen and Unwin.

BANKS, O. (1981) *Faces of Feminism*, Oxford, Martin Robertson.

BARRETT, M. (1980) *Women's Oppression Today: problems in Marxist feminist analysis*, London, Verso.

BARRETT, M. (1987) 'The concept of difference', *Feminist Review*, no. 26, pp. 29–41.

BARRETT, M. and MCINTOSH, M. (1980) 'The "family wage": some problems for socialists and feminists', *Capital and Class*, no. 11, pp. 51–72.

BARRETT, M. and MCINTOSH, M. (1985) 'Ethnocentrism and socialist-feminist theory', *Feminist Review*, no. 20, pp. 23–47.

BAUDRILLARD, J. (1975) *The Mirror of Production*, St Louis, MO, Telos Press.

BEECHEY, V. (1979) 'On patriarchy', *Feminist Review*, no. 3, pp. 66–82.

BEECHEY, V. (1987) *Unequal Work*, London, Verso.

BEECHEY, V. and PERKINS, T. (1987) *A Matter of Hours: women, part-time work and the labour market*, Cambridge, Polity.

BENGELSDORF, C. (1985) 'On the problem of studying women in Cuba', *Race and Class*, vol. 27, no. 2, pp. 35–50.

BERNARD, J. (1973) *The Future of Marriage*, London, Souvenir Press.

BEVERIDGE, W. (1942) *Social Insurance and Allied Services* (The Beveridge Report), Cmnd 6404, London, HMSO.

BIRNBAUM, B. (undated) 'Women's skill and automation: a study of women's employment in the clothing industry 1946–72', unpublished paper.

BLACK, M. and COWARD, R. (1981) 'Linguistic, social and sexual relations', *Screen Education*, no. 39, summer.

BONNER, F., GOODMAN, L., ALLEN, R., JANES, L. and KING, C. (eds) (1992) *Imagining Women: cultural representations and gender*, Cambridge, Polity.

BRANCA, P. (1975) *Silent Sisterhood: middle class women in the Victorian home*, London, Croom Helm.

BRAVERMAN, H. (1974) *Labor and Monopoly Capital: the degradation of work in the twentieth century*, New York, Monthly Review Press.

BRENNAN, T. and PATEMAN, C. (1979) '"Mere auxiliaries to the Commonwealth": women and the origins of liberalism', *Political Studies*, vol. 27, no. 2, pp. 183–200.

BRENT COMMUNITY COUNCIL (1981) *Black People and the Health Service*.

BROWN, M. (1974) *Sweated Labour: a study of homework*, Low Pay Pamphlet, no. 1, London, Low Pay Unit.

BRUEGEL, I. (1983) 'Women's employment, legislation and the labour market', in Lewis, J. (ed.) *Women's Welfare Women's Rights*, London and Canberra, Croom Helm.

BRYAN, B., DADZIE, S. and SCAFE, S. (1985) *The Heart of the Race*, London, Virago.

BUSFIELD, J. (1974) 'Ideologies and reproduction', in Richards, M.P.M. (ed.) *The Integration of a Child into a Social World*, Cambridge, Cambridge University Press.

BUTLER, N., INEICHEN, B., TAYLOR, B. and WADSWORTH, J. (1981) *Teenage Mothering*, Report to DHSS, Bristol, University of Bristol.

CAIN, M. (1986) 'Realism, feminism, methodology and law', *International Journal of the Sociology of Law*, vol. 14, nos 3/4, pp. 255–67.

CAMPBELL, B. (1979) 'Lining their pockets', *Time Out*, 13–19 July.

CAMPBELL, B. (1980) 'United we fall: women and the wage struggle', *Red Rag*, August.

CAMPBELL, B. (1984) *Wigan Pier Revisited: poverty and politics in the 80s*, London, Virago.

CAMPBELL, B. (1987) *The Iron Ladies: why do women vote Tory?*, London, Virago.

CARBY, H. (1982) 'White women listen! Black feminism and the boundaries of sisterhood', in Centre for Contemporary Cultural Studies (ed.) *The Empire Strikes Back, Race and Racism in 70s Britain*, London, Hutchinson.

CARROLL, M.B. (1983) *Overworked and Underpaid*, New York, Ballantine.

CASS, B. (1983) 'Redistribution to children and to mothers: a history of child endowment and family allowances', in Baldock, C. and Cass, B. (eds) *Women, Social Welfare and the State*, Sydney, Allen and Unwin.

CASSIDY, E. and NUSSBAUM, K. (1983) *9 to 5: the working woman's guide to office survival*, London, Penguin.

CAVENDISH, R. (1982) *Women on the Line*, London, Routledge and Kegan Paul.

CENTRE FOR CONTEMPORARY CULTURAL STUDIES (ed.) (1978) *Woman Take Issue*, London, Hutchinson.

CENTRE FOR CONTEMPORARY CULTURAL STUDIES (ed.) (1982) *The Empire Strikes Back, Race and Racism in 70s Britain*, London, Hutchinson.

CHODOROW, N. (1978) *The Reproduction of Mothering*, Berkeley, CA, University of California Press.

CLARK, L.M. and LANGE, L. (eds) (1979) *The Sexism of Social and Political Theory: women and reproduction from Plato to Nietzsche*, Toronto, University of Toronto Press.

CLARKE, E. (1957) *My Mother Who Fathered Me*, London, George Allen and Unwin.

COCKBURN, C. (1983) *Brothers: male dominance and technological change*, London, Pluto.

COCKBURN, C. (1984) Introduction to Game, A. and Pringle, R. *Gender at Work*, London, Pluto.

COCKBURN, C. (1985) *Machinery of Dominance: women, men and technical know-how*, London, Pluto.

COOTE, A. and PATULLO, P. (1990) *Power and Prejudice: women and politics*, London, Weidenfeld and Nicolson.

COWAN, R.S. (1976) 'The industrial revolution in the home: household technology and social change in the twentieth century', *Technology and Culture*, vol. 17, no. 1, pp. 1–23.

CROSSICK, G. (1977) 'The emergence of the lower middle class in Britain: a discussion', in Crossick, G. (ed.) *The Lower Middle Class in Britain 1870–1914*, London, Croom Helm.

CROWLEY, H. and HIMMELWEIT, S. (eds) (1992) *Knowing Women: feminism and knowledge*, Cambridge, Polity.

DALE, J. and FOSTER, P. (1986) *Feminists and the Welfare State*, London, Routledge and Kegan Paul.

DALLEY, G. (1988) *Ideologies of Caring*, London, Macmillan.

DALY, M. (1978a) *Gyn/Ecology: the metaethics of radical feminism*, London, Women's Press.

DALY, M. (1978b) *Gyn/Ecology: the metaethics of radical feminism*, Boston, MA, Beacon Press.

DAVIDOFF, L. (1979) 'The separation of home from work? Landladies and lodgers in nineteenth and twentieth century England', in Burman, S. (ed.) *Fit Work for Women*, London, Croom Helm.

DAVIDOFF, L. (1990) 'Beyond the public and private: thoughts on feminist history in 1990', paper given at 'The Construction of Sex/Gender: What is a Feminist Perspective?' International Symposium of the Swedish Council for Research in the Humanities and the Social Sciences, Stockholm, October.

DAVIES, M. (1978) *Maternity: letters from working women*, New York, Norton. (First published 1915.)

DAVIES, M.L. (1977) *Life As We Have Known It*, London, Virago. (First published 1931.)

DE BEAUVOIR, S. (1974) *The Second Sex*, Harmondsworth, Penguin. (First published 1949.)

DELPHY, C. (1977) *The Main Enemy*, London, Women's Research and Resources Centre.

DELPHY, C. (1984) *Close to Home: a materialist analysis of women's oppression*, London, Hutchinson.

DEPARTMENT OF EMPLOYMENT (1988) *Employment for the 1990s*, London, HMSO.

DIXON, M. (1983) *The Future of Women*, San Francisco, Synthesis.

DOYAL, L. (1985) 'Women and the National Health Service: the carers and the careless', in Lewin, E. and Olesen, V. (eds) *Women, Health and Healing*, London, Tavistock.

DUBIN, R. (1958) *The World of Work*, Englewood Cliffs, NJ, Prentice-Hall.

DWORKIN, A. (1983) *Right Wing Women: the politics of domesticated females*, London, Women's Press.

EDHOLM, F. (1982) 'The unnatural family', in Whitelegg, E. *et al.* (eds) *The Changing Experience of Women*, Oxford, Martin Robertson.

EHRENREICH, B. (1985) 'Life without father: reconsidering socialist-feminist theory', *Socialist Review*, no. 73, pp. 48–57. Reprinted in Hansen, K.V. and Philipson, I.J. (eds) (1990) *Women, Class and the Feminist Imagination*, Philadelphia, PA, Temple University Press.

EHRENREICH, B. and ENGLISH, D. (1979) *For Her Own Good: 150 years of experts' advice to women*, London, Pluto.

EISENSTEIN, H. (1984) *Contemporary Feminist Thought*, London, Unwin.

EISENSTEIN, Z. (ed.) (1979) *Capitalist Patriarchy and the Case for Socialist Feminism*, New York, Monthly Review Press.

EISENSTEIN, Z. (1981) *The Radical Future of Liberal Feminism*, New York, Longman.

ELSHTAIN, J.B. (1981) *Public Man, Private Woman: women in social and political thought*, Princeton, NJ, Princeton University Press.

ELSHTAIN, J.B. (1987) 'Against androgyny', in Phillips, A. (ed.) *Feminism and Equality*, Oxford, Basil Blackwell, ch. 7, pp. 139–59.

EMPLOYMENT GAZETTE (1983) 'Ethnic origin and economic status', *Employment Gazette*, vol. 91, no. 10.

ENGELS, F. (1942) *The Origin of the Family, Private Property and the State*, New York, International Publishers.

ERIE, S., REIN, M. and WIGET, B. (1983) 'Women and the Reagan revolution: thermidor for the social welfare economy', in Diamond, I. (ed.) *Families, Politics and Public Policy: a feminist dialogue on women and the state*, New York, Longman.

ERMISCH, J.F., JOSHI, H. and WRIGHT, R. (1990) *Women's Wages in Great Britain*, discussion paper in economics, London, Birkbeck College.

FEMINIST REVIEW (1984) *Many Voices, One Chant: black feminist perspectives* (complete journal), *Feminist Review*, no. 17.

FINCH, J. (1988) 'Whose responsibility? Women and the future of family care', in Allen, I., Wicks, M., Finch, J. and Leat, D. (eds) *Informal Care Tomorrow*, London, Policy Studies Institute.

FITZHERBERT, K. (1967) 'West Indian children in London', *Occasional Papers on Social Administration*, 19.

FOSTER, J. (1974) *Class Struggle and the Industrial Revolution: early industrial capitalism in three English towns*, London, Weidenfeld and Nicolson.

FOX PIVEN, F. (1984) 'Women and the state: ideology, power, and the welfare state', *Socialist Review*, vol. 14, no. 2, pp. 14, 17.

FRIEDAN, B. (1963) *The Feminine Mystique*, Harmondsworth, Penguin; London, Gollancz.

FRIEDAN, B. (1981) *The Second Stage*, London, Michael Joseph.

GALBRAITH, J.K. (1973) *Economics and Public Purpose*, Boston, MA, Houghton Mifflin.

GAME, A. and PRINGLE, R. (1984) *Gender at Work*, London, Pluto.

GARMENT WORKER (1970) May.

GARNSEY, E. (1984) *The Provision and Quality of Part-Time Work, The Case of Great Britain and France*, a preliminary study carried out for the Directorate-General Employment, Social Affairs and Education of the Commission of European Communities.

GITTINS, D. (1982) *Fair Sex: family size and structure 1900–1939*, London, Hutchinson.

GLUCKSMANN, M. (1990) *Women Assemble*, London, Routledge.

GOULD, C. (1976) 'Philosophy of liberation and the liberation of philosophy', in Gould, C. and Wartofsky, M.W. (eds) *Women and Philosophy: toward a theory of liberation*, New York, Capricorn Press.

GREER, G. (1985) *Sex and Destiny*, London, Picador.

HAAVIO-MANNILA, E. (ed.) (1985) *Unfinished Democracy: women in Nordic politics*, New York and Oxford, Pergamon Press.

HAGUE, D.C. and NEWMAN, R.K. (1952) *Costs in Alternative Locations: the clothing industry*, National Institute of Economic and Social Research Occasional Paper, no. xv, Cambridge, Cambridge University Press.

HAKIM, C. (1987) 'Trends in the flexible workforce', *Employment Gazette*, vol. 95, no. 11, pp. 549–60.

HALL, C. (1979) 'The early formation of Victorian domestic ideology', in Burman, S. (ed.) *Fit Work for Women*, London, Croom Helm.

HALL, S. and JEFFERSON, T. (eds) (1976) *Resistance through Rituals: youth subcultures in post-war Britain*, London, Hutchinson.

HALL, S., CRITCHER, C., JEFFERSON, T., CLARKE, J. and ROBERTS, B.

(1978) *Policing the Crisis: mugging, the state and law and order*, London, Macmillan.

HARAWAY, D. (1990) 'A manifesto for cyborgs: science, technology and socialist feminism', in Nicholson, L. (ed.) *Feminism/Post-Modernism*, London, Routledge, pp. 190–233.

HARDING, S. (1986) *The Science Question in Feminism*, Milton Keynes, Open University Press.

HAREVEN, T. (1982) *Family Time and Industrial Time*, New York, Cambridge University Press.

HARTMANN, H. (1981) 'The unhappy marriage of Marxism and feminism: towards a more progressive union', in Sargent, L. (ed.) *Women and Revolution*, London, Pluto.

HEARN, J. and PARKIN, W. (1987) *'Sex' at 'Work': the power and paradox of organisation sexuality*, Brighton, Wheatsheaf.

HEGEL, G.W.F. (1952) *Philosophy of Right*, Knox, T.M. (tr.), Oxford, Clarendon Press.

HEILBRUN, C.G. (1980) 'Androgyny and the psychology of sex differences', in Eisenstein, H. and Jardine, A. (eds) *The Future of Difference*, Boston, MA, G.K. Hall.

HERNES, H. (1987) *Welfare State and Woman Power: essays in state feminism*, Oslo, Norwegian University Press.

HEWITT, M. (1975) *Wives and Mothers in Victorian Industry*, Westport, CT, Greenwood Press. (First published 1958.)

HEWITT, R. (1986) *White Talk Black Talk. Inter-Racial Friendship and Communication amongst Adolescents*, Cambridge, Cambridge University Press.

HOLCOMBE, L. (1973) *Victorian Ladies at Work*, London, David and Charles.

HOLTER, H. (ed.) (1984) *Patriarchy in a Welfare Society*, Oslo, Universitetsforlaget.

HOOKS, B. (1982) *Ain't I a Woman? Black Women and Feminism*, London, Pluto.

HOOKS, B. (1984) *Feminist Theory from Margin to Center*, Boston, MA, South End Press.

HOOKS, B. (1987) 'Feminism: a movement to end sexist oppression', in Phillips, A. (ed.) *Feminism and Equality*, Oxford, Basil Blackwell, ch. 3.

HOSKINS, C. (1986) 'Women, European law and transnational politics', *International Journal of the Sociology of Law*, vol. 14, nos 3/4, pp. 299–315.

HUBBARD, L.M. (1872) *Work for Ladies in Elementary Schools*, London.

HUMPHRIES, J. (1988) chapter 4 in Pahl, R.E. (ed.) *On Work: historical, comparative and theoretical approaches*, London, Blackwell.

HUNT, A. (1968) *A Survey of Women's Employment*, vol. 1, London, HMSO.

INEICHEN, B. (1984/5) 'Teenage motherhood in Bristol: the contrasting experience of Afro-Caribbean and white girls', *New Community*, vol. 12, no. 1, pp. 52–8.

IRIGARAY, L. (1985) *This Sex Which Is Not One*, Porter, C. (tr.), Ithaca, NY, Cornell University Press.

JAMES, S. and DALLA COSTA, M. (1972) *The Power of Women and the Subversion of the Community*, Bristol, Falling Wall Press.

JAY, N. (1981) 'Gender and dichotomy', *Feminist Studies*, vol. 7, no. 1, pp. 38–56.

JENSON, J. (1986) 'Gender and reproduction: or, babies and the state', *Studies in Political Economy: A Socialist Review*, summer.

JENSON, J. (1989) 'The talents of women, the skills of men: flexible specialization and women', in Wood, S. (ed.) *The Transformation of Work*, London, Unwin Hyman.

JOHN, A.V. (1980) *By the Sweat of Their Brow: women workers at Victorian coal mines*, London, Croom Helm.

JOHNSON, B. (1980) *The Critical Difference: essays in the contemporary rhetoric of reading*, Baltimore, MD, Johns Hopkins University Press.

JOSHI, H. (1984) *Women's Participation in Paid Work: further analysis of the Women and Employment Survey*, Department of Employment Research Paper, no. 45.

KAMERMAN, S. (1984) 'Women, children and poverty: public policies and female-headed families in industrialized countries', *Signs*, vol. 10, no. 2, p. 250.

KEANE, J. and OWENS, J. (1986) *After Full Employment*, London, Hutchinson.

KIRKUP, G. and KELLER, L.S. (eds) (1992) *Inventing Women: science, technology and gender*, Cambridge, Polity.

KISHWAR, M. and VANITA, R. (eds) (1984) *In Search of Answers: Indian women's voices from 'Manushi'*, London, Zed.

KITTERINGHAM, J. (1975) 'Country work girls in nineteenth century England', in Samuel, R. (ed.) *Life and Labour*, London, Routledge and Kegan Paul.

KOONZ, C. (1987) *Mothers in the Fatherland: women, the family and Nazi politics*, New York, St Martin's Press.

LAND, H. (1978) 'Who cares for the family?', *Journal of Social Policy*, vol. 7, no. 3, pp. 268–9.

LAND, H. (1980) 'The family wage', *Feminist Review*, no. 6, p. 60.

LAND, H. (1983) 'Who still cares for the family?', in Lewis, J. (ed.) *Women's Welfare Women's Rights*, London and Canberra, Croom Helm.

LAND, H. (1985) 'Beggars can't be choosers', *New Statesman*, 17 May.

LAND, H. (1987) 'Social policies in France and Britain in the 1980s: their impact on the labour market', paper presented at Franco-British seminar on women's employment.

LAWRENCE, E. (1982) 'In the abundance of water the fool is thirsty: sociology and black "pathology"', in Centre for Contemporary Cultural Studies (ed.) (1982) *The Empire Strikes Back, Race and Racism in 70s Britain*, London, Hutchinson.

LEWIS, J. (1980) *The Politics of Motherhood: child and maternal welfare in England 1900–39*, London, Croom Helm.

LEWIS, J. (1984) *Women in England 1870–1950*, Brighton, Wheatsheaf.

LOACH, L. (1987) 'Can feminism survive a third term?', *Feminist Review*, no. 27, pp. 23–35.

LUKES, S. (1975) *Power: a radical view*, London, Macmillan.

MARCH, A. (1982) 'Female invisibility in androcentric sociological theory', *Insurgent Sociologist*, vol. 11, no. 2, pp. 99–107.

MARKS, E. and DE COURTIVRON, I. (eds) (1980) *New French Feminisms: an anthology*, Amherst, MA, University of Massachusetts Press.

MARSHALL, T.H. (1983) 'Citizenship and social class', in Held, D. et al. (eds) *States and Societies*, New York, New York University Press.

MARTIN, J. and ROBERTS, C. (1984) *Women and Employment: a lifetime perspective*, London, HMSO.

MARX, K. (1875) 'Critique of the Gotha Programme', reprinted in *Marx and Engels: selected works in one volume* (1968), London, Lawrence and Wishart.

MARX, K. (1954) *Capital*, vol. 1, Moscow, Foreign Languages Publishing House.

MARX, K. (1976) *Capital*, vol. 1, London, Penguin.

MARX, K. and ENGELS, F. (1968) *The German Ideology*, London, Lawrence and Wishart.

MCARTHUR, L. (1984) untitled article in Rowland, R., *Women Who Do and Women Who Don't Join the Women's Movement*, London, Routledge and Kegan Paul.

MCDOWELL, L. (1983) 'Towards an understanding of the gender division of urban space', *Environment and Planning for Society and Space*, vol. 1, no. 1, pp. 57–70.

MCDOWELL, L. (1990) 'Sex and power in academia', *Area*, vol. 22, no. 4, pp. 323–32.

MCDOWELL, L. and MASSEY, D. (1984) 'A woman's place?', in Massey, D. and Allen, J. (eds) (1984) *Geography Matters*, Cambridge, Cambridge University Press.

MCROBBIE, A. (1984) 'Dance and social fantasy', in McRobbie, A. and Nava, M. (eds) *Gender and Generation*, London, Macmillan.

MEAD, M. (1971) *Male and Female*, Harmondsworth, Penguin.

MIDDLETON, C. (1988) 'The familiar fate of the famulae', in Pahl, R. (ed.) *On Work: historical, comparative and theoretical approaches*, Oxford, Basil Blackwell, pp. 39–45.

MIES, M. (1986) *Patriarchy and Accumulation on a World Scale*, London, Zed.

MILKMAN, R. (1986) 'Women's history and the Sears case', *Feminist Studies*, vol. 12, no. 2, pp. 375–400.

MILL, J.S. (1869) 'The subjection of women', reprinted in *Three Essays* (1975), London, Oxford University Press.

MILL, J.S. (1970) 'The subjection of women', in Rossi, A. (ed.) *Essays on Sex Equality*, Chicago, IL, University of Chicago Press.

MILL, J.S. (1972) *Utilitarianism, On Liberty and Considerations on Representative Government*, London, J.M. Dent and Sons.

MILLER, J.B. (1976) *Towards a New Psychology of Women*, Harmondsworth, Penguin.

MITCHELL, J. (1971) *Women's Estate*, Harmondsworth, Penguin.

MITCHELL, J. and OAKLEY, A. (eds) (1986) *What is Feminism?*, Oxford, Basil Blackwell.

MOLLER-OKIN, S. (1979) 'Rousseau's natural woman', *Journal of Politics*, vol. 41, no. 2, pp. 393–416.

MOLLER-OKIN, S. (1980) *Woman in Western Political Thought*, London, Virago.

MOLYNEUX, M. (1981) 'Women in socialist societies: problems of theory and practice', in Young, K. *et al.* (eds) *Of Marriage and the Market*, London, CSE Books.

MOON, D. (1988) 'The moral basis of the democratic welfare state', in Gutmann, A. (ed.) *Democracy and the Welfare State*, Princeton, NJ, Princeton University Press.

MOORE, H. (1988) *Feminism and Anthropology*, Cambridge, Polity.

MORGAN, D.J.H. (1975) *Social Theory and the Family*, London, Routledge and Kegan Paul.

MORGAN, R. (1983) *The Anatomy of Freedom*, London, Martin Robertson.

MURCOTT, A. (1980) 'The social construction of teenage pregnancy', *Sociology of Health and Illness*, vol. 2, no. 1, pp. 1–23.

NEW EARNINGS SURVEY (1989) Department of Employment, London, HMSO.

NORDEN, B. (1985) in *Spare Rib*, September.

OAKLEY, A. (1974) *Housewife*, London, Allen and Unwin.

O'BRIEN, M. (1981) *The Politics of Reproduction*, London, Routledge and Kegan Paul.

OFFICE OF POPULATION CENSUSES AND SURVEYS MONITOR (1986), FMI 86/2.

OMOLADE, B. (1980) 'Black women and feminism', in Eisenstein, H. and Jardine, A. (eds) *The Future of Difference*, Boston, MA, G.K. Hall.

OMVEDT, G. (1978) 'Women and rural revolt in India', *Journal of Peasant Studies*, vol. 5, no. 3, pp. 370–403.

PARMAR, P. (1982) 'Gender, race and class, Asian women in resistance', in Centre for Contemporary Cultural Studies (ed.) *The Empire Strikes Back, Race and Racism in 70s Britain*, London, Hutchinson.

PATEMAN, C. (1980a) 'Women and consent', *Political Theory*, vol. 8, no. 2, pp. 149–68.

PATEMAN, C. (1980b) '"The disorder of women": women, love and the sense of justice', *Ethics*, 91, pp. 20–34.

PATEMAN, C. (1985) 'Women and democratic citizenship', The Jefferson Memorial Lectures, University of California, Berkeley, CA, Lecture I.

PATEMAN, C. (1987) 'Feminist critiques of the public/private dichotomy', in Phillips, A. (ed.) *Feminism and Equality*, Oxford, Basil Blackwell, ch. 5, pp. 103–26.

PATEMAN, C. (1988) *The Sexual Contract*, Cambridge, Polity; Stanford, CA, Stanford University Press.

PENGELLY, B. (1981) 'Durkheim's *Suicide*: social life without women', unpublished paper, Murdoch University.

PETCHESKY, R. (1979) 'Dissolving the hyphen: a report on Marxist-feminist groups 1–5', in Eisenstein, Z.R. (ed.) *Capitalist Patriarchy and the Case for Socialist Feminism*, New York, Monthly Review Press.

PHILLIPS, A. (1983) *Hidden Hands: women and economic policies*, London, Pluto.

PHILLIPS, A. (1987) *Divided Loyalties: dilemmas of sex and class*, London, Virago.

PHILLIPS, A. and TAYLOR, B. (1980) 'Sex and skill: notes towards a feminist economics', *Feminist Review*, no. 6, pp. 79–88.

PHIPPS-YONAS, S. (1980) 'Teenage pregnancy and motherhood. A review of the literature', *American Journal of Orthopsychiatry*, vol. 50, no. 3, pp. 403–31.

PHIZACKLEA, A. (1982) 'Migrant women and wage labour: the case of West Indian women in Britain', in West, J. (ed.) *Work, Women and the Labour Market*, London, Routledge and Kegan Paul, p. 104.

PIORE, M. and SABEL, C. (1984) *The Second Industrial Divide: possibilities for prosperity*, New York, Basic Books.

POLLERT, A. (1981) *Girls, Wives, Factory Lives*, London, Macmillan.

POMEROY, S. (1975) *Goddesses, Whores, Wives and Slaves. Women in Classical Antiquity*, New York, Schoeken Books.

RAMAZANOGLU, C. (1987) 'Sex and violence in academic life or you can keep a good woman down', in Hanmer, J. and Maynard, M. (eds) *Women, Violence and Social Control*, London, Macmillan, ch. 5.

RAMAZANOGLU, C. (1989) *Feminism and the Contradictions of Oppression*, London, Routledge.

RAPP, R. (1980) 'Family and class in contemporary America: notes towards an understanding of ideology', *Science and Society*, 42, p. 278.

RICH, A. (1977) *Of Woman Born: motherhood as experience and institution*, London, Virago.

RICH, A. (1980) 'Compulsory heterosexuality and the lesbian existence', *Signs*, vol. 5, no. 4, pp. 631–60.

RILEY, D. (1983) *War in the Nursery*, London, Virago.

ROCHE, J. (1973) 'Future trends in the clothing industry', in Barrett Brown, M. and Coates, K. (eds) *Trade Union Register*, no. 3, pp. 199–209.

ROSALDO, M.Z. (1974) 'Women, culture and society: a theoretical overview', in Rosaldo, M.Z. and Lamphere, L. (eds) *Woman, Culture and Society*, Stanford, CA, Stanford University Press, pp. 17–42.

ROSALDO, M.Z. (1980) 'The use and abuse of anthropology: reflections on feminism and cross-cultural understanding', *Signs*, vol. 5, no. 3, pp. 389–417.

ROSE, S. with ROSE, H. (1987) 'Biology and the new right', in Rose, S. (ed.) *Molecules and Minds: essays on biology and the social order*, Milton Keynes, Open University Press.

ROSENFELT, D. and STACEY, J. (1987) 'Review essay: second thoughts on the second wave', *Feminist Review*, no. 27, pp. 77–95.

ROWBOTHAM, S. (1973) *Women's Consciousness, Man's World*, Harmondsworth, Penguin.

ROWBOTHAM, S., SEGAL, L. and WAINWRIGHT, H. (1979) *Beyond the*

Fragments: feminism and the making of socialism, London, Merlin Press.

RUBERY, J. and TARLING, R. (1988) 'Women's employment in declining Britain', in Rubery, J. (ed.) *Women and Recession*, London, Routledge.

RYAN, M.P. (1975) *Womanhood in America: from colonial times to the present*, New York, New Viewpoints.

SAHLINS, M. (1976) *Culture and Practical Reason*, Chicago, IL, University of Chicago Press.

SAIFULLAH KHAN, V. (1982) 'The role of the culture of dominance in structuring the experience of ethnic minorities', in Husband, C. (ed.) *Race in Britain*, London, Hutchinson.

SALMAN, M. (1978) 'Arab women', *Khamsin*, no. 6, pp. 24–32.

SARVESY, W. (1986) 'The contradictory legacy of the feminist welfare state founders', paper presented to the annual meeting of the American Political Science Association, Washington, DC.

SASSOON, A.S. (ed.) (1987) *Women and the State*, London, Hutchinson.

SAWER, M. (1986) 'The long march through the institutions: women's affairs under Fraser and Hawke', paper presented to the annual meeting of the Australasian Political Studies Association, Brisbane.

SCHOR, N. (1987) 'Dreaming dissymmetry: Barthes, Foucault and sexual difference', in Jardine, A. and Smith, P. (eds) *Men in Feminism*, London, Methuen.

SCOTT, K.G., FIELD, T. and ROBERTSON, E. (1981) *Teenage Parents and Their Offspring*, New York, Grune and Stratton.

SEAGER, J. and OLSON, A. (1986) *Women in the World: an international atlas*, London, Pan Books and Pluto Press.

SEGAL, L. (1987) *Is the Future Female? Troubled Thoughts on Contemporary Feminism*, London, Virago.

SKINNER, C. (1986) *Elusive Mister Right. The Social and Personal Context of a Young Woman's Use of Contraception*, London, Carolina Publications.

SMITH, D. (1979) 'A sociology for women', in Sherman, J.A. and Beck, E.T. (eds) *The Prism of Sex: essays in the sociology of knowledge*, Madison, WI, University of Wisconsin Press.

SMITH, J. (1984) 'The paradox of women's poverty: wage-earning women and economic transformation', *Signs*, vol. 10, no. 2, p. 291.

SMITH, R.T. (1978) 'The family and the modern world system: some observations from the Caribbean', *Journal of Family History*, vol. 3, no. 4, pp. 337–60.

SPENDER, D. (1982) *Women of Ideas (And What Men Have Done To Them)*, London, Routledge and Kegan Paul.

STACK, C. (1974) *All Our Kin: strategies for survival in a black community*, New York, Harper and Row.

STONE, L. (1979) *The Family, Sex and Marriage in England 1500–1800*, abridged edn, New York, Harper and Row.

SYKES, B. (1984) untitled article in Rowland, R., *Women Who Do and Women Who Don't Join the Women's Movement*, London, Routledge and Kegan Paul.

TAUB, N. (1986) 'Thinking about testifying', *Perspectives* (American Historical Association Newsletter), no. 24, pp. 10–11.

TENENBAUM, S. (1982) 'Women through the prism of political thought', *Polity*, 15, pp. 90–102.

THOMPSON, E.P. (1968) *The Making of the English Working Class*, London, Penguin.

THOMPSON, W. (1970) *Appeal of One Half the Human Race, Women, against the Pretentions of the Other Half, Men, to Retain Them in Political, and then in Civil and Domestic Slavery*, New York, Source Book Press. (First published 1825.)

TONG, R. (1989) *Feminist Thought: a comprehensive introduction*, London, Unwin Hyman.

VANEK, J. (1974) 'Time spent in housework', *Scientific American*, November, pp. 116–20.

VANEK, J. (1978) 'Household technology and social status: rising living standards and status and residence differences in housework', *Technology and Culture*, vol. 19, no. 3, pp. 361–75.

WACJMAN, J. (1983) *Women in Control: dilemmas of a workers' cooperative*, New York, St Martin's Press.

WALBY, S. (1990) *Theorizing Patriarchy*, Oxford, Basil Blackwell.

WALKLEY, C. (1981) *The Ghost in the Looking Glass*, London, Peter Owen.

WARING, M. (1989) *If Women Counted*, London, Macmillan.

WATSON, J. (ed.) (1977) *Between Two Cultures, Migrants and Minorities in Britain*, Oxford, Basil Blackwell.

WEINBAUM, B. (1980) *The Curious Courtship of Women's Liberation and Socialism*, Boston, MA, South End Press.

WEINBAUM, B. and BRIDGES, A. (1979) 'The other side of the pay check: monopoly capital and the structure of consumption', in Eisenstein, Z.R. (ed.) *Capitalist Patriarchy and the Case for Socialist Feminism*, New York, Monthly Review Press.

WEITZMAN, L.J. (1985) *The Divorce Revolution*, New York, The Free Press.

WESTWOOD, S. (1984) *All Day Every Day, Factory and Family in the Making of Women's Lives*, London, Pluto.

WILLIAMS, N. (1972) 'The new sweat shops', *New Society*, vol. 20, no. 509, pp. 666–8.

WILLIAMS, R. (1985) *Keywords: a vocabulary of culture and society*, revised edn, New York, Oxford University Press.

WILSON, E. (1977) *Women and the Welfare State*, London, Tavistock.

WILSON, E. (1989) *Hallucinations: life in the post-modern city*, London, Hutchinson.

WOLF, M. (1985) *Revolution Postponed: women in contemporary China*, London, Methuen.

WOLLSTONECRAFT, M. (1975) *A Vindication of the Rights of Woman*, New York, Norton.

WOOD, E.M. (1986) *The Retreat from Class: a new 'true' socialism*, London, Verso.

WRAY, M. (1957) *The Women's Outerwear Industry*, London, Duckworth.

YOUNG, I. (1980) 'Socialist feminism and the limits of dual systems theory', *Socialist Review*, vol. 10, no. 2/3, pp. 169–88.

YUVAL-DAVIS, N. (1980) 'The bearers of the collective: women and religious legislation in Israel', *Feminist Review*, no. 4, pp. 15–27.

YUVAL-DAVIS, N. and ANTHIAS, F. (eds) (1989) *Woman-Nation-State*, London, Macmillan.

SOURCE LIST OF ARTICLES

Article 1.1 Power: now you see it, now you don't. A woman's guide to how power works   Aveen Maguire
from Steiner-Scott, L. (ed.) (1985) *Personally Speaking*, Dublin, Attic Press (pp. 216–25).

Article 1.2 Vanishing acts in social and political thought: tricks of the trade   Beverly Thiele
from Pateman, C. and Gross, E. (eds) (1987) *Feminist Challenges*, Boston, MA, Northeastern University Press (pp. 30–43).

Article 1.3 Feminist theory: the private and the public   Linda J. Nicholson
from Gould, C.C. (ed.) (1984) *Beyond Domination: new perspectives on women and philosophy*, Totowa, NJ, Rowman and Allanheld (pp. 221–30).

Article 2.1 On being a cripple   Nancy Mairs
from Mairs, N. (1986) *Plain Text: deciphering a woman's life*, Tucson, The University of Arizona Press (pp. 9–20).

Article 2.2 What is the family? Is it universal?   Diana Gittins
from Gittins, D. (1985) *The Family in Question*, London, Macmillan (pp. 60–72).

Article 2.3 Narrow definitions of culture: the case of early motherhood
Ann Phoenix
from Westwood, S. and Bhachu, P. (eds) (1988) *Enterprising Women: ethnicity, economy, and gender relations*, London and New York, Routledge (pp. 153–73).

Article 2.4 Bocas: a daughter's geography   Ntozake Shange
from Shange, N. (1985) *A Daughter's Geography*, Methuen.

Article 3.1 Classing the women and gendering the class   Anne Phillips
from Phillips, A. (1987) *Divided Loyalties: dilemmas of sex and class*, London, Virago (pp. 29–70).

Article 3.2 Contextualizing feminism: gender, ethnic and class divisions
Floya Anthias and Nira Yuval-Davis
from *Feminist Review* (1983), no. 15, pp. 103–16.

Article 4.1 Work and employment   Ray E. Pahl
from Pahl, R.E. (1988) 'Editor's introduction: historical aspects of work, employment, unemployment and the sexual division of labour', in *On Work: historical, comparative and theoretical approaches*, Oxford, Basil Blackwell (pp. 11–15).

Article 4.2 What is a housewife?   Ann Oakley
from Oakley, A. (1974) *Housewife*, London, Allen and Unwin (ch. 1).

Article 4.3 A theory of marriage   Christine Delphy
from Delphy, C. (1984) 'Continuities and discontinuities in marriage and divorce', in *Close to Home*, London, Hutchinson (pp. 94–5, 98–9).

Article 4.4   Life without father: reconsidering socialist-feminist theory
Barbara Ehrenreich
from *Socialist Review* (1984), no. 73, pp. 48–57.

Article 4.5   Women and consumer capitalism   Rosemary Pringle
from Baldock, C. and Cass, B. (eds) (1983) *Women, Social Welfare and the State*, Sydney, Allen and Unwin (pp. 85–103).

Article 5.1   Women's employment in France and Britain: some problems of comparison   Veronica Beechey
from *Work, Employment and Society* (1989), vol. 3, no. 3, pp. 369–78.

Article 5.2   Sex and skill in the organization of the clothing industry
Angela Coyle
from West, J. (ed.) (1982) *Work, Women and the Labour Market*, London, Routledge and Kegan Paul (pp. 10–18).

Article 5.3   What is a secretary?   Rosemary Pringle
from Pringle, R. (1988) *Secretaries' Talk: sexuality, power and work*, London, Verso (pp. 1–21).

Article 5.4   Private experiences in the public domain: lesbians in organizations   Marny Hall
from Hearn, J. *et al.* (eds) (1989) *The Sexuality of Organization*, London, Sage (pp. 125–38).

Article 5.5   Gender divisions in a post-Fordist era: new contradictions or the same old story?   Linda McDowell
from *Transactions of the Institute of British Geographers* (1991), vol. 16, no. 4, in revised form.

Article 6.1   Feminism, equality and difference   Anne Phillips
from Phillips, A. (1987) Introduction to *Feminism and Equality*, Oxford, Basil Blackwell (pp. 1–23).

Article 6.2   The patriarchal welfare state   Carole Pateman
from Pateman, C. (1989) *The Disorder of Women*, Cambridge, Polity (pp. 179–204).

Article 7.1   Deconstructing equality-versus-difference: or, the uses of post-structuralist theory for feminism   Joan W. Scott
from *Feminist Studies* (1988), vol. 14, no. 1, pp. 33–48.

Article 7.2   Feminism and fundamentalism in Britain   Ruth Pearson
from *Hard Times* (1990), no. 42, pp. 25–7.

Article 7.3   Declaration of an independence I would just as soon not have
June Jordan
from Jordan, J. (1988) *Moving Towards Home*, London, Virago (pp. 61–6).

Article 7.4   Feminism and liberation   Caroline Ramazanoglu
from Ramazanoglu, C. (1989) *Feminism and the Contradictions of Oppression*, London, Routledge (pp. 174–92).

ACKNOWLEDGEMENTS

Grateful acknowledgement is made to the following sources for permission to reproduce material in this book:

Text

Chapter 1: Article 1.1: Maguire, A. 'Power: now you see it, now you don't', from Steiner-Scott, L. (ed.) (1985) *Personally Speaking: women's thoughts on women's issues*, Attic Press, Dublin; *Article 1.2:* Thiele, B. 'Vanishing acts in social and political thought: tricks of the trade', from Pateman, C. and Gross, E. (eds) (1987) *Feminist Challenges: social and political theory*, Northeastern University Press, USA, and Allen and Unwin, Australia; *Article 1.3:* Nicholson, L.J. 'Feminist theory: the private and the public', from Gould, C.C. (ed.) (1984) *Beyond Domination: new perspectives on women and philosophy*, Rowman and Littlefield, USA.

Chapter 2: Article 2.1: Mairs, N. 'On being a cripple', from Mairs, N. (1986) *Plaintext*, copyright © 1986, The University of Arizona Press; *Article 2.2:* Gittins, D. 'What is the family? Is it universal?' from Gittins, D. (1985) *The Family in Question*, reproduced by permission of Macmillan Education Ltd; *Article 2.3:* Phoenix, A. 'Narrow definitions of culture: the case of early motherhood', from Westwood, S. and Bhachu, P. (eds) (1988) *Enterprising Women: ethnicity, economy and gender relations*, Routledge; *Article 2.4:* Shange, N. 'Bocas: a daughter's geography', from Shange, N. (1985) *A Daughter's Geography*, Methuen, reprinted by permission of A.M. Heath.

Chapter 3: Article 3.1: Phillips, A. 'Classing the women and gendering the class', from Phillips, A. (1987) *Divided Loyalties: dilemmas of sex and class*, Virago Press; *Article 3.2:* Anthias, F. and Yuval-Davis, N. 'Contextualizing feminism: gender, ethnic and class divisions', from *Feminist Review*, no. 15, 1983, Feminist Review Collective.

Chapter 4: Article 4.1: Pahl, R.E. 'Editor's introduction: historical aspects of work, employment, unemployment and the sexual division of labour', from Pahl, R.E. (ed.) (1988) *On Work: historical, comparative and theoretical approaches*, Blackwell; *Article 4.3:* Delphy, C. 'A theory of marriage', from Delphy, C. (1984) *Close to Home*, Hutchinson, reprinted by permission of Unwin Hyman; *Article 4.4:* Ehrenreich, B. 'Life without father: reconsidering socialist-feminist theory', from *Socialist Review*, no. 73, Jan-Feb 1984 (we were unable to contact the copyright holder); *Article 4.5:* Pringle, R. 'Women and consumer capitalism', from Baldock, C. and Cass, B. (eds) (1983) *Women, Social Welfare and the State in Australia*, Allen and Unwin, reprinted by permission of Routledge.

Chapter 5: Article 5.1: Beechey, V. 'Women's employment in France and Britain: some problems of comparison', from *Work, Employment and Society*, vol. 3, no. 3, September 1989, The British Sociological Association; *Article 5.2:* Coyle, A. 'Sex and skill in the organization of the clothing industry', from West, J. (ed.) (1982) *Work, Women and the Labour Market*, Routledge; *Article 5.3:* Pringle, R. 'What is a secretary?', from Pringle, R. (1988) *Secretaries Talk: sexuality, power and work*, Verso; *Article 5.4:* Hall, M. 'Private experiences in the public domain: lesbians in organizations', from Hearn, J. *et al.* (eds) (1989) *The Sexuality of Organization*, copyright © 1989, Sage Publications Ltd.

Chapter 6: extract on pp. 198–9: from Yuval-Davis, N. and Anthias, F. (eds) (1989) *Woman-Nation-State*, copyright © Niva Yuval-Davis and Floya Anthias, 1989, reproduced by permission of Macmillan Ltd/St Martin's Press; *Article 6.1:* Phillips, A. 'Feminism, equality and difference', from Phillips, A. (ed.) (1987) *Feminism and Equality*, Blackwell; *Article 6.2:* Pateman, C. 'The patriarchal welfare state', from Pateman, C. (1989) *The Disorder of Women*, Polity, reproduced by permission of Blackwell.

Chapter 7: Article 7.1: Scott, J.W. 'Deconstructing equality-versus-difference: or, the uses of post-structuralist theory for feminism': this article was originally published in *Feminist Studies*, vol. 14, no. 1, Spring 1988, pp. 33–50, and is reprinted here, in a revised version, by permission of the publisher, Feminist Studies Inc., c/o Women's Studies Program, University of Maryland, College Park, MD 20742; *Article 7.2:* Pearson, R. 'Feminism and fundamentalism in Britain', from *Hard Times*, no. 42, December 1990, reproduced by permission of Hard Times, Berlin; *Article 7.3:* Jordan, J. 'Declaration of an independence I would just as soon not have', from Jordan, J. (1988) *Moving Towards Home*, Virago Press; *Article 7.4:* Ramazanoglu, C. 'Feminism and liberation', from Ramazanoglu, C. (1989) *Feminism and the Contradictions of Oppression*, Routledge.

Illustrations

p. 1, Part I: Margaret Thatcher campaigning at the London Flood Barrier, 1979. Photo: Keystone/Hulton Picture Library; Pope John Paul II. Photo: Irish Times, Dublin; National Abortion Campaign demonstration, London. Photo: Chris Schwarz; *p. 45, Part II:* School child in liberated zone, Mozambique. Photo: Mozambique Information Service; Man in wheelchair at the foot of steps. Photo: The Royal Association for Disability and Rehabilitation; Primary children building an extension to a school in Yenan. Photo: Sally and Richard Greenhill Collection; *p. 119, Part III:* Textile workers, Lancashire. Photo: Judy Harrison/ Format; Women carrying water on their heads, Nigeria. Photo: Ian Watts/ Africa Journal; Ridley Road market, London. Photo: Jenny Matthews/Format; *p. 193, Part IV:* Demonstration against immigration legislation, London. Photo: David Richardson; Nelia Sancho, chair of Gabriella Women's Organisation, Philippines. Photo: Brenda Prince/Format; Catering workers voting on NUPE ballot in Portsmouth. Photo: Judy Harrison/Format.

INDEX

*(Note: Page numbers in **bold** indicate articles by these authors.)*

labour, gender division of 154
labour market 123
 dual 154–5
 feminization of 185
 and liberation struggles 289
 married women's participation
 185–8
 and political action 246–9
 restructuring 183
 segmented 154, 155
 unpaid 124–9;
 see also housework, caring
 labour process 155–7, 159–60
labour shortages
 in Britain and France 163–4
Land, H. 163, 224, 232, 233, 234
Lange, L.M. 28
language 12, 13, 254
 and power 25
 and universalisms 29
law 6
lesbian feminism 13
lesbians
 in organizations 160, 177–80
Lewis, J. 103, 164
liberal-democratic state 199
liberal feminism 13, 14, 126, 235
 and equality 206, 208, 210, 212, 213
liberalism
 and equal rights 208–10
 and family/state separation
 38–43
 feminist critiques of 214–19
liberation struggles 271–5, 276–92;
 see also Women's Movement
living standards
 and social class 90, 91
Loach, L. 281
Locke, J. 39, 43, 215, 216
low-paid workers 248–9
Lukes, S. 9, 19

Maguire, A. 9, **18–25**
Mairs, N. 51, **56–66**
male nature 30–1
'male-stream' theory 12, 26, 29,
 30, 31, 32, 33

management strategies and
 women workers 158, 166
manufacturing industry 181, 183,
 184
March, A. 26, 27, 28
marginality 4
marginalization 53
 of feminist issues 7
 of women in social and
 political theory 27
 of women in the labour market
 187–8
marital status
 and women's employment 102,
 104
market, the
 and the public/private division
 16, 38
Marks, E. 208
marriage 282
 changing attitudes, in the early
 modern period 42
 cultural differences 68
 and ethnic/gender divisions 113
 legislation 202
 and motherhood 81
 and power relations 283–4
 as work contract 125, 138–9
married women
 employment of 97, 98
 in the labour market 185–8
 and welfare 232, 233–4
Marshall, T.H. 225, 227–8, 231, 233
Martin, J. 105
Marx, K. 34, 38, 141, 167, 209, 210,
 213, 216, 240, 287
 on reproduction 29–30, 32
Marxism
 alienation of women in 28
 and family/economy separation
 38
 and patriarchy 11
 and sexual equality 213
 and socialist feminists 145
Marxist feminists 10, 13, 30, 32, 34
 and dual systems theory 36–7

masculine domain
  work as 122
masculinist values 16
masculinity 6, 14
mass production 159, 182
Massey, D. 52
maternal instinct 70–1
McArthur, L. 281
McDowell, L. 52, **181–92**, 203
McIntosh, M. 92, 105, 230
McRobbie, A. 80
men
  attitudes to women's domestic
    work 143–4
  and domestic labour 190
  and lesbians in organizations
    177–8
  and liberation struggles 290
middle class
  and the development of the
    state 41
  feminists 93–4
  nineteenth-century women
    93–4, 95–6, 98–103
  and the separation of
    male/female lives 15
  women, and housework 151
Middleton, C. 123
Mies, M. 277, 278, 284
Milkman, R. 257–8, 260, 261
Mill, J.S. 28, 31, 32, 34, 209,
  215–16, 239
Miller, J.B. 291
mind 3
Mitchell, J. 11, 140, 149, 212, 213
mode of production 11, 109
Moller-Okin, S. 29, 30
Molyneux, M. 287
Moon, D. 225, 227
Moore, H. 52, 53–4
moral majority 13, 250
Morgan, D.J.H. 66
Morgan, R. 290
mother love 50
motherhood 14, 15
  cultural definitions of 54
  and feminism 218–19, 220, 221

nineteenth century 98, 99
  as a social category 69–71
  teenage, and culture 74–87
  and welfare benefits 238
  working mothers 103, 104,
    162–5, 185–8
motherist/feminist dichotomies
  249
multiple sclerosis 56–65
Murcott, A. 81
Murdock, G. 66–8
Muslim fundamentalists 265–70,
  281
myth, construction of reality
  through 12–13

nationalism 251
nationhood 251
naturalism 29–31, 35
nature 3
Newman, R.K. 168
Nicholson, L. 16, 50, 131, **36–43**
Norden, B. 250
nursing
  nineteenth-century women in
    100–1, 102
Nusbaum, K. 176

O'Brien, M. 12, 26, 30, 33
Oakley, A. 125, **136–7**, 212
obligations 202–3
occupational segregation 154–61,
  165; see also gender segregation
Olson, A. 55
Omolade, B. 278
Omvedt, G. 115–16
oppositional consciousness 252
oppression of women
  and Marxist theory 28
'Other', women as 3–7, 12
  and lesbians 177, 178
Owens, J. 227

Pahl, R. 123, **132–5**,
  paid work 126–7, 153; see also
    employment
Palestinians 114
Parkin, W. 156

theories of discrimination 155–6
theory/theoretical constructs 52–3
Thiele, B. 12, 16, **26–35**
Third World women 279, 290–1, 292
Thompson, E.P. 95
Thompson, W. 229
Tong, R. 13
trade unions 158, 237, 247–9

unemployment
and early motherhood 81, 84, 85
male/female responses to 241
women's, in Britain and France 165
United States 235
equality issues 206–7, 209, 213
research on early motherhood 75–6
secretaries' organizations 176
welfare benefits 229
women's studies 5
universal position of women 55
universalisms 29, 35
universities
sex discrimination 160–1

Vanek, K. 143, 150
Vanita, R. 284
violence *see* domestic violence

wage labour 122, 132
and gender 153–61
wages
in contemporary Britain 185, 189
'living wage' 229–30
Walby, S. 10–11
Walkley, C. 98
Waring, M. 129–30
Watson, J. 74
wealth 52
Weber, M. 19, 26, 34
Weinbaum, B. 150
Weitzman, L.J. 229
welfare state 4, 5, 161, 182, 223–45
and gender divisions 191–2, 200–4

West Indians *see* Afro-Caribbeans
western bias 47–8, 53, 115–16
Westwood, S. 79
Williams, N. 169
Williams, R. 223
Wilson, E. 201–2, 248
Wollstonecraft's dilemma 236, 241, 242
Women Against Fundamentalism (WAF) 270
women's liberation *see* liberation struggles
Women's Liberation Movement 212
Women's Movement 274–5
women's struggles/politics 246–52
women's studies 5–7
Wood, E.M. 287–8, 291
Woolf, V. 93–4
work 4
caring work 128–9, 130, 161, 181, 231–2
defining 122–31
and employment 132–5
male/female attitudes to 91
meaning of 130–1
paid 126–7, 153
servicing work 124, 128–9, 161, 181
shorter working hours 131
unpaid 124–8, 129–30, 135, 138–9, 235–6
and the welfare state 231–4, 239–42;
see also domestic labour; employment; housework; part-time work
working class
culture 80
employment of women 123–4
nineteenth-century women 93, 96–8, 99, 101, 102–3
women 94, 151
Wray, M. 167

Young, I. 36–7
Yuval-Davis, N. 92, **107–17**, 198–9, 203